THE EMPEROR DOMITIAN

Brian W. Jones

London and New York

First published in 1992 by Routledge

First published in paperback in 1993
by Routledge
11 New Fetter Lane, London EC4P 4EE

Simultaneously published in the USA and Canada
by Routledge Inc.
29 West 35th Street, New York, NY 10001

Reprinted 2002

Routledge is an imprint of the Taylor & Francis Group

Typeset in 10 on 12 point Garamond by
Falcon Typographic Art Ltd, Edinburgh
Printed in Great Britain by
Bookcraft, Bath

British Library Cataloguing in Publication Data
Jones, Brian W. (Brian William)
The Emperor Domitian. – new edn
I. Title
937.07092

Library of Congress Cataloging in Publication Data
Jones, Brian W.
The Emperor Domitian/Brian W. Jones.
p. cm.
Includes bibliographical references and index.
1. Domitian, Emperor of Rome, 51–96. 2. Rome–History–Domitian,
81–96. 3. Roman emperors–Biography. I. Title.
DG291.J66 1992
937'.07'092 – dc20
[B]   91–22134

ISBN 0–415–10195–6

CONTENTS

CONTENTS

PREFACE

Stéphane Gsell's biography of the emperor Domitian appeared almost a century ago. So another should not be regarded as premature and needs no apology, unfashionable though biographies may well be.

Impetus for a new one comes from the additional evidence now available: the mass of epigraphic and archaeological material discovered since 1894 provides a solid basis for a broader and more detailed picture of the period. Substantial gains have been made in the past hundred years: the consular lists for the period 81 to 96 are now all but complete, whilst the names and careers of many more senators and provincial officials have been revealed. We have been made aware of the fact that Domitian was responsible for the demolition of a full-sized legionary fortress in northern Scotland erected only a few years before, and that some of his soldiers were stationed far further to the east (at Baku) than was ever thought possible. Studies by Birley, Blake, Buttrey, Eck, Syme and Waters have provided new insights into the Flavian period, whilst Anderson, Carradice, Jones, Rogers, Strobel, Vinson and Williams have all recently discussed various aspects of his principate.

The traditional portrait of Domitian as a bloodthirsty tyrant has not completely disappeared and still needs emendation. But, as well, we must now take account of his reform of the coinage, his massive building programme, his development of the 'power set' within the administration, his (rather than Trajan's) admission of a substantial number of easterners into the senate, his efforts to come to terms with various groups within the senate – in brief, his achievements were more substantial than Gsell realized.

One important aspect of the reign demands study – the role of his court and his relationship with his courtiers. For he spent most of his time at his court, not in the senate; and he was assassinated by his courtiers, not by his senators.

The abbreviations are those of *L'Année philologique*, with the exception of those for frequently used ancient sources (Suetonius, Tacitus and Pliny) whose works are abbreviated according to the recommendations of *OCD²* (1970).

It would be an overwhelming task to list all those who have helped me over the years in my work on Domitian. I can but offer them my thanks. But I must express my gratitude to Mrs Penny Peel for her preparation of the indexes and for her untiring efforts as my research assistant: her sharp eye has saved me from many an error. Thanks are also due to Professor Andrew Wallace-Hadrill for urging me to consider the importance of Domitian's court, and to both Mr Hugh Lindsay and Mr Erik Estensen for the improvements they suggested to parts of the text. Finally, I am indebted to the University of Queensland and to the Australian Research Council: the book could not have been completed without their support.

Brisbane, December 1990

ABBREVIATIONS

AAN	*Atti della Accademia di Scienze Morali e Politiche della Società Nazionale di Scienze, Napoli.*
A Arch Hung	*Acta Archaeologica Academiae Scientiarum Hungaricae.*
A Class	*Acta Classica.*
AE	*L'Année épigraphique.*
AFLN	*Annali della Facoltà di Lettere e Filosofia dell' Università di Napoli.*
AIESEE	*Association Internationale d'Etudes du Sud-Est Européen.*
AJA	*American Journal of Archaeology.*
AJAH	*American Journal of Ancient History.*
AJPh	*American Journal of Philology.*
ANRW	*Aufstieg und Niedergang der römischen Welt.*
Arch N	*Archaeological News.*
BAR	*British Archaeological Reports.*
BCAC	*Bulletino della Commissione Archeologica Communale in Roma.*
BICS	*Bulletin of the Institute of Classical Studies of the University of London.*
BJ	*Bonner Jahrbücher des rheinischen Landesmuseums in Bonn und des Vereins von Altertumsfreunden im Rheinlande.*
BMC	*Coins of the Roman Empire in the British Museum.*
CAH	*Cambridge Ancient History.*

CB	*Classical Bulletin.*
CE	*Chronique d'Egypte.*
CIL	*Corpus Inscriptionum Latinarum.*
CJ	*Classical Journal.*
Cl Ant	*Classical Antiquity.*
CPh	*Classical Philology.*
CQ	*Classical Quarterly.*
CR	*Classical Review.*
CRDAC	*Centro Ricerche e Documentazione sull'Antichità Classica.*
CW	*Classical World.*
DE	*Dizionario epigrafico di Antichità romane.*
ECM	*Echos du monde classique.*
ES	*Epigraphische Studien.*
HSCPh	*Harvard Studies in Classical Philology.*
ILS	*Inscriptiones Latinae Selectae.*
IRT	*Inscriptions of Roman Tripolitania*
JBL	*Journal of Biblical Literature.*
JDAI	*Jahrbuch des deutschen archäologischen Instituts.*
JHS	*Journal of Hellenic Studies.*
JRS	*Journal of Roman Studies.*
LCM	*Liverpool Classical Monthly.*
MAAR	*Memoirs of the American Academy in Rome.*
MDAI(R)	*Mitteilungen des deutschen archäologischen Instituts (Röm. Abt.).*
MEFR	*Mélanges d'archéologie et d'histoire de l'Ecole Française de Rome.*
MH	*Museum Helveticum.*
NTS	*New Testament Studies.*
OCD	*Oxford Classical Dictionary.*
P&P	*Past and Present.*
PBA	*Proceedings of the British Academy.*
PIR[1]	*Prosopographia Imperii Romani Saeculorum I, II, III.*
PIR[2]	*Prosopographia Imperii Romani Saeculorum I, II, III.*
QC	*Quaderni catanesi di studi classici e medievali.*
R Bi	*Revue biblique.*
RE	*Real-Encyklopaedie der classischen Altertumswissenschaft.*

ABBREVIATIONS

REG	*Revue des études grecques.*
REL	*Revue des études latines.*
RHD	*Revue historique de droit français et étranger.*
RHPhR	*Revue d'histoire et de philosophie religieuses.*
RIDA	*Revue internationale des droits de l'antiquité.*
RIL	*Rendiconti dell'Istituto Lombardo, Classe di lettere, scienze morali e storiche.*
RPAA	*Rendiconti della Pontificia Accademia di Archaeologia.*
RSA	*Rivista storica dell'Antichità.*
RSCI	*Rivista di storia della Chiesa in Italia.*
RSR	*Revue des sciences religieuses.*
SCI	*Scripta Classica Israelica.*
TAPhA	*Transactions of the American Philological Association.*
TLS	*Times Literary Supplement.*
V Chr	*Vigiliae Christianae.*
ZA	*Ziva Antika.*
ZPE	*Zeitschrift für Papyrologie und Epigraphik.*
ZSS	*Zeitschrift der Savigny-Stiftung für Rechtsgeschichte.*

1

EARLY CAREER

FAMILY AND SOCIAL MOBILITY

Domitian was born in Rome on 24 October 51, the eleventh year
of Claudius's reign. According to tradition (*Dom.* 1.1), the birth
occurred at the family home in Pomegranate Street (possibly the
Via delle Quatro Fontane) on the Quirinal Hill in the sixth Region.
Later, he converted it into a temple of the *Gens Flavia*, covered with
marble and gold,[1] and, when it was struck by lightning in 96, many
interpreted this as an indication of the emperor's mortality (*Dom.*
15); on his death (18 September 96), his ashes and those of his niece
Julia were mingled and deposited there by Phyllis who had nursed
them both (*Dom.* 17).

Suetonius (*Dom.* 1.1) repeats various rumours about his boyhood
and early youth: such was his family's poverty that there was no
silver plate, he had to sell himself to various senators, including
the future emperor Nerva. Even Suetonius does not vouch for the
accuracy of these tales and they can be safely discarded.

The family's 'poverty' is a myth. On the contrary, one of the bases
for their upward mobility was wealth, just as it was an essential
ingredient for any would-be member of the new aristocracy in the
early empire, with influence and ability being the other relevant
factors. Needless to say, the Flavians and, in particular, Domitian's
grandfather (Titus Flavius Sabinus), had (or acquired) all three.

His great-grandfather (T. Flavius Petro) had come from Reate
(Rieti), an Italian town in the Sabine territory on the Velino near
where the Via Salaria crossed the river. He had served in Pompey's
army (possibly as a centurion) at Pharsalus where his military career
came to an inglorious end as he fled from the field of battle: on the
other hand, the relationship between the Plautii and the Flavii, very

1

significant in their rise to imperial status, might well have begun during this civil war, for one of Pompey's officers at Pharsalus was A. Plautius whose great-grandson of the same name (*PIR*[1] P 344) was a patron of the Flavians – two of his three legions in Britain during Claudius's invasion were under the control of Petro's grandsons, Vespasian and his brother (Sabinus).

But Petro's reverse was only temporary. He set about acquiring what was one of the essentials for social and political success in most societies and particularly so in this one – money: he became a moneylender and married a wealthy wife. An ability to acquire money and then to retain it were qualities he handed down to his descendants. His wife Tertulla was extremely rich, owning estates at the Etruscan coastal town of Cosa and it was here that Domitian's father Vespasian was brought up (AD 10–20). Fifty years later, the family still owned it and Vespasian visited it regularly during his reign. This was not the family's only asset. There was a villa at Aquae Cutiliae on the Via Salaria between Reate and Interocrea (Antrodoco) where Vespasian spent every summer (*Vesp*. 24) and where both he and Titus died; when the family acquired it is not known. There were another three properties. Suetonius (*Vesp*. 2.1) does not record the precise nature of their estate at Falacrina (also on the Via Salaria, some 13 kilometres from Reate) where Vespasian was born, nor whether Vespasian owned the houses in Rome where Titus (*Titus* 1) and Domitian (*Dom*. 1.1) were born. Vespasian's 'poverty' during the Julio-Claudian period was an invention of Flavian propaganda of the early 70s, when the safest policy was to mention as infrequently as possible the financial, social and political successes of the Flavii during the reigns of emperors such as Gaius and Nero.

Tertulla's money and her husband's financial acumen were passed on to their descendants amongst whom was their very able son, Domitian's grandfather Titus Flavius Sabinus (Sabinus I). During the early decades of the first century, he amassed considerable wealth and possibly equestrian status from his posts of tax collector in Asia and banker in Switzerland.[2] With the practical common sense of most of the Flavii, he married well, with apparent increase in both wealth and social status, for Vespasia Polla's family was renowned and ancient: Suetonius claims (*Vesp*. 1.3) to have seen many monuments of the Vespasii not far from Nursia (Norcia), a mountain town also in the Sabine country. As Sabinus I's new brother-in-law was a senator of praetorian rank and, presumably, a member of

Augustus's senate, the Flavii had, within two generations, emerged from comparative obscurity, and the change coincided with the rise of a new aristocracy, as the old families disappeared in the series of civil wars during the last decades of the Roman Republic.[3]

The third generation saw the family senatorial: Sabinus I's wealth was sufficient to ensure that both his sons (Sabinus II and Vespasian) had the financial prerequisite for a senatorial career – some HS 1,000,000 each.[4] So, before Sabinus I, the Flavians may well have been 'obscure and without family portraits' (*Vesp.* 1.1), but, amongst his seven direct male descendants, were numbered three emperors and these seven between them amassed thirty-nine consulships.[5]

PATRONAGE

Antonia's circle

In many societies, and especially in the early empire, social and political advancement depended on access to influential patrons in the aristocracy.[6] From marriages, the Flavii had acquired money (Tertulla) and status (Vespasia). But it was through their patrons that they gained access to the imperial court and to the honours that followed therefrom.

During Tiberius's reign (14–37), both Sabinus I's sons were granted senatorial rank. So their father had by then acquired not only considerable wealth but also the advantages accruing from powerful patrons; and whilst we can not be absolutely certain of their identity, subsequent contacts made by Vespasian are suggestive. It would seem that patronage came from four powerful and eminent families (the Petronii, Pomponii, Plautii and Vitellii) who were linked together not only by marriage ties and common interests, but also by imperial patronage via Antonia Minor, daughter of Mark Antony and mother of Germanicus and Claudius.

The links between the four families were long-standing.[7] Some years before his consulship in 1 BC, an Aulus Plautius had married a Vitellia – forty or more years later, Petronia, whose mother was a Plautia, married the future emperor Vitellius. In the interval, the families' fortunes varied with those of Antonia and her sons. Observe Publius Vitellius, the uncle of the future emperor, and the trusted associate of Germanicus (*comes Germanici: Vit.* 2.3). Commander of two of his legions in 14 (*Ann.* 1.70), Vitellius led the struggle to avenge his death (*Ann.* 3.10); and, in the period of

Germanicus's greatest influence (16–19), four of the group attained the consulship. But, with his death, all that changed and from 19 to 31 only two of them were successful.[8] Sejanus's fall in 31, however, represented another turning-point and between 32 and 37, two Vitellii, a Plautius and a Petronius became consuls; similarly, with the accession of Antonia's son Claudius, seven consulships were awarded to the group in the first eight years of his reign.[9]

There is some evidence to explain the significance of Sejanus's death in boosting the families' influence. When Antonia was informed of the plot against Tiberius, she wrote a 'full and accurate account' of it to Tiberius: 'previously he had held Antonia in high regard, but now he valued her even more and put full confidence in her' (*AJ* 18.180–4). However accurate the tale,[10] it reflects the perception commonly held that Antonia's[11] influence with Tiberius increased with Sejanus's death and, with it, that of her circle.

At this same period, the Flavians acquired an even more direct contact with the imperial family in the person of (Antonia) Caenis,[12] secretary and freedwoman of Antonia and known to have been Vespasian's mistress both in his youth and in his old age (*Vesp.* 3). Presumably, he met her when he was in his early twenties. A woman of no mean ability, she had an important part in the events surrounding Sejanus's fall, for, according to Dio 60.14.1–2, it was to her that Antonia dictated the letter to Tiberius about Sejanus.

At all times, access to the court was vital, since decisions were effectively made there, not in the senate, and Vespasian acquired such access through the able and influential Caenis. As shrewd in selecting a mistress as his father and grandfather had been in their choice of wives (observe three different reasons in three generations – money [Tertulla], status [Vespasia] and influence [Caenis]), Vespasian capitalized on the advantages gained by his family's patrons.

Ten years later, with the accession of Claudius, the Flavians' patrons still retained their influence, as the evidence amply indicates. Once emperor, he immediately chose their senior members as his personal advisors – L. Vitellius for internal matters and A. Plautius for the external. As well, Tacitus has L. Vitellius reminding Claudius that not only were they both friends of long standing but also equally devoted to his mother Antonia (*Ann.* 11.3). Just as decisive is the evidence for Vespasian's connection with the group: according to one of the emperor Vitellius's supporters, 'Vespasian was a client of a Vitellius when a Vitellius was a client of a Claudius' (*Hist.* 3.66);

his first appointment to command a legion (in Germany) was due to the influence of Claudius's freedman Narcissus (*Vesp.* 4.1) – once again, Vespasian was acute enough to maintain his contacts at court (Caenis) and also to extend them (Narcissus); and when A. Plautius was appointed commander of the invasion of Britain, he had, as two of his three legionary commanders, Vespasian and his elder brother Sabinus II.

Oriental group

Another group that helped the Flavians, especially during the Jewish war and the seizure of power by Vespasian in 69, was the family and friends of the Jewish king Julius Agrippa II, all of whom had close links with members of the imperial family, especially Antonia.[13] Agrippa's father (Agrippa I), who had been educated with Tiberius's son Drusus, 'also won the friendship of Antonia, . . . for his mother Berenice[14] ranked high among her friends and had requested her to promote the son's interest' (*AJ* 18.143); in Berenice's will, one of her freedmen, Protos, was left to Antonia (*AJ* 18.156). Agrippa I was chronically hard up, and, on one occasion, sought a substantial loan from Antonia, who paid up 'because she still remembered Berenice his mother and because Agrippa had been brought up with Claudius and his circle' (*AJ* 18.165). The friendship was extended to include his son Agrippa II 'who was brought up at the court of Claudius Caesar' (*AJ* 19.360), and who, with his sister Berenice,[15] was to prove a loyal and valuable ally to Vespasian.

When war broke out in 66, Agrippa was at Alexandria with his former brother-in-law Tiberius Julius Alexander,[16] prefect of Egypt and another member of the circle. Later (1 July 69), he was to be the first military governor to declare for Vespasian, and, although Vespasian's predecessor Vitellius was destined to survive until December 69, Vespasian officially dated his reign from Alexander's proclamation in Egypt. Agrippa immediately returned to Caesarea, provided the Romans with auxiliaries (*BJ* 3.68) and served with them, being wounded at the siege of Gamala (*BJ* 4.14). Better known, perhaps, is his sister Berenice, married (or promised) to Marcus Julius Alexander (brother of Tiberius) and then to her uncle, Herod of Chalcis by whom she had two sons, Berenicianus and Hyrcanus (*AJ* 19.277; *BJ* 2.217, 221). She would have been twenty when he died *c.* 48. Subsequently, she returned to live with her brother, but the scandal and notoriety caused by their alleged incest (*AJ* 20.145) persuaded her to seek another husband. Polemo of Cilicia found her money and charms irrestible (*AJ* 20.146) and, in his late thirties, even consented to be circumcised. The marriage was brief and subsequently she became Titus's mistress.[17] Tacitus's introduction of her is memorable. Titus was obviously well aware of her physical attractions, but his father was drawn to her wealth: 'she commended herself to the elderly Vespasian by the splendid gifts she made him' (*Hist.* 2.81).

So Agrippa II, Berenice and Alexander were all part of the 'oriental group' that supported the Flavians in 69. But the relationship had been forged, almost certainly, far earlier, in the early decades of the century when Sabinus I sought and found influential patrons. Of considerable interest in this connexion is the father of Marcus and Tiberius Julius Alexander, usually known as Alexander the Alabarch (or Arabach: i.e. he was a senior customs official in the Greek administration), and one of the few Jews resident in Alexandria to hold 'Greek' citizenship; equally famous was his brother Philo whose works have come down to us. Now, according to Josephus, 'Alexander surpassed all his fellow citizens in ancestry and in wealth' (*AJ* 20.100); more importantly, he was also, 'an old friend of Claudius and looked after the interests of Claudius's mother Antonia' (*AJ* 19.276). Many imperial women owned property, so it is not surprising that Antonia (daughter of Mark Antony) should have estates in Egypt or that she should have an agent there to protect her investment.[18] Less obvious is her choice. Furthermore, it is difficult to determine just when the arrangement began, but, since one of Alexander's sons was married in 41 whilst the other was *epistrategus* of the Thebaid *c.* 42, his association with Antonia could well have begun during the early part of Tiberius's reign. So links are attested between the elder Alexander and (a) Antonia (*AJ* 19.276), (b) Claudius (*ibid.*), (c) Agrippa I (*AJ* 159–60: he tried to borrow money from Alexander, but had less success than he was to have with Antonia at *AJ* 18.165), (d) Agrippa II (his sister Berenice married Alexander's son Marcus), and (e) the Flavians (Alexander's other son Tiberius was the first military commander to declare for Vespasian in 69, served as Titus's deputy during the siege of Jerusalem and may later have become praetorian prefect). Initially, many of the links were economic – Alexander's wealth attracted Agrippa I, he kept an eye on Antonia's Egyptian investments; when Josephus introduces Alexander (*AJ* 20.100) or Tacitus Berenice (*Hist.* 2.81), they comment first on their subject's wealth. Political and social advantages follow; Alexander's sons become Roman citizens with one marrying eastern royalty, and the other gaining high equestrian office in Rome and his descendants (e.g. Ti. Julius Alexander Iulianus: PIR^2 J 142) attaining senatorial rank.

Statistics can be misleading, but to quantify Sabinus I's success in enhancing the family's status, we might consider Suetonius's statement that, over a period of some 450 years, the Claudii claimed twenty-eight consulships, five dictatorships, seven censorships, six triumphs and two ovations (*Tib.* 1.2): in less than sixty years, the Flavians numbered in their ranks three emperors who were awarded fifty-nine 'triumphs' and thirty-four consulships. The only valid conclusion to emerge from such an array of figures is that Sabinus's careful work paid dividends.[19]

FLAVIANS AT COURT

Surviving evidence suggests that neither of Sabinus I's sons had spectacular early careers as senators.[20] Under Tiberius and Gaius, both held the normal posts, though Vespasian's first attempt to become aedile ended in failure and, on his second, he scraped in last (*Vesp.* 2.3): then his well-attested neglect of Rome's streets when he became aedile earned him Gaius's ire and a mud-covered toga as well (*Vesp.* 5.3; Dio. 59.12.3). Subsequent Flavian propaganda made as little as possible of Flavian successes under the Julio-Claudians whilst maximizing any achievements under acceptable (or less disreputable) members of the family such as Claudius and Britannicus. For Tiberius's and most of Gaius's reign, though, the facts spoke for themselves.

There was a change in 39 and it involved another member of the imperial family, Gaius's sister the younger Agrippina. Despite the fact that she was closely related to some of the Flavians' strongest supporters (child of Germanicus, niece of Claudius and grandchild of Antonia), she now developed and subsequently maintained a hostility to Vespasian that was at its strongest in Domitian's early years. In 39, she joined her current lover, Gaius's nominated successor Aemilius Lepidus (*PIR*² A 371), together with the legate of Upper Germany Cornelius Lentulus Gaetulicus (*PIR*² C 1390) in planning to murder Gaius (Dio 59.22.6). He was warned, and, shortly before 27 October 39,[21] both Lepidus and Gaetulicus were executed. Agrippina was fortunate to escape with her life, for there was written evidence of her involvement (*Gaius* 24.3); but she was publicly humiliated, being forced to carry her lover's ashes to Rome in person, and then was exiled. It was around the time of the conspiracy that the praetorian elections for 40 were held and Vespasian topped the poll. Suetonius hints (*Vesp.* 2.3) at his flattery of Gaius. In fact, he was almost a spokesman for the regime,[22] congratulating the emperor in speeches to the senate and adding to the public humiliation of Agrippina by urging that Lepidus and Gaetulicus 'be cast out unburied' (*Vesp.* 2.3). She did not forget the insult. When she became Claudius's fourth wife a decade later, not long before Domitian's birth, she did her best to ensure that Vespasian suffered.[23]

Now, the accession of Claudius was a notable milestone in the fortunes of Sabinus I's descendants, for members of Antonia's circle became extremely influential and powerful. L. Vitellius was chosen as the emperor's close advisor and Aulus Plautius given charge of the invasion of Britain. Within the royal palace, virtual control lay in the hands of Pallas (*PIR²* A 858) who had been 'the most trustworthy of Antonia's slaves' (*AJ* 18.182). Very powerful too was another freedman, Narcissus (*PIR²* N 23) – L. Vitellius cherished the images of Pallas and Narcissus with his household gods (*Vit.* 2.5) – and Narcissus's influence, according to Suetonius, *Vesp.* 4.1, secured the British appointment for Vespasian. With such influence at court, it is hardly surprising that the Flavians prospered; both Sabinus II and Vespasian were granted consulships in this period and the family may even have been raised to patrician status in 47.[24]

More remarkably, Vespasian's first son, at the age of about 7, was taken from his father's house and educated at court[25] with Claudius's own son, an honour reserved for foreign princes such as Agrippa, as has been noted – though occasionally other eminent Italians (the emperor Otho's grandfather and Marcus Aurelius) were brought up at court.[26] Titus and Claudius's son Britannicus shared the same teachers and the same curriculum (*Titus* 2), with obvious political, social and even educational advantages for the future emperor. When he returned from Britain, Vespasian must have been welcome at court.

But, by the time of Domitian's birth, the Flavians were less influential at court. Once Messallina had been replaced by Agrippina, the group centred on Antonia became disunited: when Claudius sought advice about a suitable replacement for his third wife, some (e.g. Vitellius) favoured Agrippina and others (e.g. Narcissus) Aelia Paetina.[27] The victor showed little mercy to the vanquished –

8

the Plautii suffered most, with Aulus Plautius's wife, Pomponia Graecina, being charged with practising a foreign religion (*Ann.* 13.32) and two other Plautii[28] forced to commit suicide (*Nero* 35.4; *Ann.* 15.60). There were other indications of the group's lack of unity – Petronia and Aulus Vitellius (the later emperor) were divorced and, at the same time, L. Vitellius died. For the Flavians, it meant that Vespasian was no longer welcome at court.

This decline in his fortunes, coinciding as it did with the birth of his younger son, has not infrequently been pressed into service to provide an explanation of the differences in character, attitude and personality between Titus (brought up in the imperial court) and Domitian (raised in 'poverty'). Such an explanation is unsatisfactory, for much of the evidence is illusory. In the first place, there were degrees of imperial displeasure, and so, when Cornelius Gallus fell out of favour, he was invited to commit suicide (Dio 53.23–4), whereas Vespasian's son Titus remained at court, continuing his education in close association with Britannicus until about 55, when the latter was poisoned (*Titus* 2). It would be a mistake, then, to lay too much stress on the decline in the family's fortunes. Domitian's uncle remained as governor of Moesia, his father was still in Rome, serving as a consular senator, his elder brother was still being educated at court. It may have been a decline but was hardly a disaster.

By the time of Domitian's eighth birthday, the family's fortunes had fully recovered. The obvious explanation lies in the events of March 59 when Agrippina was murdered by Nero. More than one future emperor was to benefit by the removal of her influence. Galba, for instance, had had an illustrious career between 33 and 47 with a consulship, the command of Upper Germany, service with Claudius in Britain and a proconsulship of Africa; then nothing (as far as we know) for the next thirteen years until his appointment to Spain *c.* 60. The decline was due to his relationship – or rather lack of it – with Agrippina. He had rejected her open advances to him; worse still, once the story reached the ears of his mother-in-law, she is reported to have abused Agrippina in public and then to have slapped her face (*Galba* 5.1). Agrippina never forgot an insult, as Vespasian discovered (*Vesp.* 4.2).

He too prospered after 59, being appointed to the prestigious proconsulship of Africa, whilst around this time his son-in-law Petillius Cerialis was given command of *legio IX* in Britain. Imperial favour was also bestowed on various friends and relatives of the Flavii. In 61, Caesennius Paetus, married to Domitian's first cousin Flavia Sabina, was made one of the two ordinary consuls, the other being the Flavian supporter P. Petronius Turpilianus,[29] whose immediate family exemplifies very well the links between the Petronii, Plautii, Pomponii and Vitellii that were so important in enhancing the status of Sabinus I's descendants. Turpilianus's uncle was Aulus Plautius who was the son of a Vitellia, had married a Pomponia and had a sister (Plautia) married to a Petronius (i.e. Turpilianus's father).[30] Again, Plautius Silvanus was sent to Moesia at this period and not long afterwards, Barea Soranus, an attested friend of Vespasian (*Hist.* 4.7), became proconsul of Asia (*PIR*[2] B 55).

Throughout Domitian's early years and adolescence, the family's status remained high, but progress was most marked in the 60s. A number of significant marriage alliances attest to it. Domitian's brother Titus, now in his mid-twenties, found a suitable wife in Arrecina Tertulla and it seems that Domitian's first cousin Sabinus III had also married into the same family, selecting one of Arrecina's sisters.[31] The Arrecini were an equestrian family of some considerable significance, for the father Arrecinus Clemens had been prefect of the praetorian guard under Gaius, with a son of senatorial rank who was also to become praetorian prefect and then hold two consulships and the prefecture of the city during the reigns of his Flavian relatives.[32] There were other advantages in the connexion with the Arrecini. According to Suetonius (*Vesp.* 4.3), the family of Vespasian experienced grave financial difficulties after his African proconsulship, and, as a result, Vespasian was obliged to mortgage his property to his brother Sabinus II and to engage in the trading of mules.[33] This was approximately the time of Titus's marriage to Arrecina: presumably, it was economically advantageous. Perhaps, too, this is the background to Suetonius's claim that Domitian's early youth was spent in poverty (*Dom.* 1.1). But the degree and duration of Vespasian's poverty should not be exaggerated, and it need not have been the only factor in Titus's marriage into a family with Flavian connexions already. A wife whose father had been praetorian prefect was most suitable for the offspring of consular senators.

Unfortunately, Arrecina soon died and Titus sought a second wife. Marcia Furnilla, daughter or niece of Vespasian's *amicus* Barea Soranus, was an excellent choice, with consular senators in her father's and mother's family.[34] In short, she was *splendidi generis* (*Vesp.* 4.3). A final indication of Vespasian's standing in the 60s is his selection to accompany Nero on his tour of Greece (*Vesp.* 4.4). Later, pro-Flavian sources made much of his alleged banishment 'not only from intimacy with the emperor but even from his public receptions' (4.4); his offence was either falling asleep during Nero's singing or else continually entering and leaving. Tacitus has a similar story of Vespasianic behaviour, but it is set before his selection for the Greek tour (*Ann.* 16.5), and one is entitled to doubt its accuracy. He would hardly have been included if he had publicly offended Nero.

Stress on banishment by Nero was essential to explain away the fact that, when Nero needed an experienced general to deal with the Jews in the winter of 66, he sent Vespasian with three legions; and if Nero's selection of Vespasian as commander-in-chief was surprising, that of Titus, Traianus and Cerialis as his immediate subordinates, legates of his three legions, was astonishing.[35] First and foremost, it was and remained unparalleled for the leader of an expeditionary force to have his own son commanding one of his legions; yet Titus was assigned to control *legio XV*. But he was not yet 30 and so was still ineligible to stand for the praetorship, the usual (but not inevitable) prerequisite for a legionary commander. His selection, then, was doubly odd. Equally puzzling was the appointment of Ulpius Traianus as legate of *legio X*. He was married to a Marcia, the sister (so it seems)[36] of Marcia Furnilla and thereby, for a time, Titus's brother-in-law. Sextus Vettulenus Cerialis, legate of *legio V*, also had Flavian connexions: he was of Sabine origin and may even have come from Vespasian's home town, Reate. The almost inescapable conclusion is that Vespasian had a completely free hand in selecting his commanders. So, despite the fact that some of Vespasian's friends (*Hist.* 4.7) were connected with the Pisonian conspiracy, Nero never doubted the Flavians' loyalty. Very wisely, Titus had divorced Marcia Furnilla at the first sign of trouble. But despots are suspicious: Corbulo had recently been invited to commit suicide. Not so with the Flavians. Soon after the suppression of the Pisonian conspiracy, Vespasian was given command of an army that was finally to number 60,000 men (*BJ* 3.66–9) and allowed to appoint his own subordinates, and this when his brother Sabinus II was virtually in control of Rome in his role of city prefect in the emperor's absence from the capital. It is hardly remarkable that historians writing during Vespasian's principate stressed the slightest hint of Flavian disgrace in the previous reign or invented

one if none existed: so Vespasian was covered in mud by Gaius, fell
asleep when Nero sang and was banished; Titus was born in a mean
house (*Titus* 1) and Domitian spent his early years in such poverty
that he had to sell himself to survive.

EDUCATION

So Vespasian's periods of temporary financial and political embar-
rassment should be seen in the proper light. He did not neglect his
younger son's education, even though he was not brought up at
court as Titus was (*Titus* 2). His later literary efforts, whatever their
worth as literature, are proof enough of Vespasian's concern. He
gave public recitals of his works (*Dom.* 2.2) and had had the standard
training in rhetoric to judge by his performance in a turbulent senate
in January 69, at the age of 18, when his father and brother were still
in the east and senatorial feeling were running high: even Tacitus had
to describe his speech as 'brief and restrained', noting, at the same
time, his ability to field awkward questions (*Hist.* 4.40). He had, at
least, been taken through the standard authors: Suetonius attests to
his ability to quote Homer (*Dom.* 12.3 and 18.2) and Vergil (*Dom.*
9.1) on appropriate occasions. Despite Suetonius's comment (*Dom.*
20) that Domitian never bothered to become familiar with poetry, we
have definite evidence that he wrote poetry during Vespasian's reign:
when the elder Pliny, who died during the eruption of Vesuvius in
79, dedicated his *Historia Naturalis* to Titus, he praised Titus's
poetry as being as good as Domitian's (*NH Praef.* 5). He wrote
poems on the fall of the Capitol in 69 (Martial 5.5.7) and, so it seems,
on the capture of Jerusalem (Valerius Flaccus, *Argon.* 1.10–12). We
have adulatory references (written before 96) to his poetical ability
in general, from Statius (*Achil.* 1.15), Silius Italicus (*Pun.* 3.621) and
Quintilian (*Inst. Or.* 4. *proem.*), as well as to his excellence in oratory
(e.g. *Pun.* 3.618 and *Inst. Or.* 10.1.91: he is as capable a poet as he is
a warrior), and just as many hostile accounts (written after 96) by
Tacitus (*Hist.* 4.86) and Suetonius (*Dom.* 2.2), both of whom used
the same word (*simulans, simulavit*) to describe his interest in poetry
as 'feigned'. As none of it (perhaps fortunately) survives, there is no
way of judging the validity of their assessments, nor is there any need
to, for the evidence is clear: Domitian had been soundly educated in
much the same way as any member of the senatorial élite of his time.
But who were his tutors? Certainly no one of the political eminence
of Titus's (*Titus* 2); but it has been suggested[37] that one of them was

12

Statius's father, an eminent *grammaticus* who had himself competed in various Neronian literary festivals, with victories in oratory and poetry.

Now Domitian's literary productions went beyond poetry: despite his alleged sensitivity on the topic, he had written and published a book on baldness. But it is highly unlikely that Domitian was genuinely interested in literature for its own sake.[38] On the other hand, he was well educated, able to converse elegantly (*Dom.* 20) and to produce memorable comments (20). On his accession, he abandoned his literary pretensions (20), limited his reading to Tiberius's commentaries, and devoted his attention to his own stern and rigid ideal of emperorship, re-establishing Augustan standards in money as well as in morals.[39] His ideal included a specific cultural as well as political role for the emperor and his court: they were to be the source of encouragement, the fountain-head, to the ruler's greater glory. Hence his seemingly atypical gesture in spending vast sums of money to restore fully the great library at Alexandria, even sending scribes to copy works that he was unable to purchase (*Dom.* 20). It was all part of the new imperial image.

No precise details are known of the circumstances of Domitian's upbringing in the late 50s and 60s. His father's return to full imperial favour was counterbalanced, as far as Domitian was concerned, firstly, by his absence as proconsul of Africa and secondly, a few years later (December 66), by his appointment, together with Titus, to Judaea, both of them trusted agents of Nero. So, between the ages of 15 and 18, he saw neither father nor brother, and his mother had been long dead. Probably, he had been left in the care of his uncle, Sabinus II, who, as Tacitus observes, was the most senior member of the family (*Hist.* 3.75), superior in status to Vespasian. The argument that he resided in Rome at this period with his uncle is, admittedly, tenuous. Sabinus had a house on the Quirinal,[40] and both Tacitus (*Hist.* 3.69) and Dio (65.17.2) refer to the fact that he summoned his children and Domitian to the Capitol, with the implication that the latter was living with them and that their present, nearby abode was unsafe. Nor was Domitian merely there on a temporary basis, since he must have been educated in Rome: at *Dom.* 1.2, Suetonius has him crossing the Tiber and taking refuge at the home of one of his school friends.

One can but speculate on the effect that it all had on his character. His later preference for his own company is one obvious outcome: both Dio (66.9.5: *c.* 70) and Suetonius (*Dom.* 3.1: after his accession) refer to this trait in his character, and, consistent with this, was his habit of taking solitary walks after a meal (*Dom.* 21).

AFTERMATH OF CIVIL WAR

Nothing is known of Domitian during the tumultuous eighteen months when three emperors (Nero, Galba and Otho) perished. On the other hand, his role in the confused events of December 69, culminating in the death of the emperor Vitellius by the afternoon of 20 December,[41] is described in (not always consistent[42]) detail by Tacitus (*Hist.* 4.59, 69, 74) and Suetonius (*Dom.* 1.2) and briefly by Dio (65.17.2–5) and Josephus (*BJ* 4.645–9). On 18 December, according to Tacitus, Sabinus II and some supporters occupied the northern summit (the *arx*) of the Capitol[43] and sent for his family and Domitian (*Hist.* 3.69). On the 19th, the Capitol was besieged and Sabinus killed (3.70–2), with Domitian escaping in Isaic disguise to spend the night with one of his father's clients, Cornelius Primus (3.74). Suetonius, on the other hand, has Domitian taken in by the temple attendant (*aedituus*) who concealed him for the night (*Dom.* 1.2): the next day, he escaped by mingling with a procession of Isis worshippers and found sanctuary with the mother of one of his school friends. Wellesley has attempted to reconcile the two accounts, but the result is not convincing.[44] Wiseman's argument is to be preferred,[45] i.e. (in essence) Tacitus's account is accurate, Domitian stayed with an *aedituus*, not the *aedituus* (i.e. of the temple of Jupiter Optimus Maximus or of the temple of Isis), and the Flavians occupied the *arx*, not the south-western summit.[46] The next day, Domitian presented himself to the invading Flavian forces (*Hist.* 4.86) and was hailed as *Caesar*. Subsequently, he tore down the attendant's house and replaced it with a *sacellum* to *Juppiter Conservator*, later converted into a huge temple to *Juppiter Custos* (*Hist.* 4.70).

After the events of December 69, the situation was grave: wisely, Vespasian and Titus remained well away, the former returning *c.* September 70, the latter in June of the following year.[47] Apart from the immediate aftermath of the battle, with the victorious Flavians seeking the spoils of battle, with blood and bodies everywhere (*Hist.* 3.83) and cruelty on a level with that shown by Sulla or Cinna (3.83), there were longer-term problems facing the conquerors – Vitellius's praetorians sought reinstatement, legionaries recently promised praetorian status (and therefore double pay) now demanded it

(4.46) and senators, emerging from their hiding-places after ten days, sought to exercise what they imagined to be their traditional role, urging that Neronian *delatores* be dealt with.[48] In the last days of December, supreme power had been in the hands of Antonius Primus (4.2) and the praetorian prefect Arrius Varus. But Mucianus had acted promptly. Once in Rome, he assumed control and proceeded to reduce the influence of Primus and Varus (4.11). Varus, though supported by Domitian, was replaced by M. Arrecinus Clemens, a Flavian relative but also a friend of Domitian (4.68). As well, Mucianus ensured that Primus was not admitted into Domitian's circle (4.80) and, as a result, Primus sought support from Vespasian personally. He failed to get it. In short, the real power was in Mucianus's hands (4.39).

Decisions made at Berytus some six months before[49] were now ratified. More immediate problems, some requiring a diplomatic approach, were solved by Mucianus and no one else.[50] One example will suffice to indicate Mucianus's *potentia* and Domitian's comparative insignificance.

Tettius Julianus, brother-in-law of Vespasian's powerful freedman finance minister and legate of the Moesian legion *VII Claudia* in 69, had been accused of having deserted it when it declared for Vespasian (*Hist*. 4.39).[51] Designated praetor for 70, Julianus was stripped of the honour by Mucianus at the very first meeting of a Vespasianic senate (1 January) and the post given to Plotius Grypus. But, on 3 January, Mucianus reversed his decision, gave Julianus his praetorship, but also allowed Grypus to retain his, even though the latter had (so it seems) acted at the instigation of Julianus's powerful enemy, the Moesian governor Aponius Saturninus who had tried to kill Julianus (2.89). The problem was a delicate one. Mucianus knew that, on the one hand, the support of the Danubian legions and of leaders such as Aponius Saturninus was especially vital in January 70; yet, on the other, powerful imperial freedmen could not be offended. This was the sort of decision only an experienced diplomat and administrator such as he could make.

As *Caesar*, Domitian moved into the imperial residence (4.2), was appointed praetor with consular power (4.3) and represented the family in the senate, urging restraint on those wishing to deal with the *delatores* and suggesting that awkward matters be referred to Vespasian (4.40). This was his role; coached by Mucianus, he acquitted himself well. Mucianus was at the helm, Domitian the figurehead.

Domitian was eager for military glory; the criticism levelled at him on this score is quite unfair.[52] Any member of the élite, at the age of 18 at least, believed that military glory surpassed everything else, for the entire world obeyed Rome because of that very quality, according to Cicero (*Pro Murena* 22); and his enthusiasm would have been enhanced by the fact that his father, uncle, brother and four other male relatives had personally led a legion (usually into battle[53]). Like Titus, he was impatient for military glory. Some few months later, when Titus and his senior officers were stationed on the Antonia supervising the fighting near the Temple, Titus was anxious to descend and join his men but 'was restrained by his friends on account of the gravity of the risk; ... they remarked that he would achieve more by sitting still on the Antonia as director of the contest' (*BJ* 6.132–3). Titus's impatience was, in a sense, understandable: he had already said that 'rapidity was essential to military renown' (*BJ* 5.498). So Domitian's attitude was perfectly natural and even more comprehensible. Given his background and the importance placed by society on military glory, what would surely have attracted criticism would have been any indication of disinterest in acquiring it.

Apart from difficulties in the city, attention was focused on the uprising in Germany,[54] where the Batavian auxiliaries of the Rhine legions, led by Civilis, had revolted and been joined by some of the Treveri under Classicus. Seven legions were sent from Rome, commanded by Petillius Cerialis,[55] probably Vespasian's son-in-law, and, when it was mistakenly thought that reinforcements were needed, Mucianus and Domitian marched north. On their way, they were informed that the uprising in Gaul had failed; so they stayed at Lyons and, before long, Civilis was also defeated. Soon it was rumoured that Mucianus had refused Domitian a command against the Gauls, and that Cerialis would not accept Domitian's suggestion that Cerialis should hand over his army to him (*Hist.* 4.86). But, whilst the details of the revolt and its rapid suppression are beyond dispute, the rumours of Domitian's attitude and behaviour are not. Possibly, his reaction was reported to Vespasian in exaggerated terms by Mucianus himself. It has been argued[56] that Vespasian hurried back to Rome in late summer of 70, not so much because he was worried about Domitian's conduct (*Dom.* 2.1), but rather to lessen Mucianus's influence in the capital. Titus's words to Vespasian, urging him to be lenient with Domitian, might be interpreted as a reference to the prominent *amicus* Mucianus: 'as for friends [*amici*],

16

time, changes in fortune, at times their ambition or their mistakes, may lessen, alter or destroy their affection' (*Hist.* 4.52).

On the other hand, adulatory comments in the poets on Domitian's military achievements are completely inaccurate and utterly worthless as historical evidence. He did not lack courage – even Tacitus had to admit that (3.44) – but references to his defending Jupiter while still a youth (Statius, *Theb.* 1.21), regaining the Palatine when it was held by an evil power (Martial 9.101.13), holding the reins of power and then giving them up (Martial 9.10.15–16), causing the Treveri to surrender (*BJ* 7.85) and terrifying the yellow-haired Batavians (Silius Italicus, *Pun.* 3.608) are literary excesses at best.

Domitian's behaviour at this period also attracted the attention of the literary sources. According to Dio (66.2.2–3), Mucianus and Domitian appointed so many governors, prefects and consuls that Vespasian wrote to Domitian thanking him for allowing Vespasian himself to continue as emperor. Suetonius has a different version of events, but much the same anecdote: in a single day, Domitian (but not Mucianus) made twenty appointments, causing Vespasian to express surprise that one of them was not a successor to Vespasian himself (*Dom.* 1.3). But many of these decisions would have already been made, or, at the very least, firm guidelines for them laid down at Berytus six months before;[57] however, this was a barrier neither to Vespasian's sense of humour nor to the inventive minds of hostile historians. Vespasian's witticism (whether he made it or not) had to be explained, and Dio's addition of Mucianus was supposed to provide a touch of verisimilitude.

Dio outlines the Gallic war briefly, with a reference to Cerialis but none whatsoever to Domitian. On the contrary, he implies that Domitian spent all his time near Alba seducing various unnamed married women and finally marrying one (66.3.4). Suetonius, on the other hand, reverses the order and depicts an even busier Domitian – seduction and distribution of official posts (*Dom.* 1.3) followed by war (2.1). Tacitus's version only serves to complicate matters. He has Domitian living not at Alba but on the Palatine, engaged in debauchery as well as adultery (*Hist.* 4.2). Whilst the apparent chronological inconsistencies are of minimal significance, the variants resulting from differences in artistic presentation, each account is consistent with the standard literary portrait of Domitian the emperor and represents an essential prelude to it – an emperor who preached morality but practised incest and murdered his opponents would surely have revealed such tendencies earlier. So the versions ought to be considered in this light.

Two facts are clear. He was determined to achieve military glory and he persuaded Lamia's wife, daughter of the esteemed Corbulo, to leave her husband and marry him – without, necessarily, seducing her first. All the rest is of dubious value.

Domitian's choice was eminently wise. Other Flavian marriage partners, Caesennius Paetus and Petillius Cerialis, were famed for their military incompetence, Paetus at Rhandeia and Petillius consistently.[58] But Corbulo's name was synonymous with strict discipline and achievement in battle, and he was a Neronian victim as well. A better candidate would have been hard to find. So there is no need to reject completely the evidence of the Cancelleria Reliefs.[59] Vespasian did not upbraid his son publicly: what was said in private no one knows.

ROLE BEFORE ACCESSION

Certain practical considerations predetermined Domitian's official position in the 70s. Whereas the first four Roman emperors reigned for over eighty years in all, the next four perished in little more than eighteen months. The ninth, Vespasian, was already 60 on his accession, but determined to secure the succession for his sons (*Vesp.* 25; Dio 66.12.1), the elder of whom, fresh from the conquest of Jerusalem, was now just over 30. That Titus should have become Vespasian's heir, even, some would argue, co-emperor,[60] was inevitable and his position had to be made secure if the dynasty were to last. A series of ordinary consulships, tribunician power, the censorship and the praetorian prefecture,[61] all fell to him. Domitian was left with honours, but not responsibility, and it is difficult to see what else Vespasian could have done. Domitian may not have approved, but he had been done no injustice.

He held the consulship six times (71, 73, 75, 76, 77 and 79) in the reign, replacing his father or brother and assuming office usually around 13 January, i.e. whereas they held the only two available 'ordinary' or more prestigious posts, he was regarded as the first replacement or 'suffect' consul, for they would retire after a term of two weeks only.[62] In 73, however, he was ordinary consul, but, according to Suetonius (*Dom.* 2.1), only because Titus ceded the post to him. Problems have arisen with this award since some coins[63] appear to have him designated to it as early as 71,[64] i.e. he was supposed to have become consul in 72, was later snubbed and then given the senior position in 73 as recompense. But the reading on these coins should be rejected and Suetonius's statement regarded as 'malicious':[65] Domitian received an ordinary consulship since his father and brother were about to assume the censorship in the course of that year. Throughout the reign, Titus always had two consulships fewer than Vespasian and Domitian one fewer than Titus: thus, in 76, Vespasian was *COS VII*, Titus *COS V* and Domitian *COS IV*, thereby reflecting exactly the relative status of each member of the family. But it was Vespasian's intention to honour his younger son as much as possible. After all, for non-Flavians, three consulships represented the summit, the *summum fastigium* (*Ep.* 2.1.2) of one's ambition and Mucianus alone was so honoured between 70 and 79.

His other honours included the titles *Caesar* and *Princeps Iuventutis*, various priesthoods (he is attested as *augur, frater arvalis, magister fratrum arvalium, pontifex* and *sacerdos collegiorum omnium*) and, from 72, he possessed the right to have coins issued theoretically under his own aegis.[66]

Two of his four known consular colleagues, Valerius Festus and Catullus Messallinus, became imperial *amici* after 81.[67] It would not be unreasonable to assume that his experience as consul provided both valuable training in senatorial procedure and worthwhile friendships amongst sympathetic senators. He must have been well aware of the senate's role after spending a decade therein. Perhaps his reservations on its relevance were based on personal observation.

On the other hand, the sources portray him as devoting himself to literature (*Dom.* 2.2), feigning madness and spending most of his time at the Alban villa impaling flies (Dio 66.9.3,4[68]): sulking in his retreat, he even refused to kiss his father's mistress Caenis (*Dom.* 12.3). Nor was military glory to be his, though he was anxious for it still. Around 75 (Dio 66.15.3), Vespasian rejected Vologaesus's request for some *auxilia* led by Titus or Domitian to deal with an invasion of the Alani (*Dom.* 2.2); undeterred, Domitian tried to bribe other eastern kings directly affected by the attack[69] to support the Parthian request, but it was all to no avail. As an ultimate insult, even though (so he claimed) he was left a share in imperial power according to the terms of his father's will, he still received nothing, since the will had been tampered with (*Dom.* 2.3) – and Titus was known as an expert forger (*Titus* 3.2). That Domitian was dissatisfied with his lot is not unlikely, but the extent of his reaction is hard to assess, given the bias of our sources.

No change occurred in Titus's brief reign: neither tribunician power nor *imperium* of any kind was offered him. Titus did promise that he would be his *consors* and *successor* (*Titus* 9.3), but carefully avoided doing anything about it: not for nothing had that astute diplomat been trained in a Neronian court. In any case, no longer married and only 40, he was some ten years younger than Claudius had been when he took his third wife and produced two children. Possibly, Titus preferred to keep his options open. Again, the general situation in 80 was vastly different from that of 70, and, as well, he could expect to rule for at least another thirty years, given the ages at death of Augustus, Tiberius, Claudius and Vespasian. So, despite the alleged constant plots of Domitian against him (*Titus* 9.3; *Dom.* 2.3), no immediate decision was necessary.

Evidence has been adduced to show Titus's hostility to Domitian. According to Gsell, Aelius Lamia, Domitia Longina's first husband, was granted a suffect consulship by Titus as an insult to Domitian.[70] It is far more likely that Titus was trying to honour a member of a family (the Plautii) that had supported the Flavians since the time of Augustus. Similar allegations centred on the promotion of Sabinus IV, grandson of Vespasian's brother and the oldest living male Flavian apart from Vespasian's sons. Titus, it is claimed, just before his death in September 81, designated Sabinus to the ordinary consulship for 82 so as to make Domitian fear that Sabinus was to be Titus's heir, thereby making Domitian 'more submissive'.[71] But the argument is worthless.[72]

No doubt brotherly affection was at a minimum, and not unexpectedly, since they hardly knew each other. Until Domitian was 4 (c. 55), Titus remained at court, educated with Britannicus (*Titus* 2); not long afterwards (c. 59), he left Rome for three years overseas as military tribune, returning to marry Arrecina Tertulla and then Marcia Furnilla (c. 63–5); in December 66, he was appointed to Judaea and remained in the east until 71.[73] One wonders what they would have had in common, in view of the difference of eleven years in their ages, and just when they would have had the time to repair the deficiency.

But, whatever the relationship between them, Domitian seems to have displayed mimimum concern for Titus during his illness in September 81. As the emperor lay dying on the 13th, Domitian made for the praetorians' camp, promised them a donative and was hailed as emperor (Dio 66.26.3). Once the news of his death reached Rome, the senators assembled, even before an edict could be issued (*Titus* 11), not to vote the usual powers to the new emperor, but to honour the dead one (*Titus* 11), a procedure hardly likely to reassure Domitian, who had to wait until the following day to receive *imperium* and the title *Augustus* (*CIL* 6.2060) together with *tribunicia potestas*, the office of *pontifex maximus* and the title *pater patriae*.[74]

2

COURT I

Influence, ability and money had secured the throne for Vespasian and his sons. In the early part of the first century, Sabinus I, well aware of the significance of the the court, had expertly gained access to it, leaving for his sons the task of becoming part of its inner circle; and it was Vespasian, rather than his older brother (Sabinus II) who was more successful in that Titus (and not Sabinus III) was educated at court. But they all accepted the court as it was, realizing but not openly proclaiming its centrality in government. Domitian was less subtle.

His ever-growing autocracy and preference for a monarchical system of government was paralleled by an open admission of what had long been obvious, that real power resided wherever the emperor was, wherever he chose to establish his court, and nowhere else; that was not necessarily on the Palatine. During the course of his reign, it must have seemed to many that not only was the senate irrelevant but also that Rome itself was not perpetually the centre of power. Other emperors had left Rome without unduly disturbing the process of government, but none as often as Domitian, none as openly.

In the first place, it might fairly be asked how frequently Domitian bothered to attend the senate. A recent study produced somewhat pessimistic results, finding the question impossible to determine.[1] But we can at least be fairly certain that he did not emulate his father, who, we are told, lived rarely in the Palace (Dio 66.10.4), but did regularly attend meetings of the senate, until old age prevented him doing so (Dio 66.10.5). On the other hand, most of the sources are decidedly unhelpful in assessing the frequency of Domitian's attendance at senatorial meetings. According to Pliny, his senators were terrified, discussing matters of no importance or else participating in some great crime (*Ep.* 8.14.5; *Pan.* 76.3). But even that does not imply that the emperor was present, for, through his associates, he had ready access to what occurred in the Curia: elsewhere (*Pan.* 62.3–4), Pliny maintains that there were two groups in the senate, the emperor's favourites and the rest. Again, an ex-quaestor known as the *ab actis senatus* was appointed, perhaps for the first time in Domitian's reign, to supervise the senate's proceedings: possibly, like Junius Rusticus under Tiberius (*Ann.* 5.4),[2] he did more than this. Somewhat more definite, though, is Suetonius's reference to Domitian's urging the senate to accept his motion that those found guilty of treason be allowed 'free choice in the manner of their death . . . [so] all will know that I was present at the meeting of the senate' (*Dom.* 11.3). Whilst the evidence is but slight, it could well be that, on those occasions when he was in Rome, Domitian did not attend senatorial meetings on a regular basis.

ASPECTS OF DOMITIAN'S COURT

Even in the early empire, the source of all real influence and power was the imperial court, access to which was far from easy. Two possible avenues existed – via a powerful aristocratic family in favour with the Caesars or possibly through the goodwill of one of the imperial freedmen or women with constant access to the imperial family. The Flavians used both.

It can not be stressed too often that a fully developed court was in existence well before the time of Domitian: one of the more visible indications of the change from republic to empire was physical – the development of an imperial court and imperial palace.[3] Dio explains the latter term:

> The royal residence is called the 'Palatium', not because it was ever decided that this should be so, but because the emperor lives on the Palatium and has his headquarters there . . . [and], if the emperor resides anywhere else, his dwelling retains the name of 'Palatium'.
>
> (53.16.5–6)

Hence our 'Palace':[4] and Domitian frequently lived outside Rome, far more so than any of his predecessors, a fact that did not endear him to the senate, for he was publicly proclaiming its impotence.

The Palatine hill had long been the favoured residential area of the capital, but, under the empire, private homes gradually disappeared, with few surviving the fire of 64, and a complex of imperial residences, houses and gardens developed. Domitian's grandiose palace, for instance, covered the entire south-eastern half of the hill.

Palatium and aula

It is perfectly proper to speak of the imperial 'palace', for Suetonius, who was only twenty years younger than Domitian, uses the word frequently in its modern sense. Tiberius, for instance, starved Drusus to death in one of the Palace's lower rooms (*in ima parte Palatii: Tib.* 54.2), Gaius opened a brothel in his (*lupinar in Palatio: Gaius* 41.1) and Vitellius's 'abdication' was announced to his assembled troops from the Palace steps (*pro gradibus Palatii: Vit.* 15.2). On the other hand, it should be noted that eminent senators, in the republic as well as in the empire, were expected to possess a city house appropriate to their status, as Vitruvius, writing under Augustus (6.5.2), pointed out.[5] But the imperial palace differed from the elaborate establishments of the republican nobility not only in size but more importantly in function. It became the centre of political, intellectual and social life: Aulus Gellius refers to scholars conversing in the *vestibulum* of the Palatine (*NA* 4.1.1) or in the *area Palatina* (*NA* 20.1.2) while waiting for the imperial *salutatio*.[6] Already Augustus had a freedman (C. Julius Hyginus: *PIR*[2] J 357) in charge of what Suetonius (*De Gramm.* 20) called the Palatine library and, by Domitian's time, that function was performed by Sextus (*PIR*[1] S 487), whom Martial described as 'the eloquent votary of Palatine Minerva, [able to] enjoy more closely the genius of the god' (i.e. Domitian: 5.5.1–2). By his time, too, the role of the senior imperial freedmen was recognized linguistically with the adjective *Palatinus* being applied to them – Parthenius, his *cubicularius*, is described by Martial as *Palatinus Parthenius* (4.45).

It is perfectly accurate, too, to speak of an imperial 'court' (*aula*). Gaius, so we are told by Suetonius, was asked by his sister Agrippina to give her child (i.e. the future emperor Nero) a name: his suggestion, *Claudius*, was scorned since Claudius was the laughing stock of the court (*ludibria aulae: Nero* 6.1). Or again, Nero's courtiers approved of Otho – *prona in eum* (i.e. *Othonem*) *aula: Hist.* 1.13 – because he was like Nero. Such were Vitellius's attributes that he had a prominent position in the courts (*praecipuum in aula locum*) of three emperors, viz. in Gaius's (because of his ability to drive a chariot), in Claudius's (for his devotion to dice) and also in Nero's (as he arranged for Nero to be asked to play the lyre: *Vit.* 14). Vespasian was in terror (*trepidus*) at being forbidden Nero's court (*aula interdicta*) and did not know what he was to do or where to go (*Vesp.* 14).

Modern readers tend to expect ancient (and medieval) courts to have certain features. The imperial court had them too, and the adjective *aulicus* ('pertaining to a court') was used to describe them. Nero had court wrestlers (*luctatoribus aulicis: Nero* 45.1); Domitian's gladiators had all the splendour of the court (*aulico apparatu: Dom.* 4.2). Tiberius and 'one of the dwarfs standing among the jesters' discussed the fate of a man charged with treason (*Tib.* 61.6); Claudius, too, was particularly fond of his jesters (*Ann.* 12.49). Centuries later, dwarfs were still significant features in the courts of Italy and England: at the marriage of two of Charles I's dwarfs, Richard Gibson and Anne Shepherd, each a metre high, Charles himself gave the bride away.[7] Similarly, in the imperial court, we hear of Domitian's dwarf,[8] with whom he used to converse in public (*Dom.* 4.2), of an unarmed dwarf in the arena (Martial 1.43.10) and of a fighting group of dwarfs at the Saturnalia (*Silvae* 1.6.57). Like many Romans, he was fascinated by the unusual:[9] he even arranged for combats in the arena between women and dwarfs (Dio 67.8.4). In general, the imperial court of the first century had all the paraphernalia and trappings of a medieval court.

The similarity is obvious from the comments of various contemporary writers. The court had a role in the succession problems under Tiberius, encouraging Gaius's hopes (*Gaius* 12.1): Seneca claimed that it was very rare to reach old age at (Gaius's) court (*De Ira* 2.33.2); Martial complained of the traffic in empty rumour in the emperor's palace (4.5.7); and Tacitus (*Ann.* 3.55), Plutarch (*Conjug. Praec.* 17) and Pliny (*Pan.* 45.5) express the same theme as Herodian (1.2.4) that 'subjects always model their lives on the ideals of their ruler'.[10] It is not just coincidence that Cicero in 50 BC and Tacitus 150 years later both associate the words *aula* ('court') and *rex* ('king'), Cicero referring to Ariobarzanes (*Ad Fam.* 15.4.6) and Tacitus to Abdagaeses (*Ann.* 6.43).[11]

Whatever the rhetoric, the early empire was a monarchy, and, even if it had not been indicated by other evidence, the language of contemporary writers alone reveals it clearly; and as well as the consequential impotence of the imperial senate as a body, we have the fact that tremendous influence was wielded by a few favoured courtiers – senators, equestrians, freedmen and others. Access to the court was vital for social advancement, and the methods sometimes used to gain such access were certainly not for the squeamish: Suetonius relates how Otho pretended to love an influential freedwoman of Nero's court, a difficult task as she was old and all but decrepit (*anum ac paene decrepitam*: Otho 2.2), but, nonetheless, he persevered. So power was concentrated in the imperial court, not in the senate house, for the emperor was most often to be seen *in aula*, where men's real views of him were formed. Domitian illustrates this perfectly: his court not only passed judgment on him but also carried it out. Those responsible for his assassination, according to Suetonius, were his friends, favourite freedmen and his wife (*Dom.* 14.1) – in essence, his courtiers.

The court outside Italy

On five separate occasions, Domitian left Italy on military expeditions, viz. in 82/3 (Rhine), 85 and 86 (Danube), 89 (Rhine and Danube) and 92 (Danube), but not a great deal of evidence survives to enable an assessment either of the exact duration of these journeys or of the size and nature of the retinue that accompanied him. Legally, the latter was indistinguishable from the army itself, both simply part of the imperial *comitatus*,[12] but practically, any such expedition posed a variety of problems, as Suetonius instances in his *Life of Tiberius* (38). That emperor planned, but did not undertake a number of provincial tours – so much so that people used to call him 'Callipedes' after the actor of that name, famous for imitating a long-distance runner who never moved from the same spot. Nonetheless, transport always had to be chartered, sources of food and drink determined, and even vows for his safe return arranged in advance (*Tib.* 38). The prelude could also include sacrifices and visits to a number of temples (*Ann.* 15.36). Once outside the city, the emperor was legally on campaign, with the practical side of the journey in the hands of the *a copiis Augusti*, such as Plotius Grypus for part at least of his journey in 92.[13] Presumably, Domitian's retinue was large: we know that, on one occasion, it included his taster, Ti. Claudius Zosimus,[14] whilst his *comites* probably included Fabricius Veiento and Julius Frontinus in 82/3[15] and certainly Lucianus Proclus in 89 (Dio 67.11.50).

Less clear is the effect that these journeys had on his reputation. According to Pliny, they were like plundering forays, like the attacks of the very barbarians from whom he was fleeing (*Pan.* 20.4), with property being destroyed and houses emptied to provide forced lodgings. Now, in view of Domitian's well-attested concern for the provinces (*Dom.* 8.2), one is tempted to dismiss Pliny's claims as nonsense, and nonsense they may well be. But the terms (or, rather, the implications) of Domitian's *mandata* to his Syrian procurator Claudius Athenodorus ought to be borne in mind, in particular the provision that force was not to be used contrary to the emperor's wishes, or that an imperial diploma was needed before requisitioning anything:[16] perhaps it would be over-cynical to interpret this as authorizing official robbery.

So the elaborate preparations these journeys involved, the size of the retinue, and, not least, the repetition of prayers for the emperor's safe return must have served to keep on reminding members of the aristocracy that the administration of the empire could be divorced not only from the senate but also from the city itself. Nor were his absences brief: we know that his fifth expedition (in 92) lasted some eight months (Martial 9.31.3), but, unfortunately, have nothing nearly as accurate for the other four. On the basis of what we do know, though, he could well have spent the best part of three years or 20 per cent of his reign outside Rome and Italy.

The court at Alba

But a considerable amount of his time seems to have been spent at his 'villa' at Alba, some 20 kilometres out of the city on the Via Appia. The massive size of his 'retreat' (*secessus*: *Dom.* 19) there belies the name 'villa': apart from the main palace usually attributed to Rabirius, there were the reservoirs, baths, theatre, circus and 300-metre-long cryptoporticus.[17] According to Dio, he had the area set apart as a kind of Acropolis (67.1.1), and both Tacitus (*Agr.* 45) and Juvenal (4.145) refer to it as the *arx Albana*, i.e. the 'Alban citadel', with the clear implication that it was the abode of a tyrant.

Most importantly, he seems to have been happy there, for he indulged in the sport he loved, hunting and, in particular, displaying his skills as an archer: he could shoot two successive arrows into an animal in such a way that they looked like horns, as well as firing four towards the out-stretched palm of one of the slaves so that they would pass harmlessly between the fingers (*Dom.* 19). Again, it was here, during the early part of Vespasian's reign, that he conducted his affair with Domitia Longina (Dio 66.3.4).

In comparison with what we know about his five journeys outside
Italy, the evidence we have for his activities at Alba is comprehensive,
in the sense that it shows him performing a variety of obviously
imperial tasks there, rather than in Rome, as one might expect.

The 'privy council' sometimes met there. In fact, whilst it is not
very often that any meetings of an emperor's *consilium* can be
attested, two of Domitian's are known and both of them were held
at the Alban villa. In Juvenal's fourth satire, the terrified imperial
amici were summoned *Albanam in arcem* as though they were going
to discuss the fate of the Chatti or the Sycambri (145–7); and an
inscription records that, at a meeting held *in Albano* on 22 July 82,
Domitian used the 'distinguished men of each order as advisers'
to settle a land dispute between the Falerienses and the Firmani.[18]
Tacitus's comment that Catullus Messallinus's 'noisy advice' was
not heard beyond the *arx Albana* presumably refers to a private
meeting between informer and emperor rather than to an official
meeting of the 'privy council'.

Cornelia, the chief Vestal, was tried there for *incestum*. The chief
priest (i.e. Domitian), accompanied by the other *pontifices*, held
the trial at the Alban villa rather than at the Regia (*Ep.* 4.11.6),
with Cornelia being condemned in her absence. Despite Pliny's
comments, there was nothing irregular in the choice of site: it was
not being held *intra cubiculum*.[19]

Here, too, the special games in honour of Minerva were held
almost every year, with contests of poets, orators and gladiators (*Dom.* 4.4; Dio 67.1.2; Juv. 4.99): Martial comments on
the gold olive-wreath prize (5.1.1) and Statius was inordinately
proud of the victories he won there (*Silvae* 3.5.28; similarly
5.3.227–9).

Our evidence, then, suggests that a surprising variety of his
imperial duties were performed at the Alban villa. When these
are taken in conjunction with his absences on the Rhine and
Danube, it is clear that he (quite correctly) saw his powers as
being in no way limited to the *domus Flavia*. More importantly,
though, the geographical barrier between emperor and senator was
more substantial and real. There was now no subterfuge.

Evidence of Juvenal and Dio

A number of Domitian's courtiers appear in Juvenal's fourth satire,
describing what purports to have been a meeting between Domitian

and some of his *amici*, to discuss, not important policy matters, but the fate of a fish that had been presented to the emperor.[20] His description of the meeting's tone is vivid and striking: allowing for a satirist's exaggeration, we may even find a grain of truth in it. Apart from the emperor, eleven were present, all terrified, both before the meeting (4.75) and after it (4.146); not one made the slightest objection to the triviality of the matter on the agenda; courtiers of senatorial rank were kept waiting at the door until the fish was shown to the emperor (4.65) and one of them, Montanus, required six lines of verse just to say 'No' (4.130–5). And Domitian hated them all (4.73).

One of Dio's anecdotes provides corroborating evidence of a sort. In some detail, he describes the dinner party (or, rather, the funeral banquet) held for those who died in the Dacian campaign (67.9.6). Leading senators and equestrians were invited. The ceiling, walls and floor of the room were black, each guest had what looked like a gravestone for a place-tag, boys painted black danced before them, the dishes provided were those offered for the spirits of the dead, no one spoke except Domitian (and he limited his conversation to topics connected with death and slaughter) and, when the meal was over, they were sent home accompanied, not by their own slaves, but by some they did not know. Throughout the banquet, Dio asserts (67.9.3), they feared they would have their throats cut, a feeling exacerbated when, as soon as they reached their homes, a messenger came from the emperor. This time they expected to die (67.9.5), but, instead, received expensive gifts. All night, they had been 'in terror' (Dio 67.9.1–6).

Now it is hazardous to attempt to recreate the atmosphere of Domitian's court from evidence such as this; but he was assassinated by his courtiers, those who knew him best, and their motivation demands explanation. The dramatic date of Juvenal's fourth satire is *c.* 82,[21] that of Dio almost a decade later, yet both insist on the atmosphere of terror and unreality that pervaded the court. Even if one makes allowances for the elaboration and amplification to be expected from writers such as Juvenal and Dio, it does not seem to have been a product of the last years of the reign alone. Their evidence is given greater weight by Suetonius's account of Domitian's assassination: the relevant chapter (14) begins with a statement that everyone was terrified of the emperor.

Evidence of Statius and Martial

The evidence provided by the court poets Statius and Martial is consistent with this. Discussing the numerous passages in their works that praise Domitian or, on the contrary, those sections of the *Panegyricus* that laud Trajan, would be equally tedious; on the other hand, some general observations should be made. According to Millar

> If our only evidence for the regime of Domitian were the poems written during it, we should see the imperial court as a benign centre of patronage, literary as well as official, and the scene of a civilized existence carried on against a background of elegant houses and suburban estates.[22]

But we cannot simply reject the poets' evidence and assume the contrary, that, since Domitian was an autocrat, he must have imposed, through his court, his own narrow concept of artistic taste, a sort of baroque mannerism. Unlike his father, Domitian had literary pretensions, and some ability as well. His interests were not narrow: for instance, he must have encouraged Rabirius in his innovative approach to architecture. Perhaps he favoured the baroque or mannered style in sculpture, literature and architecture, in short mannerism as distinct from classicism.[23] So, for most critics, there are obvious similarities between the style of Statius's *Thebaid* and the relief panels on the Arch of Titus, both described as 'Flavian baroque'[24] and some even go so far as to imagine the existence of a close connection between autocracy and mannerism.[25]

On the other hand, evidence shows that he did not impose his preferences in cultural matters. Consider the Cancelleria Reliefs, found near the Palazzo della Cancelleria in Rome between 1937 and 1939.[26] Many scholars have remarked on their non-baroque appearance and classicizing style, so different from the panels on the Arch of Titus; others have gone further, claiming that, for this very reason, they cannot be Domitianic:

> We are [with these reliefs] in a realm of classicizing beauty behind which can be observed new principles of abstraction of forms, hieratic scale of figures and irrationality of special relationships which far remove the Cancelleria reliefs from Flavian concepts of both form and content.[27]

So, it is argued, if apparently Domitianic sculpture is inconsistent with modern canons of what his taste must have been, then it is not proper to regard it as Domitianic and better to consign it to a more suitable[28] period. The whole topic deserves more detailed treatment than can legitimately be given here, but it is relevant to an assessment of the atmosphere of the court itself, a court where, surprisingly, individuality had some scope.

Furthermore, whilst instances of Martial's and Statius's adulation of the emperor are numerous enough, on some occasions their remarks can perhaps be described as close to vicious satire,[29] as in parts of the latter's poem (*Silvae* 3.4) on the locks of the imperial favourite Flavius Earinus.[30] Born in Pergamum, Domitian's eunuch wanted to send some hair-clippings to the temple of Asclepius there[31] and Domitian asked Statius to write a poem on the topic. No commission could possibly have been more difficult – a poem on hair for an emperor who was, so it seems, notoriously sensitive[32] about his own baldness (*Dom.* 18.2) and praise of an imperial eunuch when the emperor had forbidden castration, 'immature bodies suffering an unutterable outrage.'[33]

Some passages are more significant than others. At lines 14–19, Statius introduced the comparison between Jupiter/Juno/Ganymede and Domitian/Domitia/Earinus, claiming that, whereas Juno was jealous of Ganymede ('he on whom Juno always looks in anger': 14–15), Domitian's consort had nothing but praise for Earinus ('Ausonian Jove and Roman Juno [i.e. Domitian and Domitia] alike look on [Earinus] with kindly brow and both approve': 17–19), savage irony surely,[34] when Domitia is portrayed as delighting in her husband's open display of pederasty. But the key passage is the reference to the boy's castration, performed (so we are told) by Asclepius himself –

> The son of Phoebus with quiet skill gently bids his body lose its sex, unmarred by any wound. But Cytherea is devoured by anxious care, and fears lest the boy suffer. Not yet had the noble clemency of our prince begun to keep our males untouched from birth; today it is forbidden to destroy sex and violate manhood.
>
> (*Silvae* 3.4.69–75[35])

It has been described as 'a ludicrous if not degrading conceit . . . [with] an effect hardly less than emetic';[36] and what are we to make of Venus's fear that castration might prove painful!

Perhaps it was an attack on the emperor's hypocrisy, composed along the lines recommended by Quintilian: 'you can speak well and make open statements against the tyrants we were discussing, provided the statement can be understood in another way' (*Inst. Or.* 9.2.67).[37] Imperial pederasty is hinted at by Martial in 9.36, one of his epigrams on Earinus: 'My Caesar has a thousand servants like you, and his mighty hall has difficulty in holding his divinely handsome youths' (9.36.9–10).[38] On that assessment, it has to be assumed (as Statius's and Martial's survival indicates) that all this was taken as a compliment and that no flattery was too outrageous for Domitian.

So, on the available evidence, whilst Domitian's concern for the minutiae of administration did not cause him to impose on his court his own standards of artistic taste, nonetheless the atmosphere of his court was uneasy and highly artificial at best. To that extent, Statius's and Martial's evidence is consistent with that provided by Dio and Juvenal.

Evidence of his guests

Domitian's treatment of guests invited to the palace provides an insight into the atmosphere of the court. Dio's anecdote (67.9.1–6) has already been considered. According to Pliny (*Pan.* 49), Domitian avoided his subjects and lived a life of solitude behind locked doors (49.2), whereas Trajan worked and ate in public (49.4–5). Trajan did not display meanness by cutting his banquets short (5–6) nor eat a solitary meal before his guests arrived, watch their every move, belch at them, throw food at them rather than present it and then, after entertainment provided by practitioners of some eastern superstition, depart for private excesses (6–8). On the other hand, Suetonius (*Dom.* 21) refers to Domitian's banquets as numerous, generous but not prolonged; he ate little himself, since he preferred a substantial meal in the middle of the day, there were no drinking competitions, and, after the banquet, he would indulge in a solitary walk. Martial, too, attests to his temperate drinking habits (4.8.10). Pliny's story appears to be highly imaginative, that of Suetonius more probable, given the general hostility shown to the emperor in both their accounts of him. Compare the different interpretations of Domitian's fondness for solitude, attested elsewhere as the topic of Vibius Crispus's jokes (Dio 66.9.5; *Dom.* 3.1). But a preference for his own company was one of his 'errors', a socially disastrous practice, and all the more so when coupled with an aversion to drinking heavily (unlike Trajan: *SHA*, *Hadr*. 3.3 and *Alex. Sev.* 39.1). In short, he was probably regarded as socially incompetent and, if we accept the general accuracy of Dio's account (67.9.1–6), he was at times given to bizarre practical jokes. The better one knew him, the less one could like him, for uncertainty soon gave way to fear.

COURTIERS: FAMILY

Essentially, Domitian's courtiers consisted of his family, his *amici* and his freedmen, some of whom lived permanently at court, whereas others were summoned with varying degrees of frequency. To assess the impact and significance of his court, the various members of each group merit consideration.

Domitia Longina

Daughter of Nero's general Corbulo and wife of L. Aelius Lamia Plautius Aelianus (Dio 66.3.4; *Dom.* 1.3),[39] she was one of the married women whom the 18-year-old Domitian is supposed to have seduced in the months between Vitellius's fall (December 69) and his father's return to Rome (?13 October 70).[40] With characteristic use of *vituperatio*, both Suetonius (*Dom.* 1.3) and Tacitus (*Hist.* 4.2) refer to his sexual activities at this time, the immoral prince being the precursor of the imperial monster. Probably, he married her late in 70. At *Dom.* 22, Suetonius has Domitian persistently refusing to marry his niece Julia at the same time as he was involved in an affair with Domitia. Apparently more precise, Dio portrays Domitian firstly as having various mistresses and then as devoting his attentions solely to Domitia Longina at his Alban villa, ultimately marrying her (66.3.4). Finally, Domitian's first child was born when he was consul for the second time, i.e. 73 (*Dom.* 3.1).[41] So the following timetable seems most likely: Vespasian returned to Rome in October 70 with the news of Domitian's unsatisfactory behaviour still fresh in his mind (*Hist.* 4.51), tried but failed to arrange a dynastic marriage for him with Julia and subsequently acquiesced in his son's choice. There is no reason to doubt the genuineness of Domitian's affection for his wife.

Fait accompli or not, the marriage was politically advantageous for Vespasian. Those senators less than enthusiastic at the prospect of Vespasian as emperor would have viewed his son's choice of wife

33

with cautious approval. Her ties with the so-called Stoic opposition were one advantage. Her father, brother-in-law (Annius Vinicianus) and his brother (Annius Pollio) were victims of the purge that had followed the discovery of the Pisonian conspiracy:[42] Annius Pollio, for instance, married to Barea Soranus's daughter Servilia, had been exiled, returning presumably not long before Domitian's marriage. So the expectation may have been that it would serve to counteract senatorial opposition and even help to re-establish the Flavians' connections with prominent Stoics, severed by Vespasian some six years previously when he withdrew his friendship with Barea Soranus and his ilk (*Hist.* 4.7) and had Titus divorce Barea Soranus's niece Marcia Furnilla, (*Titus* 4.2).[43]

The immediate advantage, though, was her father's name and reputation: he had been Nero's most popular and successful general and his reputation had not suffered by the manner of his death. Twelve years in the east had gained him a substantial *clientela*, not least being the numerous senior officers whose future careers had depended on him.[44] His enforced suicide was a disaster for them; his daughter's marriage in the new regime's first year represented a complete reversal of their fortunes.

In a more general way, though, marriage between Vespasian's son and Corbulo's daughter was part of wider Flavian policy: the new emperor strove to sever any Neronian ties or at least to distance himself from his family's achievements in the previous decade (thus he was portrayed not so much as a member of Nero's court but as having been expelled from it), to stress any links with the more respectable members of the Julio-Claudian dynasty (hence the emphasis on Titus's childhood friendship with Britannicus: *Titus* 2) and to rehabilitate Nero's victims or those disadvantaged by him (hence Vespasian's public statement that the award of Plautius Silvanus's triumphal *ornamenta* should not have been 'left to me': *ILS* 986).

Not long after his accession, Domitian is said to have divorced Domitia because of her adultery with the actor Paris, and then, after a brief period of separation, to have taken her back, claiming that the people demanded it (*Dom.* 3.1). According to Dio, he even planned to have her executed but was persuaded not to do so by (L. Julius) Ursus; Paris was less fortunate, being murdered by Domitian in the street (67.3.1). Soon after, despite having previously refused to marry Julia (*Dom.* 22), he proceeded to live openly with her (Dio 67.3.2) and even to set a date for their wedding (Philostratus,

Vita Apoll. 7.7). Finally, after being reconciled with Domitia, he still maintained the affair with Julia (Dio 67.3.2).

Much of this is implausible. Stories of imperial adultery are not uncommon and should be regarded with suspicion. Paris[45] was a well-known actor, to be more precise a *pantomimus*: by name, profession, origin and status, he was not the sort of lover likely to be chosen by the daughter of a Domitius Corbulo.[46] Nor is his exact role at all clear. Juvenal describes him as an influential courtier as well, 'appointing men to military commands' (7.88). More interesting is his fate. The *Lex Julia de adulteriis coercendis* permitted a husband to kill a man of Paris's class 'caught in the act of adultery in his own home'; he had also to 'divorce his wife without delay', and 'if he does not do this, he does not slay with impunity'.[47] In the latter instance, he would be guilty of *lenocinium*.[48] The sources would have one believe, however, that Domitian divorced his wife, killed Paris in the public street, was later reconciled with her and then remarried her, thereby infringing the *Lex Julia* not once but twice. So, at a time when he was about to develop moral legislation, having already been introduced as seducing 'a nameless horde of respectable matrons'[49] he is portrayed as completely disregarding the legislation he was determined to reinforce. To underline the *vituperatio*, Suetonius has Domitian hypocritically removing from the list of jurors the name of an equestrian 'for having taken back his wife after divorcing her and charging her with adultery'(8.3) – applying the *Lex Julia* to others after infringing it himself with impunity. To emphasize the point even further, Suetonius proceeds immediately to describe his *saevitia* towards the Vestal Virgins (8.4), in expected contrast to his criminal indulgence towards Domitia.[50]

The task remains to disentangle something like the truth from these improbabilities. One observation must first be made. If Domitian actually divorced his wife and then remarried her, it is surprising that the sources have not commented on the rarity of such an action, all but unprecedented in the Roman aristocracy.[51] But he did not divorce her,[52] she was probably exiled *c.* 83, as was Tiberius Julius Aug. lib.: then, after executing Sabinus IV and allowing his wife Julia to live (or remain living) in the palace, Domitian was obliged to recall her to silence the malevolent rumours of some of his courtiers. Perhaps she was guilty, not of adultery with one of the court entertainers, but of showing him sufficient favour to excite and inspire the malicious. Domitian's preference for solitude (*Dom.* 21) may well have annoyed her, possibly her failure to produce another son annoyed him. At all events, after a brief separation, she returned to the palace and lived there with him until the assassination. Dio's bizarre story of Domitian personally killing an actor in the street is highly unlikely,[53] as is the supposed affair with Julia and its later development, the abortion he forced on her (*Dom.* 22; Juv. 2.29–33 and *Ep.* 4.11.6). Rumours about Julia/Domitian and Paris/Domitia were very probably spread by the malevolent section of the court and eagerly repeated by Pliny, Juvenal and other post-Domitianic writers.

Some scholars have argued that a 'Titus faction' was in existence for most, if not all of Domitian's reign, that it was heavily involved in the early conspiracies against him and that, since Aelius Lamia, Domitia's first husband, had been executed at that time, she too was a member of it.[54] Included too was Julia, who has been seen as the faction's figurehead.[55] Subsequently, its influence spread, with the Ulpii, the Vettuleni, the Caesennii, Tiberius Julius Alexander and Flavius Silva as its more significant members; Pegasus and Ursus were moved from office as (so it is claimed) they were two of Titus's supporters and Civica Cerialis's execution was the result of his 'close ties with Titus.'[56] Included as well should be the two patricians whom Titus spared even though they had plotted against him (*Titus* 9.1).[57] Their horoscopes, according to Titus, showed that danger threatened them both, but at some future time, a prediction that turned out to be true (*Titus* 9.2). But who were they? Since L. Salvius Otho Cocceianus, Ser. Cornelius Scipio Salvidienus Orfitus and M'. Acilius Glabrio were patricians executed by Domitian (*Dom.* 10.2), they must, so it is argued, be possible candidates. All these, then, have been claimed as members of the *partes* of Titus that had Julia for a figurehead and Domitia as a supporter.

But the entire edifice is far from secure. Domitia's involvement with the *partes* of Titus is based on the early execution of Aelius Lamia and, according to Castritius, on the affair between Titus and Domitia.[58] But even the rumours of her misconduct with him were rejected by Suetonius (*Titus* 10.2); and there is no evidence whatsoever to indicate that Domitia's husband was put to death as early as 83. Equally dubious is the very existence of a 'Titus faction'. To take but one example – Ursus's removal from office can be explained by his lack of vigour as praetorian prefect. The existence of the so-called *partes* of Titus lacks ancient support: the whole theory should be discarded. Domitia was not part of the opposition.

She became pregnant again in 90, so it is often claimed.[59] The argument is based on the epigram of Martial assigned to that year beginning 'Be born . . . great child, to whom your father may entrust . . . the everlasting reins [of empire]' (6.3). Reasonably enough, most[60] have interpreted it as indicating that the emperor's wife was expecting a child. However, as has been pointed out[61] this is by no means certain. We know of only one child born to Domitia, a son in 73 (*Dom.* 3.1); he died young, as Martial's epigram 4.3 confirms, whilst, in another written after 6.3, he implies that Domitian still had lost only one child (9.86).[62] Moreover, had there been a miscarriage in 90, he would either have withdrawn 6.3 from publication or else written a *consolatio* subsequently. It would seem, then, that Martial was expressing a pious hope, nothing more.

The relationship between Domitian and his wife was officially satisfactory, though she is far from prominent in the official propaganda: Statius mentions her but once (*Silvae* 3.4.18), Martial and Silius Italicus not at all, and her image appears on no coins after 84. On the other hand, Josephus (*Vita* 429) refers to the favours he received from her, whilst Suetonius indicates that, at the very least, she accompanied her husband to the amphitheatre (*Dom.* 13.1).

There remains her supposed involvement in Domitian's murder, reported by Suetonius (*Dom.* 14.1) and Dio (67.15.2–4); but even Dio does not report her complicity or foreknowledge as a fact. Rather, according to him, there was a report that she was not unaware of the plot (67.15.2) or else, in a different version, she came upon a list of Domitian's prospective victims, passed it on to those concerned and they hurried on the plot already begun (67.15.4). The fact that Domitian was the victim of a court plot does not imply the complicity of the entire court. On the contrary, other evidence suggests she was at least moderately fond of her husband.

Twenty-five years after his death and the official *damnatio memoriae*, she still referred to herself as 'Domitian's wife': ten brick stamps of 123 bear the inscription 'from the Sulpician brickyards of Domitia, [wife] of Domitian' (*CIL* 15.548a–9d), whereas, on another dated after 23 April 140 (and after her death), she is styled 'Domitia Augusta, daughter of Gnaeus Domitius Corbulo' (*ILS* 272), no doubt the technically correct version of the name of an imperial widow whose husband had suffered *damnatio*. The inference is clear; she deliberately called herself 'Domitian's wife' when she could easily have avoided doing so.

Five centuries later, she is portrayed as devoted to her husband despite his manifold failings. In his *Secret History* (8.12–22), Procopius saw Domitian as similar in appearance and actions to his *bête noire*, Justinian, whereas Domitia was always highly respected, had wronged no one and had approved of none of her husband's actions.[63] After his death, however, she had collected the pieces of his flesh (the people had 'carved up his body'), sewed them together and had had a sculptor use the result as a model for a statue. Whatever we care to make of Procopius's version of Domitian's assassination and his explanation for the statue's appearance, it would seem that there did exist a tradition less hostile to Domitia. But, in essence, the literary sources virtually disregarded her except in so far as she was deemed useful to highlight Domitian's faults. The standard charges of adultery and promiscuity,[64] regularly made, difficult to disprove and impossible to verify, were also less firmly established than the accusations levelled against her husband, but they have served to obscure her role in the imperial court. Possibly, she urged her husband to conciliate (or compromise) members of the so-called opposition by offering them suffect consulships. We have no means of knowing.

Julia

Domitian's niece Julia[65] was born on 10 August[66] in the early 60s, daughter of Titus and (almost certainly) his first wife Arrecina Tertulla. According to the traditional view, recently restated,[67] Suetonius was referring to her in his comment that, shortly after the birth of a daughter, Titus divorced his (second) wife, Marcia Furnilla (*Titus* 4.2). But he had more than one daughter (Philostratus, *Vit. Apoll.* 7.7), and, unlike Marcia Furnilla, Arrecina Tertulla did at least have close relatives named Julius.[68] So Titus's daughters should be named (Flavia) Julia by Arrecina Tertulla and (Flavia)[69] by Marcia Furnilla.

Some ten or eleven years younger than her uncle Domitian, she was probably brought up by Julia, her maternal grandmother, and Phyllis, Domitian's own nurse: on his death, the latter mingled his ashes with Julia's, for she had reared them both (*Dom.* 17.3). In his mid-teens, he may well have helped take care of his young niece: both of them had fathers absent in Judaea and mothers who were dead. So it is not impossible that he was genuinely fond of her, but as a friend only. Thus he rejected the repeated requests to divorce his wife and marry her (*Dom.* 22), no doubt recalling as well the bitter experience of his favourite emperor Tiberius (*Dom.* 20), forced to divorce the wife he loved in order to marry the emperor's daughter, another Julia (*Tib.* 7.2). Late in Vespasian's reign or early in Titus's, she married Sabinus IV and, not long after, was granted the title *Augusta.*[70] As early as this, Domitian is said to have seduced her (*Dom.* 22), then, after executing her husband and divorcing Domitia, to have lived with her openly (even after his wife's return), finally forcing her to have an abortion which killed her (*Ep.* 4.11.6; *Sat.* 2.29–33 and *Dom.* 22). Most of this is little more than a farrago of nonsense.[71] No doubt Julia was living in the palace (as other Flavian members may well have been, given the size of the complex), for she was able to persuade her uncle to spare another of her relatives, L. Julius Ursus (Dio 67.4.2). All the rest is standard *vituperatio.*

Scholars seem not to have stressed one of the most significant factors in assessing the rumour's accuracy – Martial's epigram 6.3, written not long after Julia's death and deification.[72] In it, he expresses the hope that Domitia will produce a son, implies that the baby's name will be Julius (6.3.1) and states that (the now deified) Julia will be able to watch over him (6.3.5). Martial was neither a hero nor a fool. Had there been the slightest hint of an affair between emperor and niece, he would hardly have written those lines; had Julia's recent death been caused by an abortion forced on her by Domitian, would Martial have so far neglected the bounds of 'safe criticism'[73] and commonsense as to humiliate Domitia publicly, urging her to become pregnant, to give the child a name reminiscent of her husband's mistress and finally to remember that the same mistress, now dead and deified (thanks to her husband), would be able to protect the child?

There is a further point. Martial's sixth book contains a number of epigrams praising Domitian's renewal of Augustus's law against adultery (the *Lex Julia de adulteriis coercendis*), in particular 6.2 and 6.4.[74] Between them is the Julia epigram. The prominence given to 6.3 indicates that there was no hint of anything improper in the relationship between the emperor and his niece, as far as the court knew. Martial would not wish to suggest so obviously to his readers that Domitian was a hypocrite in renewing the *Lex Julia*, since he was involved not only in adultery but also just possibly in incest, abortion and murder. Helvidius was about to overstep the bounds of safe criticism (and he was appropriately punished: *Dom.* 10.4) by discovering and emphasizing the parallel between Paris/Oenone and

Domitian/Domitia. Obviously, the rumours linking Domitia and Paris were current during Domitian's reign, whereas those linking Julia's death with a supposed affair with her uncle were not. They were invented after his death.

L. Julius Ursus

His[75] precise connection with the Flavian family has been disputed by scholars, but it seems that he was a direct descendant of Julius Lupus (Ursus and Lupus are likely names for brothers), tribune of the praetorian guard at the time of Gaius's assassination. According to Josephus (AJ 19.191), Lupus was related (by marriage, presumably) to Gaius's praetorian prefect M. Arrecinus Clemens: so Arrecinus's wife was probably Lupus's sister Julia.[76] Ursus, then, would have been one of the sons of the tribune, the other being Ti. Julius Lupus, prefect of Egypt in the initial years of Vespasian's reign (PIR[2] J 390), proof enough of the family's reliability.[77]

We know that the Arrecini had long had close links with the Flavians.[78] Two of Arrecinus Clemens's daughters had Flavian husbands, so it seems, with Arrecina Tertulla married to Vespasian's son Titus and another (?Arrecina Clementina) the probable wife of the emperor's nephew T. Flavius Sabinus III.[79] As well, his son, also M. Arrecinus Clemens, became praetorian prefect some thirty years after his father, and, not long after that appointment, his cousin Ti. Julius Lupus was promoted to the second most important post open to an equestrian, the prefecture of Egypt. The links were maintained for more than one generation: Clementina's son (Sabinus IV) married Tertulla's daughter Julia and was Domitian's heir apparent (until executed) whilst her grandsons, named Vespasianus and Domitianus, were the emperor's designated heirs at the time of his assassination in 96. In addition, her brother Arrecinus not only became city prefect,[80] but was one of the very few persons attested in the literary sources as a friend of Domitian (Hist. 4.68; Dom. 11).

That the relationship between the Flavii and the Julii was also close and remained so is suggested by a number of factors, not least of which is the name of Titus's daughter, (Flavia) Julia, who, in view of her mother's death c. 63 and her father's absence in Judaea from 66 to 71, must have been brought up by her Julian relatives, in particular by the wife of Gaius's prefect, her maternal grandmother Julia.[81] She maintained a close relationship with the Julii, managing to persuade her uncle Domitian to grant a consulship to L. Julius Ursus in 84 (Dio 67.4.2). The following tentative stemma summarizes these connections:

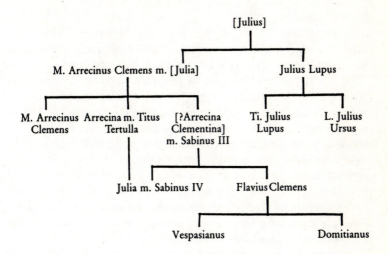

Just as L. Julius Ursus's precise relationship with the Flavian family has been the subject of scholarly debate, so too have been various aspects of his career; but some facts are beyond dispute – a Julius Ursus is attested (*AE* 1939: 60) as holding two senior equestrian posts under the Flavians, prefect of the corn supply (*praefectus annonae*) and prefect of Egypt (*praefectus Aegypti*), whilst an [U]rsus is named as consul (*c.* May 84) in the *Fasti Ostienses*.[82] If this is one and the same person, then three difficulties have to be faced: we need evidence that Ursus rose to the most senior equestrian post, the prefecture of the praetorian guard, then that he was granted senatorial status and, finally, that he was promoted very rapidly to a consulship.

Fortunately, a papyrus (*P. Berlin* 8334) provides such evidence. In it, an unnamed emperor is writing to a certain Maximus (?L. Laberius Maximus, *praefectus annonae* and *praefectus Aegypti*), informing him that he was to be made colleague of [F]uscus (?Cornelius Fuscus, prefect of the praetorian guard at the dramatic date of Juvenal's fourth satire), a promotion resulting from the transfer of a Julius to 'the most honourable order'.[83] Now whilst names such as 'Maximus' and 'Julius' are amongst the commonest, '-uscus' is amongst the rarest; so it seems that Ursus is being 'promoted' or, more realistically, moved aside (i.e. 'approbation, elevation and castration, all in one stroke'[84]) into the senate and that the consequent vacancy in the praetorian guard is to be filled by L. Laberius Maximus. Ursus, then, like his brother Lupus and cousin Arrecinus, held senior equestrian posts under Vespasian and then passed from praetorian prefect to senator and consul.

That Ursus was an intimate of the imperial court is clear from Dio Cassius. Early in the reign, when Domitian 'planned to put his wife Domitia to death for adultery, he was dissuaded by Ursus' (67.3.1); but, later, 'he came close to putting Ursus to death for failing to show pleasure at his sovereign's exploits and then, at the request of Julia, he appointed him consul' (67.4.2). So Ursus was somewhat unappreciative of Domitian's victory in Germany and therefore replaced, as leader of the praetorian guard, by someone more forceful and vigorous in the mould of Cornelius Fuscus (*Hist.* 2.86). He must have remained as an imperial courtier, though, but seems not to have held any administrative post under Domitian after his consulship; then, with the accession of Trajan, he went onto a second consulship in 98 and a third in 100.

The Julii remained prominent. Ursus's adopted son, L. Julius Ursus Servianus, married Hadrian's sister and was awarded a suffect consulship in 90, whilst his (probable) nephew, P. Julius Lupus, became the second husband of Arria Fadilla and thereby stepfather of Antoninus Pius.[85] So he was an adept courtier who retained his influence and position; nor did a disagreement with his imperial master and relative result in disgrace or death. Quite the contrary, for both problem and solution were in evidence on other occasions during the reign: freedmen deemed unsuitable (Ti. Claudius Classicus) or guilty of minor offences (Ti. Julius, father of Claudius Etruscus) were moved aside or exiled (to Campania), not done to death.[86] So too with Ursus who lacked the vigour of the Arrecini, proving unsatisfactory as guard commander, but remaining a senator and courtier.

M. Arrecinus Clemens

He was some ten years older than his cousin Ursus, more able in the military sphere (i.e. as praetorian prefect)[87] and far less so in the political and diplomatic. Tacitus introduces him with a reference to his *adfinitas* (*Hist.* 4.68) to the imperial family, a relationship explained by his sisters' marriages.[88] His career can be fairly well documented. After the period as praetorian prefect, he was replaced by Titus and, like his cousin Ursus, passed quickly to a consulship (73), thence to the governorship of Spain,[89] returning by 85 to hold a second (suffect) consulship. Not long afterwards he became city prefect, possibly succeeding Pegasus.[90] His period of eminence was brief, however, for he fell from favour.

In chapter 10 of his *Life of Domitian*, Suetonius provides a list of the emperor's consular victims. Apparently, it is meant to be complete and it does include one imperial relative (T. Flavius Sabinus IV), his brother Clemens being excluded, reserved for dramatic purposes until chapter 15, where his death is a prelude to and an explanation of the emperor's assassination by his courtiers. Arrecinus is not mentioned in chapter 10 but does appear in the next, where he is the second of three examples of Domitian's unexpected cruelty: the emperor is 'about to condemn him' (*Dom.* 11.1). The implication of the passage is that the death sentences were carried out in all cases, but Suetonius is not explicit. The passage is very reminiscent of his *Nero* 37, where he gives three instances of the emperor's lack of restraint by 'murdering whomsoever he pleased on any pretext'. Once again, as in *Dom.* 11, Suetonius means to illustrate imperial *saevitia* (*Dom.* 10.1; *Nero* 36.1), an oft-repeated vice in rhetorical invective; but, of Nero's three 'victims', only the first and third were killed, the second (Cassius Longinus) being merely exiled (*Ann.* 16.9) and later actually recalled to Rome by Vespasian (*Digest* 12.2.52).[91] Perhaps Arrecinus was also exiled, and he may well be the M. Arrecinus Clemens commemorated at Rudiae (in the extreme head of Italy) by his wife Cornelia Ocell(in)a.[92]

Whilst the reasons for Arrecinus's fall from grace are unknown, we might observe that, in 86, when Domitian was on the Danube together with his praetorian prefect, Cornelius Fuscus, he needed an urban prefect he could trust. Arrecinus fitted the bill. In 69, when 'the city must not be left without an administrator' (*Hist.* 4.68), he had been made praetorian prefect because of his *adfinitas* to the imperial house and friendship with Domitian (4.68). Once again, he was given a position of trust, and for the same reasons, no doubt. But his conduct may have been unsatisfactory. On 22 September 87, the Arval brothers offered sacrifice 'for the detected crime of wicked men', the usual euphemism for the discovery of a conspiracy directed against the emperor.[93] As well, Dio refers to the slaughter of a number of prominent men around this time (67.9.6).

Finally, there is the rather surprising selection of the *novus homo* L. Minicius Rufus as ordinary consul for 88. Possibly,[94] the senator designated to the ordinary consulship for that year perished before entering office, accused of complicity in the *scelera nefariorum*, and was replaced by Rufus. But could it not rather be that Domitian was not entirely satisfied with Arrecinus Clemens's performance as *praefectus urbi* during the events of 87, that he was suspected of inefficiency or worse, and was consequently exiled? In that case, the ordinary consulship to which he had been designated would have been awarded to the intended *suffectus*, Minicius Rufus. Such a reconstruction is highly speculative, but does at least provide an explanation for Clemens's fall from favour.[95]

Whatever his fate, he left behind a son, so it seems, also named M. Arrecinus Clemens. At some point in Domitian's reign, he held the post of assistant to the curator of the water supply, M'. Acilius Aviola.[96] Nothing else is known of him or of his mother, Cornelia Ocell(in)a; the family disappears from record.

The cousins Ursus and Clemens enjoyed their imperial relative's favour and experienced his disfavour, but Ursus, the more adept courtier and politician, not only survived, but also saw his family's connections move from equestrian rank to imperial. He certainly and Clemens possibly avoided the imperial *saevitia*. Two other imperial relatives, the brothers T. Flavius Sabinus (IV) and T. Flavius Clemens, were less fortunate.

T. Flavius Sabinus

After Domitian refused to marry his niece Julia (*Dom.* 22), she was given instead to T. Flavius Sabinus, the grandson of Vespasian's brother.[97] Tradition, however, has it that Domitian seduced her while Titus was still alive (*Dom.* 22). With this should be considered another incident from the period before Titus's death. Domitian, vexed that Sabinus IV had clad his attendants in imperial white, had delivered a Homeric warning: 'The rule of many is not good' (*Dom.* 12.3).[98] His meaning was clear and his annoyance understandable. Sabinus, as husband of the daughter of the reigning or future[99] emperor, would always be ominously senior and was prepared to advertise the fact by the colour of his attendants' clothes: such, at least, must have been the attitude of Domitian, ever suspicious over his personal safety (*Dom.* 14.1–2).

Two points need further elaboration: firstly, the precise status of Sabinus in the Flavian family, four members of which bore the name T. Flavius Sabinus. The first had two sons, Sabinus II and Vespasian. The third, *cos. I suff.* 69, *II suff.* 72, was almost certainly the son of Sabinus II. Let him be Sabinus III, with the Sabinus who married Julia (Sabinus IV) as one of his sons and the T. Flavius Clemens[100] whom Domitian executed in 95 as the other. But when did Sabinus III die? Of some importance is the Flavius Sabinus of *CIL* 6.814, according to which a temple had been constructed during the reign of Titus on a plot of ground which had been approved by Flavius Sabinus in his role of curator of public works, normally a consular post. Presumably he was one of the four Sabini. Sabinus II was killed in 69, whilst Sabinus IV's first consulship can be assigned to the year after Titus's death. Sabinus III seems indicated. Normally, the curatorship was held fairly soon after a senator's consulship,[101] which, in this case, would suggest the early 70s. If so, one is left to wonder why the construction was so long delayed. Now some scholars suggest that the Flavius Sabinus of *CIL* 6.814 was still alive in Titus's reign,[102] though that is not stated in the inscription. Indeed, the tense of the verb suggests a time-lapse of some years between the approval of the site and the actual construction of the temple. On that hypothesis, the curatorship should be assigned to Sabinus III and to the period immediately after his consulship, i.e. the years 70 or 71, when the dynasty was being established, whereas the temple itself could perhaps have been erected a decade later, as part of Titus's restoration work after the disastrous fire of 80 (*Titus* 8.3; Dio 66.24.1; *Epit. de Caes.* 10.12). This hypothesis is far from certain, but the nature of the reference to Sabinus in *CIL* 6.814 suggests strongly that he was no longer alive when Titus became emperor. He had certainly died before October 81, since it was Sabinus IV whom Domitian chose at that time to be his colleague as ordinary consul for 82. So Sabinus IV may have been 'ominously senior' for some years before 81.

The other point is his designation to the ordinary consulship for 82. For a long time, scholars believed that the appointment was due to Titus and that it had been made at the *comitia* in March 81.[103] That view is clearly erroneous; the designation was made by Domitian, at the October *comitia*, held just after his accession. The critical inscription is *CIL* 3.12218, where Titus is described as holding tribunician power for the tenth time (i.e. from 1 July 80 to 30 June 81) and as designated to his ninth consulship (so after March 81). The date must be after the designation of the brothers to the ordinary consulship for 82 (at the *comitia* of March 81) and before the end of Titus's tenth tribunician power expired (June 81).[104] So Titus had intended that he and his brother hold the ordinary consulship in 82 and the announcement was made at the March *comitia*. But Titus died on 13 September 81, and, at the second consular *comitia* for that year, held in October,[105] he was replaced by Sabinus. It was not unparalleled for designations to the ordinary consulship to be announced at the second *comitia* in October rather than at the first in March. Compare the situation in 58. In the minutes of the Arval Brethren for that year, C. Vipstanus Apronianus appears simply as a member on 25 February, 12 October and 13 October but as *cos. desig.* on 6 November, 11 December and 15 December. At the meeting of 3 January 59, he is listed as *cos. ord.*[106]

In 81, then, Sabinus was the senior Flavian after the emperor himself and so Domitian's inevitable choice as ordinary consul, for each of the Flavian emperors was concerned with establishing or maintaining a dynasty, each of them held that post in the first year of his reign with the heir-apparent as his colleague – Vespasian and Titus in 70, Titus and Domitian in 80, Domitian and Sabinus in 82. Domitian's personal attitude to Sabinus was irrelevant. Titus had died in September, Domitian had no colleague as *cos. ord.* for the first year of his reign and the October *comitia* were uncomfortably close. He had little more than a month to act.

Now, according to Suetonius (*Dom.* 10.4), Sabinus IV was executed because of the herald's unfortunate lapse at the consular *comitia* (when he announced him as *imperator*, not as *consul*), and some have posited[107] a second consular designation for him, even though there is no evidence in any of the sources that he was ever offered one. On the contrary, Suetonius and Dio together imply that he was executed very early in the reign, not long after his consulship for 82. The former claims that Julia lived openly with Domitian after her father and husband were dead (*Dom.* 22) and Dio places the couple's unconcealed living together (67.3.2) before the executions of the Vestals (67.3.3[2]) and the outbreak of the war against the Chatti (67.4.1), i.e. well before the summer of 83.[108] So the mistaken announcement at the *renuntiatio* before the people (*Dom.* 10.4) took place in October 81 and was resurrected at a later date (though not far beyond 82) when it would still have had some immediacy.

Cautiously and with due reserve, a more precise date for Sabinus's execution can be suggested. In his *Historia Ecclesiastica*, Eusebius reports that Domitian put to death and banished many prominent men (3.17) and repeats the same information in the *Chronicorum Canonum* (though executions are mentioned in the Syrian epitome only) under *A. Abr.* 2099 (i.e. 1 October 82–30 September 83). As well, before describing the executions of the Vestals, Dio says that the emperor murdered and banished many of the foremost men on various pretexts (67.3.3[1]). If we care to accept the accuracy of these statements, bearing in mind that the first comment of Eusebius is undated (3.17), that, in the *Chronicorum Canonum*, reference to executions occurs in the Syrian epitome only and that in none of them Sabinus is mentiond by name, then we could well argue that, between 1 October 82 and 28 August 83,[109] a number of leading men, including Domitian's heir, were put to death.

But, that tentative reconstruction aside, it is clear that Sabinus was dead before Domitian left for Germany. Once the consular elections of October 81 were over, Domitian set about removing a prospective rival. Self-preservation was ever uppermost in his mind.

T. Flavius Clemens

Sabinus's younger brother, Clemens,[110] is a far more shadowy figure. Presumably, he and his brother Sabinus, together with their father Sabinus III, were the *liberi* whom Vespasian's brother had managed to bring into the Capitol in December 69, accompanied by the 18-year-old Domitian (*Hist.* 3.69). Their mother was probably Arrecina Clementina, a sister of M. Arrecinus Clemens and of Arrecina Tertulla; but the name is not epigraphically attested anywhere.[111] Clemens himself married Flavia Domitilla (*PIR²* F 418), daughter of Domitian's sister (F 417) and (so it seems) Q. Petillius Cerialis Caesius Rufus;[112] the latter already had two sons by an earlier marriage, Q. Petillius Rufus (*cos. II ord.* 83) and C. Petillius Firmus (who died young),[113] both half-brothers of Domitilla. So both husband and wife were perilously close to the throne, for Clemens's brother and Domitilla's half-brother shared the ordinary consulship with Domitian in the first (Sabinus IV) and second (Rufus) years of the reign, and that honour was generally reserved for the emperor's heirs.[114]

They had seven children (*ILS* 1839), two of whom, 'though very young, were openly designated Domitian's successors' (*Dom.* 15.1) and their names changed to (T. Flavius) Domitianus (*PIR*[2] F 257) and (T. Flavius) Vespasianus (F 397). Their education had been entrusted to Quintilian, probably *c.* 90,[115] for which (presumably) he received the rare award of *ornamenta consularia*[116] (Ausonius, *Grat. Act.* 10.7.204) that provoked bitter resentment on the part of some senators at least: 'Fortune, you are making fun of us. You are turning senators into teachers and teachers into senators' (*Ep.* 4.11.2).[117] In 95, Clemens was appointed ordinary consul with the emperor, no doubt to groom his sons for the succession. He was in office until 1 May,[118] but, not long after, was charged with 'atheism': according to Dio, he was executed and his wife exiled to Pandateria (67.4.1–2). The fate of his children is unknown. Suetonius believed that it was Clemens's execution that hastened Domitian's own end (*Dom.* 15.1), and some support is provided by the fact that one of the prime movers was Domitilla's freedman, Stephanus (*Dom.* 17.1). Philostratus claims that his action was foretold by a portent – a halo (in Greek, *stephanos*) surrounded the sun and dimmed its brilliance (*Vita Apoll.* 8.23) and that Stephanus wanted to avenge Clemens or, indeed, every one of Domitian's victims (*Vita Apoll.* 8.25). Suetonius's explanation is less imaginative: Stephanus had been charged with theft (*Dom.* 17.1). Finally, the precise nature of Clemens's 'atheism' is disputed: some have argued that they were both Christians (or Christian sympathizers), others that they favoured Judaism.[119] In neither case is the evidence convincing.

Other relatives

Other members of the imperial family, less significant in court circles, can be noted briefly. Three women bore the name Flavia Domitilla – Domitian's mother, sister and niece: the first two were dead before he became emperor and the third married Flavius Clemens.[120] Early Christian writers (e.g. *Hist. Eccl.* 18.4) argued for a fourth, niece of Flavius Clemens (i.e. daughter of a supposed sister), and have won acceptance from some scholars. She can safely be discarded.[121] There was also Sabinus III's sister, Flavia Sabina, who married L. Junius Caesennius Paetus;[122] his sons (possibly by different wives) included another L. Junius Caesennius Paetus and L. Caesennius Sospes.[123] It may be simply coincidental or perhaps indicative of the emperor's determination to look for loyalty in his administrators that the younger Paetus, *cos. suff.* 79, was (so it seems) proconsul of Asia in 93/4, whilst at the same time his

48

(?half-)brother Sospes was praetorian governor of Galatia.[124] At all events, this branch of the family is the only one attested in the second century, with an L. Caesennius Sospes (the Galatian governor or, just possibly, his son) *cos. suff.* in 114 and a descendant, A Junius Pastor L. Caesennius Sospes (*PIR²* J 796), *cos. suff.* in 163.

3

COURT II

AMICI

The courtiers with the widest political and military experience were the imperial *amici*,[1] those 'friends' the emperor consulted before coming to any important decision. They were 'the most valuable instrument of good government', according to Helvidius Priscus (*Hist.* 4.7); Suetonius thought that Titus's were 'indispensable to the state' (*Titus* 7.2) and one of Domitian's *amici*, Trajan, is supposed to have said that Domitian was the worst of emperors but had good *amici* (*SHA Alex.* 65.5), perhaps a not entirely unbiased opinion. Even the astute Vespasian was not adverse to giving two of his, Vibius Crispus and Eprius Marcellus, a completely free rein (*Dial.* 8.3). But if their power and influence is well attested, their identity is often not. Most scholars agree that there was no fixed list of friends, but that, usually, the same people were summoned for consultation.[2] Most would have been senators, but prominent equestrians were frequently included: the elder Pliny, for instance, was summoned to Vespasian's presence before daybreak (*Ep.* 2.5.9) and the praetorian prefect was the 'guardian of the sacred side' (Martial 6.76.1).[3] *Amici* of senatorial rank, apart from those precisely attested as such in literary, epigraphic or papyrological sources, probably included the *consules II*, the *praefectus urbi* and the *curator aquarum*.[4] Rarely are these courtiers mentioned in the literary sources, but, with Domitian, we are particularly fortunate in that we have five references to them, the most useful being the four surviving lines of Statius's *De Bello Germanico* (naming Glabrio senior, Veiento, Messallinus and Crispus) and Juvenal's fourth satire (with those four and six more – Pegasus, Montanus, Pompeius, Rubrius, Fuscus and Crispinus).[5] Whereas members of the imperial family and the senior freedmen resided at court, his *amici* were summoned only when needed. Over twenty can be attested including politicians, generals and the praetorian prefects.[6] Amongst them were his two successors together with the grandfather of Antoninus Pius, all three given the rare honour of an ordinary consulship. An overview of what is known of these courtiers reveals the sort of expertise readily available to the emperor, though not necessarily the extent to which he availed himself of it. In theory, too, we should be able to gain an idea of the sort of person whose company he enjoyed; that information, unfortunately, emerges far less clearly.

Politicians

M'. Acilius Aviola and the Acilii Glabriones. The elder Acilius Glabrio is at times identified with M'. Acilius Aviola, but it is probably better to regard them as two different senators:[7] for what it is worth, that is the view of the scholiast on Juvenal's fourth satire, and, if true, little can be said of Glabrio senior beyond the fact that, at the dramatic date of the satire, he was about 80. Almost certainly, he can be regarded as one of Domitian's best-known *amici* since his name, together with that of Veiento, Crispus and Messallinus, appeared in Statius's poem parodied by Juvenal.[8] Aviola, on the other hand, an *amicus* of Claudius,[9] was ordinary consul in 54, served as proconsul of Asia late in Nero's reign and then as curator of the water supply from 74 to 97. Apparently, he was an experienced administrator and trusted advisor, but with no attested military experience.

The Acilii Glabriones, father and son, were of a patrician family, but that did not save the younger Acilius.[10] Appointed ordinary consul in 91 with M. Ulpius Traianus, he was the same year summoned to Domitian's Alban palace, and obliged to fight a huge lion, which he promptly killed (Dio 67.14.3); not to be outdone, the emperor then exiled him on a charge of plotting revolution (*Dom.* 10.2) and later had him put to death on the grounds of 'atheism, a charge on which many others who had drifted into Jewish ways were condemned' (Dio 67.14.2–3). So perhaps he was suspected of having Jewish sympathies; on the other hand, since a second-century Acilius Glabrio is known to have been a Christian, there are some scholars who believe that he was one as well.[11] Probably he was neither.

T. Aurelius Fulvus[12] was somewhat more active. After gaining military experience as commander of the *III Gallica* under Corbulo in the east, Fulvus, a provincial from Nemausus, continued as legate when the legion was sent to Moesia where it defeated the Roxolani (*Hist.* 1.79). Largely instrumental in persuading the Illyrian armies to join Vespasian (*Hist.* 2.74, 85), he was rewarded by being summoned to Vespasian (*Hist.* 3.10) in the critical period between the death of Vitellius in December 69 and the new emperor's departure from Alexandria for Rome in August or September[13] in the following year. Appointed consul in the early years of the new regime and raised to patrician rank in 73/4, he held various senior posts under Vespasian and Domitian, but only three are attested – a governorship of Spain, a second consulship (ordinary, with Domitian in 85) and the city prefecture. He was well connected in the local aristocracy, a prominent member of the 'Hispano-Narbonensian nexus' that developed late in the first century – becoming, in fact, the grandfather of Antoninus Pius.[14] A senior consular of wide experience, he would have been an invaluable member of Domitian's court.

M. Cocceius Nerva,[15] the future emperor, was another of his political advisors. He must have been widely identified with the pro-Domitianic group in the senate just before the emperor's death in view of Mauricus's comments not long after (*Ep.* 4.22.4–7).

As praetor designate in 65, Nerva had been honoured with a statue and triumphal *ornamenta* for his role in detecting the Pisonian conspiracy (*Ann.* 15.72; *ILS* 273) and he managed not only to survive the civil war, but also to emerge as the new regime's favourite, for he was one of only four senators in Vespasian's reign (apart from members of the imperial family) to be awarded an ordinary consulship, and the only person other than Titus to share an ordinary consulship with Vespasian. Even more significantly, he held it very early in the regime (71), about four months after Vespasian's arrival in Rome.[16] Again, he was highly honoured by Domitian, receiving yet another ordinary consulship in the year after the suppression of Saturninus's revolt. That he should have been present at the meeting imagined by Juvenal is certain, but the satirist wisely omitted from his list those Domitianic *amici* whose descendants remained powerful – hence, too, the non-appearance of L. Julius Ursus, whose adopted son, L. Julius Ursus Servianus, was Hadrian's brother-in-law.[17] Nerva appears to have been an adaptable diplomat with neither military nor administrative experience, able to influence decisions by subtle manoeuvring. It was this that gained him admission to Domitian's court and also the throne.

A. Didius Gallus Fabricius Veiento[18] was one of the most interesting of his senatorial *amici*, frequently but erroneously classified as an informer during the so-called reign of terror.[19] Praetor perhaps in 54, he had already been adopted by the eminent Claudian senator A. Didius Gallus (consul in 39, governor of Britain from 52 to 57).[20] It may also have been under Claudius, whose *comes* Gallus was, that a link was forged between his family and the Flavii, for Domitian's father and uncle commanded two of Claudius's legions in the British invasion. Later, Veiento held three consulships, two of them awarded by Flavian emperors (Titus in 80 and Domitian almost certainly in 83)[21] and is generally supposed to have been an *amicus* of all the emperors from Vespasian to Trajan.

It was under Nero that Veiento achieved some sort of eminence: during his praetorship, he became one of the earliest known strike-breakers: when the horsebreeders and charioteers were unwilling to take part in the circus races on reasonable terms, Veiento dismissed them, trained dogs to draw the chariots and used them in place of the horses (Dio 61.6.2–3).

Still not the wise statesman, he remained an intimate of Nero's court, but unable to restrain himself, incurred the penalty of exile from Italy for publishing libellous pamphlets attacking various senators and priests (*Ann.* 14.50). With age came wisdom. He retained an interest in matters religious, becoming an expert in them apparently and holding (not necessarily all at once) the exceptionally[22] large number of four priesthoods (*ILS* 1010). No doubt this endeared him to Domitian, who was genuinely concerned with such observances (*Dom.* 4–5): hence the introductory remarks assigned to Veiento by Juvenal when the fish was produced – 'You [i.e. Domitian] will have a mighty omen of a great and brilliant triumph' (4.124–5).

We need not disregard Statius's assessment of him (in the *De Bello Germanico*) as a wise and powerful statesman. Statius names him 'Fabius Veiento', recalling yet another shrewd tactician, Fabius Maximus Cunctator, whose wise (but negative) tactics overcame both Hannibal and the more adventurous Roman military commanders, perhaps just as Domitian's were destined to do. There is no evidence that Veiento ever governed a province or commanded an army; perhaps the reason for the inscription at Mainz (*ILS* 1010), where his third consulship is noted, is to be explained by his presence there as Domitian's *comes*, presumably in the Chattan war. In view of Statius's reference to him as 'Fabius', he may well have been sent to point out to the military commanders at the double camp the advantages of the imperial strategy that must have seemed close to cowardice to most of them. Convincing them needed and perhaps tested the talents of Domitian's 'sagacious' statesman. As expected, Veiento not only survived the emperor's downfall but retained his role both at court (appearing at one of Nerva's dinner parties: *Ep.* 4.22.4) and in the Senate (speaking in favour of the supporters of the *ancien régime*: *Ep.* 9.13.19). In short, he was one of Domitian's most experienced political advisors.

T. Junius Montanus's attributes included neither diplomacy nor political astuteness. Juvenal introduces him as a slow, fat epicure,[23] noted for his staying-power at Nero's banquets (4.137) and an ability to determine the origin of any oyster at the very first bite (4.138). His identity is a mystery. Some scholars favour Curtius Montanus, others T. Junius Montanus.[24] The latter came from Alexandria in the Troad where his father (*AE* 1938: 173) had established himself as a colonist in the early years of the first century, and is known to have begun his senatorial career (*AE* 1973: 500) under Nero as *triumvir monetalis*, the most prestigious section of the vigintivirate. Usually, it was reserved for patricians, which Montanus was not; perhaps an affinity with Nero helped him. At all events, his subsequent career was unspectacular, a military tribunate in Moesia with the *V Macedonica*, a quaestorship in Pontus-Bithynia, a tribunate of the people, praetorship and proconsulship of Sicily. When he held these posts is not attested, but, since he was consul in 81, his praetorship has to be assigned to the first years of Vespasian's reign (or the last part of Nero's), indicating that all the previous posts were, as one might suspect, granted by Nero. Vespasian did not think much of him, giving him merely a praetorian proconsulship, a post whose holders 'seldom came to anything'.[25] In May/June 80, the genial Montanus held a suffect consulship,[26] awarded by Titus, whose assessment, it is clear, differed substantially from Vespasian's; perhaps Montanus and Titus had known each other at Nero's court, for they must have been of about the same age. One of the first consuls ever appointed from the Greek east,[27] he must, on Titus's death, have retained imperial favour and his place at court for his conviviality rather than for any other discernible quality.

(Plot)tius Pegasus,[28] whom Domitian appointed as prefect of the city not long after his accession, was certainly more able and probably more honourable. In Juvenal's fourth satire, he was the first member of the emperor's *consilium* to be admitted to the meeting, 'the best and most righteous interpreter of the laws, a man who thought that, even in those terrible days, there should be no sword in the hands of justice' (4.78–81). He was so honourable that the city was astonished (4.77) at his appointment,[29] and there is no good reason to disregard Juvenal's assessment. Pegasus had an interesting career. He must have been awarded a consulship not long after Vespasian's accession since he had governed several provinces before becoming city prefect.[30] One of them was Dalmatia, where he appointed as a judge his military tribune C. Petillius Firmus (*AE* 1967: 355), now thought to have been the stepson of Vespasian's daughter Domitilla[31] and also acting commander of the legion *IV Flavia Felix* under Rubrius Gallus: quite often, a governor appointed one of his relatives as military tribune, so perhaps Pegasus was related to the Petillii.[32] If so, it would help to explain the activities of Pegasus's brother Grypus in 69/70, an agent of Mucianus (*Hist.* 3.52) and secret supporter of the Flavians.[33] At all events, he and his brother were committed Flavians at the right time and, despite their comparatively humble background and possibly eastern origin, were amply rewarded.

But Pegasus had other attributes as well. He was one of the leading jurisconsults of the age, head of the Proculian School of Roman law: his suffect consulship presumably followed soon after that of Nerva, whose father and grandfather were both leading Proculians.[34] It is not beyond the bounds of probability that Domitian made him city prefect and courtier primarily because of his legal ability, for the emperor was famous for his 'scrupulous and conscientious' administration of the law (*Dom.* 8.1).[35]

M. Pompeius Silvanus Staberius Flavinus[36] was probably an imperial *amicus* and member of the *consilium* for the first year or so of the reign – on the assumption that he is to be identified with the Pompeius of Juvenal 4.110.[37] Aged about 80 on Domitian's accession, he apparently died before assuming the third consulship to which he was designated for 83: on that basis, he should be classified with the regime's loyal and dependable supporters. In brief, his career was long but undistinguished. Born c. AD 3, he became consul in 45, two years before Vespasian's elder brother Sabinus II, and later governed Africa for three years (56–8). Escaping prosecution for embezzlement there, he next appears as legate of Dalmatia in 69, and as a participator in the march on Rome against Vitellius. During the 70s, he prospered, holding the curatorship of the water supply (71–3) and a second consulship (?74). For Tacitus, his most memorable qualities were his age and wealth: he twice refers to them – in 58 (*Ann.* 13.42) and in 69 (*Hist.* 2.86). Domitian, on the other hand, may perhaps have found him sympathetic through his religious interests: he held three priesthoods. More ominous is Juvenal's assessment – he was one of the *delatores*. But at least he brought to the court two essential qualities – experience and dependability.

Q. Julius Cordinus C. Rutilius Gallicus[38] was younger than Silvanus, but of much the same age as Pegasus. After commanding the *XV Apollinaris* early in Nero's reign when it was stationed at Carnuntum in Pannonia, he served under Corbulo in the Cappadocia–Galatia area, was awarded a consulship early in Vespasian's reign, held a special appointment in Africa supervising the census *c.* 73/4, governed Lower Germany towards the end of the reign and was appointed proconsul of Asia[39] by Domitian not long after his accession to the throne. After a second consulship in 85, he became city prefect, probably after Arrecinus Clemens and before Aurelius Fulvus. His practical experience, derived from service on the Danube, Rhine and in the east, must have been invaluable to the emperor.

C. Calpetanus Rantius Quirinalis Valerius Festus[40] was almost certainly the Festus whom Martial describes as an *amicus* of Domitian (1.78.10). He died by his own hand early in the reign. In the turmoil of 68/9, he appears as commander of the legion *III Augusta* in Numidia: a young man 'of extravagant habits and immoderate ambition' (*Hist.* 4.49), he was concerned about the fact that he was related to Vitellius, and rightly so. However, he proved his reliability to the new regime by arranging for the murder of Piso, the proconsul of Africa who favoured the Vitellians (*Hist.* 4.50; *Ep.* 3.7.12). In return, he was quickly honoured with a suffect consulship, which he shared with Domitian, and also with consular military *dona*; thence came the curatorship of the Tiber's banks and the command of two imperial consular provinces, Pannonia and Spain. His career stands in stark contrast with that of Montanus, for they were of approximately the same age, both praetors late in Nero's reign. But only one found favour with Vespasian, and for obvious reasons.

In Titus's reign, he may have been appointed proconsul of Asia.[41] He held two priesthoods, the most important of which was the pontificate, awarded just after his consulship. In this, his interests coincided with those of Domitian, and so it is to be assumed that, during the consulship they shared in May and June 71, the 20-year-old prince found him congenial as well as ruthless. Add to this his proven loyalty and service to the regime by the end of the decade and he was a natural choice as one of Domitian's *amici*.

L. **Valerius Catullus Messallinus**,[42] another of his consular colleagues from the 70s, was probably just as congenial: he certainly had the reputation of being ruthless. He shared an ordinary consulship with Domitian in 73 and held a second as suffect in 85 with Rutilius Gallicus. No other official post is known. Subsequently, he was regarded as the most hated of the professional accusers of the era, and feared all the more because of his blindness. According to Tacitus, his influence was confined to the Alban villa (*Agr.* 45.1); but Juvenal's verdict is harsh – Catullus is 'deadly' (*mortiferus*: 4.113).

L. **Junius Q. Vibius Crispus**[43] was one of the four Domitianic *amici* mentioned by Statius (*De Bello Germanico*) and Juvenal (4.81–93). His formal career is well attested. An experienced administrator, he held a suffect consulship and the curatorship of the water supply under Nero, continuing in the latter post until 71, when he became proconsul of Africa, then governor of Spain, returning to Rome in 74 for a second consulship. Under Domitian came the rare award of a third.

A number of ancient authorities comment on his personal qualities. Born *c.* AD 12, his wealth, acquired presumably through delation (*Hist.* 2.10), became as legendary[44] as did his usefulness to whoever was in control of the state (Juv. 4.84). A 'born playboy',[45] he was famed for his personal charm and wit.[46] The latter is better attested than the former: unable to maintain the pace during one of Vitellius's drinking bouts, he was forced by illness to absent himself for a few days and was reputed to have said that, if he had not been sick, he would have died (Dio 65.2.3). But his power, too, was a by-word, whether in 60 (*Ann.* 14.28) or in the 70s (*Dial.* 8) and we are entitled to wonder about the origin of the 'L. Junius' in his name, a prefix shared with the Flavian relative, L. Junius Caesennius Paetus. Crispus was the survivor *par excellence* – a Neronian consular official, drinking companion of Vitellius (Dio 65.2.3), senior advisor to Vespasian and *amicus* of Domitian. Juvenal attests to this same quality – Crispus never swam against the stream, and, although no one could have been a more useful advisor to Domitian, he limited his conversation with the emperor to safe topics – how wet it's been, how hot; never uttering his private opinions or staking his life on the truth, he managed to survive, even in Domitian's court (4.93), by using techniques such as these.[47]

Generals

Rubrius Gallus. Of the generals classified[48] as *amici* of Domitian, the oldest was Rubrius Gallus.[49] He had served under Nero and Otho (Dio 63.27.1; *Hist.* 2.51) and later acted as an agent for Vespasian's brother, Flavius Sabinus (*Hist.* 2.99). Appointed governor of Moesia on the accession of the Flavians, he drove out the Sarmatians and strengthened the province's defences (*BJ* 7.92–5). No doubt his specialized knowledge was of assistance to Domitian in his Danubian campaigns. Juvenal (4.106) refers to his sexual excesses and the scholiast on that author claims that Gallus seduced Domitia (presumably the empress) when she was young, a statement unsupported by any other evidence.

Cn. Julius Agricola. Some scholars[50] have argued that Agricola[51] was one of Domitian's *amici*, others[52] that he was one of those friends of Vespasian disgraced or ruined (Dio 67.2.1–3) by Domitian. That he was an *amicus* of Vespasian and Titus is a fair assumption, in view of his prolonged tenure of Britain, but the fact that Domitian was named in his will (*Agr.* 43.4)[53] is not proof that he was an imperial *amicus* in the 80s. On the other hand, he was the only one of Domitian's generals (including Funisulanus Vettonianus, Cornelius Nigrinus and, as far as we know, Tettius Julianus) to receive *ornamenta triumphalia* from him, and, so it seems, a *vir triumphalis* was not normally sent to another command[54] – another explanation, then, for his non-appointment to Syria (*Agr.* 40.2). Nonetheless, it is unlikely that he was one of Domitian's courtiers. When he finally came to Rome *c.* 84, he slipped into the Palace by night (*noctu in Palatium*: 40.3), stayed briefly and withdrew into retirement (40.4). In any case, Domitian must have regarded his expansionist projects as unattainable (e.g. his claim that Ireland could be conquered and held by one legion and a few auxiliaries: *Agr.* 24) and was surely disillusioned by his failure to complete the conquest of Britain in 82 as Agricola had promised.[55]

Sex. Julius Frontinus.[56] After military successes as a legionary commander against Civilis in 70 – some 70,000 of the Lingones surrendered to him (*Strat.* 4.3.1–4) – and a consulship early in Vespasian's reign, Frontinus was appointed governor of Britain, subsequently served in Domitian's war against the Chatti, either as an imperial *comes* or else as governor of Lower Germany,[57] and then became proconsul of Asia (*c.* 85). With the accession of Nerva, he was appointed curator of the water supply (replacing Acilius Aviola), served on the emperor's economic commission, received a second (suffect) consulship in 98 and, in 100, was granted the unusual honour of a third, ordinary, consulship which he shared with the emperor Trajan. During this time, he had also written on military strategy (*Strategemata*) and aqueducts (*De Aquis urbis Romae*), both of which works survive. A senator of many talents, loyal and experienced, he was the most capable of the generals, but the tone of his comments[58] on Domitian, written before 96, indicate that he was malleable and adaptable; whether from conviction or fear, he would have encouraged Domitian's initiatives in foreign policy.

A. Bucius Lappius Maximus and M. Ulpius Traianus. In this regard, the younger generals[59] would have been less enthusiastic but no doubt just as diplomatic. Lappius should be regarded as one of Domitian's *amici*, but, apart from the last few years of the reign, he would rarely have been present at court, since he was serving abroad in the emperor's service.[60] On the other hand, after Trajan had attained the ordinary consulship in 91 at the age of 38, he spent the rest of the reign as one of Domitian's most influential courtiers, apart, possibly, from a term as governor of Pannonia: hence his comment (*SHA, Alex.* 65.5) that Domitian had good *amici*, even though he was a bad emperor. Nor should it be forgotten that Domitian's and Trajan's family were apparently related by marriage, the alliance (Trajan's father and Domitian's brother marrying sisters named *Marcia*) being contracted some thirty years before the future emperor's ordinary consulship in 91.[61]

Praetorian prefects

It was the normal practice for the emperor to be escorted by armed soldiers, members of the praetorian guard.[62] Their leader, or prefect, was the senior equestrian official, and regularly accompanied the emperor: when Claudius went to Britain in 43/4, Rufrius Pollio went with him (Dio 60.23.2), just as Tigellinus accompanied Nero on his tour of Greece (Dio 63.12.3). So, when Domitian wanted to question the philosopher Apollonius, he immediately turned to

Casperius Aelianus (*Vita Apoll.* 7.32). No matter where the court was, the praetorian prefect (or rather prefects, since the office was collegiate at this period) was one of its regular features.[63]

Apparently, L. Julius Ursus and Cornelius Fuscus held the office early in Domitian's reign, with Ursus being replaced by L. Laberius Maximus.[64] During the civil war, Fuscus had helped to bring the Illyrian legions over to Vespasian (*Hist.* 2.86; 3.4) and went on to command the Ravenna fleet (*Hist.* 3.12; 3.42). Under Domitian, he was given control of the Dacian campaign and died fighting (*Dom.* 6.1; Dio 67.6.6). Laberius, on the other hand, had been financial procurator of Judaea in 71 and was later in control of the corn supply; in 80 he was *procurator amphitheatri Flaviani* and he is attested as prefect of Egypt on 9 June 83. So one was a soldier, the other an administrator. Later in the reign, Casperius Aelianus[65] commanded the guard, and, if we care to accept the accuracy of Philostratus's *Life of Apollonius*,[66] we have a fairly detailed account of conversations between emperor, prefect and philosopher. Dio, apparently referring to the latter part of the reign, claims that the emperor 'usually caused the [praetorian prefects] to be brought to trial during their very term of office' (67.14.4). No names (or any other evidence of this) survive but Aelianus may have been meant, since he reappears as prefect under Nerva, yet, at the time of the assassination, Norbanus and T. Petronius Secundus[67] were in office.

Traditionally, there had been a close association between the Flavians and the office of praetorian prefect. Titus had been brought up at court from the age of 7 or so, no doubt with his military training provided by Claudius's prefect Burrus, since he and the emperor's son Britannicus shared the same subjects and the same masters (*Titus* 2). Once Vespasian was emperor, he appointed Titus praetorian prefect with another Flavian relative, M. Arrecinus Clemens, as his colleague for part of the reign – appointments all the more unprecedented since, for the first time, two senators were assigned to the leading equestrian post. Clemens, whose father had been Gaius's prefect (*Hist.* 4.68), was not only one of the uncles of Titus's daughter Julia (as was Domitian), but also provided the link between L. Julius Ursus and the Flavians.[68] But the prefects appointed by Domitian himself were not members of the imperial family, though two of them, Aelianus (*Vita Apoll.* 7.18) and Cornelius Fuscus (*Hist.* 2.86), had served Vespasian loyally during the civil war.

Many accounts of Domitian's assassination assume the involvement of the two prefects. But the ancient sources are far less specific, and, whilst it would have been logical to acquire their support, it must be stressed that the ancient authorities are nowhere near as definite as are some modern ones in declaring that it was actually obtained.[69]

As for Domitian's praetorian prefects, our conclusions, like our evidence, must needs be limited. Allowing for the restraints imposed by the imperial administrative 'system' (and their extent should not be exaggerated), Domitian ensured that his prefects were sympathetic to his views; they were chosen for specific reasons, including proven loyalty (Aelianus and Fuscus in 69, Norbanus in 89), and they seem to have been the most reliable of those courtiers who had closest access to him on a regular basis, if we trust to the accuracy of Suetonius's list of imperial assassins (*Dom.* 17.2). In his choice of prefects, he differed completely from the policy of Vespasian and Titus, who obviously felt that family members were the best candidates, no doubt on the basis that they would be the most loyal. Domitian had no such illusions and removed from office a relative appointed by Titus.[70] For him, an equestrian from Amisus in Pontus was preferable to a family member.[71]

FREEDMEN

Of the residents of the imperial palace, some may possibly have been the emperor's *amici*, though they would have been very few in number, presumably residing in the palace on a temporary basis only: those required for the meeting of the *consilium* described by Juvenal were summoned from outside and those invited to Domitian's Dacian banquet were sent home when it was over (Dio 67.9.1–6). But the vast majority of those residing at court were his freedmen or *liberti*, the *familia Caesaris*.[72]

Their ready access to the emperor guaranteed that they would be influential. Vespasian's *domestici*, for example, knew that the most propitious time to approach him was after his siesta, when he went to the baths or the dining room (*Vesp.* 21). As Epictetus put it, 'tyranny would be more tolerable if the *cubicularii* did not have to be approached as well as the emperor' (1.19.17–18). A good indicator is the attitude of the court poets. Martial asked the *a cubiculo* Parthenius to ensure that Domitian saw his poems (5.6.2) and thought it politic to remain on good terms with the *a libellis* Entellus (so a poem in praise of his gardens: 8.68) as well as with Parthenius (another poem, for the fifth birthday of his son Burrus:

4.45). He also mentions (4.8.7) Domitian's *tricliniarchus* Euphemus (*PIR*² E 118), perhaps a successor of Bucolas (*ILS* 1567). In fact, according to him (9.79.5–6), all Domitian's freedmen were noted for their calm demeanour and respectful attitude to everybody. He (7.40) and Statius (*Silvae* 3.3.1–216) sent their literary respects to Claudius Etruscus, consoling him on the death of his father, Domitian's former *a rationibus* Tiberius Julius Aug. lib., and both (Martial 9.11, 12, 13, 16, 36 and Statius *Silvae* 3.4.1–106) dedicated works to the imperial eunuch Flavius Earinus. Just as telling is the tone of Statius's poem to another freedman, the *ab epistulis* Abascantus (*Silvae* 1.5): unworthy as he was, he tried to deserve well of those in the sacred palace (*domus divina*), for one who worships gods must love his priests (*intro.*); Abascantus's duties were manifold, a burden scarcely tolerable (84), as he had to deal with every problem that faced his master Domitian, from river heights in Egypt (99) to the assessment of suitable candidates for military appointments (95–8).

There were many freedmen, performing an enormous array of tasks of varying importance, from the underworked *praepositus vestis albae triumphalis* (*ILS* 1763), who had to take charge of the white robe the emperor wore on triumphal occasions, to those in charge of the departments of state. Broadly speaking, the latter fell into two categories,[73] those dealing with purely domestic matters in the imperial palaces, villas and gardens (with the *procurator castrensis* in charge of financial matters and the *a cubiculo* controlling access to the emperor) and those with general administrative tasks (the *a rationibus*, *ab epistulis* and the *a libellis* being the most eminent).

By the latter decades of the first century AD, a fairly elaborate career structure had developed, as can be seen from an examination of the posts held by Domitian's *procurator castrensis* Ti. Claudius Aug. lib. Bucolas (*ILS* 1567).[74] He began as palace taster (*praegustator*), an office once held by the eunuch Halotas in the reign of Claudius (whom he is said to have poisoned – *Claud.* 44.2); then Bucolas became superintendent of the table (*tricliniarchus*), manager of the imperial gladiatorial games (*procurator a muneribus*), supervisor of the aqueducts (*proc. aquarum*) and ultimately *proc. castrensis*. The last two posts, at least, were held during Domitian's reign[75] and his career provides some sort of indication of the sheer extent of the imperial *familia*. Domitian even used them as political agents, sending some to Britain to urge Agricola to resign his post (*Agr.* 40.2, 41.4) and possibly employing others as spies and couriers.[76]

Discovering the identity of the senior freedmen poses problems. The term *ab epistulis*, for instance, can refer to any member of the department, including its chief – thus we have an imperial slave named Libanus described as an *ab epistulis* but who died at the age of 16, as well as at least twelve freedmen *ab epistulis* (to say nothing of four *ab epistulis Latinis* and two *ab epistulis Graecis*) who worked in the period between Claudius and Hadrian when Narcissus, Abascantus and Titinius Capito are definitely attested as heads of the department.[77] Libanus obviously did not hold so senior a position, he was not even a freedman. He and the others merely worked in that department. So many of the existing lists of senior imperial freedmen must be approached with caution.[78]

Domitian's first financial secretary (*a rationibus*) was Tiberius Julius Aug. lib. dismissed early in the reign and exiled.[79] Not long after his recall some ten years later, he died at about the age of 90 and Statius's *consolatio* (*Silvae* 3.3.1–216), addressed to the freedman's son Claudius Etruscus, provides a useful, if idealized, version of his career. His replacement as *a rationibus* may have been Atticus.[80] No other holders of the office are known. A number of freedmen *ab epistulis* are attested, but how many of them were actually the imperial private secretary rather than slave members of that department cannot be ascertained. Late in the 90s, T. Flavius Aug. lib. Abascantus[81] was in office; he was possibly demoted, but certainly replaced by the equestrian Titinius Capito,[82] who retained the post under Nerva and, for a time, under Trajan. Once again, Statius is helpful. His poem of consolation (*epikeidion*) on the death of Abascantus's wife Priscilla (*Silvae* 5.1.1–262) has survived. It is the only substantial account we have of the duties of an *ab epistulis*, and, though more idealized even than the *consolatio* to Claudius Etruscus, is nonetheless an invaluable compendium of the varied tasks that Statius could claim, with some degree of credibility, were allocated to Domitian's secretary. In charge of petitions was the *a libellis*, a role filled late in the reign by Entellus, who was to be one of Domitian's assassins.[83] Hermeros[84] may well have held the post before him, but the evidence is not at all convincing and no others (unless we include Epaphroditus) are attested.[85] Apart from these officials, the only other senior administrative freedmen who may have held posts in the period 81 to 96 were T. Flavius Aug. lib. Abascantus and Astectus Aug. lib., both described as *a cognitionibus*;[86] the equestrian Titinius Capito served both as *ab epistulis* of Domitian and as *a patrimonio*,[87] but no freedmen holders of the latter office are known.

On Domitian's accession, Tiberius Claudius Aug. lib. Classicus[88] was in charge of the imperial domestic budget (*procurator castrensis*) and was promptly dismissed, with Bucolas (*ILS* 1567) as his probable successor; no other incumbents are known. Classicus was also imperial chamberlain or *a cubiculo*. We have no hint of his replacement in this role, but, by the end of the reign, the post had been assigned to Parthenius, with Siger(i)us[89] as one of his assistants (*cubicularius*); both were actively involved in Domitian's assassination.

The *Historia Augusta*'s statement that it was Hadrian who first used equestrians as *a libellis* and *ab epistulis* has long been discredited. The innovation occurred far earlier, perhaps under Claudius[90] and certainly under Vitellius, for which there is both literary (*Hist.* 1.58) and epigraphic (*ILS* 1447) evidence. But this was a temporary expedient, decided on during the crisis of civil war. Domitian went further. According to Suetonius, he 'shared certain of the chief *officia* between *libertini* and Roman *Equites*' (7.2).[91] The reference is not to the immediate creation of an entire equestrian bureaucratic class, headed by equestrians with administrative experience; rather that, in some instances, departmental heads were not chosen from freedmen but were now 'intellectuals from the Latin world'.[92] Suetonius himself is as good an example as any of such an appointment. His career was military in name only, as was that of Domitian's last *ab epistulis*, the equestrian Titinius Capito. His 'military' career stands in direct contrast with that of Vitellius's equestrian *a libellis*, Sex. Caesius Propertianus, described as *tr. mil. IIII Macedonic., praef. coh. III His(pa)nor.* (*ILS* 1447). Titinius appears merely as *praef. cohortis trib. milit.* (*ILS* 1448); no units are named, an unusual omission suggesting that the posts were assigned to him *honoris causa*. He was an intellectual, a poet and a scholar, and appointed for those very qualities.[93] The innovation, as far as can be determined from what Suetonius says, was a deliberate shift in imperial policy and not a temporary expedient.

However, this may not have been so, given the circumstances of Titinius's appointment quite late in the reign. In a recent examination[94] of Statius's *Silvae* 5.1, it has been argued that T. Flavius Aug. lib. Abascantus was still *ab epistulis* near the end of 95 when Statius wrote the *epikeidion* for the death of his wife

Priscilla and that he was not dismissed but demoted to the post of *a cognitionibus*. That idea had been rejected[95] on the grounds that the Abascantus described as *a cognitionibus* (*ILS* 1679) was married to a Flavia Hesperis, whereas the *ab epistulis*'s wife was Priscilla. But Statius describes Abascantus as *iuvenis* (5.1.247), so it would not be unreasonable to suggest that he remarried after Priscilla's death and his own demotion.[96] At all events, demoted or dismissed, he was replaced at about the time when Domitian's relationship with his senior freedmen had deteriorated – 'in order to convince his *domestici* that no one should dare to kill a patron, even on good grounds, he condemned to death the *a libellis* Epaphroditus' (*Dom.* 14.4). Epaphroditus had served as *a libellis* to Nero, took part in exposing the Pisonian conspiracy in 65 (*Ann.* 15.55), helped Nero commit suicide (Dio 63.27.3; *Nero* 49.3) and was exiled by Domitian, perhaps *c.* 93; the date of his death is fixed by Suetonius, since, in the next section (15.1), he refers to the execution of Flavius Clemens, ordinary consul in January 95. So Abascantus's demotion or dismissal may have been part of a wider problem, the dissatisfaction Domitian felt with his senior freedmen. It was in these circumstances that he turned to an equestrian *ab epistulis*.

It would seem that senators and equestrians who had held administrative posts in Titus's reign were, without exception, confirmed in their appointments by Domitian. Not so the imperial freedmen. Titus's *domestici* were promptly dismissed, as the evidence indicates clearly; in particular, a much disputed passage of Dio Cassius can be interpreted as supporting that view.[97]

> Domitian quite outdid himself in visiting disgrace and ruin on the friends [*philoi*] of his father and brother, ... for he regarded as his enemy anyone who had enjoyed his father's or his brother's affection beyond the ordinary or had been particularly influential. Accordingly, although he himself entertained a passion for a eunuch named Earinus, nevertheless, since Titus had also shown a great fondness for eunuchs, in order to insult his memory, he ordered that no person in the Roman empire should thereafter be castrated.
>
> (67.2.1–3)

Of all the possible *philoi*, Dio selected neither a senator (possibly Agricola[98]) nor an equestrian (possibly Casperius Aelianus[99]). He looked not to *amici* in a narrow sense, but to a broader group, members of the imperial court, the *domestici* – in particular, the eunuchs. Dio, then, may well not have used the word *philoi* in the sense of the Latin *amici*. Moreover, some hundred years before Dio wrote, Suetonius had already argued that Titus's *amici* were employed by subsequent emperors (*Titus* 7.2). In the absence of other criteria, a contemporary source should be preferred, and at least one later writer also seems to confuse the words *domestici* and *amici*. According to Suetonius, when Titus's *domestici* informed him that he could not possibly make good his promises, they were told that no one should leave an interview disappointed (8.2); on another occasion, at a dinner-party following a day during which he had not conferred any favour, he is supposed to have uttered the famous remark '*Amici*, I have wasted a day' (8.2). Eutropius repeats both anecdotes, but, in his version, it is the *amici* who are told that no one should leave disappointed (7.21.3). Perhaps it is hazardous to place too much emphasis on Dio's use of *philoi* and Eutropius's of *amici*. On the other hand, Dio does not seem to be referring to *amici* in the strict sense of the word, but rather to members of the imperial court in a general sense, and he may well have had a personal reason for such a view.

It is not impossible that he was a descendant of the Greek orator and philosopher Dio of Prusa,[100] described by the younger Pliny as 'Cocceianus Dion' (10.81.2) and by later scholars as 'Chrysostom' (i.e. 'golden-mouthed'), either to distinguish him from the historian or else as a tribute to his eloquence. It is not impossible that his name also included that of the emperor who had granted his family citizenship – almost certainly Claudius (*Or.* 41.6; 46.3–4). Chrysostom's name, then, may have been Claudius Cocceianus Dio, and the historian Cassius Dio Cocceianus is recorded as 'Claudius Cassius Dio' on an inscription (*AE* 1971: 430). So the two Dios, historian and philosopher, were probably related.[101]

But there is more. Dio of Prusa was a strong Flavian supporter, who approved openly of Vespasian's expulsion of the philosophers. Synesius, writing in the fifth century, names two otherwise unknown speeches of Dio, the *pros Mousonion* and the *kata ton philosophon*, the titles of which are suggestive enough, and, as well, he mentions that Dio 'hurled the coarse jests of the Dionysiac festival at Socrates and Zeno'.[102] His anti-philosophic attitude is also revealed in his attacks on the Cynics who 'do no good at all but rather the worst possible harm' (*Or.* 32.9), and who are 'creatures engaged in the work of overturning and destroying' (*Or.* 32.62). All this represents public support for Vespasian's expulsion of the philosophers from Rome and Italy at this time (Dio 66.13.2). As well, evidence for his friendship with Titus can be adduced, viz. his two obituaries of Melancomas (*Or.* 28, 29), the young athlete who, according to Themistius, was one of Titus's lovers (*Or.* 10.139a).[103] So Dio's consistent support for the Flavians throughout the 70s can be regarded as certain. He had engaged in important political activity on their behalf.

During the period before his exile under Domitian, Dio had (so he claimed) 'known the tables of rich men, of satraps and kings as well as of private individuals' (*Or.* 7.66) and it seems that it was his habit[104] to use the word 'kings' for Roman emperors and 'satraps' for imperial governors. So the reference must be to Vespasian and Titus. He was welcome at their court. With Domitian's accession, however, his fortunes changed. In the speech 'On his exile', he claims that he was banished for being the friend of someone 'very close to those who at that time enjoyed prosperity and power'; his friend was executed[105] and he himself exiled (*Or.* 13.1).

In such circumstances, Dio the historian had quite precise knowledge of the 'disgrace and ruin visited by Domitian on the *philoi* of his father and brother' (67.2.1); his ancestor, a member of the imperial court, was one of them.

Continuity of imperial administrative personnel, then, the theme advocated by a number of scholars,[106] need not and should not be regarded as applicable to Domitian's choice of *domestici*. A brief examination of two senior freedmen inherited from Titus explains why he acted so.

Tiberius Claudius Classicus was one of Titus's two most powerful freedmen, his *a cubiculo* and *procurator castrensis*.[107] As his career inscription (*AE* 1972: 574) indicates, after holding these posts under Titus, he received no appointment from Domitian, but regained favour under Nerva and may have been granted equestrian status. Now the positions held in Titus's reign were individually significant, each of them rated amongst the most senior posts available to an imperial freedman. What is surprising is that Classicus held them jointly, an unparalleled honour.[108] A *procurator castrensis* could be expected to possess considerable financial expertise; in effect, he was in charge of domestic organization within the palace and administered its budget.[109] For freedmen such as Tiberius Claudius Aug. lib. Bucolas, it represented the pinnacle of their career. But Classicus was Titus's *a cubiculo* as well. This was the most influential post in the palace available to a freedman, for the incumbent had consistent personal contact with the emperor.[110] Observe Philo's description of Gaius's *a cubiculo* Helicon (*PIR*² H 49), who

> played ball with Gaius, exercised with him, bathed with him, had meals with him, and was with him when he was going to bed ... with the result that he alone had the emperor's ear when he was at leisure or resting, released him from external distractions and so was able to listen to what he most wanted to hear.
>
> (*Legatio ad Gaium* 175)[111]

It will cause no surprise that Gaius's successor put Helicon to death. In fact, the post was quite often fraught with danger. Under Commodus, Cleander sold army commands, praetorships, prefectures and places in the senate; he had twenty-five consuls appointed in one year, acquired extreme wealth and finally married one of his master's concubines (Dio 72.12.3–5): in 190, Commodus had him executed. Equally instructive is the fate of Domitian's *a cubiculo* Parthenius at the hands of Nerva's praetorians: his testicles were cut off, stuffed into his mouth and then he was strangled (*Epit. de Caes.* 12.2, 8). In 82/3, the circumstances were different, but, nonetheless, Classicus must have wielded enormous influence in his joint role of *procurator castrensis* and *a cubiculo*. Domitian was suspicious of him, he suffered 'disgrace and ruin', but did not share the fate of Helicon, Parthenius or Cleander; rather he was moved aside to resume a successful career after 96.

So distrust of Titus's appointees prompted Classicus's sacking – or did it? Influential freedmen were not automatically efficient. Epictetus questioned that assumption: he did not believe that a freedman could 'suddenly become wise when Caesar puts him in charge of his chamberpot' (1.19.10). Classicus may not have measured up to Domitian's exacting standards.

Tiberius Julius Aug. lib., the father of Claudius Etruscus,[112] was an experienced financial administrator whose services to the Flavian cause in the civil war had not been forgotten: he was rewarded for his administration of the sinews of war (*Hist.* 2.84) by the grant of equestrian status to both his sons (between 69 and 71), by the right to appear in the lavish Jewish triumph in 71, and, in 73, by his own adlection to the equestrian order. He became *a rationibus* in Vespasian's reign and continued in that post under Titus, exerting enormous influence. Various appointments may be cited. It was probably thanks to his persuasiveness that his relative,

L. Funisulanus Vettonianus, was granted a suffect consulship in 78, some fifteen years after the debacle at Rhandeia, where he had commanded the *legio IV Scythica*. With the accession of Titus, Tiberius Julius's influence was even more obvious, and his relatives were appointed to posts of extraordinary strategic significance in 80 and 81. Vettonianus was sent to the military province of Dalmatia, Tettius Julianus (Tiberius's brother-in-law) to the senior praetorian post of Numidia, and C. Tettius Africanus became prefect of Egypt. Now the appointments to Numidia and Egypt, made in Titus's reign, were quite remarkable. Such a tight nexus was without parallel – the two Tettii had virtual control of Rome's grain supply,[113] commanding areas of considerable military significance. Neither the cautious Vespasian nor his suspicious younger son would have approved: Domitian soon broke up the nexus. But 'disgrace and ruin' were not visited on Titus's appointees. Quite the contrary. Only Tiberius Julius was punished, or rather 'caned with a feather' – dismissed and exiled to Campania. Tettius Julianus was recalled to Rome and the consulship, Tettius Africanus disappears from our records, being last attested in Egypt on 12 February 82 – perhaps he was adlected to senatorial rank – and Vettonianus was promoted to another two military provinces.[114]

Domitian's removal of his predecessors' *a rationibus* has been explained in another way.[115] Early in the reign (AD 82), the precious metal coinage was returned to the Neronian standard, in particular through a considerable increase in the fineness of the denarius that had slipped noticeably during the years of Tiberius Julius's control. Domitian would not have tolerated slackness of that sort. Possibly, too, the freedman may have objected to the new economic policy – an expensive return to the old standard coupled with the policy of cancelling debts outstanding to the *aerarium Saturni* for more than five years, of not accepting inheritances from testators with surviving children (*Dom.* 9), of confirming the rights of those squatting on the *subseciva* (*Dom.* 9) and of providing the army with a huge pay rise. He may have believed that the economy could not afford it all and been unwise enough to tell Domitian so.

OTHER COURTIERS

Lucianus Proclus (*PIR²* L 372) and L. Munatius Gallus (*PIR²* M 725) were possibly Domitianic courtiers (*comites*), but very little is known of their activities. Most elusive is Crispinus.[116] He appears not only in Juvenal (1.26–9; 4.1–33, 108–9), but also in Martial (7.99; 8.48) and has been variously identified as praetorian prefect, as prefect of Egypt, as prefect of the corn supply, as imperial freedman secretary[117] and also as one of Domitian's cronies, a sort of court parasite with no official position.[118] He is not attested epigraphically – all we know of him is provided by Juvenal and Martial. Ancient scholiasts on Juvenal were equally puzzled: they suggested that he was a slave, born in Egypt and made an equestrian or a senator by Nero or Domitian![119] Further speculation is pointless, but the least violence is done to the ancient literary evidence if we see in him one of the standard figures of any court – the ruler's personal friend, with a ready wit, meant to entertain and amuse. There is no hard evidence that he was anything more. Direct evidence of other courtiers is hard to come by.

Quintilian should be included, in view of his appointment by Domitian (*Inst. Or.* 4 *prooem.* 2) as tutor to his heirs, the two sons (*Dom.* 15.1) of Flavius Clemens and his receipt of *ornamenta consularia* through the influence of Clemens.[120] Domitian enjoyed the company of the actor Latinus (Martial 9.28.1), attested as one of Domitian's dinner guests and as a purveyor of the day's gossip (*Dom.* 15.1). As a consequence, perhaps, some have accused him of being an informer.[121] Another actor, Paris, enjoyed imperial favour for but a brief period in the early years of the reign: extremely influential at court, according to Juvenal 7.86–8, he was accused of exceeding his role by having an affair with Domitia (*Dom.* 3.1) and so he was put to death (Dio 67.3.1). Of the literary coterie, the satirist Turnus[122] is attested as being 'powerful in Domitian's court' (*PIR*[1] T 291). Included too should be the emperor's nurse Phyllis, who secretly carried his ashes to the *templun Gentis Flaviae* (*Dom.* 17.3), Andromachus, probably one of the court physicians (*PIR*[2] A 586) and his boy lover, the eunuch Earinus. But the rest – astrologers, freedmen, servants of all kinds and various guards – remain nameless.

Dio's claim that Domitian visited 'disgrace and ruin' on his father's and brother's *philoi* (if *philoi* be interpreted broadly to mean 'courtiers') is supported by the fate of Dio's own ancestor, Dio Chrysostom and by that of Tiberius Julius Aug. lib. and Tiberius Claudius Aug. lib. Classicus. They were quickly dismissed. The evidence strongly suggests that those courtiers with regular access to the emperor – the city prefect Pegasus, the praetorian prefects (Laberius Maximus replacing the family relative Julius Ursus), the *a cubiculo* and the *a rationibus* – were his appointees. On the other hand, *amici* such as Valerius Festus, Acilius Glabrio, Fabricius Veiento, Vibius Crispus and others who, appointed by his father, had shown themselves consistently loyal and dependable, were all in an entirely different category. They were retained, but summoned to court only when he needed their advice. Those courtiers with real power were those with regular access to him; his relationship with them was vital – as he discovered in 96.

4

ADMINISTRATION I

By any criteria, the Roman empire's dimensions were substantial, but, as many have observed,[1] their administrative system was not. The term 'imperial bureaucracy' is a misnomer. Administrative officials were remarkably few.[2] In practice, the emperor had to depend on the local provincial élite for many of the tasks one might have expected to be assigned to an army of 'imperial bureaucrats'. The corollary, though, is that chaos could all the more easily result from a lack of firm central control. Domitian was never guilty of that or, indeed, ever accused of it. He was personally involved (or, perhaps, engrossed) in just about every aspect of the administration of the capital and of the empire. The economy was his special concern: hence, on his accession and quite unexpectedly, he almost immediately revalued the currency by 12 per cent. He was the new Augustus, in money, morals and religion (all of which he tried to control rigorously) as well as in building and entertainment (where he spent lavishly). So aspects of his administration meriting examination include (1) the economy, (2) the building programme, his reforms affecting (3) the individual citizen as well as (4) the provinces and, finally (5) the opposition his administration aroused.

ECONOMY

Assessing the economic policy of a particular emperor is usually fraught with danger, stemming from a paucity of exact financial information. Domitian's reign is no exception. We have no idea of the exact cost of his Chattan war or, on the other hand, the value of any booty he may have obtained. Even when it seems that detailed costing is possible, difficulties emerge. Whilst the army pay rise of one-third is well attested, its exact cost is very difficult to compute: was the *V Alaudae* still in existence after 81? If not, estimates of the army's cost per year[3] would have to be reduced by HS 6.6 million; were all legions at full strength or were they rather like the severely depleted Egyptian legion of 90, with only half its normal complement of men?[4] Again, we have no idea when the full impact of the pay rise would have been felt. Since a proportion of a soldier's salary was paid over on his retirement, one would imagine that, each year between 83 and 108, extra funds would be needed since each year's retirees would have a progressively higher proportion of their accumulated funds at the higher rate. Even more difficult would be an attempt to cost accurately (or even approximately) Domitian's massive building programme.

Nevertheless, it is possible to determine broad trends in imperial economic policy and practice or, at the very least, to assess the financial position both at the beginning of the reign and at its end.

Scholars' views on Domitian's economic policy differ substantially, from Gsell (who believed that Domitian did not try to restore the finances that Titus had compromised) to Syme (who argued that he left a surplus).[5] A number of scholars have taken up a variety of positions between these two extremes, differing in their estimates of the emperor's efficiency and his policy's efficacy.[6] Overall, though, his reign should be classified as financially sound, since he started with a well-stocked treasury[7] (otherwise he would not have been able to revalue the currency just after his accession) and he left Nerva suficient funds for the normal *congiarium* and special distribution of corn as well, for the mitigation and remission of certain taxes, for the agrarian law, new colonies, various public works, and, not least, for the *alimenta*.[8]

A Domitianic balance sheet

A recent attempt to draw up a balance sheet of Domitian's reign, with estimates of his expenditure and income,[9] has revealed some interesting aspects of his finances, whilst, of course, not providing a complete picture of what happened. Vespasian's basic annual income has been estimated at around HS 1,200 million and the army's annual cost, under Domitian, in the order of HS 500 million: so, given an increase in income during Domitian's reign, about one-third or perhaps more of annual revenue was needed for the army alone. Now an army at war was presumably much more expensive than one that was not, and, for the first ten years of the reign in particular, he had substantial legionary and auxiliary forces committed to active warfare. Add to this his impressive building programme which must have been enormously expensive. One item alone cost HS 288 million, the gilding on the great temple of Jupiter; far less expensive, though, at HS 3 million, was the 19-kilometre long Via Domitiana. Other estimates have been drawn up. For his three *congiaria* (in 83, 89 and 93, probably) some HS 135 million would have been needed (i.e. the annual cost of about nineteen legions), and, for the annual subsidy to Decebalus, about HS 8 million. On the other hand, given that the properties of a moderately wealthy senator such as Pliny were worth about HS 17 million, with an annual income of HS 1 million, confiscations of property would have been worthwhile only if conducted on a very large scale. The sale of eighty properties similar to Pliny's would (very roughly) provide Domitian with his annual income – assuming that they would all be sold at market value, but if, as seems more likely, they became imperial property, then, each year, the income from about seven of them would meet the peace-time costs of only one legion.

Literary evidence

Suetonius's approach was somewhat less mathematical. Domitian's finances are mentioned on four separate occasions, the first (*Dom.* 3.2) being the most vital, since, according to Suetonius, it was contrary to Domitian's nature that he became greedy through need. In chapters four to six appears a list of his expenditure – costly entertainment in the circus and amphitheatre, games (secular, Capitoline and Quinquatria), *congiaria*, public banquets, the restoration of many buildings and the erection of new ones, various wars and the army pay rise of one-third. At 9.1 is a very laudatory version of his finances: his honesty, integrity and generosity are noted and examples provided (he refused inheritances from those with children and punished delation). But, at 12.1, the tone changes. The 'achievements' of 4–6 exhausted the treasury and, as a result, property was confiscated on any pretext, he resorted to every kind of robbery, including the vigorous exaction of the *fiscus Iudaicus*.

Dio's account is far briefer but supportive. He adds to the list of expenses the annual subsidy to Decebalus (67.7.4) and assigns the confiscations to *c.* 84 (67.4.5). On the other hand, despite his six years in the treasury (three of them under Domitian), Pliny is comparatively unhelpful and disappointingly vague. At 12.2 and 20.4 of the *Panegyricus*, for instance, he comments on the extent of Domitian's expenses, and, although he refers often to the confiscations, he rejects Suetonius's explanation that they were based on need (*Dom.* 3.2), suggesting rather that he was motivated by envy (50.5). The consistent themes emerging from the literary evidence, then, are that his enormous expenses caused him to revise his early generosity and that, to balance his budget, he was obliged to resort to confiscations and rigorous collection of taxes.

Numismatic evidence

Other evidence confirms some of this. A detailed numismatic analysis has revealed that Domitian's reign was one of the most important in the history of Roman imperial coinage.[10] At some time between Vespasian's accession and the first months of 82, the Neronian standard had been abandoned, but, although most coins were issued at a lower or debased level, some were still minted at the higher. Domitian put a stop to all that. For the first few months of his reign, he retained the old debased Vespasianic standard, but, as soon as possible, revalued his coinage to the much higher level[11] of Augustus. Another reform occurred in 85, a reversion to the Neronian level of 64, which was still higher than Vespasian's and one that he meticulously retained until the end of the reign.

The reform of 82 can be dated precisely. The first coins of the year, with Domitian merely *COS VIII*, are of 'Vespasianic' quality, but those appearing *c.* March, with Domitian now *COS VIII DES VIIII*, are remarkably finer, a 'dramatic and entirely unexpected'[12] change. Everywhere, Domitian's influence was evident. Having dismissed the financial secretary, he was now determined to see to it that what he wanted done was done: the silver content of the denarius was lifted by about 12 per cent; with only one exception, there appeared, on both the gold and silver issues, an entirely new series of reverse types; the four reverses of Domitian's favourite goddess Minerva, which later became standard,[13] were soon established on the denarii and retained for the entire reign; finer portraits of the emperor appeared on the obverses; and, as well, the mint at once stopped issuing bronze coins, resuming some two years later.[14] After the comparatively haphazard performance of the mint under Vespasian, the rapid improvement in efficiency was plainly due to Domitian, who must have been involved in the minutiae of administration.

Then, in 85, came the second reform, a devaluation: coins appearing between April (Domitian as *CENSOR*) and September (Domitian with *TR P V*) were of both standards, but the precision and exactness of manufacture was such that no confusion between the types is possible.[15] Once again, one of the interesting (if hardly surprising) facets of the second reform is the interest shown by Domitian: not only is there a remarkable 'uniformity and consistency'[16] of coin quality, but also a regular and careful reproduction of the details of the imperial titles and the ever-present Minerva/Jupiter reverses. No detail was too small for him.

Now the second reform (or devaluation) of 85 coincided with a change in Domitian's attitude and policy noted by both Suetonius (*Dom.* 12.1–2: 'reduced to financial straits') and Dio (67.4.5: confiscations). The phrase *me adulescentulum* (12.2) in the anecdote concerning the exaction of the Jewish tax enables the change, noted at 12.1, to be dated to around 85, i.e. when Suetonius was approximately 15. So, by 85, imperial income must have proved inadequate to meet the expenses of the army pay rise, the Chattan and British wars, the *congiaria*, the triumph, the imperial shows and the building programme. Earlier in the reign, he had dismissed his financial secretary, Tiberius Julius Aug. lib., because he had either regarded as unwise the revaluation of 82, or else permitted a remarkable degree of slackness to permeate the mint.[17] But now any doubts he may have had were proved valid. Changes were needed: confiscations and rigid enforcement of taxes followed.

Two other points are relevant to the financial crisis that became evident in 85. Early in that year, Domitian received censorial power, upgrading it to a perpetual censorship by the end of the same year;[18] as a consequence, he hoped to 'legislate morality', especially by enforcing laws such as the *lex Voconia* and the *lex Julia de adulteriis coercendis* (*Pan.* 42.1), as well as the *lex Scantinia* (*Dom.* 8.3), thereby, according to Pliny (42.1), enriching the treasury. Furthermore, for what their evidence is worth, later writers assigned the decline in the standard of Domitian's administration to this period, rather than to the more obvious 'turning-point', the revolt of Saturninus. Eutropius, for instance, has him *moderatus* at first, but finds a decline to *ingentia vitia* once he began to call himself *dominus et deus* (7.10.1–2), a title that Dio (or rather his editor, Boissevain) assigns to the period *c.* 85/6: in fact, it is preserved by the epitomator Zonaras and appears immediately after his account of the Chattan war and the army pay rise. But the extent of the decline or crisis should not be exaggerated: as is clear from an examination of his coinage, Domitian was still able to maintain a standard higher than Vespasian's.

Less easy to determine is the extent of and motivation for the confiscations, since the income they produced for the new imperial owner was presumably welcome but hardly enormous: each year of the reign, he would have had to confiscate the property of seven senators such as Pliny just to maintain one legion throughout the period. It was an additional gain from the successful prosecution of an opponent, but not the reason for the prosecution.[19] Even Pliny believed that Domitian was motivated by envy rather than need – 'he possessed far more than he needed but always wanted more. It was fatal at that time . . . to own a spacious house or an attractive property' (*Pan*. 50.5).

So the confiscations began as early as 85 and must be separated entirely from the events of 93, crucial though these may have seemed to Tacitus and Pliny because of their intimacy with those who suffered death or exile.[20] Gsell and others regarded the year 93 as a turning-point in the reign, inaugurating a reign of terror ('période de terreur') including confiscations, banishments and executions.[21] But not so: confiscation preceded the so-called terror by about eight years.

Vine edict

One of the most discussed of Domitian's economic measures has been his vine edict.[22] Suetonius (7.2) reports that, when a glut of wine coincided with a shortage of corn, Domitian

> thought that the corn-fields were being neglected as a result of too much concentration on vineyards, and issued an edict that no more vines were to be planted in Italy and that vineyards in the provinces were to be cut down, leaving no more than half standing, but he did not go through with the measure.

Then at 14.2, we are told that he dropped the proposal after a poem appeared comparing him to a vine-eating goat. Statius also comments on it, praising Domitian who, 'to chaste Ceres, restores acres long denied her and a sober countryside' (*Silvae* 4.3.11–12) and proceeds immediately to glorify Domitian's achievement (as Censor) in forbidding castration (13–15).

Two general observations should be made. The vine edict constitutes the only instance we have of Domitian legislating for the entire Roman empire rather than for an individual province, as, for example, with the edict of L. Antistius Rusticus (*AE* 1925: 126). Secondly, both Suetonius and Statius regarded it not as an economic reform but as a moral one;[23] and similarly, Philostratus (*Vit. Soph.* 520) reports that Domitian ordered the destruction of the vines in Asia through fear of *stasis* induced by too much wine, but was dissuaded from it by the orator Scopelian.

Undoubtedly, he wanted to encourage cereal-production both in Italy and in the provinces, for shortages were not unknown. The vine edict (of *c.* 90–1) had been issued just before the severe famine in Pisidian Antioch (92–3)[24] But there was more to it than this; the cities of Asia had been growing and their populations expanding for many years, but the emperors were reluctant to allow the local élite to assume complete control over the production of corn, for fear it would result in a concomitant loss of imperial authority.[25] In fact, what it did produce was famine. Domitian tried to deal with the problem: hence, perhaps, his popularity amongst the provincials.

The theory that he meant to assist the Italian vine-grower by reducing competition from outside[26] is not tenable, for the Italian grower needed little help at this period. Italy was experiencing a boom in wine-production; it seems that increasing consumption was resulting in more extensive markets at home,[27] and that they were even able to absorb quite easily the increasing quantity of imported wines. From a different point of view, the problems involved in implementing the policy and destroying the vines in both Italy and the provinces would have been formidable. Who would do it and what would be the attitude of the Italian and provincial élite at the loss of part of their livelihood?

Despite Suetonius's repeated claim (7.2, 14.2) that the proposal was soon abandoned, some scholars believe that it was put into effect in some of the imperial estates of Africa, and subsequently reversed by an edict of the emperor Probus. Levick has discussed the evidence and convincingly dismissed it.[28]

All the indications suggest that Domitian inherited and bequeathed a balanced budget. However, the most striking aspect of his economic policy was his (perhaps not unexpected) personal involvement and insistence that the coinage be of a consistently high standard, that Minerva (in precise guises), Jupiter and *Germanicus* should appear consistently, and that the regular changes in imperial titulature be recorded precisely. This was very much his policy, as Tiberius Julius Aug. lib. soon discovered. Moreover, he refused to 'take the easy option' and devalue the currency, as Trajan and his successors did.[29] On the other hand, there is evidence to suggest that a decline in his relationship with sections of the aristocracy can be assigned to the period immediately following the devaluation of 85, but none to show that the prosecutions of the latter part of the reign were motivated by need of money. In short, his autocratic conception of government was nowhere more evident than in his economic policy.

BUILDING PROGRAMME

Part of the debate between Syme and Sutherland over Domitian's finances dealt with the supposed decline in his building programme in the latter part of the reign.[30] That decline was illusory. Domitian maintained the programme just as he maintained the currency standard established in 85. This very consistency in both building and currency control suggests, though does not prove, that his was always a balanced budget.

In the years after 64, the physical appearance of Rome was drastically changed. Natural circumstances, in particular two major fires lasting for many days, together with a civil war in which four emperors died, had made restoration and rebuilding essential, and, when combined with Domitian's determination to make Rome a capital worthy of the empire, the result was a very different city. A magificent palace on the Palatine with its impressive, original design and the restored temple of Jupiter on the Capitol were but the highlights: some fifty structures were either erected, restored or completed by him in a massive and spectacular programme of public building equalled by hardly any other emperor.[31]

Now the fire of 64 had been a disaster: in nine days (*ILS* 4914), it had completely destroyed three (3, 10 and 11) of Rome's fourteen

Regions, sparing only four (1, 5, 6 and 14) in all. Nero's work of restoration was apparently well planned, praised even by Tacitus for combining both beauty and utility (*Ann.* 15.43), but it was not completed on his death four years later, nor on Domitian's accession in 81 (*ILS* 4914).

Further damage had occurred during the civil war (e.g. *Vit.* 15.3) and, whilst repairs and new programmes had been undertaken by Vespasian (not least of which being the *Amphitheatrum Flavianum*), another disaster occurred early in 80 whilst Titus was in Campania, checking on the damage caused by the eruption of Vesuvius (*Titus* 8.3; Dio 66.24.1). For three days and nights (*Epit. de Caes.* 10.12), fire raged in Rome, particularly from the Capitoline temples to the Pantheon, consuming whatever was in its path, including

> the temple of Serapis, the temple of Isis, the Saepta, the temple of Neptune, the Baths of Agrippa, the Pantheon, the Diribitorium, the theatre of Balbus, the stage buildings of Pompey's theatre, the Octavian buildings together with their books, and the temple of Jupiter Capitolinus with its surrounding temples.
>
> (Dio 66.24.2)

Some work was done by Titus, but the major burden of rebuilding fell on his successor, who 'restored very many splendid buildings that the fire had destroyed' (*Dom.* 5). According to Suetonius, Domitian's name only was inscribed on the restoration, with no reference to the original builder (*Dom.* 5), a policy completely opposed to that of his father, if we are to believe Dio (66.10.1a). Suetonius's claim may contain some truth, but not the complete truth: where Domitianic restorations are actually attested epigraphically, they are indicated by the words *Domitianus . . . restituit*[32] with no hint whatsoever of the identity of the emperor originally responsible, but also with not the slightest attempt to claim the structure as 'his', an omission on Suetonius's part that may well be only unintentionally misleading.

Archaeological investigation has shown that most of the buildings on Dio's list were restored by Domitian, with the possible exception of the temple of Neptune, the *scaena* of Pompey's theatre and the *diribitorium*. The temple, built by Agrippa in 25 BC, was restored by Hadrian (*SHA, Hadr.* 19.10), but that does not rule out earlier Domitianic work; on the other hand, Pompey's theatre (55 BC) had been restored by Augustus at great expense (*RG* 20.1), and later by either Gaius (*Gaius* 21) or Claudius (*Claud.* 21.1). But in 80 only the *scaena* was burned down and quickly restored, perhaps by Titus – after all, the theatre itself was built of stone. The *diribitorium* is a puzzle. It may well have been the upper level of the *Saepta* rather than a separate building. Nash's illustration, where the two relevant sections of the Severan marble plan[33] have been placed placed together, would give some support to this theory.[34] In that case, Domitian may well have restored them both.

The Chronographer of 354 credits him with quite a few monuments, as does Eusebius. Their lists are important; according to the Chronographer, his buildings included

> *atria vii, horrea piperataria ubi modo est basilica Constantiniana et horrea Vespasiani, templum Castorum et Minervae, portam Capenam, gentem Flaviam, Divorum, Iseum et Serapeum, Minervam Chalcidicam, Odium* [sic]*, Minuciam veterem, stadium, et thermas et Titianas et Traianas, amphitheatrum usque ad clypea, templum Vespasiani et Titi, Capitolium, senatum, ludos iiii, Palatium, metam sudantem et Panteum* [sic].

Eusebius adds three to the Chronographer's list,[35] omits eight[36] and refers to the *ludus matutinus* rather than to *ludos iiii* and to the *templum Vespasiani* (omitting any reference to Titus). But though many topographers have been loath to accept their accuracy, recent archaeological excavation together with a study of the relevant brickstamps[37] has forced a re-evaluation of their claims. Almost all of the buildings they attribute to him can be shown by other evidence to have been his: apart from archaeological evidence and brickstamps, information can be gleaned from inscribed water pipes, coins, architectural styles (e.g. Flavian cornices with their twin rings), later reliefs (e.g. those from the Haterii Mausoleum) and the Severan marble plan.[38] Furthermore, the chronographers' lists were far from complete. To the structures mentioned by the Chronographer and Eusebius, more than thirty should be added: basic information on all these, together with the appropriate illustrations, is provided by Platner and Ashby (1929), Blake (1959) and Nash (1961–2), as the following summary indicates.

Domitian's building programme: summary of sources (page nos)[39]

	Platner and Ashby	Blake	Nash
Altars	30	100–1	I: 60–2
Amphitheatrum Flavianum	6–11	91–6, 109–10	I: 17–25
Arches and Gates	38–9, 45	112	
Arcus Neroniana	22, 41	123–4, 141	I: 37
Arcus Titi	45–7	98, 111–12	I: 133–5
Atria Septem	57	115	
Atrium Vestae	58–9	115	I: 154–9
Bibliotheca Apollonis Palatii	84, 161	118	I: 204–5
Bibliotheca Templi Divi Augusti	63, 84		
Casa Romuli	101–2, 377		II: 164–5
Circus Maximus	114–20	104–5	I: 236
Curia Julia	143–4	102–3	I: 301–3
Domus Flavia, Domus Augustana, Hippodromos	158–66	115–24	I: 316–38
Domus Tiberiana	191–4	118	I: 365–74
Equus Domitiani	201–2	112–13	I: 389–90
Forum Caesaris	225–7	102–3	I: 424–32
Forum Traianum	237–45	105	I: 450–6
Forum Transitorium	227–9	105–6	I: 485–7
Horrea Agrippiana	260	114	I: 475–80
Horrea Piperataria	262–3	114	I: 485–7
Horrea Vespasiani	263	99, 114	
Ludi	319–20	110	II: 24–6

	Platner and Ashby	Blake	Nash
Meta Sudans	340	110	II: 61–3
Mica Aurea	341	115	
Naumachia	358	109	
Obeliscus: Isis Campensis	369	107	II: 148–54
Odeum	371	108–9	
Pantheon	382–5	110	II: 170–5
Porta Capena	405	115	
Porticus: Dei Consentes	421	97, 100	II: 241–3
Porticus: Minucia Vetus	424–6	103	
Porticus Octaviae	427	103	II: 254–8
Saepta Julia	460–1	100	II: 291–3
Stadium	495–6	107–8	II: 387–90
Templa:			
Castorum et Minervae	102–4, 342–3	114–15	I: 210–13
Divi Vespasiani	556	97–8	II: 501–4
Divorum	152–3	113	I: 304
Divi Augusti	62–5	124	I: 164
Fortuna Redux	218	113–14	I: figure 115
Gentis Flaviae	247, 326	114	
Ianus Quadrifons	280	106	I: 504–5
Iseum et Serapeum	283–5	106–7	I: 118–19
Iuppiter Custos	292	101	I: 518–20
Iuppiter Optimus Maximus Capitolinus	297–300	101	I: 530–3
Iuppiter Tonans	305–6	101	I: 535–6
Minerva Chalcidicia	344	104	II: 66–8
Pacis	386–8	89–90	I: 439–45

	Platner and Ashby	Blake	Nash
Veiovis	548–9	102	II: 490–5
Theatrum Balbi	513	103	II: 414–17
Thermae Agrippae	518		II: 429–33
Thermae Titianae et Traianae	533–6	98	II: 469–77
Tribunal Vesp. Titi Dom.	541		

For a more precise assessment of his massive achievement, it is proposed to examine his building programme under four headings, viz. the structures he erected, those he restored, those he completed, together with those (probably correctly) attributed to him. Let it be noted in passing that he did not restrict his efforts to any one particular section of the capital. Probably most money was spent on the Palatine and the area of the Campus Martius, but he did not neglect the Capitoline, the Forum region, the Quirinal, the valley of the Flavian amphitheatre or the Esquiline.

Structures erected by Domitian

Altars. The conflagration of 80 probably served as a reminder that the altars voted to commemorate the fire of 64 and ward off similar destruction in the future had never been erected (*ILS* 4914). Domitian remedied the defect, setting one up in (presumably) each Region, dedicated to Vulcan. They were quite substantial, that on the Quirinal being more than 6 metres long.

Arches and Gates. According to Suetonius, Domitian erected commemorative arches and monumental gates in the various Regions of the city, adding that an ancient graffito scrawled on one of the arches (*arcus*) read *arci*, a transliteration of the Greek *arkei* meaning 'enough' (*Dom.* 13.2). Dio also mentions his arches (68.1.1). None of these have been identified. However, representations of them appear on coins from 83, 89 and 93, one is mentioned by Martial (8.65), the Cancellaria Reliefs may have decorated one of them and another may be represented on the Haterii Relief.[40] Again, the *arcus Tiburii* or *Diburi* was the medieval name assigned to an arch that may well have formed the entrance to Domitian's *porticus Divorum*.[41] Perhaps it was another of his many arches.

Atria Septem. The Chronographer of 354 mentions these amongst Domitian's *operae publicae* but nothing else is known of them.

Equus Domitiani. In 89, the senate voted that a massive equestrian statue of Domitian be erected in the Forum to commemorate his victories over Germany and Dacia and, not long afterwards, the emperor himself dedicated it in a ceremony that inspired Statius's 107-line poem (*Silvae* 1.1.1–107).[42] Some idea of its size emerges from the dimensions of its concrete base, discovered in 1903 – 11.80 metres by 5.90 metres.[43] Despite the pious hopes of Statius that it would 'stand as long as earth and sky abide and as long as the light that shines on Rome endures' (*Silvae* 1.1.93–4), it was destroyed some five years later, following the *damnatio*.

Forum Nervae or **Forum Transitorium.** The best sources claim that it was built by Domitian but bore the name of Nerva (*Dom.* 5),[44] since he dedicated the temple of Minerva in it (*CIL* 6.953), a claim that was confirmed by archaeologists in the 1930s.[45] Some scholars, though, preferring the evidence of Aurelius Victor (who states that Vespasian built a forum next to the temple of Peace: *De Caes.* 9.7), believe that Domitian merely continued his father's work,[46] but this is not generally accepted.[47] It was very narrow, 120 metres by 40, and served as the main thoroughfare between the *Subura* and the *Forum Romanum* – hence its alternative name. Since it was adjacent to the *Forum Augusti* and the *Forum Iulium*, Domitian may well have intended to combine all three into one massive complex, but this is purely speculative. Its most notable feature was the temple of Minerva, an imposing building represented on the Severan marble plan. As well, there seems to have been architectural features similar to those of Domitian's palace.[48]

Horrea Piperataria. A warehouse and market for the sale of pepper and spices from Arabia and Egypt (Dio 72.24.1),[49] it is assigned to Domitian by both the Chronographer of 354 and Eusebius; the former even gives its location – *ubi modo est basilica Constantiniana*. Excavations under the central nave of the basilica of Maxentius satisfied scholars that the brickwork was Domitianic,[50] but no stamps seem to have been published to confirm this assessment.

Horrea Vespasiani. Only the Chronographer of 354 allocates the construction of these warehouses to Domitian. Their location is not known.

Ludi. The Chronographer of 354 credits Domitian with the erection of four gladiatorial training schools (*ludos iiii*), Eusebius with one (*ludus matutinus*). The Regionaries provide the names of four such schools in the area of the *Amphitheatrum Flavianum*, viz. *ludus* *magnus* (presumably the principal establishment), *ludus gallicus* (for Gallic gladiators), *ludus matutinus* (perhaps for participants in the beast hunts, held 'in the morning') and *ludus dacicus* (for gladiators from Dacia);[51] it seems reasonable to assume that these were the four referred to by the Chronographer and that they were established on the site of the *domus aurea* as part of a huge entertainment complex. Archaeological investigation has revealed the existence of foundation walls and other remains of *ludi* to the east and south of the Amphitheatre.[52] The evidence of the Chronicles, then, ought not to be rejected.

Meta Sudans. Just to the south-west of the *Amphitheatrum Flavianum*,[53] Domitian erected a large fountain, according to the Chronographer of 354 and Eusebius. Although it appears on the obverse of one of Titus's coins,[54] it is generally attributed to Domitian on the evidence of the brickwork.

Mica Aurea. According to Eusebius (but not the Chronographer of 354), Domitian was responsible for the construction of what was presumably a building, the *mica aurea* (*mica* = ?a small dining-hall). Its location is a mystery. In the Regionary Catalogue, reference is made to a *mica aurea* on the Caelian (in the second Region).[55] On the other hand, Martial refers to a *mica* 'from which one looks upon Caesar's dome' (2.59.2), which must mean Augustus's mausoleum in the Campus Martius; but it is hardly visible from the Caelian. So both the nature and location of Eusebius's *mica aurea* remain unknown.

Naumachia. Domitian constructed an artificial pond for sham naval battles (*Dom.* 4.2; Dio 67.8.2–3; and, possibly, Martial 1.5.1–2), probably on the bank of the Tiber. Stone from it was used to restore the Circus Maximus (*Dom.* 5).

Obeliscus Isis Campensis. A number of obelisks came from the *Iseum et Serapeum* (the temple of Isis) in the Campus Martius. Four of them can be found in various parts of Rome.

Odeum. It was apparently a very impressive building, for, even in the fourth century, it was regarded as one of the most conspicuous and famous monuments in Rome (Amm. Marcell. 16.10.14). Built by Domitian in the Campus Martius, probably near the Stadium (*Dom.* 5; Eutropius 7.23), it was intended for musical performances and apparently could hold some 5,000 spectators.[56] Apollodorus restored it during Trajan's reign (Dio 69.4.1). Unfortunately, but a few fragments of it remain.

Stadium. In the Campus Martius, Domitian built a stadium for athletic contests with a capacity of 15,000 (*Dom.* 5; Eutropius

7.23). The arena itself, about 250 metres long, is now covered by the Piazza Navona which preserves quite strikingly the shape and size of Domitian's building. It, too, was still regarded in the fourth century (by the emperor Constantius) as one of Rome's most outstanding buildings (Amm. Marcell. 16.10.14). Following the fire of 217 in the Colosseum, it was, for some time, used for gladiatorial contests and, until the nineteenth century, was unanimously identified by scholars as the Circus of Alexander Severus.

Templum Divorum. Situated in the Campus Martius, this structure (so named by the Chronographer of 354) was part of Domitian's rearrangement of the entire Region.[57] Until the excavation of 1925, its general shape was known only from fragments of the Severan marble plan. In essence, it consisted of a *porticus* (hence Eusebius's reference to the *porticus Divorum*: 7.23) 200 metres long and 55 wide[58] together with two *aedes*, one to the deified Titus and another (presumably) to the deified Vespasian. Domitian may have developed the site because the Judaean triumph of Vespasian and Titus started from this point. If this was the motivation, his own triumph probably commenced from here too; hence the suggestion that the Cancelleria Reliefs may have decorated this *templum*.[59]

Templum, Fortuna Redux. After his triumphant entry to Rome in 93 after the Sarmatian campaign, Domitian built a temple in the Campus Martius. According to Martial, even the approach to it was magnificent, with its consecrated arch (8.65.8), two chariots and many elephants (8.65.9). However, its precise site remains conjectural, the suggestion that it is the apsed building south of the *Templum Divorum* on the Severan marble plan being open to question.[60] Neither Eusebius nor the Chronographer mention it.

Templum Gentis Flaviae. Domitian apparently erected a dynastic mausoleum (Martial 9.3.12; 9.34.2; *Silvae* 4.3.19), a sumptuously decorated building (Martial 9.20.1) on the site of Vespasian's house on the Quirinal, just south of the *Alta Semita* where he himself had been born (*Dom.* 1.1).[61] Completed by 94,[62] it was struck by lightning in 96, foreshadowing (so he thought) his own death (*Dom.* 15.2). Not long after, his own ashes were placed there by his nurse Phyllis (*Dom.* 17.3) together, probably, with those of his father and brother which he had removed there already; such at least is the obvious interpretation of Statius's comment that Domitian had 'recently founded a sacred shrine for his everlasting family' (*Silvae* 5.1.240–1). Although no definite traces of it have been found, most topographers locate it under San Carlo alle Quatro Fontane.[63]

Templum, Ianus Quadrifrons. In the *Forum Transitorium*, Domitian erected a shrine to 'four-faced Janus'; it was square, with four doors, and the statue of Janus was supposed to look out on four *Fora* (Martial 10.28.6), *Romanum, Augustum, Pacis* and *Transitorium*.[64] Its precise location has never been discovered, but topographers suggest it must have been in the centre of the *Forum Transitorium*.[65]

Templum, Iuppiter Custos. Domitian had built a small chapel, a *sacellum*, to Jupiter the Preserver (*Conservator*) on the site of the house where he had hidden from the Vitellians on the night of 19 December 69 (*Hist.* 3.74). On its altar, according to Tacitus, Domitian's exploits in escaping death were represented in marble. Later, on his accession, he replaced the *sacellum* with a large temple (*Hist.* 3.74; *Dom.* 5) to Jupiter the Guardian (*Custos*). It may be represented on a relief in the Conservatori Palace portraying Marcus Aurelius; on the other hand, some identify it with a temple on the Haterii Relief.[66]

Templum, Minerva Chalcidicia. A temple of this name is attributed to Domitian by the Chronographer of 354; and, in the Regionary catalogue, he is assigned a temple in the Campus Martius, linked, in the Severan marble plan, to the *porticus Divorum* by a flight of steps.[67] In view of Domitian's attachment to Minerva's worship, the proximity – her temple and the *aedes* of his deified father and brother – would be entirely appropriate.[68]

Tribunal Vespasiani Titi Domitiani. Somewhere on the Capitoline, a platform was erected, perhaps supporting statues of the three Flavian emperors and certainly providing lists of discharged soldiers. The name appears on a military diploma of 82 (*ILS* 1992).

Structures restored by Domitian

Arcus Neroniana. Archaeological investigation has indicated that Domitian was responsible for reconstruction and restoration work on part of this aqueduct (a branch of the *aqua Claudia* built by Nero) between the Caelian and the Palatine.[69] He was the first to bring the water of the *Claudia* to the Palatine,[70] and as well, according to epigraphical evidence, his reign saw the completion of work on a tunnel for the *aqua Claudia*, under the *mons Aeflanus*, near Tibur (3 July 88: *ILS* 3512).

Atrium Vestae. Originally, the term referred to the entire precinct associated with the Vestals, but, by the end of the republic, it was applied only to their dwelling house. Situated at the foot of the Palatine, the *atrium* was probably destroyed in Nero's fire, rebuilt by him and again severely damaged in 80. Domitian restored and enlarged it.

Bibliotheca Apollonis Palatini. This library, established by Augustus in the temple of Apollo, was apparently situated to the south-west of the triclinium of the *domus Flavia*. Destroyed by fire in 64, it was restored by Domitian.

Bibliotheca Templi Divi Augusti. This library, established by Tiberius and dedicated only after his death (*Tib.* 74; Pliny, *NH* 34.43), was destroyed with the temple and completely restored by Domitian.

Casa Romuli. He restored the hut of Romulus on the south-western corner of the Palatine. Built of straw, with a thatched roof, it was revered as the legendary dwelling-place of Rome's founder (Martial 8.80.6).[71]

Circus Maximus. Severely damaged in the fire of 64 (*Ann.* 15.38), it again suffered damage under Domitian, especially on the long sides (*Dom.* 5). The restoration was not completed until Trajan's reign, but it seems highly likely that Domitian planned and commenced it.

Curia Julia. Begun by Julius Caesar just before his assassination, it was dedicated by Octavian on 28 August 29 BC (Dio 44.5.1–2). Its precise location is a matter of dispute. Recently, it has been convincingly argued that the Curia Julia had been situated to the north and west of the Diocletianic Curia and that it had been moved to its present site by Domitian as part of his reorganization of the Argiletum.[72] Doubts have been expressed,[73] but both Eusebius and the Chronographer include the *senatus* amongst Domitian's works, and ancient sources minimize rather than exaggerate anything that might be included amongst his achievements.

Domus Tiberiana. Built on the north-western part of the Palatine, Tiberius's palace[74] became the imperial residence and is mentioned by all the major sources for the events of 69 (*Hist.* 1.27; *Vit.* 15.3 and Plutarch, *Galba* 24.2). It was apparently destroyed in the fire of 80[75] and reconstructed by Domitian, who built the great reception hall in front of it, added a façade as well as connecting it to Nero's cryptoporticus and the Flavian buildings to the south-east.[76] Also, Domitianic brickwork has been found in various parts of the *domus*.[77]

Forum Caesaris. Late in Domitian's reign, the reconstruction of this forum was begun and substantially completed by him,[78] though the new Temple of Venus Genetrix therein was not dedicated until 12 May 113.[79] Both it and Trajan's forum were, in essence, Domitianic structures.

Horrea Agrippiana. These warehouses, built in the eighth Region by (presumably) Agrippa, were partly reconstructed by Domitian when erecting the *templum divi Augusti*.[80]

Pantheon. Damaged in the fire of 80 (Dio 66.24.2), Agrippa's Pantheon in the Campus Martius was restored by Domitian. Both chronicles refer to his work, but some scholars are inclined to doubt their accuracy.[81] However, this entire area was reconstructed by Domitian and a number of his brick tiles have been discovered in its walls under the parts of Hadrian's building.[82] There is no need to reject the ancient testimony.

Porta Capena. The Chronographer, but not Eusebius, credits Domitian with this structure, referring to a gate in the Servian wall on the south-western slope of the Caelian. This hardly makes sense; it would not have been a city gate in Domitian's time. But since a branch of the *aqua Marcia* (the *rivus Herculaneus*) ended just beyond the *porta Capena* (Frontinus *De Aq.* 1.19), it is generally thought that Domitian was responsible for restoration work in connection with this extension.[83]

Porticus, Dei Consentes. The *porticus* was originally built in the second or third century BC, but restored and extended by Domitian. Archaeological investigation has revealed the extent of his work.[84]

Porticus, Minucia Vetus. Situated in the Campus Martius near the *Porticus Octaviae* and the theatre of Balbus, it was presumably destroyed like them in the fire of 80 (Dio 66.24.2) and restored by Domitian. Recent work on the Severan marble plan confirms the Domitianic activity[85] and it is listed by the Chronographer of 354 amongst his works.

Porticus Octaviae. Built by Augustus in the name of his sister, it was damaged, as were its libraries, in the fire of 80 (Dio 66.24.2); the restoration was almost certainly due to Domitian. The Severan marble plan differs considerably from the visible remains and it has been suggested that it represents his work, later destroyed by the fire of 203.[86]

Saepta Iulia. Usually referred to simply as the *Saepta*, this was a large enclosed section of the Campus Martius where the people assembled to vote and which contained a number of shops.[87] It was also used for other purposes: Augustus held gladiatorial contests there, as did other emperors; in his reign, the senate once met there; Gaius used it for artificial naval combats (*naumachiae*), it probably contained works of art and, under Domitian, it seems to have been a fashionable meeting-place (Martial 2.14.5, 2.57.2 and 9.59.1). Completed and decorated by Agrippa, it was damaged in the fire of 80 (Dio 66.24.2) and, in view of Martial's references to it, quickly restored by Domitian.

Templum, Castorum et Minervae. It was one of Domitian's buildings, according to the Chronographer of 354. This odd collocation of divinities has prompted considerable scholarly debate: some have even suggested that Domitian restored the temple of Castor and Pollux and rededicated it to them and Minerva combined.[88] Presumably the relationship was topographical, i.e. a temple of Minerva near to/in the same Region as the temple of Castor and Pollux. The latter, officially named the *aedes Castoris*[89] (*Jul.* 10) and situated at the south-eastern end of the *Forum Romanum*, was supposedly dedicated in 484 BC (Livy 2.42.5) and long served as one of Rome's most important and best-known temples. That it was restored by Domitian is implied by Martial (9.3.11) – immediately after a reference to his dedication of a temple to Minerva (9.3.10) and immediately before one to the *Templum Gentis Flaviae* (9.3.12). So there is no reason to doubt the ancient testimony that is also confirmed by archaeological investigation.[90] Various attempts have been made to locate the appropriate temple of Minerva, the most attractive suggestion being a site near the *domus Augustana*.[91]

Templum, Divus Augustus. The temple on the Palatine to the deified Augustus, built by Tiberius and Livia (Dio 56.46.3) or by Tiberius alone (Dio 57.10.2), was destroyed by fire before 79 (Pliny, *NH* 12.94) and rebuilt by Domitian in connexion with a shrine to his favourite goddess Minerva (Martial 5.53.1–2). Both temple and shrine are referred to in military diplomas issued after 90, the originals of which were set up *in muro post templum divi Augusti ad Minervam*.[92] It has been convincingly demonstrated by Lugli[93] that Domitian completely rebuilt the earlier temple of Augustus as a memorial to four deified emperors, including Vespasian and Titus: so it is to be identified with the *aedes Caesarum* of *Galba* 1.1 and the *aedes divorum* of CIL 6.2087.

Templum, Iseum et Serapeum. The cult of Isis, privately encouraged by all the Flavians, was long associated with the Campus Martius area. Tiberius is supposed to have destroyed a temple of

Isis and to have thrown her statue into the Tiber (*AJ* 18.3.4), but, by 65, the cult had been officially accepted (Lucan 8.831) and a (new) temple built in the Campus Martius, possibly by Gaius. Burned down in 80 (Dio 66.24.2), it was restored by Domitian (Martial 2.14.7, 10.48.1; Juv. 9.22 and Eutropius 7.23).[94] The *Serapeum* was a separate building. The location is certain, thanks to the discovery of numerous obelisks in the area and to the Severan marble plan, where the complex appears with the name *Serapaeum* only.[95]

Templum, Iuppiter Optimus Maximus Capitolinus. The first of the great temples on the Capitoline dedicated to Jupiter, Juno and Minerva (the Capitoline triad) was burned down on 6 July 83 BC,[96] and the second destroyed in December 69 (*Vit.* 15.3; Dio 65.17.3). Rebuilt by Vespasian (*Vesp.* 8.5), it was burned down once again in 80 (Dio 66.24.2), partly restored almost immediately[97] and rededicated early in Domitian's reign. His building was magnificent, with a hexastyle Corinthian façade of white Pentelic marble (*Dom.* 5; Plutarch, *Publicola* 15.4), a material used in no other Roman building; doors plated with gold (Zosimus 5.38.4) and roof covered with gilt tiles (Procop. *Vand.* 3.5). It has been estimated that the gilding alone cost some 288 million HS.[98] As expected, the court poets were enthusiastic (Martial 9.1.5, 9.3.7, 13.74.2; *Silvae* 1.6.102, 3.4.105, 4.3.160), with Silius Italicus, for instance, claiming that its summit reached heaven itself (*Pun.* 3.622).

Templum, Iuppiter Tonans. Built (so it seems) on the western edge of the *area Capitolina*, it was dedicated on 1 September 22 BC. According to the elder Pliny, it was one of the very few buildings in Rome to be built entirely of marble and not just faced with it (36.50). Nash argues that it was reconstructed by Domitian after suffering in the fire of 80, suggesting that the Domitianic reconstruction is that represented in the Haterii Relief.[99]

Templum Pacis. Statius (*Silvae* 4.3.17) ascribes this temple's completion to Domitian, but the topographers tend to reject his evidence.[100] Vespasian's building, begun in 71 (*BJ* 8.158), had been dedicated in 75 (Dio 65.15.1; Martial 1.2.5). Some fifteen to twenty years later, however, it seems that Domitian altered it radically: clearing all traffic from the Argiletum, he meant to join it to the other *fora* by means of the *Forum Transitorium*, thereby greatly enhancing the general overall effect.[101]

Templum Veiovis. The interior and ceiling of this temple, damaged by fire (presumably in 80), was restored by Domitian, making liberal use of different types of marble: the result, according to Blake who summarizes the archaeological investigation, 'must have been garish to say the least'.[102]

Theatrum Balbi. Built by L. Cornelius Balbus (the younger) and dedicated in 13 BC (*Aug.* 29.5), this stone theatre was damaged in the fire of 80 (Dio 66.24.2) and restored, presumably by Domitian.[103]

Thermae Agrippae. These, the earliest of Rome's famous baths, were begun by Agrippa in 25 BC (Dio 53.27.1), destroyed in the fire of 80 (Dio 66.24.2) and immediately restored by Domitian.

Structures completed by Domitian

Amphitheatrum Flavianum. Domitianic brickstamps and analysis of masonry styles confirm that Domitian completed the Amphitheatre by adding the fourth level, finishing off the interior and seating areas. The Chronographer of 354, though, states that he completed the building *ad clipea*, referring presumably to the bronze shields that were placed immediately beneath the uppermost cornice. If the *naumachia* of *Dom.* 4.1 was held there, then he must also have added the passages and rooms under the arena.[104]

Arcus Titi. This fine monument, erected *in summa sacra via*, commemorates Titus's victory in Judaea and his defication.[105] It belongs to the early years of Domitian's reign, despite attempts to assign to Trajan's. The principal objection to a Domitianic dating, that of ill-feeling between the brothers, is an inadequate reason for rejecting the evidence of architectural styles.[106]

Templum Divi Vespasiani. Titus began and Domitian completed a temple referred to as the *templum Vespasiani et Titi* in the Chronographer's list of Domitian's buildings, although only Vespasian's name appeared on the original inscription (*CIL* 6.938).[107] It had been completed by 3 January 87 since it is mentioned in the *Acta* of the Arval Brethren for that day.[108] The fine entablature fragment and three columns remain *in situ* on the south-eastern section of the Capitoline;[109] the ornamentation resembles that of the Arch of Titus and the remains are an excellent example of early Domitianic work. Archaeological investigation has indicated that most of the temple should be credited to Domitian as should the work on the adjacent buildings.[110]

Structures attributed to Domitian

Thermae Titianae et Traianae. The literary sources indicate the location of Titus's baths – quite close to the western side of the Esquiline wing of Nero's Golden House (*Titus* 7.3; Martial, *De Spect.* 2.5–8). They were still popular under Domitian (Martial 3.36.6). Unfortunately, no physical traces remain, and so it is impossible to substantiate archaeologically the statements of both the Chronographer of 354 and Eusebius ascribing them to Domitian. We do know that Titus's builders worked hastily (*Titus* 7.3); presumably, Domitian's finished what they had begun. More controversial is the claim in both chronicles that Domitian also built the nearby baths of Trajan. In the early church writings, they were known as the *thermae Domitiani*, whereas Pausanias (5.12.6) and Dio (69.4.1) attribute them to Trajan. Until recently, all topographers except Platner and Ashby have rejected outright the claims of Domitian,[111] but the evidence of his brickstamps can be adduced in support.[112] Moreover, work on the so-called Esquiline wing of the Golden House has suggested that the eastern half of the wing (where the rooms had been converted to form passageways under Trajan's baths) is quite unlike the western, that it contained the *domus Titi* mentioned by the elder Pliny (*NH* 36.37) and that the work was never finished.[113] Presumably, Domitian's other projects diverted his attention and caused him to abandon his brother's palace.

Forum Traianum. Dedicated by Trajan on 1 January 112, it was the last and finest of the imperial *fora*.[114] Deliberately integrated with its four predecessors, its complex of buildings served as a city centre. Some sources attribute it to Trajan alone (e.g. Dio 68.16.2), but Aurelius Victor (13.5) and Eusebius assign it to Domitian. Archaeological investigation has shown that Domitian removed the saddle of land that had connected the Capitoline Hill to the Quirinal, that the enclosure wall behind the Temple of Venus Genetrix contains Domitianic brickstamps and that the odd bastion-like building, three stories high, abutting the north-western corner of the *Forum Augusti* was also built by him. So it seems most likely that this was to be the culmination of Domitian's plan for the reorganization of the imperial *fora*. Trajan and Apollodorus improved and completed it.

Domitian's palace on the Palatine[115]

When in Rome, Domitian lived on the Palatine, and, by the end of 92,[116] his entirely new palace complex there, just south of the *domus Tiberiana*, was all but completed; it became, and remained for centuries, the centre of the Roman empire.[117] But more than that, its style was unique, with the great visual and spatial effects Rabirius produced therein. Much of the Palatine Hill was levelled. No effort was spared. A spectator in the Circus Maximus would have looked up at a huge curved terrace in front of the palace and at buildings that towered over the terrace: as Martial correctly put it, 'You would think that the seven hills were rising up together' (8.36.5).[118]

In the complex of some 40,000 square metres[119] were four major structures, viz. (a) the *domus Flavia* or official palace; (b) the *domus Augustana*[120] or private palace, on the same level as the *domus Flavia*; (c) the lower level of the *domus Augustana*, and (d) the *Hippodromos* or *Stadium*, on the same level as (c). A few of its major elements deserve mention, e.g. the immensity of the *domus Flavia*'s four halls (vestibule, *basilica, aula regia* and *cenatio Iovis*, the first measuring, in metres, 23.5 by 32.5 with a height of over 27.5![121]) and the peristyle, the so-called *Sicilia*, separating the *aula regia* from the *cenatio Iovis*, with the walls of highly coloured polished stone mentioned by Suetonius as enabling the emperor to see a reflection of what was happening behind him: *Dom.* 14.4. One of the most remarkable features of the four halls was apparently the vaulted ceilings, which, by Hadrian's time or even earlier, had already needed additional support.[122]

About twice as large as the *domus Flavia*, the *domus Augustana* is both impressive and architecturally significant.

> [Its] importance ... lies both in the design of the rooms themselves and the unique ways in which they were grouped, for here Rabirius repeatedly departed from anything seen in the Esquiline wing of the *domus aurea* or known from previous Roman buildings. ... [In the upper level, he] utterly abandoned the vocabulary of the past, [leading] the visitor through bewildering chains of spaces that now expanded, then contracted ... as if he wished to show what new kinds of spatial and visual sensations were possible. ... [He had light] coming from varying heights and directions [so as to emphasize] the various shapes of the rooms.[123]

Somewhere in the *domus Augustana* there must have been a hall, the *aula Adonidis*, where Domitian received Apollonius (*Vita Apoll.* 7.32); its walls were decorated with garden scenes. On the lower level, innovation again: there was neither precedent nor parallel for the fact that 'identical octagonal rooms [were arranged] symmetrically on either side of a square chamber'.[124] The rooms designed for Domitian's use were virtually a palace within a palace: hence Pliny's reference to 'the secret chambers [*arcana cubilia*] into which he was driven by his fear, pride and hatred of mankind' (*Pan.* 49.1). Yet the general effect does not seem to have been oppressive, as Pliny virtually admits (*Pan.* 49.2) in his description of the 'same palace' (*eadem domus*) as 'safer and happier' (*tutior . . . securior*) once Trajan was emperor.

Finally, the *hippodromos*: completed between 93 and 95, it was comparatively small (50 by 184 metres), too small to have been used or intended for racing (80 by 400 metres would be the norm) and so was presumably meant to be a private garden for the imperial family.[125] Later, the combination of villa and circus-shaped structure was to be fairly common:[126] perhaps the *domus Augustana* had set the fashion.

MacDonald sees the palace as typical of Domitian's 'semi-orientalized, quixotic despotism'.[127] An ancient commentator, Plutarch, was hardly more kind: 'it was a disease of building, and a desire, like Midas's, of turning everything to gold or stone' (*Publicola* 15.5). In both cases, the judgement on the building programme is tightly linked to the author's assessment of the emperor's character, and Pliny's view of Trajan's buildings, some at least of which were also planned by Rabirius,[128] reflects the same procedural method: according to Pliny, a 'good' emperor's architectural achievements were 'appropriate for a nation that has conquered the world' (*Pan.* 51.3); but, with a 'semi-orientalized despot', work even by the same architect reflected the character of the emperor, not that of the nation. Rabirius, then, must have been 'asked to create a tangible rhetoric of power, a panegyric in architecture of the emperor's claim to omniscience'.[129] One wonders: perhaps it is not only beauty that is in the eye of the beholder.

Alban villa and others

During Vespasian's reign, Domitian acquired the villa of Pompey at Albanum and made it his home, whilst his own, new villa was being constructed nearby.[130] It was fairly close to the Capital, being only 20 kilometres away on the Via Appia, but distant enough to permit him to conduct his affair with Domitia Longina in privacy (Dio 66.3.4). It is almost certain that the huge villa he built there was the work of Rabirius, with its three massive terraces together with aqueducts, reservoirs, baths, *nymphea*, theatre, circus and 300-metre-long cryptoporticus.[131] The palace itself was large, built along the lines of the *domus Flavia*.[132]

There are many references to it in contemporary literature (*Dom.* 4.4, 19; *Agr.* 45.1; Dio 67.1.2; Juv. 4.99–101; Statius, *Silvae* 2.5.28, 4.2.66); and the evidence suggests, but does not prove, that this was his favourite official residence.

But he had other villas as well. The complex near Circeo was almost as large as the *arx Albana* and very similar to it in style. From here, the *Lex Irnitana* was promulgated. Nearby too were a number of other residences built for those accompanying him.[133] As well, there were imperial villas at Tusculum, Antium, Gaeta, Anxur (Martial 5.1) and Baiae (Martial 4.30; *Pan.* 82.1) together with the substantial property around Orbetello formerly belonging to the Domitii Ahenobarbi and passing to the emperor through his wife Domitia Longina: once again his courtiers were catered for, with other sumptuous villas built nearby.[134]

It would seem that Domitian's determination to exercise as much control as possible over the entire administration of the empire and city extended to the supervision of building projects. Under the Flavians, and probably in his reign, the *opera Caesaris* (or Department of Public Works) increased its influence markedly and was, at the very least, consulted on all programmes of any size.[135]

Finally, the indications we have suggest that Domitian's massive programme continued throughout the reign, with some work almost certainly ascribable to the last years – the Hippodromos on the Palatine was constructed after the completion of the palace in 92, as was the *Forum Transitorium*, the *Templum Gentis Flaviae* and Temple of *Fortuna Redux*. Possibly, too, the Odeum, the Baths of Titus, the Forum of Trajan and the Meta Sudans were all being erected during this period.[136]

Precise evidence for the erection of so many buildings is impossible to discover, but the general stability of coinage argues for consistency in the building programme, rather than a sudden halt in 93. In any case, the selection of 93 as a turning-point seems to have originated in the belief that a sudden deterioration in his attitude to the aristocracy occurred in that year and that there was a concomitant decline in economic activity; perhaps it would be more logical to posit 85 as a turning-point, given the devaluation occurring in that year, and to suggest that there was a cessation of building then!

5

ADMINISTRATION II

THE INDIVIDUAL

Domitian seems to have been genuinely concerned with the beliefs and behaviour of his subjects, for obviously that is how he regarded the citizens of the empire. Stern and somewhat forbidding, he saw himself, like Augustus, as the supervisor of laws and morals (*curator morum et legum. RG* 6.1). But the similarity went further than mere words. His ideal seems to have been a return to Augustan standards, and not only in monetary matters. He was just as uncompromising in his approach to religion; and he was further influenced by two factors, the Flavians' need to bolster the new dynasty with supernatural support and his personally sincere belief in the traditional religion.

Jupiter and Minerva

Vespasian and Titus had stressed the family's connection with the more reputable Julio-Claudians,[1] and thus, indirectly, with Venus. But this was far from enough. In Flavian propaganda, Jupiter regularly appeared: on Vespasian's coinage, for instance, he was associated with the benefits the new regime provided – victory, peace and food.[2] Domitian went further. As Jupiter had saved his life in 69, he had a shrine erected to *Iuppiter Conservator* (replaced by a temple to *Iuppiter Custos*) and, as well, arranged at great cost the restoration of Jupiter's Capitoline temple. Throughout the reign, whether on coins or in the works of Statius, Silius Italicus or Martial, Domitian was linked with Jupiter and portrayed as his subordinate, his 'warrior vice-regent'.[3] More than this, in instigating the Capitoline Games in 86, he associated Jupiter publicly with the regime, just as his reorganization of the *sodales Flaviales* resulted in the cult's activities being directed more towards the same God.[4]

So much for his public stance. In private, his devotion to Minerva[5] was absolute: Suetonius called it superstitious veneration (*Dom.* 15.3). That his reverence was genuine appears from the fact that he kept a *sacrarium* or shrine to her in his bedroom (*Dom.* 15.2). Domitian even claimed to be her son: he is said to have imprisoned a magistrate at Tarentum because he had forgotten to include that 'fact' in a prayer (*Vita Apoll.* 7.24). Early in the reign, he named his new legion neither *Flavia* (cf. *IV Flavia Felix*) nor *Domitiana* (cf. *III Augusta*) but *Minervia*; and, just before the end, she came to him in a dream, so he claimed, with the news that she was no longer able to protect him, since Jupiter had disarmed her (*Dom.* 15.2). She appeared consistently on his coins, four different types being assigned to her each year,[6] and was also portrayed prominently with Domitian on the Cancelleria Reliefs. It was in her honour that he erected the temple of Minerva Chalcidicia, restored the *templum Castorum et Minervae*, set up a shrine to her in or near the *templum divi Augusti* (Martial 5.53. 1–2; *ILS* 1998), began work on the *Forum Transitorium* (*Dom.* 5) with its temple to Minerva (*CIL* 6.953), and, at the Alban villa almost every year between 19 and 23 March, presented a special festival (*Quinquatria*), controlled by a college of priests he established (*Dom.* 4.4). Here, there were splendid shows of wild beasts, plays and contests in oratory and poetry (*Dom.* 4.4; Dio 67.1.2). Statius was more successful at the Alban contests than at the Capitoline, winning the golden olive-crown on three occasions (*Silvae* 3.5.28–31; 4.2.63–7).[7] But there was no theological dichotomy between his private devotion to her and his public role of Jupiter's representative on earth: presumably the coins depicting her bearing a thunderbolt were meant to show that his private veneration to her was but part of a deeper feeling for Jupiter.

Isis

Genuine and intense belief in the traditional Roman religion did not cause Domitian to expel from Rome the followers of Isis, for Egyptian religions were supported by all three Flavian emperors to an extent not seen again until the end of the second century.[8] Vespasian believed that, at Alexandria in 69, he had healed a blind and a crippled man through the intervention of Serapis (*Vesp.* 7.2; *Hist.* 4.81 and Dio 66.8.1) and that Serapis in fact had appeared to him[9] (*Vesp.* 7.1). In December 69, Domitian saved himself by mingling in an Isaic procession, appropriately disguised (*Dom.* 1.2; *Hist.* 3.74); before returning to Rome after capturing Jerusalem, Titus participated (*Titus* 5.3) in the consecration of the bull Apis at Memphis and, not long after, he and Vespasian spent the night preceeding their joint triumph in the temple of Isis (*BJ* 7.123: it was, presumably, in commemoration of this that a temple of Isis appeared for the first time on a Roman coin.[10] Then, once Domitian was emperor, he had the temple restored and a number of obelisks erected in the city and elsewhere. Presumably, they identified Serapis with Jupiter and Isis with Minerva, and their devotion must have been real, for it is hard to believe that they even expected it to attract support in the Capital. With Domitian, there is no reason to doubt that his reverence was genuine: he was certain that Isis's support would come to him as Jupiter's earthly representative. It is worth observing that imperial interest in the worship of Isis was minimal after Domitian's death, and it was not for another hundred years that the sort of interest shown by all three Flavians was to appear again, with the advent of Commodus.

Vestals

Not long after his accession, the behaviour of the Vestal Virgins attracted his attention.[11] Since they were technically daughters of the community, any moral transgressions on their part constituted *incestum*: hence Suetonius begins his account of their behaviour in the 80s with the word *incesta* (*Dom.* 8.3). An investigation into allegations of this nature was the responsibility of the *pontifex maximus* and so Statius describes Domitian as the 'investigator [*explorator*: *Silvae* 5.3.178[12]] of the hidden fire'. Suetonius, Pliny and Dio also stress his personal involvement: rigorous enforcement of the law was to be expected from an emperor such as he. Unlike Vespasian and Titus, he had no intention of turning a blind eye to incest (*Dom.* 8.3).

Two separate incidents are recorded. On the first occasion, early in the reign, Domitian found three of the six Vestals (the Oculata sisters and Varronilla[13]) guilty of incest, but allowed them to choose the manner of their deaths, and merely exiled their lovers – generosity indeed, since the customary penalty was to be hung from a cross and beaten to death with rods.[14] The senior Vestal, Cornelia,[15] was apparently not involved on this occasion, though Suetonius refers to her acquittal at a trial held well before 89 (*Dom.* 8.4). She was less fortunate in the middle of Domitian's reign.[16] Accused of incest, she was found guilty at a trial held at the Alban villa (rather than at the *Regia* of the *pontifices*)[17] and condemned to be buried alive. Her lovers, including the equestrian Celer, were beaten to death, with the exception of one, Valerius Licinianus, who admitted his guilt and was exiled.[18] But it was perfectly clear that they were guilty and no criticism should be levelled at Domitian on that score. What apparently horrified Pliny was the thought that someone of his status should have to face the same penalty as any other malefactor. But, that aside, the entire affair exemplifies the attention Domitian paid to the letter of religious law.

He was also preoccupied with its minutiae. When the *flamen Dialis*, one of the most important priests in the state,[19] wanted to divorce his wife, Domitian finally agreed but insisted it be done in the time-honoured way, with 'horrid rites and incantations'.[20] Or, when one of his freedmen erected a tomb for his son with stones meant for the temple of Jupiter Capitolinus, Domitian had it destroyed (*Dom.* 8.5). Presumably, he recalled the decision of the *haruspices* (at the time when Vespasian was restoring the same building) forbidding the builders to use stone that had been destined for some other purpose (*Hist.* 4.53). Again, even long-forgotten vows were officially remembered. After the fire of 64, Nero had promised to have altars erected to ward off future fires, a vow long-neglected and unfulfilled (*diu neglectum nec redditum. ILS* 4914). Now, it was scrupulously discharged.

Ludi Saeculares (Secular Games)

That Domitian delighted in the enforcement of the regulations governing Roman religion is exemplified by the fate of the errant Vestal Virgins and by the efforts of a *flamen Dialis* to secure a divorce. But he was also preoccupied with the strict interpretation of its ritual; as well, he was not unaware of the possibility of using religion to publicize his regime. Hence his celebration of the *Ludi Saeculares* in 88,[21] under the control of the *quindecimviri sacris faciundis*,[22] a prestigious priestly college that included the historian Tacitus (*Ann.* 11.11). As the name implies, these *Ludi* could be held only once a century, and, according to tradition, a century was a period of

110 years. Augustus had celebrated the games in 17 BC, Claudius[23] in 47 AD. The year selected by Domitian, 88 rather than 93, was technically correct, since Augustus had intended to hold them in 22 or 23 BC and the postponement to 17 BC needed justification.[24] Domitian's precision in such matters is typical: holding them in 93 would not have been 'correct'.

Ludi Capitolini

In 86 (Censorinus, *De Die Natali* 18.15), Domitian instituted the Capitoline Games,[25] based no doubt on the *Neronia* (*Nero* 12.3) that had been discontinued at Nero's death but revived later and celebrated by Gordian III.[26] Held every four years early in the summer, they attracted competitors from many nations: Martial (9.40) refers to Diodorus coming from Egypt and, in the *Ludi* of 94, there were fifty-two contestants for the Greek poetry prize alone (*ILS* 5177). Everything was done on a grand scale. Not unlike the modern Olympics, vast sums were expended on new buildings, especially designed for each contest and no doubt the resultant financial problems were identical. Domitian could attest to that; according to Suetonius, his buildings and shows exhausted his treasury (*Dom.* 12.1). In the Campus Martius, the Odeum (for musical performances) and the Stadium (for athletics) were erected, magnificent buildings still regarded three hundred years later as two of Rome's finest (Amm. Marcell. 16.10.14). Once again, he was determined to make known both Rome's importance and his own as well.

As with the *Neronia*, the contests were of three major types – chariot-racing, athletics/gymnastics and music/singing/oratory/poetry, with the prize, a wreath of oak-leaves, being presented by the emperor himself.[27] Domitian maintained the Greek tenor of it all, wearing a purple toga and a golden crown bearing representations of Jupiter, Juno and Minerva (*Dom.* 4.4). The assessors or judges (*ILS* 5178) included the *flamen Dialis* and the *Flaviales*, similarly dressed, apart from the fact that their crowns also bore Domitian's image. In all, it was a display arranged to show the regime to the world.

Some information about the performers and their achievements has survived. Winners in four events are attested, viz. Collinus (86: Martial 4.54.1) and Scaevus Memor (*PIR*[1] S 188) in Latin poetry; Palfurius Sura (P 7) in Latin oratory; T. Flavius Metrobius of Iasos in long-distance running;[28] and, in the pancration, T. Flavius

Artemidorus of Adana and Antioch (*PIR²* F 221) and T. Flavius
Archibius of Alexandria.²⁹ Amongst the losers were both P. Annius
Florus (A 650) and Statius (*Silvae* 3.5.31–3; 5.3.231–3) in Latin
poetry, and Q. Sulpicius Maximus in Greek poetry. In one sense,
those who failed to win the prize were the more interesting. Florus
was still a boy when he competed, and, even though the audience
had unanimously demanded he be declared victor, he lost, not
because the emperor was envious of his youth, but because he
was afraid that a competitor from Africa might gain the '*corona*
of mighty Jove'.³⁰ Sulpicius was also young when he presented his
(still surviving) forty-three hexameters. The details are recorded on
his tombstone (*ILS* 5177), set up not very long afterwards by his
parents, a touching memorial to their precocious son who died 'at
the tender age ... of eleven years, five months and twelve days'.

According to Suetonius (*Dom.* 4.4), a number of the items were
omitted from these *Ludi* on Domitian's death: epigraphical evidence
suggests that these included the competitions in Latin and Greek
oratory, in choral and solo singing to the lyre and, so it seems,
the girls' race. On the other hand, most were retained, including
contests in Greek and Latin poetry, singing, lyre and flute playing, dramatic recitations, organ playing (probably), chariot-racing,
boxing, wrestling and the pancration together with the competition
between the heralds.³¹

At these and other spectacles, Domitian was an interventionist. At
the gladiatorial *munera*, it was (literally) fatal to voice support for
the Thracians (*Dom.* 10.1); at the Circus, flatterers such as Martial
urged on the Blues if Domitian was emperor (6.46.1–2) and the
Greens (11.33.1–4) when Trajan was; and, at the *Ludi Capitolini*,
Domitian expressed his annoyance at Palfurius Sura's success and
refused to let the herald announce his name: perhaps Domitian's
pique is to be explained by the fact that the senator Palfurius Sura
had had a somewhat varied career, including a period in exile and
a wrestling-bout in the arena with a Spartan woman (*Dom.* 13.1;
PIR¹ P 7). But the most significant aspect of these *Ludi* was the
influence they had on Rome's standing as the capital of the world.
This was what Domitian intended. A striking instance of his success
is the fact that memories of the ceremonial endured for centuries and
that, after nearly 1300 years, part of the ceremony itself was revived
and brought up to date – but in a way that would hardly have
pleased Domitian. On Easter Sunday 1341, Petrarch was crowned
on the Capitol by the Roman senator Ursus and then the poet

went in procession to place his laurel wreath on the high altar of St Peters.[32]

Shows

Few emperors were ignorant of the problems caused by the sheer size of Rome's population and the concomitant need to provide entertainment, customary in the empire's capital by Domitian's reign. Given his view of Rome's status in the world and his own not unimportant role in maintaining it, he was hardly likely to shirk this responsibility – and, unlike Tiberius, he seems to have enjoyed it. As well, the search for popular favour was not cheap. Suetonius introduces his chapter on the public entertainment provided by Domitian with a concise, if somewhat blunt, statement: his shows were frequent, elaborate and expensive (*Dom.* 4.1). On the other hand, they were nowhere near as costly as Trajan's: on his return from the conquest of Dacia, his *Ludi* lasted either for 123 days involving 11,000 animals and 10,000 gladiators (Dio 68.15.1) or for 117 days with 4,941 pairs of gladiators (*AE* 1933: 30).

According to Suetonius (*Dom.* 4.1) and Dio (67.8.2–4), Domitian sought to innovate. He added to the usual chariot races a genuine battle. So there were naval contests in the *Amphitheatrum Flavianum* and, later, a special lake had to be dug near the Tiber, presumably because of the popularity of this form of entertainment. Gladiatorial combats were also held at night, sometimes with female competitors and even dwarfs (Dio 67.8.4). Quaestors were now forced to provide entertainment, a custom long-neglected and perhaps revived to assist the public treasury. Again, at the Saturnalia of (December) 88, the emperor showered a great variety of presents on the audience, including figs, plums, dates, cakes and partridges from Numidia (*Silvae* 1.6.75–8). Animal shows were always popular, and, again, no expense seems to have been spared: we hear of leopards, tigers, bears, bison, boars and elephants (Martial 1.104), and of bulls and deer fighting each other (4.35.1–5). He introduced three new gladiatorial schools (*ludus magnus, Gallicus, Dacicus*)[33] and additional regulations to make the combats themselves more difficult (Martial 8.80.1–4). In the circus, he brought in two new factions, gold and purple (*Dom.* 7.1), and charioteers such as Scorpus and Incitatus were famous throughout the city.[34] As far as the theatre was concerned, the least popular form of public entertainment, accusations of obscenity kept actors from the public stage,[35] but

Domitian allowed them to perform in private houses (*Dom.* 7.1). Paris, Latinus, Thymele (Latinus's mistress) and Panniculus were the best-known performers, Canus, Glaphyrus and Pollio the most famous musicians.[36]

Censor

Domitian's autocracy was illustrated in other ways. Dio Cassius, in a passage assigned by Boissevain to 84, claims that Domitian was then designated consul for ten years in succession, appointed censor for life and also received the right to be accompanied by twenty-four lictors and to wear triumphal dress into the senate (67.4.3–4). As far as the censorship is concerned, Dio's date is wrong. The numismatic evidence is clear: Domitian became *CENSOR* in April, 85 and *CENSOR PERPETUUS* (censor for life) towards the end of the same year.[37]

Despite Suetonius's apparent silence on these matters and despite the fact that the constitutional difficulties posed by Dio are not easily solved,[38] his statement is further proof, if such were needed, that Domitian had not the slightest intention of disguising his autocracy. On the other hand, whilst Suetonius mentions by name neither Domitian's censorial power nor his perpetual censorship, he does devote three chapters (*Dom.* 7–9) to an account of his innovations, be they censorial, legislative, jurisdictional or pontifical (with little attempt to separate them[39]), and, at *Dom.* 8.3, does refer to his *correctio morum* ('correction of morals').

The ancient office of censor was held by various emperors, including Vespasian and Titus in 73/4.[40] Domitian's assumption of censorial power, followed soon after by his appointment as censor for life, was widely advertised on coins and inscriptions[41] and represented in a sense a turning-point in the constitutional development of the office: subsequently, no emperor formally assumed it, for, if they were ever worried about the point, they regarded its specific powers as having already been conferred by their initial grant of *imperium*. Its most significant powers were control over admission to and expulsion from the senatorial and equestrian orders together with a general supervision of conduct and morals.

A few interesting points emerge. At times, Martial's treatment of Domitian's innovations as censor is less than respectful, and certainly not eulogistic, an attitude he displays elsewhere.[42] The post receives a casual mention in 1.4.7 (dated to 85/6), but nothing more until four years later. At first, his tone is laudatory; the 'Master and God' has restored to the equestrians the seats in the theatre reserved for them (5.8.1–3), but then Martial concludes with an account of Phasis trying to flaunt Domitian's 'new' regulations. Moreover, another seven epigrams in the same book refer to others behaving as Phasis did. He is similarly 'disrespectful' in his descriptions of the behaviour of those who, despite Domitian's renewal of the *lex Julia de adulteriis coercendis*, publicly scorned it.[43] Next, Suetonius's account: in 8.3, beginning with a reference to Domitian's *correctio morum*, he refers to the condemnation of senators and equestrians who offended against the Scantinian law (i.e. sexual intercourse with free-born males) and discusses in considerable detail the punishment of the errant Vestals. But the former presumably had to face the relevant *quaestio perpetua*,[44] whilst the latter were dealt with well before 85 (Dio 67.3.3–4) and by Domitian as *pontifex maximus*: they were neither investigated nor punished by him as censor. Again, in 7.4, we are told that Domitian (presumably as censor) forbade actors appearing on stage in public, but Suetonius's next item is the emperor's prohibition of castration, which is dated to 82 or 83.[45] Suetonius's apparent confusion of pontifical, legislative and censorial material was hardly the result of rapid composition, but rather a reflection of reality. He felt that Domitian's various reforms were issued essentially on the basis of his *imperium*.[46]

Listed in *Dom.* 7–9, they indicate his obsessive concern with administrative detail – the dole was to be replaced with a proper meal, two new factions were added to the Circus, prostitutes could not ride in litters (perhaps an early instance of restriction of trade[47]), lampoons on prominent people were forbidden and an ex-quaestor was expelled from the senate for acting and dancing. As well, there were a number of legislative reforms[48] used by Suetonius to show that Domitian administered justice 'scrupulously and conscientiously' (8.1): corrupt jurors were punished and strict control exercised over officials in the city and in the provinces, so much so that they became more honest and just than they had ever been, and more so than they were to be after Domitian's death (8.2). Suetonius was in a position to know what he was talking about: he had been Hadrian's private secretary, his *ab epistulis*. Besides, such rigour is consonant with Domitian's single-minded approach to other aspects of his role as emperor. Intense imperial scrutiny no doubt gave offence, but that would not have bothered him.

Dominus et Deus

Many scholars, but not all, have accepted the claim that Domitian insisted on being addressed as *Dominus et Deus* ('Master and God').[49] A brief review of the evidence is in order.

According to Statius (*Silvae* 1.6.83–4), he rejected the title *Dominus*, just as Augustus had done (*Aug.* 53.1). Slaves used it of their masters, and Domitian is called *Dominus* by them on inscriptions.[50] But there is no epigraphical evidence whatsoever of its being used of him in any other sense. On the other hand, Suetonius (*Dom.* 13.2) reports that Domitian dictated a letter that began 'Our Master and God orders' and that, from this, the habit developed of addressing him in this way: Dio (67.4.7) supports the story. Later writers repeat and embellish it: Aurelius Victor (*De Caes.* 11.2), the *Epit. de Caes.* 11.6, Eutropius 7.23 and Orosius 7.10 all claim that he 'ordered' its use. As well, they couple it with a change in his character,[51] unlike Suetonius who refers to the deterioration elsewhere and on two separate occasions (*Dom.* 3.2, 10.1).

In view of Domitian's concern for theological niceties, the story is all but incredible. The best that an emperor could expect after death was to be declared a *divus*, never a *deus*: a living one had to make do with even less. If an emperor such as Domitian could overcome that barrier, why should he hesitate to proclaim it publicly (and epigraphically)? Senatorial abhorrence would not have concerned him. However, in common with all educated Romans, and as expressed by Aelius Aristides in his Cyzicus speech, he was aware of the clear difference between the old pagan gods (*Dei*) and deified emperors (*Divi*) – no one ever prayed to a *divus*.[52] Again, some have made capital out of the fact that, on some of his coins, Domitian was portrayed with a thunderbolt;[53] but so was Trajan.[54]

A number of sources report that Domitian was addressed as *Dominus et Deus* by others. The jurist Juventius Celsus hoped to persuade the emperor that he was not part of a conspiracy against him: as others were doing, he called Domitian *Dominus et Deus* (Dio 67.13.3–4); the crowd in the amphitheatre hailed the imperial couple as *Dominus et Domina* (*Dom.* 13.1); and, according to Dio Chrysostom (45.1), Domitian was 'an enemy who was called *Master and God* by all'. But terms used by flatterers such as Martial, Statius, Juventius Celsus (or Pliny) to secure a favour from an autocrat hardly constitute proof that they were instructed or required to use them.[55]

Did Trajan insist on the 'grovelling'[56] tone of the *Panegyricus*? Are we to believe that a 6-year-old Duke insisted on the words of Purcell's 'Ode for the Birthday of the Duke of Gloucester, 1695' ('Who can from joy refrain?'), a libretto described by a recent reviewer as 'ridiculous even by the worst standards of seventeenth-century eulogistic court poetry, wildly over-praising a six-year-old Duke and his family'?[57]

Domitian was both intelligent and committed to the traditional religion. He obviously knew that he was not a God, and, whilst he did not ask or demand to be addressed as one, he did not actively discourage the few flatterers who did.

PROVINCES

The first assessment we have of Domitian's administration of the provinces is Suetonius's statement (*Dom.* 8.2) that Domitian took care to control his officials and that, during his reign, administrators in Rome and in the provinces were more honest and more restrained than ever before: since his time, the situation had changed and such officials had been guilty of all manner of offences. In similar vein, Silius Italicus praised Domitian for preventing land and sea from being stripped bare by greedy robbers (*Pun.* 14.688).

Most, but not all, scholars have accepted Suetonius's praise at face value.[58] We can easily discard Gsell's attempt to impugn the accuracy of *Dom.* 8.2 with his suggestion[59] that the extortion trial of Baebius Massa in 93 was not the only one attested in the period 81–96 and that both Marius Priscus and Caecilius Classicus had been Domitianic officials: the offences for which they were tried occurred in 97/8,[60] when Nerva was emperor. Furthermore, Suetonius's assessment was soundly based, presumably on knowledge gained during his time as Hadrian's *ab epistulis* and, had it been made of one of the 'good' emperors, it would probably never have been questioned.

It is worth considering briefly one aspect of the mechanics of imperial administration, i.e. the number of administrators. Hopkins suggests a figure of one senatorial or equestrian official for every 300,000 people and compares the situation in a similarly sized empire, south China in the twelfth century, where the proportion was one for every 15,000 people.[61] Moreover, in many provinces of the Roman empire, the governor's main function was control of the army rather than the administration of justice or the supervision of tax collections: he was stationed where the army was, near the frontiers. Hence much was left to the local officials, in the main members of the local élite, who could hope for senatorial status for themselves or perhaps for their children so long as the emperor was satisfied with their loyalty. The scope for extortion must always have been enormous. But, in view of Domitian's fondness for the minutiae of administration coupled with his suspicious nature, it would not be surprising if both imperial and local administrators were comparatively honest (or rather if they avoided blatant dishonesty), the former from fear of detection, the latter through hope of promotion as well.

That the provincials were taxed rigorously during his reign is beyond dispute: Suetonius himself was present (*Dom.* 12.2) at a sitting of the procurator's court when a man of 90 was examined to see if he was circumcised and so eligible for the Jewish tax. Yet that is not inconsistent with the attitude of the Alexandrian Jew who, more than a century after Domitian's death, praised him as the benefactor of all the provincials, as he whom 'all men worship and gladly obey',[62] a 'comprehensible'[63] verdict, but not what one would expect from a Jew in view of Titus's destruction of the Temple in 70 and Domitian's own very rigorous (*Dom.* 12.2) enforcement of the Jewish tax. On the other hand, it is not reasonable to dismiss the author's praise of Domitian as 'just one more sign of his eccentricity'.[64] The assessment is comprehensible if, for instance, the taxes actually collected did not require further 'enhancement' to accommodate greedy senatorial, equestrian or local officials. On the other hand, it could well be that the author's enthusiasm was based, not so much on Domitian's alleged concern for the ordinary provincials, but rather on his well-attested philhellenism.[65]

East

Both factors are relevant to his administration of the eastern provinces, attested in another five documents, the interpretation of which has been the subject of some dispute.[66] Pleket tries to associate them with the Sibylline Oracles, seeing in them some evidence of Domitian's concern for the disadvantaged majority:[67] Levick is rightly sceptical. In general, they show Domitian's interest in the details of provincial administration coupled with a very strong determination to impose his will on officials, be they senatorial, equestrian or local. Any gratitude reflected in the Sibylline oracles would be due to the latter factor, in that the only taxation burden they had to face was Domitian's, without further (or, perhaps, with far fewer) contributions demanded by corrupt officials.

We have the text of a letter Domitian wrote to his equestrian procurator of Syria, Claudius Athenodorus.[68] It contains none of the courtly politeness of Trajan's requests to Pliny,[69] but autocratically instructs Athenodorus to follow the orders issued by Vespasian and not allow provincials to be burdened with demands for transport or lodgings – unless accompanied by a *diploma* issued by the emperor himself. Domitian was mainly concerned with efficient communications, far less with the comfort of the Syrians: Athenodorus was being told bluntly just what he had to do.

In 85, the city of Acmonia in Phrygia voted to prevent the embezzlement by local officials of endowments made by wealthy provincials (such as T. Flavius Praxias in this case) to their native cities and, moreover, the decree was to last as long as Roman rule.[70] Again, one suspects the emperor's hand in it all. His main concern was to keep a firm control over local administrators and the class from which they were likely to come; genuine concern for the lower classes is hard to believe.

The next document concerns measures taken by L. Antistius Rusticus, governor of Cappadocia–Galatia during the famine of 92/3.[71] He limited speculation in grain, ordered reserves to be declared and fixed a maximum price, enabling land-owners to make a profit twice as high[72] as before. Presumably, Rusticus acted on his own initiative; he would not have had time to consult Domitian.[73] Nonetheless, he was well aware of the attitude of an emperor who expected prompt action as well as honesty from his subordinates.

Further Domitianic activity in the east is attested by the fate of Hipparchus, the wealthy Athenian whose 'tryannical behaviour'[74] resulted in his estates being confiscated to the imperial treasury.[75] How far Domitian was motivated by a desire to assist smaller property owners who had suffered at Hipparchus's hands is difficult to assess. But anyone in the local élite planning a little embezzlement now knew what to expect.

Finally, Domitian was asked to settle a dispute concerning the reorganization of the Pythian games:[76] he ordered that they be maintained in the ancient manner, according to the Amphictyonic laws. Apart from the autocratic tone, the most interesting aspect of the document is that it attests to the high regard in which Domitian was held in the east, the result, no doubt, of his genuine philhellenism.

His concern for Greek culture is abundantly attested. He was the first emperor to become eponymous archon at Athens where his cult was associated with that of Zeus Eleutherios;[77] he was also eponymous *strategos* at Pergamon and *hieromnamon* at Byzantium.[78] At his own expense he saw to the restoration of the temple of Apollo at Delphi in 84 (*ILS* 8905) and to extensions at Ephesus to the temple of Artemis: hence the many references to him in inscriptions there. He also encouraged the cult of Asclepius at Pergamon and that of Demeter at Ephesus.[79] Apart from these, he contributed to works of various kinds at Anazarbus, Aphrodisias, Cyrene, Isauria, Limyra, Lindos, Megalopolis, Priene, Sebaste, Stratonicea and Termessus.[80]

Domitian seems to have made a very significant contribution to the development of urban life in Asia Minor.[81] During his reign, city status was possibly granted to Creteia–Flaviopolis, Lora–Flaviopolis and Flavio–Caesare; Sala began to issue coins under the name Sala Domitianopolis; of the main cities of the Moccadeni, Silandus and Temenothyrae seem to have received city status from him together with the right to issue coins; Laodicea was granted city status and, at the same time, Diocaesarea in Cilicia began to issue its own coins.[82]

Spain

Domitian continued with his father's policies in Spain, with particular attention to the development of local government. Towns of a certain size could be granted the status of a municipality or even of colony. Substantial fragments of the charters of three such towns have survived – Salpensa (*Municipium Flavium Salpensarum*), Malaga (*Municipium Flavium Malacitanum*) and Irni (*Municipium Flavium Irnitanum*). The first two were discovered in 1851,[83] the last[84] in 1981, near Seville, but neither the exact position of Irni nor even its name is certain.[85] On the other hand, its charter is a particularly interesting and immensely valuable historical document – and a fairly large one as well: about two-thirds of it have survived, consisting of six bronze tablets about 60 cm by 90 cm each, with letters 4 to 6 cm high and a total length of some 9 metres. It is quite noticeable that Domitian's name survives on very few inscriptions from Spain, no doubt owing to the effectiveness of the *damnatio memoriae*.[86] In this case, however, the date is clear and indicates that Domitian did more than just formally approve the innovations of his father (*NH* 3.30[87]), granting Latin rights to Salpensa and Malaga. He continued with the policy, possibly honouring some 129 towns[88] in exactly the same way. It is clear evidence of his concern for the provinces and, much more importantly, for the efficient administration of them. It was a clever policy and, in a sense, typically Flavian. A degree of self-government in no way diminished the emperor's control, whilst the grant of Latin rights (i.e. partial rather than full citizenship) encouraged further Romanization with the hope of even greater honours.

All sorts of administrative matters are dealt with on the charter – manumission, general administration, roads, games, financial affairs, jurisdiction and public works, concluding with a letter from Domitian, written in 91. Again, the document shows that the local communities had considerable discretion, e.g. in sending and paying ambassadors (chapter G), inspecting sources of revenue (chapter 76) and the arrangement of seats at the games (chapter 81).[89] On the other hand, the influence of Rome is far from intrusive: there is no hint of a *curator rei publicae* or of any other form of Domitianic watchdog, and, in the entire document, the governor is mentioned only twice (80 and 86), together with another two references to his edicts (70 and 85).

Other areas

Apart from the Greek world and Spain, we have evidence for substantial road-building in Asia Minor (under A. Caesennius Gallus and T. Pomponius Bassus), as well as in Sardinia, Baetica and near the Danube; he also saw to the excavation of a canal in Egypt.[90] In Africa, Romanization continued rapidly and the province prospered under Domitian who made contributions to its roads, buildings, defence, commerce and colonies.[91]

As was to be expected of an emperor concerned with the details of administration, a number of essential changes were made to the organization of the provinces. Those most effected were the most senior, i.e. the imperial (or military) provinces staffed by governors of consular rank. Germany was no longer divided into two military areas, but received the same administration as the other senior provinces; Moesia was split into two, Dalmatia reduced to praetorian status,[92] and Galatia briefly (*c.* 93/4) separated from

Cappadocia and governed by L. Caesennius Sospes, a legate of praetorian rank. In his reign, too, the same Sospes was appointed to a new office, that of *curator*, his task being to investigate the particular city's misuse of public funds.[93] There were a few other changes. After the death of Agrippa II *c.* 92, Domitian annexed his kingdom (including Auranitis and Batanaea) to Syria.[94] As for the Bosporan kingdom,[95] Rome seems to have been supporting it, for, under Domitian, the client-state issued gold coins with the king's head on one side and Domitian's on the other, a concession granted to no other area. No doubt control over the Black Sea district was facilitated by this unusual arrangement: Scythian pirates were a problem and, if necessary, the Bosporan kings constituted a useful buffer against the Alani.

As for the equestrian procuratorships, Domitian created a number of new posts, possibly moved towards a more clearly defined equestrian cursus and, most importantly, extended the powers of the procurators for all to see, when the senatorial proconsul of Asia was executed and his post transferred, for the time being, to a procurator (*ILS* 1374).

OPPOSITION

The extent of opposition to Domitian is as much a vexed question as is its nature. Broadly speaking, we may for convenience consider three groups, viz. Christians, Jews and philosophers.

Christians

In Christian tradition, Domitian has often been portrayed as the second persecutor (after Nero) of the early church, and, despite the paucity of evidence, the tradition persists,[96] a tradition that reached its full extent not on Domitian's death, but fifteen hundred years later, in the writings of Cardinal Caesar Baronius. From a frail, almost non-existent basis, it gradually developed and grew large.

No pagan writer accused Domitian of persecuting Christians, though Nero's activities in this regard were recorded as was Domitian's determination to tax the Jews. Pliny (*Ep.* 10.96.1) did claim that he had never attended a *cognitio* of Christians (i.e. a trial presided over by a magistrate with *imperium*): so, presumably, such examinations were conducted during Domitian's reign. That aside,

114

the ancient pagan sources have not a single word on Domitian's alleged attacks on the Christians.[97]

Were Flavius Clemens and Acilius Glabrio Christians? According to Dio (67.14.1–2), Clemens and his wife Domitilla were accused of atheism and found guilty: Clemens was executed and Domitilla banished to Pandateria. In the Christian tradition (i.e. the *Acta* of Saints Nereus and Achilleus), she and two of her eunuch servants, Nereus and Achilleus, were exiled to Terracina, where the servants were beheaded and she was burned to death. All three became official martyrs, with a feast day on 12 May (until 1969, when hers was abolished).[98] Neither his death nor that of Acilius Glabrio was linked in any way with Christianity. Suetonius describes Clemens as a 'contemptibly lazy man . . . killed on the slightest of suspicions' (*Dom.* 15.1). Perhaps he inherited some of his father Sabinus III's cowardice, if a recent survey of his activities in December 69 is to be believed.[99] But, again, there is no reference to Christianity, and, not unexpectedly, in an ordinary consul of the Roman empire in 95, though Christian apologists have seriously argued that Flavius Clemens and bishop Clement (author of *1 Clement*) should be identified.[100] The only 'evidence' that Clemens and Glabrio were Christians is archaeological,[101] but the relevant Christian cemeteries bearing the names of Domitilla and Acilius Galbrio could well[102] be assigned to the end of the second century AD.

Now early Christian writers were nowhere near as certain as are some of their modern counterparts that Domitian persecuted the early church. Phrases from *1 Clement*, such as 'sudden and repeated misfortunes and calamities' or 'unexpected and repeated troubles'[103] have often been cited as evidence of a Domitianic persecution, for the work is at times ascribed to his reign (e.g. in *Hist. Eccl.* 3.15, 16) – and at others to the period between 70 and 140.[104] Just possibly, the phrases in question might refer to prominent Christian sympathizers denounced by informers late in the 90s: three or four executed or banished could well have represented a calamity to a comparatively small group.[105] However, the first precise reference to Domitian attacking the church appears in Eusebius's citation of some comments by Melito, bishop of Sardis *c.* 170, to the effect that Nero and Domitian were persuaded by evil advisers to slander Christian teaching (*Hist. Eccl.* 4.26). Towards the end of the second century, Tertullian is quoted (again by Eusebius) as claiming that Domitian 'almost equalled Nero in cruelty, but, because he had some commonsense, he soon stopped what he had begun and recalled those he had exiled' (*Hist. Eccl.* 3.20). All this is comparatively mild – and so is sometimes dismissed as 'rhetorical' and 'not essential' by modern writers convinced of the existence of a Domitianic persecution.[106]

Eusebius's own account, though, is vastly different. Domitian had 'promoted persecution' (3.17), banished Clemens's niece, Domitilla, to Pontia (3.18: not his wife to Pandateria, as Dio had it) and, for good measure, had persecuted the Jews as well (3.20). In his *Chronicorum Canonum*, he added Domitian's banishment of John the Apostle to Patmos and cited a certain Bruttius[107] as his authority for Domitilla's relationship to Clemens and for her banishment to Pontia (*A. Abr.* 2110). The legend then grew apace. In the *Acta* of Saints Nereus and Achilleus, Domitilla was not only Clemens's niece, but also niece to the father of bishop Clement (author of *1 Clement*) and had also been assigned a mother, Plautilla. By the time of Orosius, the assessment of Domitian by Melito and Tertullian had been substantially 'modified': Domitian 'issued edicts for a general and cruel persecution' (7.10). Finally, in the *Annales Ecclesiastici* of Cardinal Caesar Baronius, written between 1588 and 1607, Domitian was charged not only with exiling John to Patmos, but also with killing Cletus (second bishop of Rome); Baronius was the first to link the execution of Flavius Clemens to a general persecution of the church and the first to believe in the existence of two Domitianic victims named Domitilla (4.586).[108]

One other Christian document, John's *Apocalypse* or *Revelation*, has also been used as evidence for a Domitianic persecution. But not all scholars assign it to his reign; it could well belong to Nero's.[109]

The only direct evidence that it dealt with events occurring during the 90s is the testimony of Irenaeus, a somewhat unreliable second-century source,[110] who merely stated that John's apocalyptic vision occurred recently and that he composed his work during Domitian's reign (Irenaeus, *Adv. haer.* 5.30.3 and *Hist. Eccl.* 3.18). Nowhere does Irenaeus try to connect John's work with any alleged Domitianic persecution of the Christians. On the other hand, a number of factors point to Nero's reign.[111] Firstly, there is the identity of the 'fifth head' at *Rev.* 17.9–11. Various solutions have been proposed to avoid the obvious choice (if Augustus is the first emperor, Nero must be the fifth), e.g. some scholars starting the count at Gaius (the first emperor to demand divine honours) or at Nero; others include only deified emperors or exclude Galba, Otho and Vitellius; others resort to any combination of these![112]

The second factor is the identity of the mortally wounded beast whom 'the earth followed with wonder' (13.3): the 'false Nero' of 69 (*Hist.* 2.1), whose appearance coincided with the vicious civil war, is a likelier candidate than the third pretender (of 88: *Nero* 57.2), attested during a lull in Domitian's Danubian campaigns. Such an extensive civil war coming after a century of peace could well have convinced John that the second coming was nigh and motivated him to write the *Apocalypse* to prepare his people.

No convincing evidence exists for a Domitianic persecution of the Christians. The growth of the legend may well be impressive, but the consistent development only serves to weaken the case, as must happen when Flavius Clemens's wife (and mother of his seven children) is transformed into his virginal niece and claimed as one of the first virgin martyrs or when, in the eighth century, Flavius Clemens is, for the first time, hailed (by Syncellus) as a Christian,[113] four centuries after his wife had been so acclaimed. Perhaps a few Christians were amongst those executed or banished during the 90s: that hardly constitutes persecution.

Jews

The situation with the Jews was vastly different. Not only were they far more numerous, but there had also been hints of anti-semitism, in Latin literature at least, for over 150 years, from Cicero (*Pro Flacco* 67) to Tacitus (*Hist.* 5.5). Neither Martial nor Quintilian was free of it.[114] So, given Domitian's general background and his devotion to the traditional Roman religion, he may well have had views very similar to those of Tacitus or Quintilian.

In Talmudic and Midrashic sources, reference is made to a Jewish proselyte named Onkelos, described as a son of Kalonikos or Kalonymos and as a nephew of Titus: on three occasions, the emperor tried to arrest him, but failed.[115] In view of the vague similarity between Clemens and Kalonymos together with the reference to the imperial family, Cassius Dio's comment on Clemens's atheism or adoption of Jewish ways (67.14.2) should not be rejected out of hand. Furthermore, the Midrash and the Babylonian Talmud refer to a senator named Keti'ah bar Shalom who, converted with his wife to Judaism, was put to death by an emperor.[116] All this is not hard evidence for the existence or extent of Clemens's sympathy with Judaism; probably it was only slight, but zealous *delatores* may well have found it enough to enable them to denounce him to the highly suspicious Domitian.

The Talmud also refers frequently to a visit to Rome at this period by four Rabbis, including Gamaliel II and Akiba. A 'God-fearing senator' (and Keti'ah bar Shalom is often so described) had informed them of a decree aimed at expelling all Jews from the Roman empire,[117] a story reminiscent of an account in the apocryphal *Acta* of St John, in which Domitian, learning that Rome was full of Jews and wanting to expel them, was persuaded by one of their number that it was the Christians who were wicked: so he turned on them.[118] However unreliable these stories may be, they do support the view that, during Domitian's principate, many Jews felt very uneasy about their future, fearing expulsion at the very least; Josephus, too, seems to see similar unease amongst the Jews towards the end of the reign. A comparison of his two different versions of the same event (in the *BJ* and *AJ*) suggests that Jews were concerned for their future: hence, in the *AJ*, written in Domitian's reign, Gaius's murder is portrayed as the result of an emperor trying to attack Judaism.[119]

This Jewish unease is reflected in the classical sources. Suetonius's account of the rigorous collection of the *ficus Iudaicus* (*Dom.* 12.2) has already been mentioned, and, since Suetonius described himself as *adulescentulus* at that time (and as *adulescens* c. 88: *Nero* 57.2), it seems reasonable to conclude that the 90-year-old man was examined at least ten years before Domitian's assassination.

Domitian's policy towards the *ficus Iudaicus* is a matter of dispute.[120] According to Suetonius (12.2), he imposed the tax (a) on those living as Jews but not acknowledging the fact publicly and (b) on those concealing their Jewish origin. Probably, Suetonius meant simply Jewish converts and Jews by birth[121] and was stressing the emperor's utter determination to collect the tax. There were to be no exceptions, especially in regard to converts. No doubt the Jewish policy of active proselytizing aroused Domitian's anger. So, not only in his last years, but also for a considerable part of the reign, the tax was rigorously collected, and Nerva was able to boast that he had abolished the concomitant abuses (*BMC* 2: 15–19). But harassment of Jewish tax-dodgers does not constitute persecution of Jews: at the same time, though, their general unease or fear of expulsion may perhaps have been well-founded.

The only Jewish (or, far less likely, Christian) sympathizers with reason to fear for their lives were men of wealth and property, those of senatorial or equestrian rank, for this was the only group to interest the *delatores*, who could make use of it to play upon the emperor's prejudices and so, perhaps, devise charges of *maiestas*.[122] Belief in Judaism by itself, though, was obviously not an offence, otherwise the existence of the *fiscus Iudaicus* would have been impossible. That possession of wealth could prove dangerous is well-illustrated by Eusebius's account of the grandsons of Jesus's brother. According to legend, Domitian had them brought before him, and seeing that they were very poor, immediately dismissed them, 'finding no fault with them and despising them as beneath his notice' (*Hist. Eccl.* 3.20). Had they been senators or equestrians, the verdict would have been different.

So the tradition of Domitian the persecutor has been vastly exaggerated. The evidence we have suggests that, towards the end of the reign, some very few Jews or Christians of high rank (if there were any) may have had to face prosecution (i.e. for alleged *maiestas*) and, as well, that many Jews just may have feared expulsion. On the other hand, Jewish tax-dodgers of the lower classes were certainly harassed for at least the last ten years of the reign.

Philosophers and astrologers

But 'opposition' came from the (pagan) aristocracy as well, and it was sternly punished. The sources make that absolutely clear. The major difficulty in this area seems to be, not so much what motivated his opponents (the possibilities are just about endless), as to determine the charges he brought against them and precisely when, in his reign, he decided to deal with them.

Why, for instance, were Arulenus Rusticus, Helvidius (Priscus) and Herennius Senecio executed?[123] Not even the chronology of his actions against his opponents is firmly established: Dio (67.3.3) and Eusebius (*Chronicorum Canonum, A. Abr.* 2099, i.e. 1 October 82/30 September 83) both report executions and banishments not long after his accession, an assessment supported by Tacitus in his comment that the emperor's *saevitia* lasted for fifteen years (*Agr.* 3.2), whereas, in another tradition, he is depicted as merciful and moderate in the first part of the reign (*clementia*: *Dom.* 10.1; *moderatus*: Eutropius 7.2) and as *saevus* only *c.* 85/6, on his assumption of the title *dominus et deus* (e.g. Eutropius 7.2–3). Just as disputed is the chronology of his later behaviour towards the opposition. Some sources clearly refer to two separate expulsions of philosophers and/or astrologers. Eusebius, in his *Chronicorum*

Canonum, has him exiling both groups in 88/9 and again in 95/6 (or, in the Armenian version, 93/4[124]) and Dio similarly, after referring to the execution of Senecio and 'many others', adds that 'all the philosophers left in Rome were banished again' (67.12.2–3): the chronology is clear, for the comment occurs after the Pannonian war of 92 and before the events of 95/6 leading to the assassination. His 'again' can hardly be explained by reference to one of Vespasian's expulsions in 70 or 71 (Dio 66.9.2, 13.2). On the other hand, Suetonius (*Dom*. 10.3), Pliny (*Ep*. 3.11.2) and Apollonius (*Vita Apoll*. 7.3) mention but one attack on his opponents, with Suetonius referring to banishment from Rome and Italy but Pliny from Rome only. Finally, we might note that the only authors to have him expelling astrologers are Eusebius and the Suda.

But such expulsions were nothing new.[125] Astrology itself had had a long history, even by Domitian's time: for centuries, it had been believed that a man's entire life was determined by the stars and their position at his birth. But, in the Hellenistic period, it began to appear more 'scientific' on account of the extraordinary advances in mathematics that enabled the accurate determination of the position of the stars and hence predictions of greater 'precision'. In the second century BC, scientific astronomy really came into its own with the emergence of Hipparchus of Rhodes, the first scientist to produce a theory explaining the motion of the sun and the moon based solely on precisely observed and recorded data; an eminent mathematician, he was a pioneer of the scientific method. But, at the same period, the so-called science of astrology gained, not only an aura of 'scientific precision', but also intellectual respectability, when it was taken over by the famous Stoic Posidonius, who wrote five books on the topic.[126]

In the early empire, it was widely practised and its predictions accepted by emperors (e.g. Augustus: *Aug*. 94.12), by their close associates (e.g. Maecenas: Horace, *Od*. 2.12) and by leading courtiers (e.g. Vitruvius: 9.6). Nor was their eminence a disadvantage to their families. Observe the court astrologer Thrasyllus (*PIR*[1] T 137), one of Tiberius's 'intimate friends' (*Ann*. 6.23): his granddaughter married the praetorian prefect Macro.[127] However, it also acquired political overtones during this period. As Ulpian noted, consulting an astrologer about an emperor's health was punishable by death,[128] a logical provision, since, in the empire, only by removing the emperor could political change be brought about, and a conspiracy would always benefit if a suitable reading could be obtained. For the emperor himself, and especially for one who believed in this 'science' as firmly as did Domitian, astrological predictions were vital; he saw them as more 'scientific' and more disinterested than the advice given by his *amici* or his *intimi* or his freedmen. Alternately, such an emperor's fears would have been immediately aroused at the mere hint of someone else, particularly an eminent senator, consulting an astrologer. For Domitian, it would have been the prelude to conspiracy – hence Mettius Pompusianus's fate (exile to Corsica: Dio 67.12.3, and death: *Dom.* 10.4).

Before his accession, astrologers had been expelled from Rome on nine occasions.[129] There was not the slightest possibility that such orders would be applied to the colleges of augurs or haruspices: divination had always been an inherent part of the state religion and so these practices, be they public or private, were perfectly respectable. Astrology, though, could be misused, especially in times of unrest: such was the official view. The first expulsion may have been prompted by Domitian's increasing autocracy or could, in some way, have been connected with the aftermath of either the conspiracy in September 87 or the revolt of Saturninus in January 89. On the second occasion, the executions of 93 are explanation enough.

The term 'philosophic' opposition has sometimes been misunderstood, especially when applied to those executed or banished in 93. None of them were punished just because they were Stoics. Domitian apparently had no quarrel with Stoicism (appropriately practised). In his first book, Martial praised a certain Decianus for being a follower of the maxims of great (*magni*) Thrasea and Cato the perfect (*consummati*) – as well as for not seeking easy fame by committing suicide (1.8.1, 5–6). Open reference to these Stoic luminaries by a writer with Martial's obsequious attitude to the emperor is evidence enough of what was permitted. Again, there was Flavius Archippus, to whom Domitian gave 100,000 sesterces of his own money so that he could buy a farm near his native town of Prusa: Archippus was, in Domitian's own words, a 'philosopher, an honest man, his character in accord with his profession' (Pliny, *Ep.* 10.58, quoting in full two of Domitian's letters). Teachers of philosophy were perfectly respectable, entitled to special grants and immunities.[130] Again, there is the *Punica*, an epic poem written by the eminent senator Silius Italicus (*PIR²* C 474), proconsul of Asia under Vespasian, with a son, L. Silius Decianus, himself consul in the last years of Domitian's reign.[131] He was wealthy, influential and, in view of his son's consulship in 94, highly acceptable to the emperor. Nonetheless, in the *Punica*, Stoic ideas abound.[132] So Domitian's quarrel was not with Stoicism.

On the other hand, if philosophers came to Rome and practised their philosophy 'with insolence and defiance' (Seneca, *Epistulae Morales* 103.5), they were in danger of being destroyed. It was ever a matter of emphasis or discretion. Stoic philosophers had no quarrel with the concept of monarchy; thus Seneca criticized the murder of Caesar – Brutus was acting contrary to the teachings of Stoicism if he feared the name of king, for the best condition of the state is under a just king (*rex iustus*: *De Ben.* 2.20.2). But not everyone would have agreed on what constituted the latter. Briefly, aspects of Stoicism that could cause problems for an adherent included their cult of Cato, any open display of free speech, any criticism of the imperial government and obvious withdrawal from public life.[133] So Dio cites as one of the reasons for the death of Senecio in 93 was that 'he stood for no office after the quaestorship' (67.13.2).

Late in 93 (*Ep.* 3.11.2–3),[134] not long after the death of Agricola (*Agr.* 45) on 23 August,[135] seven people were brought to trial, probably for making derogatory remarks either on the principate or on the Flavian dynasty or else on Domitian himself.[136] Three were put to death, Herennius Senecio and two senators – Arulenus Rusticus and Helvidius (Priscus) – whose long-attested connections with executed members of the opposition had not deterred Domitian – in fact, both had received suffect consulships from him, Arulenus most recently, in the previous year. The four other accused were exiled and their possessions confiscated (*Ep.* 7.19.6) – Arulenus's brother (Junius Mauricus) and wife (Gratilla) together with that 'tedious pair'[137] Arria and Fannia (mother and daughter, wives of Thrasea Paetus and the elder Helvidius Priscus). Some of the accused were but part of a long-standing family tradition of hostility towards the principate, whatever the dynasty: Arria's mother (i.e. Fannia's grandmother) was the wife of Claudius's victim, A. Caecina Paetus (*PIR*[2] A 1140, C 103), whilst Fannia was the daughter of Thrasea Paetus (C 1187) who perished in Nero's reign, wife of the elder Helvidius Priscus (H 59) whom Vespasian had put to death and stepmother of Domitian's consular victim, Helvidius (Priscus). Fannia's exile in 93 was her third (*Ep.* 7.19.4)! On the other hand, the not normally patient Domitian had just awarded consulships not only to Helvidius and Arulenus, but in that very year, 93, to T. Avidius Quietus, another attested friend of Thrasea Paetus, Arria and Fannia (*Ep.* 6.29.1, 9.13.16), whilst, earlier in the reign, he had similarly honoured Helvidius's son-in-law Herennius Pollio (AD 85) and had made Arria's brother, the aged senator C. Laecanius Bassus Caecina Paetus, assistant to the *curator aquarum*.[138] In 93, they must have provoked him beyond endurance.

The accounts of the charges provided by the sources are not consistent: Suetonius is the only one to claim that Arulenus was accused of having published eulogies of both Thrasea and Helvidius (*Dom.* 10.3), whereas others state that Herennius Senecio was the one to praise Helvidius (*Agr.* 2.1, *Ep.* 7.19.5 and Dio 67.13.2). On the other hand, they do make it clear that, in essence, the major charge was that they had published attacks on the dynasty, or had aided such publication: at Fannia's trial, for instance, she was obliged to admit that she had lent her husband's diaries to Senecio (*Ep.* 7.16.5).[139]

Consistent with this interpretation are a number of other passages from Suetonius, suggesting that, as time went on, Domitian became less able to cope with criticism, especially if it were directed in any way against his position as emperor. At *Dom.* 8.3, Domitian as censor punished libels on prominent people by destroying the offending works[140] and issuing the writer with a censorial *ignominia*. The date is unknown, but at least he was still acting as censor as late as 93, since he then expelled Caecilius Rufinus from the senate for 'acting and dancing' (8.3; Dio 67.13.1). On the other hand, at 12.2, in reference to the emperor's confiscations, we are told that 'it was enough to allege any action or word whatsoever derogatory to the majesty [*maiestas*] of the emperor': so, if the confiscations began not long after the currency devaluation of 85, we may well be able to assign a very approximate date to Domitian's hardening attitude.[141] The change was obvious. He began to place less reliance on censorial *ignominia* and more on the deterrent effects of a *lex maiestatis*. Its penalties were persuasive. At 11.2–3, Suetonius has Domitian referring to the fate of those guilty of *maiestas*: they should be punished *more maiorum*, i.e. 'in the ancient way'. Not even Nero knew what that meant when told that the senate had recommended it for him; and, on being informed that the victim was stripped, fastened by the neck to a wooden fork and flogged to death, he thought that suicide was preferable (*Nero* 49.2).

Precise details exist of Domitian's harshness when faced with personal attacks. Suetonius reports (10.1) that Hermogenes of Tarsus was executed because of certain *figurae* (i.e. 'indirect attacks') in his history and that the slaves who copied it out were crucified. Again, at the gladiatorial games (*munera*), the father of a family made the mistake of supporting the Thracians (whom Domitian despised: hence Martial 9.68.7 and 14.213) and then he compounded his error by claiming that the *munerarius* was biased (10.1). Now the *munera* at this period were usually the responsibility of the quaestor, but, on this occasion, the *munerarius* may have been the emperor himself; for, according to Suetonius (4.1), Domitian could be 'persuaded' to provide gladiators, at his own expense, for the last event of the day. The unwise spectator was thrown to the dogs, with the following sign attached to his back – 'A Thracian supporter who spoke impiously' (10.1). Much the same version appears in Pliny ('no one [under Trajan] risked the old charge of *impietas* if he disliked a gladiator': *Pan.* 33.3), though, with one variant, the garrulous spectator was burned alive.[142] Then, at 33.4, Pliny accuses Domitian of 'using the arena to collect charges of *maiestas*'.

The pattern seems clear. Early in the reign he was *moderatus* in various ways, but soon found that he was unable to mollify or even cope with those who disagreed with his vision of what the empire, its leader and its capital should be. In particular, he ruthlessly suppressed any criticism from members of the aristocracy, whether or not they happened to be Stoics.

'Intellectual' opposition

Some have discovered the existence of an 'intellectual opposition' to Domitian,[143] a description meant to cover not only Tacitus and Pliny, but also such lesser lights as Philostratus, Epictetus, Sulpicia, Chio of Heraclea and the author of the 'letters' between Seneca and St Paul: the thread linking this ill-assorted group would have to be the theme of Domitian as the stock tyrant of history.

Now the 'five good emperors' laid as much stress as was possible on Domitian's autocratic methods so as to highlight their own restoration of 'freedom'. This was a phenomenon that few writers dared to ignore, just as they cared not to emphasize the fact that the new dynasty was equally intolerant of opposition. Witness the fate of Calpurnius Crassus, nephew of Galba's Piso. Granted the *fasces* by Domitian in 87, he was exiled by Nerva, then by Trajan and later killed by Hadrian, who also inaugurated his reign by executing four consular generals, one of whom, C. Avidius Nigrinus, was the nephew of T. Avidius Quietus, known for his close links with the

Stoics who perished under Domitian.[144] In these circumstances, the 'intellectual opposition' to Domitian could well have flourished.

However, in Epictetus's *Discourses*, it is often difficult to distinguish between what may be references to Domitian and to the tyrant who is the 'stock ogre of Stoic thought':[145] at times, he obviously does not mean Domitian, but simply 'the emperor'.[146] At 4.1.60, Epictetus argues that nobody is frightened of Caesar but rather of death or exile or loss of property; and that nobody loves Caesar, only the wealth or offices he can provide. As well, the phrase 'intellectual opposition to Domitian' is something of a misnomer: it appeared in the post-Domitianic era, and, like much of the adulatory output of Statius and Martial, whilst not being officially inspired or authorized, always reflected with considerable accuracy the spirit of the imperial court. Efforts to include in this category the works of Sulpicia, Chio of Heraclea and the 'correspondence' between Seneca and St Paul[147] only serve to weaken the case further, and are little more than testimony to the strength and persistence of anti-Domitianic propaganda, undeterred by lack of evidence.

6

WAR I

Tacitus's assessment of imperial foreign policy from 69 to 96 was distinctly hostile:

> There was success in the east, failure in the west. Illyricum was disturbed, the Gallic provinces wavered in their allegiance, Britain subdued and immediately let go. The Sarmatians and Suebi rose against us; the Dacians won fame by defeats inflicted and suffered; even the Parthians were almost aroused to arms through the trickery of a false Nero.
>
> (*Hist.* 1.2)[1]

Most, if not all, Tacitus's barbs were directed at Domitian, and the imperial general staff would almost certainly have concurred. Thanks to the epigraphical and archaeological discoveries of the past hundred years or so, however, it has to be substantially revised.[2]

The military ability of Vespasian and Titus is beyond dispute. Both were attested experts in siege warfare: Vespasian would have been equal to the generals of old had it not been for his *avaritia* (*Hist.* 2.5), and Titus was graceful and energetic in war (*Hist.* 5.1). Not so Domitian. His first efforts to secure military glory proved abortive – in Vespasian's absence, he 'began an expedition against Gaul and the Germanies, which was unnecessary and from which his father's friends dissuaded him, just so that he might make himself equal to his brother in power and rank'. Vespasian reprimanded him (*Dom.* 2.1) and, later, also squashed his attempt to lead a force in support of the Alani (*Dom.* 2.2). Now, emperors with no military experience tended to seek it once they gained power,[3] and it need cause no surprise if Domitian be included in their number. In fact, he was the first emperor to spend a substantial part of

126

his reign outside of Rome personally involved in his military ventures.

A number of scholars have been working on the notion of imperial foreign and frontier policy and just how it was formulated.[4] The evidence is not extensive, but, with Domitian, some points emerge clearly. What is surprising, perhaps, is that his practice in Britain and Germany differed openly from the accepted Roman norm, for he rejected the idea of expansionist warfare, seeing it as 'anachronistic and contrary to the interests of the state'.[5] Without doubt, the policy was his, even though he had his advisors. When war in Germany was imminent, he summoned his *amici* to the Alban villa to discuss the situation (Juv. 4.144–6), including three with military experience in the Balkans (Pegasus, Rubrius Gallus and Cornelius Fuscus) together with other advisors, accomplished politicians such as Acilius Glabrio, Fabricius Veiento and Vibius Crispus.[6] It is impossible to assess the extent of their input into the ultimate decisions; and, caution is necessary in attempting to assess it, since, in a rudimentary state, one man can obviously have far more influence than in a complex modern society. But, that aside, in a number of instances, the evidence we have shows that the decision was Domitian's, and Domitian's alone. Julius Ursus, imperial relative and praetorian prefect, was promptly eased out of his influential post and 'promoted' to the senate and a consulship for failing to agree with imperial policy in Germany (Dio 67.4.2); Cornelius Fuscus, the equestrian, was given supreme control of the Dacian campaign (*Dom.* 6.1) and therefore of the senatorial legates commanding the various legions; and who else but the emperor could have ordered the construction of a legionary fortress (Inchtuthil) and, then, some four years later, its complete demolition? Finally, Frontinus seems to indicate that Domitian himself made the important decisions during the Chattan war[7] and did not, as Dio alleges in reference to his presence on the Danube, simply 'remain in one of the cities . . . indulging in riotous living' (67.6.3). On the contrary, according to Frontinus, he attempted to conceal his aggressive intentions towards the Chatti by pretending that he was about to conduct a census in Gaul (*Strat.* 1.1.8); to uncover the enemy's hiding-places, he had 75 kilometres of roads constructed through their territory (1.3.10); on another occasion, he ordered his men to dismount and fight on foot because of the difficult terrain (2.3.23) and he even paid compensation for the damage his army caused (2.11.7).[8]

CHATTI

Much has been written on the Chattan war, when it began and what it achieved.[9] Very early in the reign, Domitian went to Gaul, pretending to conduct a census, but suddenly turned on the Chatti, constructing military roads into their territory and taking various measures designed to control them for the future. For this, he quickly claimed an undeserved triumph.

His departure, so it is thought, is depicted on the second frieze of the Cancelleria Reliefs, the *profectio* scene: *virtus* pushes him forward, Mars and Minerva turn to him in appeal.[10] He and his court, once on the Rhine, may even have stayed for some time at Mainz, headquarters of the two legions *XIV Gemina* and *XXI Rapax*: we have the tombstone of his official taster, Tiberius Claudius Aug. lib. Zosimus.[11]

There is much to be said for 82, rather than 83, as a commencement date, though this is not generally accepted.[12] In brief, three pieces of evidence have been used to support 83, viz. *ILS* 1995, Dio 67.3.4–5 and Domitian's four salutations between June 83 and September 84. The first, a military diploma of 20 September 82, refers to the discharge (*dimissi honesta missione*) of a number of auxiliary soldiers serving in (Upper) Germany; as a result (argued Henderson and many others) 'it can hardly have been in this year that Domitian attacked or meant to attack the Chatti'.[13] The argument depends on the phrase *dimissi honesta missione*, interpreted as indicating a state of peace, i.e. soldiers would not be discharged during a war.[14] But what are we to make of the two diplomas issued on the same day to different groups of soldiers in Syria (7 November 88) when only one contains the phrase in question? That there was a state of peace and war at the same time?[15] Even if we were to accept Henderson's argument, we would then have Domitian discharging soldiers at the end of 82 and, at the very same time, assembling a huge force to support the 83 campaign.

Dio's evidence seems more promising. He, or rather his epitomator Zonaras, refers to the emperor's northern expedition only after discussing his divorce of Domitia Longina and his affair with Julia, whereas Xiphilinus also notes the punishment of the Vestal Virgins before commenting on the war.[16] No precise dates can be assigned to any of these, however. There is some evidence (quite conflicting) for the affair of the Vestals: Eusebius, for instance, in the Armenian version, dates it to the period October 81/September 82,[17] and this could perhaps suggest that Domitian moved north in 82, but other sources prefer a later date. Scott accurately summarizes the ancient evidence in assigning the affair to either 81 or 82 or 83.[18]

Finally come the imperial salutations, awarded whenever the emperor or one of his *legati* won a victory. Traditionally, the first was received on his accession to the throne (so September 81) and the second, noted by March 82, may well be explained by one of Agricola's successes in Britain; the third appeared in January 83 (and was still there on 9 June: *ILS* 1996), the fourth is unattested, the fifth was awarded in January 84 and, by September of that year, he had received his seventh.[19] On that basis, the war could well have begun in Spring 83 and salutations four to seven been awarded for success in Germany: such is the contention of some.[20] On the other hand, as Syme pointed out long ago,[21] three of the four might belong to other areas such as Britain and Mauretania. In any case, triumphs were far more prestigious than salutations.[22]

In 83, he celebrated a triumph for his victory and ensured that all were aware of his achievements by claiming a new title, *Germanicus* (i.e. 'Conqueror of Germany'), which appeared on official documents and coins for the first time during the period 9 June/28 August 83 and remained part of his official titulature throughout the reign.[23] Consistent with his determination to secure a military reputation, he preferred to advertise his success with a triumph, just as his father and brother had done in June 71. Neither triumph indicated the completion of the campaign – after the fall of Jerusalem, the fortresses of Herodium, Macherus and Masada remained to be taken and Vespasian received seven salutations between June 71 and 74.[24] But neither Vespasian nor Titus claimed the title *Judaicus*; so it is tempting to believe that Domitian was determined to better them by adopting the *Siegerbeiname* 'Germanicus'. As well, he wanted it thought that the victory was his, not that of his *legati*: salutations first would spoil the effect – hence a triumph to rival his father's and brother's with the added glory of the title, 'Conqueror of Germany'. Subsequent victories in Germany, like those in Judaea, would be noted by salutations.

Some evidence can be adduced in favour of the earlier date. There is a definite indication in *ILS* 1995 that Domitian had moved into Germany well before September 82. In that document, three of the seventeen units assigned to Germany had already been moved to Moesia. It is certainly unusual to find mentioned in the one diploma units from two different provinces, but, as early as September 82, Domitian presumably felt confident enough to continue his movement eastwards by releasing a small number of his German auxiliary forces for service in Moesia. It does not indicate that the war was over by September 82; rather it had begun successfully and the emperor was already continuing his father's policy of strengthening the frontier where the real danger lay, the Danubian. Conversely, it is hardly likely that, before the advance into Germany, Domitian was transferring soldiers into Moesia. A German campaign beginning in 83 presupposes preparations before the end of 82, the precise time when auxiliaries were being moved out of Germany. The diploma of September 82, then, provides solid evidence that the Chattan war began before 83.

Apart from Frontinus's account, the literary evidence for the war provided by Pliny, Tacitus and Dio is, at best, unhelpful, along the lines of Tacitus's comment that, 'in recent times, the Germans were more triumphed over than conquered' (*Germ.* 37). Even Frontinus's comments do not get us very far, and one of his key phrases, *limitibus per centum viginti milia passuum actis* (*Strat.* 1.3.10), has been interpreted as meaning either that he drove 75 kilometres of military roads into enemy country[25] or else that he constructed fortified boundaries extending for 75 kilometres.[26] If we assume that the former interpretation is correct,[27] then Domitian's military roads were intended to open the way to the Chattan fortresses, massive stone structures difficult of access. For this, a large force was needed and so a new legion, *I Minervia*, was raised and sent to Bonn in Lower Germany, replacing the experienced *XXI Rapax* which moved to Upper Germany where *I Adiutrix, VIII Augusta, XI Claudia* and *XIV Gemina* were already stationed. We know that soldiers from all five Upper German legions (*vexil. legionum I, VIII, XI, XIV, XXI: ILS* 2285) were busy manufacturing tiles at Mirebeau-sur-Bèze (22 kilometres from Dijon in Upper Germany) and scholars usually (but not always[28]) assign this activity to the period of the Chattan war. Again, there were vexillations of nine legions, four of them from Britain, which may have been in Germany as early as 83 (*ILS* 9200). Commanded by Velius Rufus, this mysterious force apparently had a roving commission, and the extraordinary nature of his position is indicated by the fact that he was the first Roman of equestrian rank since the time of Augustus to be recorded as possessing the *ius gladii*.[29] But, however we date Velius Rufus's force, it does seem from L. Roscius Aelianus's career inscription (*trib. mil. leg. IX Hisp., vexillarior(um) eiusdem in*

expeditione Germanica: ILS 1025) that vexillations were taken f
the four legions in Britain for the German campaign.[30] Even tho
the *IX Hispana* alone was mentioned, it is generally accepted that
basis of the vexillation system was that equal drafts from each legi
in a province were meant to take the place of a complete legion.
all, it must have been a substantial force.

Rewards were considerable – an increase of a third in the soldier
pay,[31] a *congiarium* and also, possibly a donative.[32] Attempts hav
been made to assess the costs involved in all this. It would seen
that, on a yearly basis, a legion would now cost 6.6 million HS
the whole army 450–500 million HS (or one-third of the total state
revenues) and a *congiarium* some 45 million HS.[33] On the other
hand, the achievements were impressive,[34] at least in the long term,
though not likely to find favour with the aggressively minded general
staff. The literary, epigraphical and archaeological evidence suggests
that Domitian was now able to devote his attention to the Moesian
front, since he could strengthen the Rhine defences in the Taunus
and Wetterau region,[35] giving Rome better control of the tribal
movements to the east of the Rhine and providing a quicker route
between Mainz and the Danube. This was the main achievement, the
commencement of a defence system of forts, roads and watch-towers
that was to be continued for decades. The Chatti, however, were
not conquered, as is indicated by their role in Saturninus's revolt
(*Dom.* 6.2) and their interference with the Cherusci (Dio 67.5.1).
But Domitian's primary aim was military glory. He wanted it at
once – and a commencement of hostilities even in 82 meant that he
had already been waiting twelve years for his opportunity.

BRITAIN

One of Appian's comments on Britain is not without interest.
According to him, '[the Romans] have taken possession of the
better and larger part [of Britain], not caring for the remainder.
Indeed, the part they do hold is not very profitable to them' (*Praef.*
5). Domitian would have agreed with him wholeheartedly.

During the reigns of Vespasian and Titus, Agricola[36] had made
substantial advances in Britain. The chronology of his campaigns,
though, is still a matter of dispute,[37] some favouring the earlier
dating 77–84, others 78–85. But the most persuasive argument[38]
seems to be Tacitus's comment in *Agricola* 39.2, that 'Domitian
knew in his heart that his recent counterfeit triumph over the

Germans made him a laughing-stock', and, since the comment was made in connection with Agricola's victory at Mons Graupius (which occurred in his seventh and last season), it would appear preferable to accept the earlier dating, i.e. Domitian's accession to the throne coincided with the end of his fifth year in Britain, with Mons Graupius and Domitian's celebration of a triumph occurring in 83.

The sixth season was long and eventful, fully described in chapters 25 and 26 of the *Agricola*. Tacitus's account concludes with a very significant comment: if the Caledonii had not managed to escape into the *paludes et silvae* ('marshes and forests'), *debellatum illa victoria foret* ('that victory would have ended the war'). The impression given is that, after a 'crowded summer and a long campaign',[39] Agricola had hoped that the entire island would be his and, more importantly, that this is precisely what he had told Domitian in 81,[40] at the end of the fifth season, just after the emperor's accession to the throne. Agricola must have expected to be transferred, for he had already spent five years in the command, two years longer than usual for consular legates during the Flavian era.[41] For the same reason, the construction of the new legionary fortress at Inchtuthil was undertaken in this, the sixth season.[42] Agricola was fully confident that ultimate victory was within his grasp and Domitian was convinced. Whatever his defects, Agricola was never short of confidence. Only once does Tacitus report his father-in-law's views directly, and this was Agricola's often repeated claim that Ireland could be 'conquered and occupied' by one legion with auxiliaries (*Agr.* 24.3).[43] So extending the command for a sixth year would be consonant with the emperor's major concerns – immediate glory for himself and, as well, the subsequent and immediate freeing of at least one British legion for service on the Danube.

But he was to be disappointed. Agricola needed yet another year and reinforcements were required in Germany and then in Moesia; so he lost vexillations from each of his four legions and, despite his victory at Mons Graupius (wherever it was[44]), the movement eastwards became irrepressible. Numismatic evidence[45] has now made it clear that, at some time between the middle of 87 and the middle of 88, drastic changes occurred in Britain. Shorn of Domitianic propaganda, it was a massive withdrawal. *Legio II Adiutrix* was permanently moved from Chester (and Britain), the new legionary fortress at Inchtuthil was completely dismantled and all the northern Scottish forts as well as the

'Gask Frontier' watch towers (Ardoch, Strageath and Bertha) were abandoned.[46] Domitian apparently intended to move some 120 kilometres south of Inchtuthil, as far as the forts of Glenlochar, Dalswinton, Milton, Oakwood and Newstead, with support from the forts at Broomholm, High Rochester and Learchild. Later, Trajan went even further south, in fact to the Stanegate: so perhaps Tacitus's famous comment, *perdomita Britannia et statim omissa* (*Hist*. 1.2) ought to be applied to him.[47] The retreat was conveniently disguised – but not from the general staff: at this very time (87/8), as the distribution pattern of coins indicates, the magnificent arch at Richborough was erected.[48] Apparently it was meant to symbolize the completion of the conquest of Britain. Built on a cruciform foundation 9 metres below ground level, 41 metres long and 32 metres wide, the main arch alone was 9 metres wide and 29 metres high. Strong describes it as follows:

> In scale of building, it rivals all the great monumental arches constructed in the Roman world, and its massive severity must have been as effective and impressive a piece of propaganda as one could find throughout the Roman empire.[49]

Two incidents (possibly connected) that occurred after Agricola's departure deserve brief mention. According to Suetonius, the governor of Britain, Sallustius Lucullus, was executed by Domitian for allowing a new type of lance to be named after himself (*Dom*. 10.3). Lucullus is an enigma. We must assign his command to the years after Agricola (no other governor of Britain is known for the years between 86/7 and 94/5),[50] but can be no more precise than that, since neither the year of his consulship, nor even his full name is known – unless he is to be identified with the suffect consul of 89, P. Sallustius Blaesus.[51] Various solutions have been proposed, one being that his demise is to be connected with the hostility shown by the general staff to Domitian's rejection of expansionist warfare in Germany and Britain. Perhaps Lucullus had been appointed to supervise the destruction of Inchtuthil, the withdrawal south, the establishment of a new frontier and the elaborate pretence at Richborough:[52] opposition to what must have seemed a cowardly policy would have been interpreted by Domitian as treason.

Connected with this reconstruction could be the unusually generous awards (*AE* 1951: 88) of three crowns and a silver spearshaft granted to Gaius Julius Karus for his activities in a *bellum Brittannicum* (sic).[53] He almost certainly[54] received his reward for his actions in Domitian's reign, possibly some outstanding act of loyalty towards the emperor at the time of Lucullus's 'treason'. There certainly are parallels for officers receiving exceptional awards for their part in crushing conspiracies and rebellions – Valerius Festus was given decorations appropriate to a consul whilst he was still a praetor, presumably for having Piso killed and thereby removing the major opposition to Vespasian in Africa;[55] and, in Domitian's reign, the phrase *bellum Britannicum* is both ominous and significant, for A. Bucius Lappius Maximus, who suppressed the revolt of Saturninus, is attested as *confector belli Germanici*, whereas Suetonius, avoiding the official euphemism, refers to the revolt as a *bellum civile* (*Dom.* 6.2). Karus's tombstone (*AE* 1951: 88) contains other unusual features. The unit in which he served (*coh. II Asturum eq.*) at the time of his memorable activities is named, but no honours were awarded it, no title such as *felix* or *invicta*;[56] even more surprising is the omission of precisely what Karus did to have received such lavish honours. Moreover, no wars are attested in Britain at this time. So far, then, we have only negative evidence. Two facts, though, can be added. The British governor's foot guards, the *pedites singulares Britanniciani*,[57] were around this time moved from Britain and given 'separate but inferior status'[58] – perhaps for remaining loyal to their governor rather than to their emperor. Again, a diploma of 98 (*CIL* 16.43) contains a unit named *cohors I Fida Vardullorum civium Romanorum*. The title is doubly unusual. The cohort was one of the very few British units to receive Roman citizenship *en bloc*. As well, *Fida* appeared not at the end of the cohort's name, as was normal, but in the most prominent position, where one would expect the imperial name: i.e. compare units such as *coh. I Aelia Dacorum* (*ILS* 9150) or *coh. II Flavia Brittonum* (*ILS* 1999).[59] Perhaps it too had been loyal to Domitian.

All this evidence, positive and negative, should be considered in the context of the military situation in Britain during Domitian's reign after the departure of Agricola. The legionary fortress at Inchtuthil was demolished not long after it had been built and Roman forces in Scotland moved south. Many generals must have resented Domitian's rejection of expansionist warfare and despised him, the governor of Britain more than most, perhaps. Lucullus's objections may have been reported by Karus, with appropriate rewards and punishments following. But the connection with Lucullus is far from inevitable;[60] possibly, the *bellum Britannicum* should be assigned to the last years of Domitian's reign. Either reconstruction must be regarded as speculative.

DANUBE

Domitian's sternest test was on the Danube, where he had to face three opponents – the Sarmatians (Iazyges and Roxolani) moving ever westwards, the Suebic Germans (Marcomanni and Quadi) to the north of Pannonia as well as the Dacians, emerging after a century as a united group once again. Whilst the three were never linked in solidarity through hatred for Rome or else distrust of her, nonetheless preparations for war against the first two inevitably involved defensive measures against the third. The problem was not new,[61] but it had reached its zenith by the last fifteen years of the century, and Domitian was well aware of it from the beginning of his reign.

It was not purely coincidental that, of the courtiers he summoned to the Alban villa (Juvenal, *Sat.* 4), four of them had attested military experience – not in Germany or Britain, but in the Danubian area. Pegasus (4.77) had governed Dalmatia, Rubrius Gallus (4.105) had avenged the death of the Moesian governor Fonteius Agrippa, slaying many of the Sarmatians (*BJ* 7.91–5), Cornelius Fuscus (4.112) had been procurator of Pannonia and Pompeius (4.110), if he was indeed M. Pompeius Silvanus Staberius Flavinus, had also governed Dalmatia (*Hist.* 2.86, 3.50) during the civil war at the same time as Fuscus was in Pannonia. As far as we know, no one else listed by Juvenal had any military experience at all: Montanus (*Sat.* 4.107), if he was T. Junius Montanus, had served as military tribune of the *V Macedonica* under Nero (*AE* 1970: 500), but it, too, was stationed in Moesia. Some of his other courtiers had also served in the Balkans: Valerius Festus, described by Martial (1.78.10) as an *amicus* of Domitian, had governed Pannonia early in Vespasian's reign and was responsible for a considerable amount of construction work in the area;[62] Rutilius Gallicus had commanded the *XV Apollinaris* early in Nero's reign when it was stationed at Carnuntum, and held his second consulship and city prefecture around the time of Domitian's first Danubian campaign;[63] and T. Aurelius Fulvus was legate of the *III Gallica* when it was sent to Moesia during the civil war, defeating the Roxolani (*Hist.* 1.79), and later, like Rutilius Gallicus, was consul for the second time and city prefect in the late 80s.[64] So, during Domitian's absences from Rome supervising operations against the Dacians, two of the three city prefects probably representing him in Rome had had considerable experience on the Danube. His courtiers' expertise lay mostly here.

Of the three actual (or potential) opponents – Suebi, Dacians and Sarmatians – the latter were by far the most formidable. In general, the Suebian Marcomanni and Quadi were unreliable Roman clients, 'likelier to be loyal to Rome than to take orders from others' (*Hist.* 3.5): the reference is to the civil war period, when one of their kings was Italus (*PIR*[2] I 60), father (so it seems) of Chariomerus (C 714), who sought Domitian's help (*c.* 90–1) against the Chatti, sending him hostages and receiving money in return but no soldiers (Dio 67.5.1). More dangerous were the Dacians, long weakened after the downfall of Burebista but soon to regain prominence under Decebalus:[65] they too were Roman clients and about as reliable as the Suebi. But the Sarmatians posed more serious problems. As early as the fifth century BC, Herodotus (4.21.110–17) had been aware of the Indo-European Sauromatae (or Sarmatae) who, for centuries, controlled the area from the Hungarian plain to the lower Volga. At various periods, both groups of Sarmatians, western (Iazyges and Roxolani) and eastern (Alani) represented an actual menace as they moved westwards, and remained so until finally dispersed by the Huns.[66]

The official attitude to them in the civil war is significant: whereas the Suebi did provide some assistance (*Hist.* 3.5), the Flavian generals would not use the Iazyges in a force against Vitellius for fear that they would immediately desert on receiving a better offer (*Hist.* 3.5). As well, at this very period, occurred the first recorded contact between Rome and the Roxolani.[67] With the passage of time, the situation became more critical as Sarmatian pressure westward increased, forcing Rome to reassess its relationship with the Dacians and Suebi. The most efficient (i.e. cheapest) solution would have been the development of a secure client–king system, supported by generous subsidies. Annexation was both dangerous and expensive, and all the more so since Rome would have to provide garrisons large enough to control not only the Suebi and Dacians but also both the Iazyges to the west and the Roxolani to the east.[68]

Recent archaeological investigation has revealed that Vespasian consistently strengthened the Danubian defences.[69] It seems[70] that Vespasian did not increase the total military establishment there but rather redeployed it, adopting different tactics by relying more on infantry than on cavalry and by concentrating his forces close to the river, more or less along the lines adopted by Rubrius Gallus (*BJ* 7.94–5). In the 70s, new work was undertaken at the legionary (*XV Apollinaris*) base at Carnuntum (*CIL* 3.11194–7) and at the auxiliary fort at Aquincum (where the Danube could be forded) directly opposite the area occupied by the Iazyges. A whole series of forts at Hurlec, Leskovec, Nikopol, Donji Milanovac, Orehovo (*AE* 1957: 307: AD 76) and Adony, long thought to have been Domitianic, are now known to have been undertaken by Vespasian.[71] Again, this substantial increase in fort construction must have placed additional pressure on the Danubian fleet, so the naval bases at Zemun (Pannonia), Noviodunum (Moesia) and possibly those at Arcar (Ratiaria) and Sexaginta Prista (Ruse) may well have been due to Vespasian's initiative.[72] The Romans did have ships on the Danube in the first half of the century, but now both the Pannonian and Moesian fleets were named *Flavia*, possibly due to Domitian's initiative. He seems to have added to the personnel and increased the status of the officers: particularly significant in this regard is the *cursus* (*AE* 1972: 572) of M. Arruntius Claudianus from Ephesus, one of the emperor's senior equestrian officials (*praefectus classis Moesiacae et ripae Danuvi*[73]) to whom he subsequently granted senatorial rank. Finally, as the shortest route from Italy to the Lower Danube was via the river Save, it is hardly surprising that Vespasian established colonies at either end of the river, at Siscia and Sirmium.[74]

From the start, Domitian persisted with his father's policy of strengthening the Danubian defences and especially the river crossings. Auxiliary units were sent to Pannonia in the early 80s, as is indicated by a comparison of three Pannonian diplomas, viz. *CIL* 16.26 of 13 June 80 (with four *alae* and thirteen *cohortes*), *CIL* 16.30 of 3 September 84 (with five *alae* and thirteen *cohortes*) and *CIL* 16.31 of 5 September 85 (with six and fifteen respectively); as well, the *ala Claudia nova*, *cohors III Gallorum* and *cohors V Hispanorum* had arrived in Moesia from their German bases by 20 September 82 (*CIL* 16.28 = *ILS* 1995). Not too much should be made of this, however, as the legionary complement in the Danubian area was still as it had been almost twenty years before, late in Nero's reign, when there had been two legions in Pannonia (*XV Apollinaris* at Carnuntum and *XIII Gemina* at Poetovio), one in Dalmatia (*XI Claudia* at Burnum) and three in Moesia (*VII Claudia* at Viminacium, *III Gallica* at [possibly] Oescus and *VIII Augusta* at Novae): by 81, though, the *V Macedonica* had replaced the *III Gallica* at Oescus, *IV Flavia* was at Burnum and *I Italica* at Novae.[75] Domitian's Danubian experts looked towards a continuation of Vespasian's policy of fortifying the river-bank area and developing stronger client–king relationships with the Suebi and Dacians. But Domitian, eager for military glory, and having quickly claimed a probably undeserved triumph in Germany, may have favoured or have been suspected of favouring direct intervention. On the other hand, the recently united and strengthened Dacian tribes may have been under pressure from outside. Whatever the truth, the Dacians acted.

FIRST DACIAN WAR, 84/5[76]

In the winter (*Pan.* 12.3–5) of 84/5,[77] the Dacians, possibly under the leadership of Diurpaneus (or Dorpaneus),[78] crossed over the Danube and attacked the Romans, killing the Moesian governor Oppius Sabinus (*PIR²* O 122) and wreaking considerable destruction: some claim that the legion *V Alaudae* perished then too. But Suetonius makes no reference to the loss of a legion at that time, though a few lines lower (*Dom.* 6.1) he notes the destruction of one (?*XXI Rapax*) by the Sarmatians. The lost standard (*semeion*) referred to by Dio (68.9.3) probably belonged to the praetorian guard, not to a legion, and was lost by Cornelius Fuscus.[79] Oppius was probably replaced, for the moment, by one of the Moesian *legati legionis* until M. Cornelius Nigrinus could be sent to the area[80] as governor. Domitian, accompanied by his praetorian prefect Cornelius Fuscus, came to the Danube, basing himself at Naissus, probably.[81]

The Dacians had to be forced back across the Danube, a task made all the more difficult by the emergence of their new leader Decebalus. It used to be thought that one of Domitian's measures at this time was the construction of a huge earth rampart in the Dobrudja,[82] but it is now known that it belongs to the ninth century.[83] Not far from it, though, is the village of Adamklissi, with the nearby *Tropaeum Traiani*,[84] Trajan's memorial to the ultimate conquest of Dacia and, as well, an altar with the names of 3,800 or more Roman soldiers who died in a battle. Some have dated it to Oppius Sabinus's defeat,[85] others to Cornelius Fuscus's,[86] and usually it is assumed that the dead belonged to the legion *V Alaudae*. But the theory that this legion survived after 70 was devised solely as an explanation for the dead on the Adamklissi altar – set up in an area first visited by a Roman army, not in Domitian's lifetime, but during Trajan's first Dacian war.[87] So the whole edifice is fragile – *V Alaudae* did not survive 69/70, Domitian did not get as far as the Dobrudja and Adamklissi had nothing to do with him.

Domitian, then, visited Moesia for the first time in 85, immediately after Oppius Sabinus's defeat (*expeditione . . . in Dacos . . . prima, Oppio Sabino oppresso*: *Dom.* 6.1), refusing to accept peace overtures from the Dacians and ultimately sending Fuscus out against them (Dio 67.6.3–5). His initial success enabled Domitian to return to Rome by late summer or early autumn and claim his tenth and eleventh salutations[88] for driving the invaders from Moesia. As well, he was now declared censor for life.[89]

Early in the following year, possibly in conjunction with his twelfth salutation, which appeared between 17 March 86 (*CIL* 16.32) and 13 May of the same year (*CIL* 16.33),[90] he celebrated his second triumph, on this occasion for his victory over the Dacians. Some have disputed the existence of this event,[91] others strongly champion it.[92] Suetonius is the problem: at *Dom.* 6.2, he has Domitian celebrating a *duplicem triumphum* (i.e a 'double triumph') over the Dacians and the Germans, whereas, at 13.3, Domitian changes the names of the months[93] after *duos triumphos* (i.e. 'two triumphs'). But the first is the double triumph of 89, the latter his previous two triumphs, one in 83 over the Chatti and the other in 86 over the Dacians.[94] There is no reason to doubt his clear testimony. This was Domitian's second triumph, probably less undeserved than his first.

AFRICA

In Africa, such evidence as we have suggests that campaigning and frontier consolidation occurred in Domitian's reign. Ptolemy (1.8.4) discusses two separate expeditions into the hinterland, to Ethiopia and the territory of the Garamantes, both assigned to the Flavian era and led by Julius Maternus and Septimius Flaccus respectively.[95] But, whenever they occurred, the obvious implication is that the relationship between Rome and the Garamantes was friendly.

Not so with the Nasamones, a tribe living to the north-east of the Garamantes and south-east of Leptis. Dio alone (67.4.6–7) provides evidence of their encounter with Domitian's forces. In 86, probably, whilst Cn. Suellius Flaccus[96] was in command of the legion assigned to Numidia, the *III Augusta*, many (Dio 67.4.6) of the desert tribes of proconsular Africa, including the Nasomones (he names them alone) revolted on account of the severity of their taxes, killed the tax collectors and defeated the Roman forces sent out against them. But they grew careless, allowing Flaccus to counterattack and, ultimately, to wipe them out: hence Domitian's boast that he had forbidden the Nasamones to exist. It seems not unlikely that the revolt was sparked by the vigorous methods employed by the financial agents of an emperor facing financial difficulties and forced (in the middle of 85) to devalue the currency he had revalued a few years previously, in the summer of 82.[97]

To the west lay Numidia and Mauretania. Lack of direct evidence makes it difficult to assess Domitian's policy towards the troublesome Numidian tribes, but Trajan's measures – a fort at ad Maiores, the establishment of new colonies (e.g. at Thamugadai in 100) and the ultimate encirclement of the Aurès Massif[98] – all presuppose preparatory work by Domitian. Originally, the *III Augusta* was stationed at Ammaedara, then at Theveste and later at Lambaesis, probably by 80[99] – and certainly by Trajan's reign. The move was significant, for, at Ammaedara and Theveste, the legion was, so to speak, looking back towards proconsular Africa, but not so at Lambaesis, much closer to Mauretania and so strategically more important; its establishment should be taken as proof of the continuing Roman advance towards the Aurès Massif. How much credit belongs to Domitian is difficult to assess.

The situation in Mauretania was somewhat more serious. Ten years or so previously, in Vespasian's reign, the two equestrian procurators of Caesariensis and Tingitana were replaced by an imperial *legatus* Sex. Sentius Caecilianus.[100] No further information is available on the reasons for his appointment or of its outcome, but wars in Mauretania were notoriously long and difficult. Between 85 and 87,[101] Velius Rufus, 'tribune of the thirteenth Urban cohort' (at Carthage) was appointed 'commander of the armies of Africa and Mauretania to crush the tribes in Mauretania' (*ILS* 9200). No doubt he was successful: his was an outstanding career. Corroborating evidence of the campaign may be provided by a number of diplomas from Mauretania Tingitana, which suggest that there was a serious war in the area at some time between 88 and 109;[102] possibly, this was the same as that recorded in *ILS* 9200. However, it is hard to see that Domitian did anything specific to precipitate war in the area, beyond the depredations of the imperial tax-collectors.

SECOND DACIAN WAR, 86

For the first half of the year, Domitian remained in Rome. According to the *Acta* of the Arval Brothers, Domitian was there early in January 86;[103] and he was certainly in Rome during the early part of the same summer to celebrate the inaugural Capitoline Games.[104] It was during this period that Cornelius Fuscus attempted to avenge Sabinus's death by invading Dacia itself. With his well-attested impetuosity (*Hist.* 2.86) and, perhaps, a sense of history, he not only crossed the Danube by means of a bridge of boats (Jordanes, *Getica* 77), but also plunged into Dacia itself – and perished: Tacitus's comment in *Agricola* 41.2, *tot exercitus amissi temeritate . . . ducum* (i.e 'so many armies lost through the rashness of their commanders') is directed at Fuscus.[105] The result of this was Domitian's second journey to the Danube (*expeditio . . . in Dacos . . . secunda Cornelio Fusco* [*oppresso*]: *Dom.* 6.1).

Assigning a date to it poses problems. Domitian was in Rome until the early part of summer (86), and the following year, 87, has to be ruled out altogether, since no imperial salutations were then awarded, Domitian being *IMP. XIV* in September 86 and still so in January 88,[106] and, as well, the *Acta* of the Arvals, complete for 87, have no hint of prayers for an imperial expedition. So, presumably, the emperor went back to the Danube *c.* August 86. Immediately, he divided the province into two, retaining Cornelius Nigrinus in Lower Moesia (to the east) and, for Upper Moesia (to the west), moving L. Funisulanus Vettonianus from Pannonia. Apparently, the recent dismissal[107] of Vettonianus's powerful relative, Tiberius Julius Aug. lib., did not prejudice the emperor against him: an experienced commander was needed and Vettonianus had been serving in the Balkans (Dalmatia and then Pannonia) since 79.[108] Nigrinus and Vettonianus must have achieved some success against the Dacians, to judge by the substantial military awards they received and by Domitian's thirteenth and fourteenth salutations which were proclaimed late in the year.[109] Before returning to Rome late in 86, he probably ordered three additional legions to be moved to the Danube, viz. *IV Flavia* from Dalmatia to, perhaps, Upper Moesia; *I Adiutrix* from Germany to Brigetio or Sirmium and *II Adiutrix* from Britain to (possibly) Sirmium as well, going later to Aquincum.[110] Similarly, *mandata* would have been sent at this time to Agricola's successor in Britain, ordering withdrawal from northern Scotland, demolition of Inchtuthil and construction of a huge arch at Rutupiae (Richborough) to disguise the whole operation.

After a year's inaction (87), Domitian was ready to avenge Fuscus. A new governor was appointed to Upper Moesia. Vettonianus's long Balkan posting (Dalmatia, Pannonia and Upper Moesia in succession from 79/80 to 87/8)[111] was over and he was replaced by his relative Tettius Julianus, another commander with Danubian experience. He had been legate of the *VII Claudia* in 69, defeating the Roxolani when they tried to invade Moesia (*Hist.* 1.79, 2.85), and, whereas Fuscus had been noted for his impetuosity, Tettius had the reputation of being a stern disciplinarian (Dio 67.10.1). From Viminacium, he led his army across the Banat to the Iron Gates of Transylvania *en route* for Sarmizegetusa, Decebalus's capital, and defeated the Dacians at Tapae, presumably late in 88.[112] In Rome, Domitian had celebrated the Secular Games, probably in the middle of the year,[113] and also his sixteenth and seventeenth salutations;[114] he may even have been considering another journey to the Danube to accept in person the Dacians' surrender. Trouble in Germany forced a change of plan.

It was around this time that he issued an edict conferring (or perhaps confirming[115]) a series of benefits to former soldiers. He decreed that they all

> shall be freed and exempt from all public taxes and harbour dues, and that they themselves, the women who married them, their children and their parents shall be Roman citizens with full rights and shall be free unconditionally and have every immunity, and that the above-mentioned parents and children shall have, in the matter of full immunity, the same rights and status.[116]

Reassurance of imperial support for the soldiers might have seemed desirable in view of the recent emergence of a 'false Nero' (*Nero* 57.2) or, just possibly, due to hints of problems on other fronts – on the Rhine, where Saturninus's revolt was about to break out (1 January 88) or the Danube, with trouble from the Marcomanni and the Quadi (*c.* May 89[117]). On the other hand, since his fourteenth salutation had been celebrated about two years before (*c.* October 86) but his fifteenth and sixteenth (appearing on the edict) within the space of the last four months,[118] following Tettius Julianus's victory at Tapae, it is far more likely that the situation was not unlike that of 83: military success had to be seen to be rewarded to guarantee the soldiers' continued loyalty and, as well, to enhance the image of the warrior emperor.

7

WAR II

SATURNINUS'S REVOLT

Very little precise information has come down to us about Saturninus's revolt.[1] The basic facts seem to be these. On the first of January 89,[2] the governor of Upper Germany, L. Antonius Saturninus, seized the savings of the two legions (*XIV Gemina* and *XXI Rapax*) stationed at Mainz and revolted against Domitian. He could count on the support of his own legions and had, apparently, reached an accommodation with some nearby German tribes, including the Chatti.[3] It was a critical time for Domitian, as he was facing problems on two other fronts, the aftermath of the false Nero's appearance in the east and further unrest on the Danube. However, the commander of Lower Germany, Aulus Bucius Lappius Maximus,[4] moved quickly to the seat of the revolt and, with the aid of the equestrian procurator of Rhaetia, Norbanus,[5] soon suppressed it. Trajan was summoned from Spain with the *VII Gemina*, whilst Domitian came from Rome with his praetorians. But the uprising, such as it was, was short-lived. The rebels' leaders at Mainz were promptly and savagely punished.

One of the many difficulties presented by this uprising is its precise cause. As the soldiers had received a substantial increase in pay only five years before and, more recently, had had their privileges and immunities as veterans confirmed,[6] they should have had little cause for dissatisfaction. Seven years later, the soldiers alone regretted Domitian's assassination: they wanted to deify him, and, so we are told, they would have avenged him, had they not lacked leaders (*Dom.* 23.1). It may have been the same in 89. The men, but not all their officers, were enthusiastic supporters of the emperor. Pressure for revolt may have come from above rather than from below.

144

Germany was probably still under military administration in 89. The first *legatus Augusti pro praetore provinciae Germaniae Superioris*, L. Javolenus Priscus,[7] is attested on 27 October 90 (*ILS* 1998). Saturninus, his immediate predecessor, was in command of the four legions stationed in Upper Germany. His headquarters and two of his legions, were in Mainz, his other two being at Strassburg (*VIII Augusta*) and Windisch (*XI Claudia*). Lappius resided in Cologne, with his legions at Nymwegen (*X Gemina*), Xanten (*XXII Primigenia*), Neuss (*VI Victrix*) and Bonn (*I Minervia*). Now a case could be made for the growth of dissatisfaction amidst the senatorial officers in Germany. For some one hundred years, the chief emphasis of imperial military policy had been in this area; its commanders had great political influence and power. Precisely twenty years before the outbreak of Saturninus's uprising, Vitellius had announced his imperial candidature: he had held the post now occupied by Saturninus. But, if the commanders' futures depended on military successes, they may well not have agreed with Domitian's German policy. A quick campaign followed by a much advertised triumph and a series of defensive works to enable emphasis to be placed on the Danube front may have been sound general policy, but not one to impress an aggressive commander. Even less reassuring was the emperor's withdrawal from Inchtuthil:[8] dismantling a full-sized legionary fortress was hardly the policy of an Agricola. Again, Domitian's lenient treatment of the conquered German tribes, including compensation for lost crops (Frontinus, *Strat.* 2.11.7) was, to put it mildly, open to misinterpretation. That this was the attitude of some within the empire can be attested. Pliny assailed the 'sham trappings of false victory' (*Pan.* 16.3); Agricola's son-in-law Tacitus complained that 'in recent times the Germans had provided more triumphs than victories' (*Germ.* 37). It is hard to believe that similar views were not held by some of the commanders of Germany's eight legions as they saw their hopes of military success diminish.[9]

But there is another factor. The date of Saturninus's appointment to the Upper German command is not known; it must have been after his consulship which almost certainly can be assigned to 82.[10] It may be that, when he arrived, the legionary complement was five rather than four. Domitian had moved the *XXI Rapax* from Lower to Upper Germany at the time of the Chattan war and, so it seems, stationed it at Mainz with the *I Adiutrix* and *XIV Gemina*:[11] so, for a brief period *c.* 83–5, three legions were in the one camp. In any case, the unusual situation was not destined to last long: in the middle of 86, *I Adiutrix* was transferred to the Danube, but the effect on Saturninus could have been disastrous. His huge army of five legions was larger than the normal maximum for a province at this time and surely tempting to an ambitious officer, yet it was not acquiring military glory for its commander, but, as far as he was concerned, did little more than make tiles. Then, to make matters worse, one of the legions was moved to another province, to fight. The difficulty with this reconstruction is the nature of the evidence: *I Adiutrix* may have been transferred before Saturninus's arrival.

On the other hand, the situation in the double camp at Mainz could well have been explosive. With Vespasian's reorganization of the Rhine armies, *XIV Gemina* and *I Adiutrix*, had been assigned there, a reasonable decision since both units had fought for Otho and against Vitellius in the civil war, e.g. at Cremona (*Hist.* 2.43). Sixteen years in camp together must have strengthened their solidarity: at the very least, a certain *esprit de corps* had surely developed. Neither would have welcomed the arrival of *XXI Rapax*, a Vitellian unit against whom they had both fought together: a legionary legate of *I Adiutrix*, Orfidius Benignus (*PIR*² O 136) had been killed at Cremona by members of the *XXI Rapax*. Veterans tend to have long memories.

The insurrection was brief and miscarried. It began at Mainz, such at least is what Suetonius (*Dom.* 7.3) implies, and presumably Saturninus would have sought help from his other two legions at Strassburg and Windisch: none came. At least, no evidence is available to suggest that the legates of the *VIII Augusta* or *XI Claudia* sided with Saturninus, and neither legion was moved from Germany after the revolt had been suppressed. There must have been a similar reaction from Bonn, where the closest of the Lower German legions was stationed. Unfortunately for the rebels, this was the *I Minervia*, Domitian's own recent creation and no doubt at all the more loyal to him. The rest of the legions there followed suit; worse still, they marched against Saturninus and defeated him, somewhere between Coblenz and Bonn, possibly in the plain near Andernach.[12] He had also been disappointed by the non-arrival of the recruits from the Chatti on the right bank of the Rhine, for a sudden thaw prevented them from crossing the river: and it must have been quite unexpected, since, according to Herodian, horses used to cross the Rhine in winter just as if it were firm ground (6.7.7).

It seems reasonable to assign the commencement of the uprising to 1 January 89, the twentieth anniversary of Vitellius's proclamation by the two legions at Mainz (*Hist.* 1.55). The minutes of the Arval Brethren for January 89 (*CIL* 6.2066) indicate that, as early as the 12th of the month, prayers were being offered for the emperor's return, similarly on the 17th, and that, by the 25th, they were celebrating his victory,[13] a timetable consistent with the outline provided by Plutarch in his *Life of Aemilius Paullus* (25). So it seems clear that the uprising was of extremely short duration, that Lappius's reaction was remarkably swift and that therefore rumours of at least what was likely to happen in Mainz on the twentieth anniversary of Vitellius's proclamation had reached most, if not all, the Upper and Lower German legions in advance of 1 January 89. By the end of February, the armies from the capital and Spain had met in Mainz,[14] but, before long, Domitian had left for his third journey to the Danube.

This was a military revolt, nothing more. We should reject the notion that Saturninus had considerable support from the senate, that the uprising was part of a widely organized conspiracy against Domitian, that many senators were executed by him once the revolt was suppressed and that, after it, he became bitter, suspicious and cruel towards them.[15]

Saturninus's background was hardly comparable with that of a Vitellius. Granted senatorial rank by Vespasian in 69 or 73, he was probably sent to the senatorial province of Macedonia to serve for a year as proconsul (? 76/7) and thence, perhaps, to Judaea, replacing the conqueror of Masada, L. Flavius Silva.[16] A consulship came early in Domitian's reign, probably in 82. He may well have been a competent officer, but hardly *capax imperii*. Despite Martial's comment (4.11), he was no descendant of Antonius the triumvir. Nor were his morals acceptable to an emperor who condemned several senators and equestrians for breaking the Scantinian law (*Dom.* 8.3), since Saturninus was 'a notorious and untrustworthy pervert',[17] an assessment supported by Dio (67.11.4).

With the evidence we have, it is difficult to assess the extent of the support Saturninus received or at least counted on. Suetonius refers to the various forms of torture meted out to 'many of the opposite party' (*Dom.* 10.5), but of the 579[18] certain and probable senators of Domitian's reign, only two, Julius Calvaster (*PIR*² J 231) and Lappius,[19] appear in the ancient sources as possible supporters of Saturninus, and neither was in Rome at the time of the revolt.

Again, some scholars associate Domitian's execution of the senators Civica Cerialis and Sallustius Lucullus with the suppression of Saturninus's revolt, despite the silence of the ancient sources on this point: but there is no evidence whatsoever to support such a claim.[20]

Perhaps the most significant statement in any assessment of the senate's involvement appears in Pliny's account of Trajan's military prowess. In the *Panegyricus*, delivered on the occasion of his consulship in 100, Pliny refers to Trajan's role in helping to suppress Saturninus's revolt: '[Domitian] had called you from Spain to be his surest support during these very German wars, unwilling as he was to bestir himself and jealous of another's virtues even when he was in dire need of them' (*Pan.* 14.5). Now Pliny failed to accuse Domitian of a widespread massacre of senators, even though the Domitianic 'terror' was one of the regular themes of the *Panegyricus*. His reticence was prompted by Trajan's readiness to come to Domitian's aid. If a single senator had been involved in a conspiracy against the emperor or had been executed as a result of his participation in it, there would have been no mention whatsoever of the revolt. In the senate and in front of the emperor himself, Pliny would have been more discreet, and, by referring openly to Trajan's role in the affair, he provided the strongest possible evidence of its purely military nature; his audience was only too well aware of the fact that the emperor had been promoted with almost unprecedented rapidity, from legionary legate in 89 to ordinary consul in 91,[21] for his part in helping to suppress what was an army mutiny at Mainz, but not a widespread senatorial conspiracy. So there is no evidence to suggest that Saturninus had widespread support or that his revolt caused the deterioration in Domitian's relationship with the senate.

The epigraphic and literary evidence for Lappius's career may be summarized as follows: towards the end of Vespasian's reign, when he was in his mid-thirties, he was commander of the legion *VIII Augusta* stationed in Strassburg; a few years later, possibly *c.* 82, he was appointed proconsul of Pontus–Bithynia (*Ep.* 10.58.6); then, in September 86, he became consul; his role in suppressing Saturninus's uprising can most logically be explained by assigning to him the governorship of Lower Germany in the years immediately after his consulship – but there is no epigraphic evidence for his tenure and Dio, who had most to say about him, merely claimed that he 'overcame and destroyed

Saturninus' (67.11.1); finally, after being appointed governor of a second consular province, Syria, he was recalled to a second consulship in May 95 and then to the pontificate, a position he still held in 102.

What were the results of the uprising? That it represented a turning-point in the reign has often been maintained, yet it is clear that Domitian persisted with the policy he had been pursuing since the beginning of his reign of admitting to consular rank senators with ties to the 'opposition': Arulenus Rusticus and Avidius Quietus received the *fasces* in 92 and 93 respectively.[22] On the other hand, it is easy to believe that it exacerbated his suspicious nature. The exceptionally large number of suffect consuls appointed in 90 suggests that he was more and more anxious to surround himself with committed supporters but not that a 'reign of terror' was about to commence.[23]

Punishments and rewards were announced. To the four Lower German legions and their auxiliaries, the honorific title *pia fidelis Domitiana* was awarded; on the emperor's death in 96, the *Domitiana* was dropped but the remainder retained.[24] Lappius and Norbanus were promoted, the latter perhaps to the prefecture of Egypt. Once the mutinous leaders had been dealt with severely (*Dom.* 10.5), the two Mainz legions were transferred to the east. The legion *XXI Rapax* went to Pannonia and was virtually obliterated by the Sarmatae in 92 (*RE* 12.1789); *XIV Gemina* was moved to the Danube and stayed there.[25]

There were other administrative changes.[26] Since the uprising was at least partly financed by the soldiers' savings, it was decided that no more than 1,000 sesterces per man could be deposited in the camp fund and Mainz became a one-legion camp (*Dom.* 7.3); a Lower German legion was moved there and both Germanies became three-legion provinces. The political predominance of the Rhine legions was no more. One other innovation may perhaps be assigned to this time. The commanders of what were two separate army groups became regular provincial governors at some time between 82 and 90. Presumably, the Rhine hinterland formerly controlled by the *legatus* (governor) of Gallia Belgica now passed to the new German governor, but it appears that the financial administration remained with the equestrian procurator in Trier.[27] One can but speculate on the motives behind such an arrangement. Perhaps an attempt was being made to discourage administrators in Germany from assuming that they had a predominant political position.

CHATTI, 89

Before leaving Mainz, Domitian turned his attention once more to the Chatti. Famous for their fighting ability – 'You would see other Germans going to battle, but the Chatti going to war' (*Germ.* 30.3) – they had not been conquered in 83, and their intervention in 89 had, at the very least, resulted in the destruction of part of the recently constructed frontier fortifications.[28] Lappius defeated them and a peace treaty was signed: hence Statius's reference to Domitian 'giving the conquered Chatti terms of mercy' (*Silvae* 3.3.168). Lappius could now, with some justification, be described as the *confector belli Germanici* (*ILS* 1006) rather as the victor in a *bellum civile* (*Dom.* 6.2).

Domitian was the first emperor since Tiberius to spend long periods of time outside Rome. One of the remarkable features of the wars during the first half of the reign was the presence of the emperor in the military zone on four separate occasions – 82/3, 85, 86 and 89. He was not unattended: the court came with him. In either 83 or 89, his chief taster Tiberius Claudius Zosimus accompanied him to Mainz and died there.[29] On the other hand, Dio may well be going too far in claiming that Domitian returned from the first Chattan war 'without ever seeing hostilities' (67.4.1). The imperial court was sometimes established in Rome, sometimes at the *arx Albana*, sometimes at Circeo and sometimes far further afield. This was an innovation.

FIRST PANNONIAN WAR, 89

Domitian was probably still in Mainz when reports came of hostile activity on the part of the Suebian Germans and so, whilst the Dacian king and his capital remained to be taken, he was faced with the prospect of war on two fronts. He proceeded at once to the Danube and came to terms with Decebalus who escaped the fate that most of the general staff surely thought he deserved, and all the more so in view of what had happened to Oppius Sabinus and Cornelius Fuscus. His position was recognized and he sent Diegis (Martial 5.3), a member of the Dacian royal family, to Rome so as to accept the diadem from Domitian's hands: no doubt he was wise not to go there himself. As well, he received practical assistance in the form of men and money (Dio 67.7.2–4);

in the official propaganda (but nowhere else), Fuscus's death had been avenged (Martial 6.76). Tactically, it was an eminently sensible arrangement, since it rendered highly unlikely the possibility of war on two fronts. Moreover, it was consistent with Roman diplomatic practice.[30] For his achievements in Dacia, a huge equestrian statue was decreed by the senate (*Silvae* 1.1.1–107). As well, according to Dio (67.8.1–3), gold and silver statues were erected throughout the empire, magnificent games were instituted under the direction of L. Arruntius Stella (*Silvae* 1.2.180), and, in the Circus, infantry, cavalry and naval battles were fought. The poets were as adulatory as ever, e.g. Martial (5.19.3, 6.4.2, 6.10.8) and Statius (*Silvae* 1.1, 4.2.66).

Details of the conflict with the Suebian Marcomanni and Quadi are obscure. According to Dio (67.7.1), Domitian himself began it by attacking both tribes for not providing him with assistance against the Dacians; he then rejected two separate attempts by the Germans to treat for peace and even executed the members of a second embassy; and, after (Dio 67.7.2) the Marcomanni defeated him, he granted Decebalus a generous settlement.

By November 89, Domitian was back in Rome, celebrating his double triumph over the Chatti and the Dacians (*Dom.* 6.1);[31] and so, if we accept Dio's chronology, Domitian's first recorded conflict with the Suebi must have occurred earlier in that year before the settlement and the triumph. If indeed Domitian was the aggressor, his intention may have been to forestall a German attack.[32] It has been argued that, throughout the 80s, Domitian had in mind the Marcomanni and Quadi alone, as he increased the Pannonian auxiliary forces; and that he was able to move three additional legions to the Danube so quickly in 86 simply because they were already being prepared to attack the Suebi. If so, the Dacians had merely seized the opportunity that was being offered to them,[33] attacking suddenly and unexpectedly.

No activity is recorded for the years 90 or 91, for Domitian had been taking various diplomatic initiatives (recorded by Dio) in an attempt to isolate the Suebi.[34] The Marcomanni and Quadi had long been settled in Bohemia and Moravia (*Germ.* 42), but it was the Semnones, from the north of Bohemia, who 'considered themselves the leaders of the Suebi, (for) they were their oldest and noblest tribe' (*Germ.* 39.1, 4), exercising a sort of religious supremacy over them all (*Germ.* 39.1–2). It was hardly coincidental that their king Masyus and priestess Ganna, successor of Veleda, visited Domitian and were received with honour (Dio 67.5.3) or that he offered military assistance (Dio 67.5.2) to the Lugii of Silesia (*Germ.* 43.3). One wonders, too, about the attitude of the Hermunduri who were known for loyalty to Rome (*Germ.* 41.1) and willingness to intervene in Bohemia on her behalf;[35] but Dio has no comment on their attitude in the early 90s. All this was standard Roman diplomatic practice, isolating the enemy by encircling him with hostile neighbours, and it neatly complemented the neutralizing of the Dacians.

SECOND PANNONIAN WAR, 92

Early in May 92,[36] Domitian left Rome for yet another expedition to the Danube where the Sarmatians had now joined the Suebi to oppose Rome's interests (*Hist.* 1.2), influenced, according to Dio (67.5.2), by Rome's offer of military assistance to the Lugii. Thanks to the settlement with Decebalus, the Romans were allowed to march through Dacia, 'through the kingdom of Decebalus' (*ILS* 9200), and attack the Sarmatian Iazyges from the rear – Domitian sent an expeditionary force consisting of vexillations from nine legions (*ILS* 9200), led by Velius Rufus.[37] But disaster struck again, for the Sarmatians destroyed a legion, presumably *XXI Rapax*.[38] Little else is known of the war. If, as some believe, Trajan governed Pannonia in 93 (*AE* 1985: 722), then he presumably played a prominent part in this campaign. Perhaps this was the point of Pliny's comment (*Pan.* 14.5) that, after the defeat of Saturninus, Trajan had been found worthy to conduct a series of campaigns. It also seems likely that Domitian's relative L. Caesennius Sospes commanded the *XIII Gemina* at the time, for he was highly decorated in an *expedit[ione] Suebic[a] et Sar[matica].*[39]

The campaign lasted but eight months and, by January 93, the emperor was back in Rome,[40] where he celebrated an *ovatio* but not a triumph. The literary sources tried hard to explain it away. According to Suetonius and Silius Italicus, he was content to dedicate a laurel wreath[41] to Jupiter Capitolinus (*Dom.* 6.1; *Punica* 120), which, as Pliny (*NH* 15.30) asserts, was part (but only part) of a regular (*iustus*) triumph. For Martial, it was a concealed triumph, and the laurel marking the peace achieved by Domitian was just as important (8.15.5–6), whereas Statius offered the fact of the emperor's clemency (*Silvae* 3.3.171) as an explanation for the absence of a triumph, but, later, did urge

Domitian to accept a triumph (4.1.39). Despite it all, the implication was clear. Domitian deliberately rejected a triumph: perhaps he was not fully satisfied with what had happened, knew that a triumph could ultimately be achieved, and so was prepared to bide his time, strengthening the Danubian front until he felt able to move once again. On the other hand, reports may have reached him on the Danube concerning the behaviour of certain members of the 'philosophic opposition', a group he imagined that he had under control: if so, a prompt conclusion of the war would have been essential.

THIRD PANNONIAN WAR, ?95

Various pieces of evidence suggest strongly that, towards the end of the reign, *c*. 95–6, yet another Sarmatian campaign was in progress. Until recently, its existence was not even recognized.

Since the early 90s, the forces in Upper Moesia and Pannonia were being substantially increased, as an Upper Moesian diploma of 12 July 96[42] indicates. A long-known diploma (*CIL* 16.46) of 100 listed a large number of auxiliary units as serving in Upper Moesia, many more than were there in 93 (*CIL* 16.39), and the increase has usually and plausibly been explained as being part of Trajan's preparations for the first Dacian war.[43] That will no longer do: most of them were already there on 12 July 96. Again, close co-operation between the two Danubian provinces is indicated by the temporary transfers of units from Pannonia to Moesia Superior and vice versa, e.g. the cohorts *V Gallorum*, *I Montanorum c. R.*, *I Lusitanorum* and the *ala Praetoria*. There seems to be no reason to accept the old hypothesis that it was not these units that were being moved but the provincial boundaries, i.e. that Upper Moesia was being briefly expanded to include the area of Syrmia (Srem).[44]

Of some relevance too is the honorific inscription of L. Aconius Statura who was rewarded by Trajan for his achievements in the Dacian war (of 101/2) and 'by previous emperors ... for the German and Sarmatian war' (*CIL* 11.5992). The obvious (but not only) explanation of the last phrase would be that Statura was honoured for his exploits in Nerva's 'German' war and in Domitian's 'Sarmatian' campaign immediately preceding it. A plausible reconstruction of Statura's *bellum Germanicum et Sarmaticum*, then, would be a war in 95 or 96 in the vicinity of Singidunum against the Iazyges with the front moving to the north of the province against the Suebi for reasons unknown, but, presumably, because of another Germanic-Sarmatian alliance against Rome: victory was achieved by the summer of 97 (*Pan.* 8.2). Far less likely is a reference to Domitian's earlier Sarmatian war. In any case, his choice of a mere *ovatio* at that time (93) is very significant. But there are other indications of a concentration of forces in the area *c.* 95–6: Dio Chrysostom (12.16–20) describes what was probably a large number of (Upper Moesian) troops, perhaps a legion, at Viminacium in September 96.

Four inscriptions from the Moesian city of Scupi (*AE* 1910: 173; 1972: 512; 1973: 477; and 1977: 730) could well support the contention[45] that Domitian undertook another Sarmatian campaign towards the end of his reign. They may[46] be late-Domitianic (even though lacking precise dating criteria), and they reveal the presence in Scupi of soldiers from four legions (or from vexillations of four legions) normally stationed outside of Upper Moesia during the period from 70 to 120. On the other hand, if the four inscriptions are not Domitianic but Vespasianic (and that is not impossible, given the imprecision of the dating criteria), then they would have to be seen as connected with his foundation of the *colonia* at Scupi.[47] They should not, and need not, be used to prove the existence of Domitian's third Pannonian war.

Finally, the senatorial officers appointed to the area in 96 deserve attention. The diploma of 12 July 96 indicates that Pompeius Longinus was still governor of Moesia Superior at that time; he had been serving there on 16 September 94 (*CIL* 16.39) and had been moved to Pannonia (together with his tribune and some auxiliary units) by 20 February 98 (*CIL* 16.42). It used to be thought that he had left Upper Moesia in 95 to be replaced by Trajan.[48] Involved, too, was the early career of Hadrian. According to *ILS* 308, he served as tribune in legions *II Adiutrix*, *V Macedonica* and *XXII Primigenia*, and, when taken with the account of his activities given in *SHA, Hadr.* 2.2–5, it was deduced that he served successively in provinces governed by his relatives, Trajan and L. Julius Ursus Servianus.[49] That reconstruction can now be safely discarded, but not the comment that he was transferred to Lower Moesia *extremis iam Domitiani temporibus* (*Hadr.* 2.3). Perhaps it was in the middle of 96 that Julius Mar[inus] came to Lower Moesia as governor, with Hadrian as his *laticlavius* for the *V Macedonica* (at Oescus), whilst the capable Pompeius Longinus (Dio 68.12.1) was moved from Upper Moesia to Pannonia as the emphasis of the war shifted. With him went his tribune and a number of auxiliary units, three of which can be identified, viz. the *cohortes I Hispanorum, I Lusitanorum* and *I Montanorum.* These three were still in Upper Moesia on 12 July 96, but in Pannonia before 20 February 98 (*CIL* 16.42). Moreover, Attius Priscus, honoured by Nerva for services in a *bello Suebico*, is on record (*ILS* 2720) as having led what appears to be an expeditionary force of the three.[50]

In the last years of Domitian's reign, then, there was a notable concentration of forces on the middle Danube. Five legions in Pannonia,[51] numerous auxiliaries in Upper Moesia (presumably to deal with the possibility of intervention from Dacia) and vexillations from legions normally stationed outside the province assume a foe, not Dacia, but the *Germani et Sarmatae.* Appropriate senior appointments and transfers were made. Attention was paid first to the Sarmatians and later to the Suebi. By October 97 it was all over.

THE EAST

Domitian's eastern policy[52] differed little from that of his father who had been obliged to acquiesce in Nero's settlement of 66, whereby the relative position of the two great powers was indicated by the decision to have the Parthian king's brother crowned in Rome as king of Armenia, and on this he had to build. In brief, his aim had been to bar Parthia's progress either by annexing nearby territories or else by developing new client–king relationships with them: and, at the same time, the defences were strengthened. So Commagene and Armenia Minor was annexed and the latter added to the new Cappadocia–Galatia complex, now extending over some 112,000 square miles;[53] two legions were stationed there (*XII Fulminata* at Melitene and *XVI Flavia Firma* at Satala) and numerous roads were constructed.[54]

Of the nearby tribes, the Iberians, Hyrcanians and Albanians were most likely to be of use to Rome. Settled in the vicinity of modern Tiflis, the Iberi[55] were close to and in control of the vital Darial Pass. Whatever Iberia's previous relationship with Rome, it now became a client-kingdom, with its ruler Mithridates declared *philocaesar kai philoromaios*, as the Harmozica inscription indicates:

> The emperor Caesar Vespasian Augustus, pontifex maximus . . . [various titles appropriate to the period 1 July 75 to 31 December 75] and the emperor Titus Caesar, son of Augustus . . . and Domitian Caesar . . . strengthened these fortifications for Mithridates, king of the Iberians, son of king Pharasmenes and Iamaspus, friend of Caesar and friend of the Romans, and for the people of the Iberians.[56]

So the Romans had built fortifications there, i.e. in Iberia (and not in Armenia Maior where Harmozica is sometimes wrongly located[57]), and since Harmozica is near both Armenia and the Darial Pass, its strategic significance (Strabo 11.3.5 [501] and Pliny *NH* 6.29–30) is obvious, and the fact that the Romans were erecting military structures in Iberia is proof enough of the success of Vespasian's policy.

The Hyrcanians,[58] from the south-eastern shore of the Caspian sea, were an unknown factor and remained so. Early in Vespasian's reign, they had allowed the Alani to pass through their territory and attack Parthia and Armenia (via the Rayy Pass) and Vespasian refused to intervene when asked by the Parthians to do so (*BJ* 7. 244–54; Dio 65.15.3), for hostility between them and the Hyrcanians was very much to Rome's advantage. Consequently, whilst we have no direct evidence of Rome's attitude to the Hyrcanians, it stands to reason (arguing, unfortunately, *ex silentio*) that neither Vespasian nor Domitian would have tried to discourage their anti-Parthian attitude.

Equally significant is the attitude of the Albani.[59] Since their territory bordered on Armenia Maior and Iberia, with the Caucasus and Caspian sea to the north and east, they controlled the Derbend Pass and could stop the Alani moving south of the Caucasus. If Albania were to become a reliable client-kingdom of Rome, the policy of encirclement would be complete. This, almost certainly, was Domitian's achievement.

His relationship with Albania requires examination. For some time, a Roman force had been stationed right in the heart of Albania. It is first attested in Domitian's reign, at Bejuk Dagh,[60] where an inscription (*AE* 1951: 263) records the presence of a unit of the *XII Fulminata*,[61] normally based at Satala in Cappadocia–Galatia. There is, however, no indication of when the unit arrived in the area; we are only told that it was there by 84. The position was as strategically significant as Harmozica's,[62] for it provided control of the Derbend Pass, even though there is no indication of military fortifications as at Harmozica. According to *AE* 1951: 263, the unit of the *XII Fulminata* was commanded by the centurion L. Julius Maximus 'under the emperor Domitian Caesar Augustus Germanicus', but there is no hint whatsoever of its purpose. Now Grosso refers[63] to another Latin inscription (lost and not even fully recorded) from the village of Karjagino in Azerbaijan that also mentioned the legion *XII Fulminata*. One can but guess at their purpose. Just possibly, Maximus's unit was part of the army sent into *A[. . .]* under the command of M. Hirrius Fronto Neratius Pansa (*AE* 1968: 145): the inscription is incomplete, but the general sense is that an army was sent against either the Alani or the Albani or else into Armenia.[64] Be that as it may, the unit's physical presence in the heart of Albania is proof positive that, whatever the status of the Albanian king during the reign of Domitian (assuming that there was one then), Albania was within Rome's sphere of influence. Domitian had completed the encirclement of the Parthians.

Finally, the Alani: that they were regarded by Vespasian or Domitian with the same wariness as the Parthians is highly unlikely.[65] Early in Vespasian's reign, the Flavians' attitude to both of them became apparent when, at the invitation of the Hyrcani, the Alani invaded Parthian territory (*BJ* 7.244–51) and created havoc, taking captive Pacorus of Media Atropatene together with his wives and concubines (7.247) and then almost capturing Tiridates of Armenia (7.249). Both Tiridates and Pacorus were brothers of Vologaeses of Parthia, and, when Vologaeses asked Vespasian for help, he was told that 'it was not proper [for Rome] to interfere in others' affairs' (Dio 65.15.3). Vespasian had no quarrel with the Alani and no reason to assist the Parthians. As a result, relations between them could at best be described as strained.

However, the options open to Vologaeses were severely limited, and it is hardly surprising that he welcomed the appearance of the false Neros. Various factors, not least of which was Nero's popularity in the east, had given rise to hopes that he was still alive, and three pretenders claiming descent from him are attested under the Flavians. Pretenders posed a number of problems for local and imperial officials. In his account of the appearance of a false Alexander in 221, Dio reports that 'accommodation and provisions were provided for him at public expense [and] not a soul, neither governor nor soldier nor procurator, not the magistrates of the local communities, dared to withstand him or say anything against him' (79.18.1–3).

The first of the three caused panic in Asia and Africa c. 69 (Hist. 2.8), but the second and third became directly involved with the Parthians. In Titus's reign, a certain Terentius Maximus gained a few followers in Asia, advanced to the Euphrates and finally sought refuge with Artabanus IV, the Parthians' *archegos* (Dio 66.19.3), becoming involved in their internal politics by siding with him in his contest with Pacorus, the king (*basileus*).

When a third pretender appeared in 88, the Parthians were involved once again. According to Suetonius,[66] they 'supported him vigorously and surrendered him reluctantly' (*Nero* 57.2). Worse still, for the emperor's peace of mind at this time, Rome's energies were concentrated on the protracted Dacian campaign, with at long last some indication of success after early disasters. So, at the very least, Pacorus had the chance to embarrass Rome with little risk by supporting the pretender. As well, there had been a conspiracy against the emperor in Rome (22 September 87[67]) and the merest hint of trouble in the east would have aroused imperial ire. Possibly, 'accommodation and provisions (had been) provided for him at public expense'; possibly, the local, or, more importantly, the imperial officials had preferred to turn a blind eye to his activities. In either case, Domitian would have been far from satisfied. The parallel cannot be pressed very far, but Domitian's proconsul of Asia may well have thought that the pretender and his support would wither away even more quickly if dealt with in a non-violent fashion, whilst fearing that intervention might exacerbate the situation, involve war with Parthia and prejudice the successful conclusion of the Dacian campaign.

Although the precise year of the pretender's appearance is not known, Suetonius's *viginti annos* (*Nero* 57.2) suggests either 87/8 (when the proconsul of Asia was C. Vettulenus Civica Cerialis) or 88/9 (term of L. Mestrius Florus[68]). It seems reasonable to assign him to Cerialis's term and to see in his rising and the proconsul's reaction to it the cause of Domitian's apparently precipitate action in executing Cerialis (*ILS* 1374; *Agr.* 42.1).[69]

Some support for the earlier date can be gained from the fact that, by November 88, Domitian had increased the auxiliary forces in Syria, possibly as a reaction to earlier unrest nearby. Two military diplomas are of some interest in this regard: the first (*CIL* 16.35), issued on 7 November 88, lists twenty units stationed in Syria, whilst the second, issued in the same province and on the same day, lists seven units, all different from the first.[70] The number of units is possibly significant, since only ten of these twenty-seven appeared on a Syrian diploma of 12 May 91.[71] This might well indicate that, with the easing of tension, troops were able to be moved elsewhere, to more dangerous fronts.

If the Syrian legions were involved in suppressing the false Nero,[72] they must have been led by the Syrian governor P. Valerius Patruinus, who seems to have been in control of Cappadocia–Galatia before Syria[73] and so could be regarded as something of an expert on eastern affairs. Perhaps Valerius's victory caused Domitian to claim his seventeenth salutation, awarded in September/October 88.[74] But, whatever force was needed to deal with the false Nero, Domitian had no need to be concerned at the resultant deteriorating relationship with Parthia, for Roman control of the Caucasus remained as firm as ever.

There are also indications in contemporary literature that Domitian planned a military expedition to the east. In a poem addressed to Vitorius Marcellus (*Silvae* 4.4), Statius suggests areas where the young officer might serve, such as the *metuenda portae limina Caspiacae* (63–4). This passage and others like it have been pressed into service[75] to prove that, in the 90s, Domitian proposed to mount an expedition to the east. But, given Roman policy in the Caucasus, the emperor had to have some units in Iberia and Albania if only to guard the passes; there is no evidence and no need to postulate a grandiose eastern campaign. For one thing, Domitian could not afford it. Foreign policy may well have been made in the court but not by the court poets.

8

ARISTOCRACY I

One view of Domitian's relationship with the aristocracy was established by Nerva's senators. It was unambiguous. They failed to deify him and then officially condemned his memory. How his death was regarded by the other section of the aristocracy, the equestrian order, is not known. Perhaps, like the city population (*Dom.* 23.1), they were indifferent. Both groups demand attention.

SENATORS

For contemporary and near-contemporary historians, only senatorial opinion mattered, and there can be no dispute that, in September 96, the *damnatio memoriae* had the enthusiastic support of most senators. They had no choice, unless they themselves sought the purple, for Domitian had left no adult heir. So his statues were destroyed, or rather, with almost Flavian avoidance of waste, the heads were removed and recycled, 'his baleful, fearsome visage being cast into the fire to be melted down' (*Pan.* 52.5).

Such was the almost inevitable fate of the last member of a dynasty in the Roman imperial period. Denigration and vilification served to justify the military or political *coup* (more usually assassination) that removed him. Once a few minor measures were be countermanded (e.g. excesses involved with the collection of the Jewish tax[1]) and a few cosmetic changes introduced, the administration of the city and empire would continue as before with precisely the same officials.[2]

Unfortunately for Domitian's reputation, the dynasty that propounded the hostile view of him was to endure, not for one or two generations, but until well into the third century AD, until in fact the death of Severus Alexander. Septimius Severus, who died in 211, included in his official title the phrase 'great-great-great-grandson of the deified Nerva' (*ILS* 420), with the last member of Nerva's dynasty, Severus Alexander, claiming to be 'the son of the deified Antoninus the Great [i.e. Caracalla] and the grandson of the deified (Septimius) Severus' (*ILS* 5759a). Domitian's assassins and those behind them had to argue that he had been

> an abominable and intolerant tyrant for only [then] could his assassination be not merely justified but glorified, as the essential act for inaugurating the Golden Age. . . . On the other hand, if the utility and necessity of the assassination were questioned, then the legitimacy of the dynasty which Nerva founded would be impugned. Therefore, as long as that dynasty lasted, no rehabilitation of Domitian could be undertaken.[3]

By the middle of the third century AD, the anti-Domitianic tradition had become long-established and, by then, re-assessing it was not one of the primary concerns of the Roman aristocracy. On the other hand, the view of his reign propounded by Nerva's senate and repeated throughout the dynasty could even be accurate – although inevitably hostile, it was not inevitably wrong.

According to Dio, 'Domitian did not care that the senate frequently saw fit to pass decrees that it should be unlawful for the emperor to put to death any of his peers' (Dio 67.2.4). Such were his introductory remarks on Domitian, written a century after his death during the reign of Nerva's 'descendants'. He may well, as Suetonius noted, have administered justice 'carefully and conscientiously' (*Dom.* 8.1): but, apparently, he made the mistake of being consistent, treating aristocrats and others in the same fashion. Thus was his reputation amongst the senators established and written into the tradition.

From the beginning, Domitian's terms were clear and the aristocracy were well aware of them. He stressed the reality of his autocracy. Lacking the experience of Vespasian and the diplomatic talents of Titus, he made no effort to disguise what he regarded as the nature of the principate. His was a personal monarchy and he saw himself as a benevolent despot.

By the end of his second week as emperor, his wife Domitia had been assigned the title *Augusta* (*CIL* 6.2060); coins soon appeared with her image actually on the obverse;[4] she was honoured as a goddess[5] in the east (*IGRR* 3.444: from Termessus); her name appeared with that of her husband in the prayers offered by the

Arval Brothers for his safety (*CIL* 6.2060–8), and their son, who had died apparently some years before his father's accession, was now quickly[6] deified. There was no delay whatsoever in stressing his view of the imperial position, no attempt to disguise how he felt.

As the reign progressed, he continued to proclaim the reality of his personal autocracy. 'He was elected consul for ten years in succession and censor for life', according to Dio (67.4.3). All this was without precedent. Worse still, he then declined to assume these consulships; in fact, he held only half of them and, in the period from 90 to 94, none at all. Furthermore, he usually relinquished the post after holding it for only a week or so. Nor was the perpetual censorship likely to cause less offence, since it gave him the right to adlect men to the senate whenever he chose, and not merely, as Vespasian and Titus had done, during the eighteen months of the normal censorship.[7] Presumably he had the right anyhow, thanks to the grant of *imperium* on his accession. No subsequent emperors needed to be appointed specifically as censors to add members to the senate. But Domitian's attitude to republican titles of this type was simply foolish. Assuming a title only to abandon it meant that all he achieved was a loss of good will without increasing his power.

In the same vein, he renamed two months of the year,[8] with September becoming *Germanicus* and October *Domitianus*; he insisted on being accompanied by twenty-four lictors, twice the regular number, so it seems,[9] and went so far as to include amongst the lictors a number of Roman knights selected by lot together with other attendants, all bearing military spears (*Dom.* 14.3). Just as offensive was his attitude to the imperial cult. Titus had already been responsible for one innovation, in granting divine honours to his sister Domitilla as well as to his father Vespasian. Domitian went further, in that he deified his brother Titus and also his niece Julia.[10] As well, the house where he was born was converted into a temple for the Flavian family, the *Templum gentis Flaviae*; according to Statius, he 'founded a sacred shrine for his eternal family' (*Silvae* 5.1.240–1), whilst, not to be outdone, Martial described the building as the 'towering glory of the Flavian family [which] shall last as long as the sun and the stars and the light that shines on Rome' (9.1.8–9). So the aristocracy as a whole could not have failed to recognize his conception of an emperor's role.

A highly tendentious version of the atmosphere permeating Domitian's senate appears in Pliny, so tendentious that it is difficult to assess its worth as historical evidence. Pale and apprehensive (*Ep.*

162

8.14.8), no senator there dared open his mouth (*Pan.* 76), and any who were not his favourites he hated, treating them like slaves (*Pan.* 62.3, 68.2). Those admitted to the palace were no better off. There he plotted the massacre of the most distinguished members of the aristocracy; locked in by walls and treachery, he provoked terror in those he admitted as well as in those he excluded (*Pan.* 48.3–5, 49.1). Now this assessment was delivered before Trajan's senate and before Trajan himself, an emperor not only probably related to the Flavians,[11] but also one whose administrative policies were similar to Domitian's and, in many ways, a continuation of them. Any difference was superficial. Both sought to reduce the senate's real power and, at the same time, to pay a certain amount of lip-service to its traditional significance. But Domitian was doubly unfortunate. Apparently unable or unwilling to communicate effectively with individual senators, with people whose background and education were similar to his own, he completely lacked the diplomatic skills of Titus and had inherited none from those expert practitioners Vespasian and Sabinus I; worse still, he left no heir to deify him and so, unlike Nerva, he was not able to 'guide' the literary tradition to the 'correct' interpretation of events.

Consulship

He did make concessions to senatorial opinion. Consider his attitude to the consulship. Of all the official posts surviving from the republic, this was the one most prized by senators; to be granted three of them was the highest distinction available to someone not a member of the imperial family (*Ep.* 2.1.2).

During the reigns of Vespasian and Titus, members of the family had held all but six of the twenty-four 'ordinary' consulships available.[12] Those who held this office were the senior consuls, two being appointed each year; after a brief tenure, they were replaced by up to ten 'suffect' consuls. Pliny bewails the consistent tenure of the ordinary consulship by the Flavians – it was the result of 'their wretched ambition to match their lifelong power with a perpetual consulship ... [and] to appropriate every year and pass on the official purple only when its lustre was tarnished after use' (*Pan.* 58.4). So the policy of excluding virtually all non-Flavians from this prestigious post was resented. However, alluding to Trajan's alleged reluctance to hold the post, Pliny enthusiastically proclaimed that now 'ordinary people enjoyed the honour of opening the year and heading the official calendar, and this too was proof of liberty restored' (*Pan.* 58.3). But, unlike Vespasian and Titus, Domitian did precisely this. Presumably some senators appreciated it.

For the first two years of his reign, his practice was much the same as Vespasian's – in 82 and 83 he held the ordinary consulship with two relatives, Petillius Cerialis and Flavius Sabinus (IV), and, at the same time, three well-known Flavian supporters were granted suffect consulships – Fabricius Veiento, Vibius Crispus and Pompeius Silvanus (who died before assuming office) – each for the third time.[13] During the next five years (84–8), he abandoned Vespasian's practice and allowed Flavians to hold only five of the ten posts available: the rest were distributed with some care, to a senator of provincial origin (Aurelius Fulvus), two to 'new men' (Oppius Sabinus and Minicius Rufus) and two to eminent patricians (Volusius Saturninus and Cornelius Petronianus). His determination to allow 'ordinary people to open the year' was particularly obvious in 85, when a close relative and friend (*Hist.* 4.68) Arrecinus Clemens,[14] who was about to be appointed city prefect, had to be content with a suffect consulship and play second fiddle to a senator from Nemausus.

During the last eight years of the reign, he departed even further from Vespasian's norm: Flavians held only four of the sixteen ordinary consulships, three of them falling to Domitian himself and the other to Flavius Clemens (brother of Sabinus IV). After 84, then, Domitian completely abandoned Vespasian's practice and regularly allowed a clear majority of non-Flavian senators to 'open the year and head the official calendar'. According to Pliny's argument, this should have been proof of liberty restored. Yet, as far our evidence goes, it had no effect on Domitian's reputation.

There were other criteria for assessing an emperor's relationship with the senate. In the *Panegyricus*, Pliny praised Trajan for

> offering young men of noble birth the position which was their family right. . . . The light of the nobility is not dimmed by Caesar but made to shine more brightly; at least the grandsons of great men, the descendants of liberty, are restored to their ancestral glory.
>
> (69.5)[15]

Domitian did this too; candidates from senatorial and, in particular, patrician families were highly favoured when 'recommendations' for the ordinary consulship were required.

Hopkins has shown recently that, in the first two centuries of the empire, well over half and at times three-quarters of the ordinary consuls were descended from consuls.[16] This was certainly the case in Domitian's reign: of the thirty ordinary consuls of his reign, all but seven had consular fathers and, for five of these seven, we have no evidence at all of their origin.[17] As for patricians, the proportion is also significant: only ten were not of that rank, and two of these may well have been adlected patricians by Vespasian, viz. T. Aurelius Fulvus, father and son. As well, one of Domitian's ordinary consuls (Ser. Cornelius Dolabella Petronianus) was descended from a patrician family of the republic.[18] Inevitably, a few patricians had to be content with a suffect consulship, but, in each case, they held office, not at any time of the year, but immediately after the *ordinarii*, both of whom were also patricians – e.g. in 94, M. Lollius Paullinus D. Valerius Asiaticus followed the ordinary consuls L. Nonius Calpurnius and T. Sextius Magius Lateranus (similarly in 87 and 95).[19]

These senators, then, had no cause for complaint. At the very least, Domitian was trying not to offend this influential group. They were, in Hopkins's language, the grand set, aristocrats who had been given rapid promotion, from praetor to consul, in perhaps three rather than thirteen years; they had had no time to govern an imperial province, command a legion or to gain experience. The power set did that. The irony is that, whilst the early emperors did their best to dispense with the grand set, Domitian positively encouraged them, without, of course, giving them any real power. The most startling example of this occurred in 87 and 88.

On 13 January 87, C. Calpurnius Piso Crassus Frugi Licinianus (*PIR*[2] C 259) became suffect consul, replacing Domitian and holding the post with another patrician, L. Volusius Saturninus, who may well have been married to Calpurnius's cousin, Licinia Cornelia.[20] In the following year, a similar award was made to Calpurnius's brother, Libo Frugi[21] (*PIR*[2] L 166). Given their pedigree and the family's history, Domitian's decision to grant them the *fasces* is quite remarkable. Apart from the fact that they were descended from Pompey and Crassus, their father was one of the four sons of M. Licinius Crassus Frugi (L 190), consul in 27, and of Scribonia (S 211), both of whom were put to death by Claudius *c*. 46 together with one of the four sons, Cn. Pompeius Magnus (P 477).[22] Of the surviving three, M. Licinius Crassus Frugi (L 198: ordinary consul in 64 and father of the consuls of 87 and 88) was killed by Nero towards the end of his reign, L. Calpurnius Piso Frugi Licinianus (C 300: the Piso adopted by Galba) perished with him in 69 (*Hist.* 1.44) and Crassus Scribonianus (L 192) was assassinated in 70.

The consul of 87 did his best to live up to his pedigree. After a peaceful existence as part of Domitian's grand set, he conspired against Nerva and was banished to Tarentum (Dio 68.3.2: *Epit. de Caes.* 12.6); conspired against Trajan and was banished to an unknown island (Dio 68.16.2) and was killed by one of Hadrian's procurators 'whilst trying to escape' (*SHA, Hadr.* 5.5). Some might regard his brother as more successful: his grandson was the emperor Marcus Aurelius.

Domitian's appointment of Calpurnius Crassus as consul parallels his promotion of Salvidienus Orfitus and Helvidius (Priscus), for their fathers too had been executed by former emperors, a factor that might well render the sons suspect to an emperor such as Domitian. But a senator with the pedigree of Calpurnius and his brother was a far more dangerous prospect, as Nerva, Trajan and Hadrian soon discovered. Even the careful editing of material by post-Domitianic historians was unable to conceal the apparently genuine efforts he made to come to terms with (rather than execute) senators of patrician rank. Few other emperors were so patient.

He resorted to other measures to gain support in the senate. A number of his suffect consuls (and also one ordinary consul) had had a particularly long praetorian career, well over the legal minimum of twelve years. We have evidence of thirteen such appointments.[23] Two in particular are worth noting – Arulenus Rusticus (*PIR²* J 730), already a praetor at the time of the civil war (69), did not become consul until the last four months of 92: Manlius Valens (M 163), commanding a legion *c.* 50 (before Domitian was born), became ordinary consul in the last year of his reign, some forty-six years later. So it could well be that Domitian was trying to win supporters from the disappointed, those who had been passed over for one reason or another; Rusticus, for instance, was a committed member of what passed for the opposition. On the other hand, the selection of Manlius Valens is incredible. He was 89 (Dio 67.14.5). In view of the emperor's deteriorating relationship with the aristocracy during the 90s, Syme's explanation, that 'selection of that relic could scarcely have been taken by the high assembly as other than affront and contempt', could well be the right one, though it has been suggested, less convincingly, that honouring the old man should have won him some sympathy in senatorial circles.[24]

On the other hand, such 'overdue' promotions may not have been uncommon. As there were seventeen praetors each year (under Domitian) but only seven to eight consuls, a number of senators must always have experienced difficulties in gaining the *fasces* at the legal minimum age, even if we allow for premature deaths and for those who had no interest in pursuing a senatorial career beyond the praetorship. So, whilst the legal minimum age for the consulship was 42, the actual age may always have been somewhere between 50 and 55, for instance. We simply do not know; and, after all, age is one of the essential demographic variables.[25] Furthermore, it is simply fortuitous that, for Domitian's consuls, a precise date can be assigned to their praetorship. Usually, there is simply no way of acquiring such information, short of a chance reference in our literary sources (as with Rusticus). But, in 73/4, a number of adlections were made, many of them to the praetorship, and these were recorded on inscriptions; all would have been eligible for the consulship in Domitian's reign. An approximate age of 30 in 73 can be assigned to these *adlecti*, and the consular *fasti* for Domitian's reign are fairly full. At no other time, however, can the length of so many praetorian careers be attested, since adlections are usually both far fewer and not dateable. If we had a similar quantity of data from other reigns, perhaps Domitian's promotions may not have been as unusual as appears. But, even if they were, any gratitude that resulted did not help his reputation.

Other senators were also awarded belated consulships by Domitian, e.g. when a son gained the *fasces* fairly soon after his father. The normal interval between the consulships of father and son should be about twenty-five to thirty years[26] but, in some cases, the interval is substantially less than that, suggesting that either the son was favoured with an early consulship (and this would have been less likely, given the number of praetorian candidates [seventeen] theoretically seeking the seven or so consulships available each year), or else, more probably, that the father's post was belated. With Domitian, the latter is almost certain, since the fathers seem to have been the first in their family ever to enter the senate. Ti. Julius Celsus Polemaeanus, for example, first senator in his family, obtained the *fasces* in 92 and his son eighteen years later; similarly with C. Cilnius Proculus and his son who were consuls (for the first time) in 87 and 100. Seven other Domitianic consuls fall into this category.[27] Once again, he was trying to gain supporters in the aristocracy by admitting new families to the senate and promoting them quickly.

A number of his suffect consuls were closely associated with the so-called opposition, a remarkable circumstance, one would have thought, in view of his suspicious nature. At times, associating with senators such as Barea Soranus and Thrasea Paetus was not to be discouraged – Vespasian numbered them amongst his friends (*Hist.* 4.7), but, once the political climate changed, such friendships were sundered. At the first hint of the Pisonian conspiracy, Titus had to divorce Soranus's niece (Marcia Furnilla) and Vespasian ceased to be an *amicus* of that family.[28] Even when he became emperor, he made no attempt to conciliate such people, for their opposition to the dynastic policy he openly proclaimed (Dio 65.12.2; *Vesp.* 25) put them beyond the pale. So Helvidius Priscus was executed (*Vesp.* 15).

Domitian's attitude, on the other hand, is less clear. His first attested association with them occurred around the time of Vespasian's accession, when he married Domitia Longina. The political advantages of an alliance with the daughter of the great Corbulo were not to be ignored – nor were the numerous connexions her family had with the opposition.[29]

But, even after 81, his attitude to them remained unchanged in that he promoted to the consulship a number of senators with 'unsatisfactory' pedigrees. Early in the reign, Salvidienus Orfitus (*PIR*[2] C 1445) was awarded a suffect consulship, even though Nero had executed his father (C 1444) for treason. Around the same time, the son of the Helvidius Priscus whom Vespasian had put to death was similarly honoured by Domitian. Observe the difficulty Pliny had in explaining away the younger Helvidius's acceptance of a consulship from Domitian – 'fear of the times made him hide his name and virtues in retirement': *Ep.* 9.13.2). Given his father's fate and the family connections of his stepmother Fannia, daughter of Thrasea Paetus, it is remarkable that Helvidius sought and accepted a consulship from the son of the emperor who had ordered his own father's death and even more remarkable that Pliny could use the word *secessus* ('retirement') in this context. But this was not all. In 85, Helvidius's son-in-law M. Annius Herennius Pollio (almost certainly married to Helvidius's daughter Helvidia[30]) also received the *fasces*.

He persisted with this practice, even after the revolt of Saturninus in 89, wrongly assumed to mark the inauguration of a 'reign of terror'. In 92, Arulenus Rusticus, a well-known adherent of Stoicism and a pupil of Thrasea Paetus, became suffect consul; as tribune in

66, he had intended to veto the senate's condemnation of Thrasea, but the latter forbade him to do so. Domitian was not deterred: as well as promoting Arulenus, he may have made a similar award to Arulenus's outspoken brother, Junius Mauricus.[31] Nor did this mark the end of this apparent flirtation with the opposition, for yet another friend of Thrasea, T. Avidius Quietus, received the *fasces* as late as 93.[32]

All this is variously instructive. Domitian's attitude to the senators with links to the opposition differed from his father's. That careful administrator took few risks and so it is hardly surprising that no one from the opposition received the *fasces* from him. He would not have agreed with what happened in the 80s and 90s. Quite deliberately, Domitian offered and continued to offer potential opponents one of the highest posts available. Less clear is his motivation. Perhaps he wished to compromise them in the eyes of their supporters, perhaps he merely hoped to gain their support. In any case, his behaviour here is consistent with his attitude to other groups within the senate. Again, it did not help his reputation.[33]

THE POWER SET

Senators had reason to dislike Domitian: for one thing, he accentuated, though he did not initiate, their loss of real power. If Hopkins is correct in seeing the disappearance of hereditary succession to senatorial status,[34] then factors other than direct imperial intervention were in operation – low fertility rate, sons of senators opting out of politics (despite imperial assistance in meeting the financial qualifications of the census) or the general expense of a senatorial career.[35] We have no evidence that Domitian ever came to their aid; on the contrary, he may have deliberately exacerbated the situation by reviving the old custom by which quaestors were obliged to provide special games – and pay for them as well (*Dom.* 4.1). But this was not the whole story. Emperors such as Domitian sought to diminish senatorial power by direct action, assigning real power to fewer senators (Hopkins's power set) and creating new posts that were allocated to equestrians or freedmen but rarely to senators.

Domitian was heavily involved in the development of a power set. He would have concurred with Louis XIV's observation on appointees of this sort: 'since they were conscious of who they were, they had no higher aspirations than those I chose to permit'.[36]

Consider his attitude to senatorial proconsulships. Each year of his reign, proconsuls were appointed to the eight provinces of praetorian status (e.g. Baetica, Cyprus, Pontus–Bithynia) and one each to Africa and Asia, both governed by ex-consuls. The former posts were not particularly prestigious and their holders 'seldom came to anything'.[37] An examination of known praetorian proconsuls between 70 and 81 confirms Syme's statement: of the twenty attested, just three went on to a consulship and only one of these (i.e. Pliny's consular colleague, Cornutus Tertullus)[38] to an imperial province. Under Domitian, the position was quite different: twenty-five are known, twelve of whom became consuls (and eleven of them received the *fasces* from Domitian) and six subsequently governed imperial consular provinces (Britain, Cappadocia–Galatia, Syria [twice], Lower Moesia and both Germanies).[39] Apparently, there were a number of senators who, for various reasons, had no wish to pursue a career of (essentially) provincial administration, preferring the comfort and atmosphere of the capital; but they would have been quite prepared to spend one year as proconsul in a minor province, a not unrewarding experience financially, and then retire to Rome. They probably constituted a majority in the senate, and, convinced that they were entitled to the status of proconsul, would have resented Domitian's undermining of their 'rights'.[40] In this context, it is worth remembering that, around the end of the first century, only 155 posts of all kinds were available to senators in any one year, that at least fifty of them (i.e. the 'imperial' as distinct from the 'senatorial' appointments) were normally held for three years;[41] and that therefore, each year, only 17 per cent of senators (whether they were part of the power set or not) could possibly receive a post of any kind.

Domitian believed that administrators should be appointed on the basis of neither birth nor efficiency, but on trust, i.e. those he could trust, those who 'had no higher aspirations than those he chose to permit'. Such officials constituted the power set, others were eased out, even out of posts with more prestige than power.

Far more significant was his policy towards senators of eastern origin, some of whom moved into the power set after the upheaval of Saturninus's revolt. Firstly, some general observations; given the period of at least seventeen years between quaestorship and consulship, it follows that the full impact of an increase of senators from one particular area could often not be realized during the reign of the emperor responsible for their admission to the senate. This is particularly true of Vespasian and Domitian, in view of the length of their reigns: Domitian's was the longer, fifteen years and five days. His father had contracted a variety of debts in the east for the support he had received in 69; hence the adlection in 73/4 of a number of easterners. But they could receive little more from him, and, with the accession of Domitian, there were no signs of a change in policy, not even when the eastern *adlecti* came of consular age *c.* 85/6. Immediately after Saturninus's revolt, though, two of them, Ti. Julius Celsus Polemaeanus and A. Julius Quadratus, were appointed to the 'military' provinces of Cilicia and Lycia–Pamphylia,[42] posts of importance in themselves and even more so as they usually led to a consulship.[43]

Far more momentous was the promotion now accorded to another senator from Asia Minor, Ti. Julius Candidus Marius Celsus,[44] the first easterner to be appointed to a military province of consular rank. He received Cappadocia–Galatia at the same time as Polemaeanus and Quadratus were appointed to the lower-ranking military provinces. The full ramifications of his appointment have only recently been realized. Candidus was long thought to have been of western origin (*PIR*[2] J 241) and hence promotion to Cappadocia–Galatia was not rated as unusual. As well, his term was thought to have begun in 87,[45] but it, too, must be assigned to the July following Saturninus's revolt (i.e. July 89).[46] It follows, then, that, whilst the admission of the three to the senate was due to Vespasian, the sort of senatorial post to which they were assigned was the decision of Domitian, and one probably not made on the grounds of efficiency. He sought senators he could trust.

Of considerable importance is his policy towards new senators or *novi homines*, i.e. those who were the first of their family to gain admission to the senate. An emperor could admit them in two different ways: he could assign them one of the twenty preliminary posts (vigintivirate) available each year, thereby making them eligible to stand for election to the quaestorship and so a seat in the senate; or else, more rarely, he could (as censor) revise the senatorial roll, admitting (or 'adlecting') them immediately to whatever level he thought appropriate. Since twenty quaestors were needed each year, admission to the vigintivirate all but guaranteed the candidate a place in the senate. Consequently, so it seems,[47] an emperor's policy towards new senators is most accurately determined by looking, not so much at those of them who held the quaestorship in the course of the reign, but rather at the ones then allocated a place in the vigintivirate. Thus a senator elected to the quaestorship early in Trajan's reign must have received the vigintivirate from Domitian and would therefore be best regarded as a Domitianic appointee, whereas a quaestor of 82 or 83 must have held his vigintivirate post late in Vespasian's reign and would have to be included amongst that emperor's *novi homines*.

On this basis, it seems that Vespasian admitted between six and thirteen new men of eastern origin, Domitian perhaps as many as twenty-four and Trajan no more than thirteen and possibly as few as six.[48] Hence we must firmly reject the standard view that 'the influx of orientals . . . does not become really important before Trajan'.[49] Domitian, and not Trajan, was directly responsible for the influx of easterners in the latter part of the first century. He was determined to change radically the composition of the senate.

Some of the newcomers merit a brief examination. One of the few easterners he adlected to the senate was the capable Lycian fleet commander, M. Arruntius Claudianus (*AE* 1972: 572; 1974: 619).[50] He was part of the power set. Utterly different was the aged 'King Alexander' (C. Julius Alexander)[51] together with his two sons, C. Julius Agrippa and C. Julius Alexander Berenicianus. They constituted an interesting group. Late in the reign, possibly *c.* 93/4, the father was adlected (presumably to praetorian rank), with the two sons becoming *vigintiviri* around the same time, and, although the appointments were essentially honorific, they were also indicative of Domitian's quest for support in non-traditional areas during the 90s, among princelings of the east, men of enormous wealth, power and influence in their own districts. Alexander was one of the four consular cousins of the famous and wealthy C. Julius Severus of Ancyra whose relatives and ancestors included, according to *OGIS* 544, two kings (Attalus and Deiotarus) and two tetrarchs of Galatia together with four consular cousins (C. Julius Quadratus Bassus, Julius Aquila and Claudius Severus as well as Alexander).[52] It was under Domitian that senators of this sort gained admission, and under Trajan that some of them joined the power set.

In at least four areas, substantive changes occurred in the actual composition of the senate during his reign.[53] A comparison with the position under Vespasian is most instructive. With Domitian, the proportion of non-Italians increased from 33 per cent to 38 per cent, whilst, amongst the Italians themselves, central Italy's pre-eminence was weakened, from 62 per cent to 57 per cent. On the other hand, the percentage of senators of Spanish and Gallic origin amongst the non-Italians dropped from 76 to 60, with a corresponding increase in easterners (15 per cent to 26 per cent). But a decrease in numbers under Domitian did not always result in loss of power.[54] Consider the composition of his general staff, consisting of the consular governors of the military provinces where the legions were stationed. In 82/3, six are attested, four Italians (Caesennius Gallus, Corellius Rufus, Civica Cerialis and Atilius Rufus) and two westerners (Julius Agricola and Funisulanus Vettonianus),[55] whilst his last appointees (96/7) included one Italian ([Metilius] Nepos), one easterner (Julius Mar[inus?]) and four westerners (Licinius Sura, Trajan, Pompeius Longinus and Cornelius Nigrinus) with one of unknown origin (Pomponius Bassus).[56] So the 5 per cent decrease in the proportion of Italian senators becomes significant when their concomitant substantial loss of power is considered; yet the lower proportion of senators of Gallic and Spanish origin was accompanied, not by a decrease, but instead by a significant increase in real power. Obviously, Domitian's role was paramount: as well as diminishing the influence of the senate as a body, he increased enormously the importance of those in it he trusted, the power set.

Whatever the size of any aristocracy, real power inevitably becomes concentrated into the hands of comparatively few. The Roman empire was no exception as the size of the power set indicates. That intermarriage was an integral part of the narrowing of the power basis has long been an assumption, but only an assumption, since, unfortunately, not a great deal of work had been done in this area until recently. Now, however, much more is known about the marriage patterns and partners[57] of Domitian's senators and, in particular, about the extent of intermarriage within the power set.

Now the senate consisted of some six hundred members, and it must be admitted that, in comparatively few instances, do we know even the name of a senator's wife; and, of these few, sometimes that is all we do know, e.g. Cornelia Ocel[ina] and Arrecinus Clemens (Raepsaet-Charlier, 1987: 257–8) or Attica and Fabricius Veiento (135–6), or perhaps her municipal status as well, e.g. Salvius Liberalis's wife Vitellia Rufilla, a *flamen* at Urbs Salvia (641). But, in at least twenty-eight instances, epigraphic or some other indication exists of the social status as well as the family connections of both the partners. These have been arranged in alphabetical order, according to the female partner.

1 **(Aelia) Domitia Paulina**. Sister of the future emperor Hadrian, military tribune late in Domitian's reign and later governor of Lower Pannonia, she married the consul of 90, L. Julius Ursus Servianus, governor of Upper Germany and Pannonia and adopted son of L. Julius Ursus, Domitian's relative, praetorian prefect and consul in 84 (35–7).

2 **Annia Quartilla**. Daughter of the Flavian senator Ap. Annius Marsus, she married Galeo Tettienus Severus M. Eppuleius Proculus Ti. Caepio Hispo, proconsul of Baetica in 95, consul in 102 or 103 and later proconsul of Asia, who had been adopted by Galeo Tettienus Petronianus, consul in 76.

3 **(Arria)**. Presumed sister of M. Arrius Flaccus, consul in 79, she married L. Nonius Calpurinus Asprenas Torquatus, patrician, proconsul of Africa c. 92; their son was ordinary consul in 94 (111–12).

4 **Ar(ria) Calp(urnia)**. Daughter of L. Nonius Calpurnius Asprenas Torquatus, patrician, proconsul of Africa c. 92, and sister of L. Nonius Calpurnius Torquatus Asprenas, patrician, ordinary consul in 94, she married C. Bellicus Natalis Tebanianus, consul in 87: both their sons held the *fasces*, one being suffect consul in 118, the other ordinary in 124 (113–15).

5 **Arria Fadilla**. Daughter of Arrius Antoninius, proconsul of Asia in 78/9 and consul II in 97, she married P. Julius Lupus, consul in 98,[58] after the death of her first husband, T. Aurelius Fulvus (ordinary consul in 89), and so provided a link between the Flavians and the 'five good emperors', since her son by her first husband was the future emperor Antoninus Pius (115–16).

6 **Caecilia (Maior)**. Presumed daughter of Cn. Caecilius Simplex, consul in 69, she married Ti. Julius Candidus Marius Celsus, consul in 86 and governor of Cappadocia–Galatia from 89 to 91; their two (or three) sons were senators (152–3).

7 **Caecilia (Minor)**. Another presumed daughter of Cn. Caecilius Simplex, she married L. Julius Mar[inus], consul in 93 and governor of Lower Moesia from 95 to 97: their son, L. Julius Marinus Caecilius Simplex, was governor of Lycia–Pamphylia from 96 to 98 (153–4).

8 **Caepia Procula**. Daughter or sister of Galeo Tettienus . . . Ti. Caepio Hispo, proconsul of Baetica in 95, consul in 102 or 103 and later proconsul of Asia, she married M. Aquillius Regulus, presumably consul early in Domitian's reign[59] (162–3).

9 **Corellia Hispulla**. Daughter of Q. Corellius Rufus, governor

of Upper Germany from 79 to 82, she married L. Neratius Priscus, consul in 97, later governor of Lower Germany (98–100) and Pannonia (102–4) and brother of L. Neratius Marcellus, governor of Britain (101–3). Their son was ordinary consul in 122 (237–40).

10 **Dasumia Polla.** Daughter or sister of L. Dasumius Hadrianus, suffect consul in 93 and proconsul of Asia *c.* 106, her husbands included Cn. Domitius Tullus, proconsul of Africa in 85, as well as, possibly, P. Tullius Varro, proconsul of Macedonia late in Vespasian's reign and L. Catilius Severus, quaestor late in Domitian's reign and later governor of Cappadocia–Armenia and Syria (272–4).

11 **Domitia Vettilla.** Daughter of L. Domitius Apollinaris, governor of Lycia–Pamphylia from 93 to 95, she married the patrician L. Neratius Marcellus, consul in 95 and governor of Britain from 101 to 103: Marcellus's uncle and adoptive father (M. Hirrius Fronto Neratius Pansa) had been consul in Vespasian's reign (then governor of Cappadocia–Galatia from 77 to 79), his natural father (L. Neratius Priscus) consul in 87 (then governor of Pannonia from 91 to 93)[60] and his brother (also L. Neratius Priscus) consul in 97 (then governor of Lower Germany from 98 to 100 and of Pannonia from 102 to 104) (293–4).

12 **(Fabia?) Fabulla Asiatica?** Daughter or possibly sister of M. Fabius Fabullus (a senator of praetorian rank in 69 and commander of the Vitellian legion *V Alaudae*: his subsequent career is unknown),[61] she married the patrician consul of 94, M. Lollius Paullinus D. Valerius Asiaticus Saturninus, later proconsul of Asia and ordinary consul, for the second time, in 125 (306–7).

13 **Funisulana Vettula.** Daughter or sister of L. Funisulanus Vettonianus, governor of Dalmatia, Pannonia and Upper Moesia continuously from 79 to 87 and then proconsul of Africa in 92, she married C. Tettius Africanus, prefect of Egypt in the first years of Domitian's reign – and, presumably, brother of L. Tettius Julianus, governor of Upper Moesia immediately after his relative Funisulanus, in 88 and 89 (341–2).

14 **Helvidia.** Daughter of Domitian's victim Helvidius Priscus, consul before 87, she seems to have been the wife of M. Annius Herennius Pollio, consul (together with his father P. Herennius Pollio) in 85 (354–5).

15 **(Julia).** Daughter of the Flavian general Cn. Julius Agricola, governor of Britain in the early part of Domitian's reign, she

married Cornelius Tacitus, legionary legate (presumably) in the early 90s,[62] consul in 97 and proconsul of Asia in 112 (362).

16 **Julia Frontina.** Daughter of Sex. Julius Frontinus, *comes* of Domitian during the Chattan war and proconsul of Asia in 85/6, she married Q. Sosius Senecio, governor of Belgica in 97 and ordinary consul in 99 (377–8).

17 **Julia Tertulla.** Daughter of C. Julius Cornutus Tertullus, proconsul of Narbonensis under Vespasian or Domitian and consul in 100, she married L. Julius Marinus Caecilius Simplex, governor of Lycia–Pamphylia from 96 to 98 (396).

18 **Julia Procula.** Presumed sister of C. Julius Proculus, *ab actis* of Domitian late in the reign and consul in 109, she married M. Flavius Aper, consul *c.* 103 (390–1).

19 **Laberia Mar(cia) Hostilia Crispina Moecia Cornelia.** Daughter of M'. Laberius Maximus, consul in 89 and son of Domitian's prefect of Egypt in 83, L. Laberius Maximus, she married Bruttius Praesens, military tribune of the *I Minervia c.* 93[63] and later governor of Cappadocia, Lower Moesia and Syria as well as proconsul of Africa (408–10).

20 **Licinia Cornelia Volusia Torquata.** First cousin, so it seems, of Lucius Volusius Saturninus, patrician and ordinary consul in 87 (and of his brother Quintus, ordinary consul in 92), she married the patrician C. Calpurnius Piso Crassus Frugi Licinianus, consul in 87 (420–3).

21 **(Metilia Maior).** Presumed sister of P. Metilius Nepos, consul in 91 and governor of Britain from 95 to 97, she married M. Atilius Postumus Bradua, proconsul of Asia in 94 (451–2).

22 **(Metilia Minor).** Another presumed sister of P. Metilius Nepos, she married the patrician ordinary consul of 86, Ser. Cornelius Dolabella Petronianus (452).

23 **Mummia Nigrina.** Wife of L. Antistius Rusticus, consul 90 and governor of Cappadocia–Galatia in 92 and 93, she was related (by marriage) to Q. Valerius Vegetus, consul in 91 (459–60).

24 **Pompeia Celerina.** Daughter (probably) of L. Pompeius Vopiscus C. Arruntius Catellius Celer, consul *c.* 77 and governor of Hispania Citerior from 85 to 89, her first husband seems to have been L. Venuleius Montanus Apronianus, consul in 92, and her second the consul of 98 (or 99), Q. Fulvius Gillo Bittius Proculus, adopted son of M. Fulvius Gillo, proconsul of Asia in 89/90 (507–9).

25 **Sergia Paulla.** Sister of L. Sergius Paullus, consul *c.* 70, she

married C. Caristanius Fronto, governor of Lycia–Pamphylia from 81 to 83 and consul in 90 (561–2).

26 **Sosia Polla**. Daughter of Q. Sosius Senecio, ordinary consul in 99, she married Q. Pompeius Falco, quaestor late in Domitian's reign, later governor of Lower Moesia and Britain as well as proconsul of Asia (576).

27 **Ulpia Marciana**. Sister of the future emperor Trajan, patrician and ordinary consul in 91, possibly governor of Pannonia c. 92 and of Upper Germany in 96, she married C. Salonius Matidius Patruinus, a senator of praetorian rank in Vespasian's reign and possibly governor of Upper Germany in 70/1 or in 82/3[64] (646).

28 **Valeria Vetilla**. Daughter of P. Valerius Patruinus, consul c. 82, then governor of Cappadocia–Galatia (?83–5) and Syria (86–8), she married L. Domitius Apollinaris, governor of Lycia–Pamphylia from 93 to 95 (609–10).

Various conclusions emerge. Apart from these twenty-eight, the only Domitianic senator actually attested as having copied Titus and Sabinus III and married into an equestrian family is Sex. Vettulenus Cerialis, proconsul of Africa (probably) in 83: his wife Lusia Paullina's father and brother were prominent equestrians (434–5). On the other hand, a member of Funisulanus Vettonianus's (13) family married the equestrian prefect of Egypt. Again, it is noticeable that members of the power set often tended to intermarry, viz. 1, 5, 6, 7, 9, 11, 13, 15, 16, 19, 21, 26 and 27 and that some of the links between these powerful families were complicated, viz. 2 and 8; 3 and 4; 16 and 26; 6, 7 and 17; 9, 11 and 28. Observe, for example, that the easterners (6 and 7) to whom Domitian turned after Saturninus's revolt, the first to be appointed to consular military provinces, probably married sisters; and that Corellius Rufus, the four Neratii, Domitius Apollinaris and Valerius Patruinus (9, 11 and 28), who between them governed some eight imperial consular provinces, were linked together in a fairly complicated marriage pattern.

EQUESTRIANS

Pflaum has argued that Domitian's reign was of primary importance in the development of the equestrian order and in the extension of its role to the detriment of senators and freedmen.[65] His reforms were continued by Trajan and redounded to the credit of Hadrian.

Of particular importance is Domitian's appointment of the equestrian Titinius Capito as *ab epistulis et a patrimonio* (*ILS* 1448). This was an innovation, for the brief experiment with the equestrian Sex. Caesius Propertianus (*ILS* 1447) under Vitellius had quickly been abandoned, with both Vespasian and Titus reverting to bureau-chiefs of freedman rank. He also created seven new equestrian posts, or, rather, they are first attested epigraphically in his reign;[66] Ti. Claudius Pollio (*ILS* 1418),[67] for instance, a Domitianic appointee, appears to have been the first *procurator Alpium Graiarum*. Another interesting appointment was that of L. Bovius Celer (*ILS* 1397)[68] as *procurator familiae gladiatoriae* at Alexandria, a new post that was, by its very nature, indicative of Domitian's determination to control personally every aspect of government, even the recruiting of gladiators in Egypt. But he was particularly concerned with this form of entertainment, as is shown by his erection of four gladiatorial training schools in Rome.[69] Again, he instituted the post of *procurator ad Mercurium* at Alexandria to ensure the provision and storage of an adequate food supply for the city, appointing to the post Sex. Attius Suburanus, who was later to be granted senatorial status and two consulships by Trajan.[70] His concern with the minutiae of administration together with the creation of new sources of power that led to him alone marked his reign out as the turning-point in the growth of the equestrian order's importance in the government of the empire.

At times, Domitian's attitude to the equestrian order and preference for officials of equestrian rank must have offended many senators. In political and administrative matters, he tended to ignore the traditional hierarchical distinctions between them and the equestrians. Now, whilst the differences between the constituent sections of the aristocracy should not be exaggerated,[71] certain niceties had to be observed.

The first 'incident' occurred less than a year after his accession. In August 82, he publicly promulgated a judgement of his privy council or *consilium* (held at the Alban villa, not in the palace at Rome) as to whether squatters could retain land they were occupying, and in the preamble he referred to the fact that he had 'assembled the excellent men from both orders'.[72] In one sense, there was nothing new in this. Senators and equestrians were appointed to the *consilium* according to the emperor's whim; this was no innovation of Domitian. But if the presence of equestrians was unexceptional, the emperor's phrase was less so. It was a public statement, made very early in the reign, and could well have offended senatorial dignity. The more sensitive members of the order would not have welcomed it.

Consistent with this was his rapid promotion of one of the imperial relatives, L. Julius Ursus. In quick succession, he passed from prefect of Egypt to prefect of the praetorian guard and from there (thanks to Domitian's *imperium*) to a consulship.[73] There was no adlection in his case: Domitian was censor in April 85 and not in 84.[74] In addition, Ursus was elevated not to quaestorian rank, as was customary, but almost immediately to the consulship. Within the space of less than one year, he had passed from the leading equestrian post to one of the most senior senatorial positions. Once again, tradition had been disregarded. Ursus's elevation was consistent with Domitian's creation of a power set, in that a more vigorous and reliable praetorian prefect was needed and needed at once; hence Ursus had to be quickly moved aside, whatever tradition demanded.

A few years later, his attitude was even more obvious in his appointment of a commander for the Dacian war. Without exception at this period, legions were commanded by a senatorial officer, the legionary legate, and the command of a number of legions in a war was, at this time, always given to a senator of consular rank. In the Judaean war, Nero had assigned three legions to Vespasian (*Hist.* 1.10), consul fifteen years before, and each legion was under the control of a less senior senator.[75] In the Dacian campaign, though, complete control was given to Domitian's praetorian prefect, the equestrian Cornelius Fuscus (*Dom.* 6.1).[76] This was an innovation. In 87/8, he went even further. The proconsulship of Asia was the most prestigious post available to a member of the senate, and, in that year, the incumbent was Civica Cerialis. For some reason, Domitian had him executed, and, to add insult to injury, he was replaced for the rest of his term by the equestrian procurator of Asia, C. Minicius Italus. It may well have been administrative common-sense, but one is entitled to wonder why Domitian did not resort to one of Civica's three senatorial assistants rather than appoint, even on a temporary basis, a member of the equestrian order.[77]

On these occasions, then, Domitian's lack of concern for senatorial sensitivities is evident. Tradition had given way to greater centralization of power in the hands of those the emperor felt he could trust. Another emperor may have attempted to sugar the pill. In effect, this was an indication of why Domitian failed as a politician. He lacked hypocrisy.

9

ARISTOCRACY II

RELATIONSHIP WITH THE SENATE

Domitian's unpopularity with the senatorial members of the aristocracy had a substantive basis – he executed at least eleven senators of consular rank and exiled many others; and, so it seems, he often had (what was for him) equally substantive reasons for his actions – they were guilty of treason. He took absolutely no notice whatsoever of repeated senatorial decrees that an emperor should not execute anyone of his own rank (Dio 67.2.4). The result was that his reputation suffered, especially amongst the senatorially biased sources, whether the reasons for the executions were valid or not.

Undoubtedly, Domitian's reputation was also damaged by his readiness to accept the information provided by informers or *delatores*. The name arose from the practice of giving the name (*delatio nominis*) of an alleged malefactor to the president of the appropriate *quaestio perpetua*. They were the curse of the judicial system. Tacitus put it more strongly: they were a class of men invented to destroy the state and never adequately controlled, even by penalties (*Ann.* 4.30). A number of emperors who at first discouraged them later found them useful, especially in times of financial crisis. Domitian was no exception. He too began by punishing false accusations, maintaining that not to punish informers only encourages them (*Dom.* 9.3), a remark recorded also by Dio (67.1.4). But, not long after the devaluation of 85, financial problems encouraged a change in that policy (*Dom.* 12.1–2): as Suetonius claimed earlier (3.2), Domitian became greedier through *inopia*, i.e. lack of money.

The identity of the informers is less easy to determine. The fullest account of their activities under Domitian appears in *Agricola* 45 –

armed men surrounding a senate where terrified members passed death-sentences desired by the emperor. But the only solid facts that emerge are the names of three informers (Baebius Massa, Mettius Carus and Catullus Messallinus[1]) and three victims (Helvidius, Herennius Senecio and Arulenus Rusticus). Other senators such as Regulus, Vibius Crispus and Fabricius Veiento may well have been *delatores* in other reigns, but there is no evidence that they engaged in similar activities under Domitian; on the other hand, amongst the guilty, we should probably include Palfurius Sura, Publicius Certus, Pompeius (possibly M. Pompeius Silvanus)[2] and Arrecinus Clemens (*Dom.* 11.1).

Senators obviously resented his growing readiness to resort to informers (and, ultimately, to banishments and executions); and, were this the explanation for the reputation he acquired, it would seem perfectly comprehensible to the modern observer with some regard for human life. But this was far less true of Roman society. It was militaristic, cruel and brutal. Public executions were regarded as necessary: thus, after Spartacus's rebellion, some six thousand slaves were crucified along the road to Capua (Appian, *BC* 1.120).[3] Disregard for human life was as apparent in individuals as it was in the governments that controlled them, and regularly seen in emperors and senators to whom ancient sources assign an excellent reputation. In his *Res Gestae*, Augustus boasted that he had 'captured about 30,000 slaves who had escaped from their masters [and that he had] handed them over to their masters for punishment' (25); further details are provided by Dio – those for whom no masters could be found were impaled (49.12.4). Another 'good' emperor, Trajan, provided public entertainment to celebrate his victory in Dacia: during the twenty-three days it lasted, ten thousand gladiators fought (Dio 68.15), and, presumably, some five thousand of them perished. Entertainment of this nature met with the approval not only of the 'common people' but also of senators such as Pliny, for it 'inspired [Trajan's] subjects to face honourable wounds and look with scorn on death, by exhibiting love of glory and desire for victory even in the persons of criminals and slaves' (*Pan.* 33.1). For Pliny, then, such a death could almost raise a slaves's status! Again, he saw no problem whatsoever in executing Christians who had broken the law (*Ep.* 10.96.3). The death penalty was regarded by senators as obnoxious only when applied to them.

On numerous occasions, Dio accuses Domitian of executing senators, at 67.3.3 (AD 83), 67.4.5 (84), 9.6 (before 89), 11.2–13 (89),

12.1–5 (91/2), 13.1–4 (93) and 14.1–3 (95). Similar, but undatable charges are made by Eutropius (7.23.2) and Orosius (7.10.2). Such vague allegations have minimal evidential value. There may have been one victim, there may have been one hundred. When no names are recorded, we are entitled to conclude that the charges are based possibly on fact but essentially on the hostile tradition, and reveal later generations' attitudes towards the memory of Domitian. No other deductions can reasonably be drawn from vague allegations of this sort.

In the minutes for the Arval Brothers for 22 September 87, reference is made to sacrifices held *ob detecta scelera nefariorum*, without any indication of the identity of the 'wicked men' or of their fate. There may, however, be a clue in the rather surprising selection of L. Minicius Rufus as ordinary consul for 88. As far as can be determined, he was a *novus homo*, whereas his counterparts in 86 and 87 (Ser. Cornelius Dolabella Petronianus and L. Volusius Saturninus) were patrician members of consular families. It has been suggested that the senator designated to the post for 88 may perhaps have perished before entering office, accused presumably of complicity in the *scelera nefariorum*, and that Rufus replaced him.[4]

More precise evidence is provided by Suetonius. In chapter 10 of his *Life of Domitian*, he attempts to show that the emperor's character declined from *clementia* to *saevitia* (10.1), and, as proof, names ten former consuls whom he executed. The implication of Suetonius's introduction has not always been stressed: the words 'he put to death many senators, including several ex-consuls' (10.2) indicate that only the most eminent of his senatorial victims will be named. We could add this to the vague statements of Dio, Eutropius and Orosius noted above, but with a similar note of caution, for no other senators are mentioned by name.

CONSULAR VICTIMS

C. Vettulenus Civica Cerialis, first of the three on Suetonius's list accused of plotting revolution, perished in 87/8 whilst proconsul of Asia and was replaced by an equestrian, C. Minicius Italus; so the argument that he was executed for being involved in Saturninus's revolt[5] can be safely disregarded, for it occurred in January 89. But that does not mean that the charge of *maiestas* was groundless. It might have been connected with an event not in Germany but in

Asia itself, the appearance of a 'false Nero' *c.* 88.[6] Little is known of the pretender's movements in 88, but it seems reasonable to suppose that he would not have avoided Asia, for it must have seemed ideal for his purposes. Cerialis could well have hoped that he and his support would wither away, and do so even more quickly if ignored. But masterly inactivity would not have been enough as far as the emperor was concerned – note how readily Trajan moved from Spain to Germany (*Pan.* 14.5) early in 89 to assist in suppressing Saturninus's revolt. With the memory of the September conspiracy still fresh in his mind, Domitian could well have regarded the instigator of such a policy as a *molitor rerum novarum* and accordingly had him executed.

Ser. Cornelius (Scipio) Salvidienus Orfitus, next on Suetonius's list, was also executed on a charge of planning revolution. His father, of the same name, had been one of Claudius's consuls (in 51, the year of Vespasian's consulship) and had held the proconsulship of Africa under Nero (61/2 or 62/3).[7] But, in 66, he was executed for allegedly 'leasing to certain states three shops that were part of his house near the Forum' (*Nero* 37.1); Dio has a similar report (62.27.1). The real reason may have been his patrician rank or his connexions with the 'opposition', for he was a grandson of Vistilia whose descendants included, as well as Corbulo who committed suicide in 66, the Q. Pomponius Secundus who was probably involved in Arruntius Scribonianus's conspiracy against Claudius, and the father of the P. Glitius Gallus who was exiled in 65.[8]

In his consular posts at least his career was remarkably similar to Vespasian's. The parallel with the Flavians is instructive. With immaculate timing, they had severed their ties with the 'opposition' (*Hist.* 4.7) once it became clear that friends like these would be fatal, to future preferment at the very least. The Orfiti were less politically aware. In the long term, though, they were the winners since a Ser. Cornelius Scipio Salvidienus Orfitus held the consulship in 110, 149 and 178. Given his pedigree, it ought to be remarkable that a son of Nero's Orfitus was elevated to the consulship by Domitian early in his reign (before 87).

Apart from Suetonius, the only ancient author to refer to him is Philostratus who links him with Rufus (perhaps L. Verginius Rufus) as being no more capable of planning treason[9] than Nerva (*Vita Apoll.* 7.8, 7.33, 8.7.10), a back-handed compliment in view of that senator's reputation for treachery. With Tigellinus, he had been rewarded for revealing details of the Pisonian affair: he had his bust placed in Nero's palace and triumphal statues of himself in the Forum (*Ann.* 15.72). But Philostratus's portrait of Orfitus is meant to be laudatory – he was not interested in wealth and was indifferent to public affairs. Yet that was the charge made against Flavius Clemens (*Dom.* 15.1). Such indifference could be used against senators by ill-natured opponents or by suspicious emperors as evidence of treason (e.g. *Ann.* 15.44). Quintilian objected to those who refused to participate in 'the administration of the state, from which those who are called philosophers have very far withdrawn themselves' (*Inst. Or.* 11.1.35). So non-participation could, if the emperor or one's opponents wished, be a serious matter indeed: Flavius Clemens's *inertia* was *contemptissima* (*Dom.* 15.1) and he was executed.

According to Philostratus (7.8), Orfitus was also thought to be a suitable candidate for imperial power, and, if this was known to Domitian, especially after 93 when he was particularly suspicious of the philosophic opposition, it is all but inevitable that a ruler such as he would connect an aristocrat's lack of interest in public office, his philosophic beliefs and his reputation for being *capax imperii*. Exile and death followed.

M'. Acilius Glabrio (*PIR*[2] A 67), third on Suetonius's list of alleged revolutionaries, was exiled by Domitian and later executed. Some believe that he was a Christian convert,[10] which might perhaps explain his fate, but the evidence is slight and we have no other indication of anti-imperial activities.

L. Aelius Lamia Plautius Aelianus was the most eminent of the consular victims;[11] according to Suetonius (*Dom.* 10.2), he perished because of his harmless witticisms directed against Domitian some years previously (*veteres et innoxios iocos*). Early in 70, when Vespasian was still in Egypt, Domitian had taken Aelius's wife Domitia Longina as his mistress, later marrying her (Dio 66.3.4). But Aelius kept his sense of humour if not his wife: his excellent singing voice, he said (*Dom.* 10.2), was the result of abstaining from sex and, when urged by Titus to remarry, asked whether he too was looking for a wife.

His was a noble family, for he was related to Ti. Plautius Silvanus Aelianus,[12] and the Plautii had long been patrons of the Flavians. His descendants included a son, L. Lamia Aelianus, ordinary consul in 116, a grandson (Lamia Silvanus) betrothed to Aurelia Fadilla (daughter of T. Aurelius Fulvus, later the emperor Antoninus Pius) and a daughter, Plautia, whose husbands were L. Ceionius

Commodus (*cos. ord.* 106), C. Avidius Nigrinus (*cos. suff.* 110) and Sex. Vettulenus Civica Cerialis (*cos. ord.* 106).[13] Small wonder, then, that Juvenal used his family as representative of Domitian's most noble victims (4.152).

Aelius Lamia had enjoyed Titus's favour in so far as his was by far the longest suffect consulship during the entire Flavian period. He is attested in office as early as 14 January 80 and was still there on 13 June, having had three different consular colleagues: normally at this time, the consular term was only two months.[14] Perhaps this would not have endeared him to Domitian, but, in itself, it is hardly an adequate explanation of his fate. Again, Domitian lacked a sense of humour: when his father had been treated with disrespect by Mucianus, a notorious homosexual, Vespasian laughed it off with the comment 'At least I am a man' (*Vesp.* 13). But Domitian was unable to cope with personal criticism of any sort. Even jokes about baldness are supposed to have offended him; he regarded any reference to it as an insult directed at him personally (*Dom.* 18.2). So it is not inconceivable that the ever suspicious Domitian could, in time of crisis such as the uncovering of a conspiracy (22 September 87) or during the executions of 93, imagine or be persuaded that apparently harmless jokes directed at an emperor should be taken seriously and especially so when coming from an aristocrat with imperial connections. After all, he had punished those publishing lampoons on distinguished people (*Dom.* 8.3), and, in any case, justification for firm action already existed: libellous verse had attracted the death penalty as early as the Twelve Tables (Cicero, *De Republica* 4.10.12) and Augustus had been the first (but not the only) emperor to apply the laws of treason (*maiestas*) to writings of this sort (*Ann.* 1.72). So there was ample precedent for Domitian to be 'persuaded' that Aelius's *iocos* were far from *innoxios*.

(L.) Salvius (Otho) Cocceianus[15] was put to death for celebrating the birthday of his paternal uncle, the emperor Otho (*Dom.* 10.3). Such remembrances were not, in themselves, unusual. Julius Caesar's birthday was officially celebrated after his death (Dio 47.18.5–6), as was that of other emperors; conversely, Domitian had forbidden memorial games on Titus's (Dio 67.2.6). Salvius was a consular patrician and well connected, a nephew of Otho and, to judge from his *cognomen* 'Cocceianus', of Nerva as well.[16] In view of the latter's popularity with the Flavians in general and with Domitian in particular, this should have stood him in good stead. But he would have done better to have heeded both parts of the advice given him by his uncle in 69 – 'My boy, this is my last charge to you; do not altogether forget, and do not too well remember, that you had a Caesar for an uncle' (Plutarch, *Otho* 16.2).

Mettius Pompusianus[17] was executed (*Dom.* 10.3) because (a) according to his horoscope, he would one day be emperor, (b) he carried with him a map of the world on parchment (painted on the walls of his bedroom, according to Dio 67.12.2), (c) he had with him speeches of kings and generals from Livy (also Dio) and (d) he called two of his slaves 'Mago' and 'Hannibal'. Few of those executed by Domitian have the details of their indictment (or at least some sort of reason for their deaths) recorded by both Suetonius and Dio; in this case, the latter also adds that Mettius was first banished to Corsica and then killed (67.12.2–3). Now after Vespasian, less superstitious than his son, had been warned about Mettius's horoscope, he made him consul nonetheless and (typically) reminded Mettius that he now owed him a favour (*Vesp.* 14). But Domitian was both superstitious and suspicious. It could well be that the details recorded by Suetonius and Dio were part of the charges officially brought against Mettius: perhaps it had been alleged that he was plotting to seize power, since he had a map outlining possible conquests, speeches at hand to urge on his warriors and their leaders, to say nothing of slaves with Punic names and a horoscope indicating that he would one day be emperor.[18]

Sallustius Lucullus[19] was executed for naming newly designed lances 'Lucullan' (*Dom.* 10.3). Nothing else is definitely known of him, but much has been conjectured. The most promising hypothesis centres on the unusually generous awards (*AE* 1951: 88) of three crowns and a silver spearshaft granted to Gaius Julius Karus for his activities in a *bellum Brittannicum* (sic). The legionary fortress at Inchtuthil had been demolished not long after the departure of Agricola, and Domitian moved the Roman forces in Scotland south. Let us assume that Lucullus was then governor and Karus one of his subordinates. Since many generals must have resented Domitian's rejection of expansionist warfare[20] and accordingly despised him, the governor of Britain more than most, Lucullus's objections may have been reported by Karus, with appropriate rewards and punishments following. As with Pompusianus, Suetonius may have had access to the charges officially laid against Lucullus and may be reporting one, but not all, of them.

Q. Junius Arulenus Rusticus and **Helvidius**, two of Domitian's consular victims, were members of the so-called 'philosophic opposition', senators who, despite that, had been elevated to consular rank by him.[21] Arulenus Rusticus was executed for 'publishing eulogies of Thrasea Paetus and Helvidius Priscus and for calling them the most upright of men' (10.3). Suetonius's account is not fully accurate: Tacitus (*Agr.* 2.1), Pliny (*Ep.* 7.19.5) and Dio (67.13.2) agree that it was Herennius Senecio who was executed for eulogizing Helvidius. But, that apart, it is clear that, not long after Agricola's death (23 August 93), Domitian's relationship with the opposition deteriorated, seven of them were brought to trial, three (Arulenus Rusticus, Senecio and Helvidius Priscus's son) were executed with the others being sent into exile. The younger Helvidius (*PIR*[2] H 60: his *cognomen* is nowhere attested) had been charged with composing a farce attacking Domitian's separation from his wife (10.4). It was cleverly chosen, for the chief characters were Paris and Oenone. She was Paris's first wife whom he had deserted for Helen and who, on learning that he had been wounded by an arrow, refused to return and cure him. The parallels are obvious – Paris is Domitian, Helen Julia and Oenone Domitia – and rendered all the more piquant by two factors: Paris was also the name of Domitia's alleged lover (*Dom.* 3.1) and Domitian himself was known to be particularly fond of archery (*Dom.* 19).

T. Flavius Sabinus, the last consular victim listed by Suetonius in *Dom.* 10, was executed because, at the consular elections, he had been announced not as 'consul' but as 'imperator' (10.4). He was also heir-apparent: perhaps that was enough for Domitian.[22]

M. Arrecinus Clemens and **T. Flavius Clemens**, two other victims of consular rank, are discussed separately by Suetonius in *Dom.* 11.1 and 15.1. We are told that the emperor was on the point of condemning Arrecinus (but not why, or, indeed, whether he actually did have him put to death) and that Flavius Clemens was executed on the slightest of suspicions. With regard to the latter, Dio adds that 'the charge was atheism, on which many others who drifted into Jewish ways were condemned' (67.14.1).

M?. Cornelius Nigrinus Curiatius Maternus has recently been seen as another of Domitian's consular victims, identified with the sophist Maternus (*PIR*[2] M 360) executed *c.* 91 (Dio 67.12.5) and with the Curiatius Maternus of Tacitus (*Dial.* 11).[23] It is just possible that Nigrinus served briefly in Syria (*AE* 1973: 283) in the latter half of 91, for there could be a very brief gap in the Syrian *fasti* between the terms of P. Valerius Patruinus (attested 7 November 88) and of A. Lappius Maximus (attested 12 May 91). But the hypothesis is not without its difficulties. Why should Suetonius omit such an illustrious consular 'victim'? It is more likely that Nigrinus served Domitian in some other capacity during the 90s and followed Lappius as governor of Syria, emerging as the mysterious commander of an army in the east whose activities were causing concern in Rome (*Ep.* 9.11.13).[24] Tacitus's Curiatius Maternus was probably his uncle, i.e. brother of Curiata, Nigrinus's mother.[25] Nigrinus should not be included amongst Domitian's consular victims.

Thus, of the twelve ex-consuls, three were charged with revolution (Cerialis, Orfitus and Glabrio), one with atheism (Flavius Clemens) and the rest with what Suetonius twice describes as 'trivial' matters (*tenuissima*: 15.1 and *levissima*: 10.2). On the surface, his description of the accusations levelled at the ex-consuls is completely at variance with his previous comment that the emperor's administration of justice was 'careful and conscientious' (8.1). Yet terms such as *tenuissima* and *levissima* are consonant with the post-Domitianic literary tradition and all part of the pattern of *vituperatio*[26] directed at Domitian by Nerva and his successors. Domitian was suspicious by nature and perhaps with justification: Suetonius reports his comment that princes are unfortunate in so far as no one believes in the existence of conspiracies against them unless they happen to be killed (*Dom.* 21). At least some of the ex-consuls may have been guilty of conduct any autocrat would interpret as treasonable: not every Domitianic senator would, for instance, have been as sensible or restrained as Trajan or Tacitus or Pliny in their remarks (before 96) on his 'cowardly' foreign policy. He erred, perhaps, in being consistent, in dealing as 'carefully and conscientiously' with senatorial malefactors as he did with those of lower status.

EXILES

As well as those whose execution is recorded in the sources, various members of the aristocracy were exiled[27] by Domitian. The sources refer to such action fairly frequently, though only rarely do they provide the names of the alleged victims, viz. Mettius Pompusianus to Corsica (Dio 67.12.4); Domitilla to Pandateria (Dio 67.14.2); Valerius Licinianus to Sicily (*Ep.* 4.11.1); and Salvidienus Orfitus (*PIR*[2] C 1445), Apollonius (*Vita Apoll.* 7.8) and Acilius Glabrio (*Dom.* 10.2) to unknown islands. According to Eusebius, the emperor banished countless prominent men early in the reign for no reason whatsoever (*Hist. Eccl.* 3. 17), a claim repeated and made more precise ('for those that have unlimited faith'[28]) in the *Chronicorum Canonum*, where 'numerous proscriptions' are assigned to the period 1 October 82/30 September 83. Dio has a similar report for the same period (67.3.3[1]). At this time, too, the paramours of the Vestal Virgins (Varronilla and the Oculata sisters) were merely banished and not, as was customary, beaten to death (*Dom.* 8.4), and Valerius Licinianus was equally fortunate, escaping the death penalty by a timely admission that he was one of Cornelia's lovers (*Dom.* 8.3; *Ep.* 4.11).

Many more banishments, it is alleged, occurred later. Yet it is difficult to assign names to the supposed victims, apart from (for the early years) the finance minister Tiberius Julius Aug. lib., one of his subordinates (*Silvae* 3.3.160–2), perhaps Dio Chrysostom, and just possibly Domitian's other senior freedman Tiberius Claudius Classicus, though there is no evidence as to his fate until his re-emergence in Nerva's reign. Epaphroditus, another prominent freedman, was also banished by Domitian (Dio 67.14.4), whilst the exile of Epictetus is probably to be assigned to 92/3 (*PIR*[2] E 74) and linked to one of the two expulsions of philosophers and astrologers: according to late sources, both groups were expelled in 88/9 and again in 93/4 (or 95/6)[29] and at least four names are known, viz. Junius Mauricus, Gratilla, Arria and Fannia (*Ep.* 3.11.3). Property was confiscated as well (*Dom.* 12.1; *Ep.* 7.19.6). Unusually, one might think, two of those banished in the 90s were Domitian's own supporters – C. Julius Bassus, exiled by Domitian even though he was one of his friends (*Ep.* 4.9.1)[30] and Baebius Massa, said to have been one of Domitian's *delatores* (Juv. 1.35), and relegated for extortion (*Ep.* 7.33.4).[31] Perhaps Domitian's reputation for scrupulous and conscientious administration of justice (*Dom.* 8.1) was not undeserved. Ultimately, many of those exiled were recalled by Nerva (Dio 68.1.2).

C. Salvius Liberalis Nonius Bassus,[32] we can be reasonably certain, was one of those, banished *c.* 87, to return on Domitian's death. The literary sources attest to his outspokenness as an advocate both in Vespasian's reign (*Vesp.* 13) and on his return from exile (*Ep.* 2.11.17). At least he was consistent. Members of the élite accused of robbing the provincials during their term as proconsul (or in other ways) could depend on his support in the 70s (Hipparchus: *Vesp.* 13) and in the 90s (Marius Priscus: *Ep.* 2.11.17), and any provincials daring to bring in such accusations received no mercy from this 'forceful and eloquent' speaker (*Ep.* 3.9.36), as the Baeticans seeking to arraign Caecilius Classicus soon found out (3.9.29–36).[33]

He was not without ability. An equestrian from Urbs Salvia in Picenum, he was adlected *inter tribunicios* by Vespasian and Titus in 73/4 and immediately promoted to praetorian rank, appointed legate of the *V Macedonica* in Moesia and then *legatus iuridicus* in Britain, being probably the first ever to hold this type of post in the empire: those appointed *iuridici* in Britain at this period were men of recognized legal ability.[34] On Domitian's accession, he was in Rome (*CIL* 6.2060), serving as one of the Arval Brothers, and was subsequently appointed to the proconsulship of Macedonia, probably for 83/4.[35] In Moesia and Macedonia, he was accompanied by his son, C. Salvius Vitellianus (*PIR*[1] S 117), attested (so it seems) as military tribune in the *V Macedonica* and as assistant (*legatus*) to the proconsul of Macedonia.[36] More famous was his cousin, L. Flavius Silva Nonius Bassus,[37] conqueror of Masada and holder of an ordinary consulship in Titus's reign, a rare honour indeed: ominously, perhaps, nothing is known of his career under Domitian.

The precise cause[38] of his exile is uncertain; it must have occurred after 87 (last appearance in the *Acta* of the Arvals during Domitian's reign). Presumably, he was either involved in the aftermath of the September 87 conspiracy or else condemned for extortion during his proconsulship.[39]

Whatever the reason, he retained his individuality. Back in Rome after Domitian's death, he was awarded the proconsulship of Asia, one of the most prestigious prizes left for a senator, but then declined it. Perhaps he was influenced by a sudden illness. On the other hand, it seems somehow perfectly consistent with the character of this outspoken senator whose frankness, especially when coupled with a rather flexible attitude to senatorial corruption, could (apart from any other reason) easily have caused him to fall foul of Domitian.

D. Plotius Grypus, suffect consul in 88, was almost certainly the brother of the city prefect [Plo]tius Pegasus (Juv. 4.77) and father of the Plotius Grypus in whose honour Statius wrote *Silvae* 4.9,[40] a fifty-five-line poem with references to the Sarmatian campaign of 92 (so written after the consulship of 88), and with indications that Grypus was a young man (so clearly he was not the consul of 88); for the latter would have been about 50 on reaching that post, having been adlected to the praetorship some eighteen years before.[41] On the other hand, given the rarity of the name, the relationship itself is all but certain.[42]

Statius's description of young Grypus contains no reference whatsoever to his consular father, even though the young man was very much a court favourite (4.9.15–18).[43] It is not impossible that his father had died after the belated consulship, but that would not have prevented Statius from mentioning him. The most likely explanation of the omission is that the elder Grypus had been exiled. Involvement in the revolt of Saturninus has been put forward[44] as a possible reason, but, were that true, it is highly unlikely that he would have escaped so lightly. Another possibility is a revival of the rivalry between him and Tettius Julianus that had seen Julianus dismissed and then reinstated as praetor in 70 (*Hist.* 2.89, 4.39). In 88, though, the position was vastly different: Julianus was the hero of Tapae, victor over the Dacians, whereas it had taken Grypus eighteen years to reach the consulship. Jealousy may have caused him to attempt to undermine his former rival, and failure led to his being banished. But since evidence is lacking, further speculation is pointless.

The **Mettii** of Arles definitely felt the force of Domitian's disfavour. Three generations are known.[45] M. Mettius Modestus (*PIR*[2] M 566), equestrian procurator of Syria under Claudius, seems to have left two sons who held important posts during Domitian's reign, viz. Mettius Modestus (M 565 and ?567), suffect consul in 82 (and possibly later governor of Upper Germany[46]) and M. Mettius Rufus (M 572), prefect of Egypt (*Dom.* 4.2: attested on 3.8.89 as well as in 91/2), and, earlier in the reign, prefect of the corn supply.[47] Furthermore, the latter's two sons held senatorial offices after Domitian's death and the return from exile of their father and uncle, C. Trebonius Proculus Mettius Modestus (governor of Lycia–Pamphylia from 99 to 102 and suffect consul in 103) and M. Mettius Rufus, proconsul of Achaia at an unknown date.[48]

During the 90s, the Mettii must have fallen into disfavour, for the consular Modestus was exiled (*Ep.* 1.5.5, 13) and, in a number of papyri, the name of his brother, the prefect, has been erased. Stein and others[49] have argued that the Mettius Modestus referred to by Pliny (1.5.5) as having been exiled by Domitian was the future Lycian governor, but his uncle, the consul of 82, is a far likelier candidate: Pliny describes Mettius as *optimus* ('eminent') and the tone of the latter suggests that the person exiled was a senior senator. Perhaps he and his brother had come to grief through involvement in the fall of Mettius Pompusianus (*PIR*² M 570), who was, presumably, one of their relatives.

SUMMARY

So Domitian's attitude to the aristocracy was that of a benevolent despot. Real power was concentrated in the hands of those he trusted, the power set, senators who seemed suitable because of their background (e.g. Ti. Julius Candidus Marius Celsus) or equestrians whose entire career depended on imperial whim (e.g. Titinius Capito). As for the rest, the grand set, harmless patricians (such as T. Sextius Magius Lateranus) were treated with deference and given ordinary consulships, unacceptable equestrians were 'promoted' to the senate (e.g. L. Julius Ursus), potential opponents were compromised with offers of a suffect consulship (e.g. T. Avidius Quietus) but executed if that did not prove satisfactory (e.g. Arulenus Rusticus); other unco-operative aristocrats, arraigned rightly or wrongly on a variety of charges, were put to death or exiled (e.g. Salvius Liberalis). But stress on this last measure results in an entirely unbalanced view of his relationship with the aristocracy. After all, Claudius executed 35 senators and 300 (or 221) equestrians (*Claud.* 29.2; *Apocol.* 13), yet was still deified by the senate.

10

CONCLUSION

ASSASSINATION

On 18 September 96, Domitian was murdered in a palace conspiracy
and replaced, on the very same day (*eodem die*), by one of his *amici*,
the senator M. Cocceius Nerva: the *Fasti* of Ostia record precisely
what happened.[1] It was not unplanned. According to Suetonius
(*Dom.* 17.1), when the plotters were hesitating about when and
how to kill him, they were approached by Domitilla's steward
Stephanus: for some days, he feigned an injury, covering his arm
with bandages so as to conceal a dagger. So it was not done on
the spur of the moment. There is no doubt that the conspirators
had the time to secure the support of Nerva and of the praetorian
guard. That they did so (as is generally assumed[2]) is by no means
certain.

Suetonius's account is surprisingly detailed, given the comparative
brevity of the *Life* as a whole. Chapter 14 begins with a reference
to the murderers – Domitian's intimate *amici* and *liberti* as well as
his wife – and proceeds to explain that Domitian was hated for
the reasons given in the preceding four chapters, viz. executing
senators (10, 11), rigorous enforcement of his financial policy
(12) and increasing arrogance (13). What persuaded them to act
when they did was his execution of two of his courtiers, Flavius
Clemens and Epaphroditus. Dio's account is supportive and he
includes Glabrio's execution in the preceding year as another
factor. But there are discrepancies. Each gives a list of conspirators.
Stephanus and Maximus (one of Parthenius's freedmen) appear
on both; Suetonius has Satur (one of the *cubicularii*), Clodianus
(a *cornicularius*) and an unnamed gladiator, Dio the *cubicularius*
Sigerius and the *a libellis* Entellus. But, whereas Dio (67.15.1) and

193

the later historians name the *a cubiculo* Parthenius as the instigator of the plot and as one of the actual murderers (*interfector Domitiani*: Eutropius 8.1), Suetonius is a little more reticent, portraying him as the organizer (*Dom.* 16.2) who leaves the actual murder to someone else. Presumably, he was also one of the 'intimate freedmen' (14.1): Dio is far more helpful, naming three of them (Parthenius, Sigerius and Entellus).

Whilst the support of the praetorian prefects would obviously be one of the primary concerns of any would-be imperial assassin, the ancient sources are nowhere near as unanimous as their modern counterparts in claiming that it was obtained on this occasion.[3] Suetonius makes no mention of them whatsoever, and Dio's account of their part in it is far from convincing: according to him (67.15.2), 'it was said that' Domitian's wife and praetorian prefects were aware of the plot. Later sources, so often repeating almost verbatim Suetonius's account of any incident, differ from him somewhat in this matter, referring to Parthenius as the killer, and to the praetorian prefect Petronius Secundus as his assistant (Eutropius 8.1). Dio alone mentions the other prefect, Norbanus. Nerva's role is dealt with in much the same way, in that he does not appear in Suetonius's version, whereas Dio claims that the conspirators warned him of their plans in advance (67.15.5).

The discrepancies are interesting since both Suetonius and Dio must have had detailed information of what happened, even of comparatively minor details. Both, for instance, refer to the fact that Domitian kept a dagger under his pillow and that, when he went to retrieve it, he found that the blade had been removed. In Suetonius, no culprit is named (17.2), whereas Dio assigns the credit (or blame) to Parthenius (67.17.1). Suetonius's omission of Nerva's role (and name) is perfectly understandable: it would have been worse than tactless for him, as Hadrian's secretary, to suggest that the present dynasty owed its existence to a murder committed with the active support of Hadrian's (adoptive) grandfather (though the only time he does mention Nerva is to report the rumour that Nerva seduced the young Domitian: *Dom.* 1.1). Perhaps his comparative reticence with regard to Parthenius is to be explained as an atempt to disguise Nerva's weakness as emperor, being forced to hand Parthenius over to the praetorians.

Nerva's role in the murder is difficult to assess. The speed with which he was nominated emperor indicates that the assassins had a likely candidate ready, and, presumably, in the palace itself. Yet Nerva's past activities would not have recommended him to them. Rewarded for betraying the Pisonian conspirators, Nerva was one of the few non-Flavians to receive an ordinary consulship from Vespasian and it was awarded very early in the reign, for services unspecified but presumably against Nero. Domitian rewarded him with a second ordinary consulship, in the year immediately after the suppression of the revolt of Saturninus: once again, betrayal may have been the explanation. A well-meaning later writer, Philostratus, has Domitian exiling him in the 90s (*Vita Apoll.* 7.8), a 'fraudulent invention'.[4] Equally unlikely is Dio's story of Domitian's alleged plan to execute Nerva, cancelled because an astrologer told him that Nerva was doomed to die anyhow (67.15.6). Both were invented to disguise what even Pliny could not hide: Nerva was a committed Flavian. Once emperor, Nerva maintained his friendship with the pro-Domitianic faction in the senate – and was notorious for it (*Ep.* 4.22.7). Would Parthenius and the others have even considered approaching a pro-Domitianic senator with such a record of betrayal?

On the other hand, Domitian's *amici* may have been consulted. Suetonius maintains that they were involved. One of them, his accomplished general, Lappius, was in Rome at that time: now *pontifex*, he had been consul in 95, and was the only senator to whom Domitian himself gave two consulships. Undoubtedly, he would have been welcome at court. However, two other senior members of the general staff, Trajan and Cornelius Nigrinus, were in Upper Germany and Syria[5] and no doubt they too considered themselves as worthy replacements for Domitian: and in view of that emperor's record (Inchtuthil built and abandoned, compensatation paid in Germany, Oppius Sabinus as well as Cornelius Fuscus unavenged and, instead, payments made to the Dacians), most of the generals would probably have agreed with the principle if not the candidate. It could well be that, through fear of civil war, someone such as Lappius may have persuaded Parthenius and the others to urge the nomination of someone uncontroversial, 'malleable, flexible, likeable, [with] no firm opinions, no bright ideas, not intellectually committed and without the strength of purpose to change anything, ... someone [who] ... can be professionally guided'.[6] A known Flavian supporter, old, sick and childless, Nerva was the perfect choice: the real struggle would have been postponed.

All the ancient sources stress that this was a palace plot,[7] though Suetonius alone uses the word *amici*. None refers to the involvement of the senate and there is no real need to assume one. The impotent senate did not remove an unsatisfactory emperor. On the contrary, Domitian's fate was determined essentially by his inability to work with his courtiers. His suspicious nature caused him to begin executing members of his personal staff, those closest to him wherever the court was. The outcome was inevitable.

CHARACTER

Assessing Domitian's character and that of his reign is bedevilled by two separate factors, the bias of the literary sources and the judgemental standards adopted by the aristocracy. Martial illustrates the first admirably: writing under Domitian, he praises the new palace as surpassing the pyramids (8.36.1), but, once the emperor was dead, dismisses it as the 'extravagance of a haughty king' (12.15.4–5). So, no matter who was emperor, the existing regime was untouchable and its predecessor fair game. There was nothing unexpected in the senate's failure to condemn Claudius, even though he executed so many of its members, far more than Domitian did: he was not the last of the dynasty. The second problem is linked to the first, in that the literary evidence emanates from a tiny section of the Roman world, the aristocrats, whose view of an emperor, inevitably narrow, was determined solely by his attitude to them. Hence Dio's insistence on the decrees frequently passed by Domitian's senate to the effect that an emperor should not put to death any of his peers (67.2.4): what he did to anyone else was far less important.

These factors have been responsible for much, but not all, of the hostility directed at Domitian. He risked obloquy through his utter determination to govern according to his own standards, to ignore tradition whenever it did not suit him and to proclaim the senate's impotence rather than disguise it through polite platitudes. He was a monarch, who lived in his court, visiting the senate on rare occasions, so it seems: he did not bother to pretend otherwise.

One criticism[8] made against his foreign policy is that, by not completing the conquest of Britain, he caused 10 per cent of Rome's legions and 14 per cent of her auxiliaries to be concentrated in that island. On the other hand, Domitian would have done better to withdraw from Britain completely, for it is hard to believe that it ever represented anything other than a loss for the Roman treasury. Always prepared to cast tradition aside, he was just about the only emperor with sufficient courage to adopt such a policy, but, obviously, such a drastic reversal could not even be contemplated. Nor, indeed, did he make any effort to reduce the drain the army imposed on the treasury; quite the contrary, he added to the burden by increasing the army's pay. Such is the sort of criticism that can be levelled at one of the very few emperors (if not the only one) with both the ability and the courage to impose substantial basic reforms on the system, and yet who did not do so.

On the other hand, the evidence we have, both literary and epigraphic, indicates not only his close personal involvement with various aspects of the administration but also the comparative efficiency and justice of the system itself. Senatorial and other malefactors expected and received no mercy, though relief came with the 'five good emperors' – a difference hinted at in the bluntness of the orders given to Claudius Athenodorus compared with the studied courtesy of Trajan's requests to Pliny. Domitian's administrators may not have liked him, but they would have obeyed him.

The emphasis he placed on the development of a power set, with the concomitant exclusion of more and more senators from the slightest contact with the administration of the empire, was unlikely to win him many friends – those selected felt that they had earned it, the rest must have felt resentful or uninterested – but it meant a reinvigorated aristocracy. His policy of encouraging senators from the east, and it was clearly his and not Vespasian's or Trajan's, deserves special commendation.

It is by no means certain that his efforts to win support in the senate were to no avail. We cannot tell what the outcome would have been of his determination to honour patricians with ordinary consulships and to reward those with long-standing praetorian careers behind them. But, if we separate the reality of the Nervan senate from the façade created by the official propaganda, we are left, as far as most people were concerned, with a Domitianic senate inefficiently led. The Nervan dinner-party anecdote attests to the first point:

[The emperor] Nerva was dining with a few companions, Veiento next to him and actually leaning on his shoulder. The conversation turned to Catullus Messallinus . . . and when the emperor asked what he thought would have happened to him if he were still alive, Mauricus said that he would be dining with us.

(*Ep.* 4.22.4–7)

The comments of Nerva's consul, Fronto, attest to the second:

Fronto is said to have remarked that it was bad to have an emperor under whom nobody was permitted to do anything, but worse to have one under whom everybody was permitted to do everything.

(Dio 68.1.3)

In many ways, Domitian remains an enigma.[9] His interest in libraries and passion for literary contests, his knowledge of Homer and Vergil as well as his fondness for epigrammatic expression[10] all sit ill with the philistine of *Dom.* 20. The lazy emperor of *Dom.* 19 can hardly have been the same person who kept so close any eye on the minutiae of administration, who even checked the accuracy of the coins.

Assessing his personality is a more difficult task, hardly facilitated by the hostility of the literary sources. Some aspects emerge, though. By nature, he was both superstitious and suspicious, completely lacking a sense of humour. His preference for his own company and inability to mix widely amongst the aristocracy were fatal defects, enabling his opponents to describe him as morose and gloomy, quite unlike his gregarious father and brother. He lacked the ability to be at ease with people: unlike Augustus, he would not have attended the birthday celebrations of members of the aristocracy, nor would they, one suspects, have paid courtesy calls on him in the palace on those days on which the senate did not meet (*Aug.* 53). His remoteness must have been only too evident: on five occasions, he was outside Italy for substantial periods, and, within the country, he had three palaces (Rome, Alba and Circeo): his was a mobile court and the word *rex* could quite reasonably have been applied to him.

NOTES

1 EARLY CAREER

1 Martial 9.20.1; Scott, 1936: 64–6.
2 *Vesp.* 1.2–3; Berchem, 1978: 267–74; and Birley, 1986:6.
3 Jones, 1984a: 1–3.
4 Talbert, 1984: 10–11.
5 The seven were Sabinus II, his son (Sabinus III), his two grandsons (Sabinus IV and T. Flavius Clemens), his brother Vespasian and Vespasian's two sons. Sabinus II and his descendants secured five consulships (two to Sabinus III and one each to the rest), with the remaining thirty-four held by Vespasian, Titus and Domitian (Buttrey, 1980: 6–7, 18–20, 28–31).
6 Saller, 1980: 44–63 and 1982; as well as Wallace-Hadrill, 1989.
7 Nicols, 1978: 13–20; Jones, 1984a: 4–7.
8 Between 16 and 19, Pomponius Graecinus, Pomponius Flaccus, P. Petronius and Vibius Marsus (father-in-law of P. Plautius Pulcher) held consulships but, between 19 and 31, only C. Petronius and A. Plautius did.
9 Between 32 and 37, consulships came to A. Vitellius, L. Vitellius, Q. Plautius and C. Petronius Pontius Nigrinus and, during the first eight years of Claudius's reign, to L. Vitellius II, L. Vitellius III, Q. Pomponius Secundus, P. Pomponius Secundus, L. Plautius Silvanus Aelianus, A. Vitellius and L. Vitellius.
10 Nicols, 1975: 48–58.
11 *PIR*[2] A 885; Nicols, 1975: 48–58; McGuire, 1980: 190–2; and Raepsaet-Charlier, 1987: 90–1.
12 *PIR*[2] A 888; Braithwaite, 1927: 26; Mooney, 1930: 386; and McGuire, 1980: 190.
13 For the details of the cordial relationship between Herod the Great, Salome, Agrippa I, Berenice and various members of the imperial family, see Jones, 1984a: 59–60. Augustus, for one, had few illusions about Herod: he is supposed to have said that he would rather be one of Herod's pigs than one of his sons (Macrobius, *Sat.* 2.4.11). All members of the family had been entitled to call themselves Julius (or Julia) since Antipater received the citizenship from Caesar.

14 *PIR²* B 108 (grandmother of Titus's mistress Berenice).
15 *PIR²* J 651; McDermott and Orentzel, 1979b: 32–8; P.M. Rogers, 1986: 80–95; McGuire, 1980: 97–9, 107–8; Martinet, 1981: 68–70, 73–4; and Jones, 1984a: 74 n. 94.
16 *PIR²* J 139; Houston, 1971: 292–4 with 292 n. 16 for earlier studies; and Jones, 1984a: 69 n. 57.
17 For their relationship (not mentioned, naturally, by Josephus), see Rogers, 1980: 86–95; Braund, 1984: 120–3; and Jones, 1984a: 91–3.
18 E.g. *P. Oxy.* 244; *P. Ryl.* 2, 140, 141, 171.
19 According to Buttrey, Vespasian received twenty imperial salutations and nine consulships (1980: 6–7), Titus seventeen and eight (1980: 18–20), Domitian twenty-two and seventeen (1980: 28–31).
20 Jones, 1984a: 6, 10, 24–5 with notes 20–7.
21 *A.d. VI K. Novembr. ob detecta nefaria con[silia in C. Germani]cum Cn. Lentuli Gaet[ulici . . .]*: Smallwood, 1967: no. 9.
22 Jones, 1984c: 583.
23 i.e. 'The rest of the time up to his proconsulate he spent in rest and retirement, through fear of Agrippina, who still had a strong influence over her son and hated any friend of Narcissus, even after the latter's death' (*Vesp.* 4.2, Loeb trans.).
24 See Jones, 1984a: 7 and 25 n.30. A.R. Birley examines Sabinus II's career (arguing for a consulship in 47, not 44; in more detail, 1986: 66) and that of Vespasian (1981: 224–8). A number of scholars have suggested that the Flavians were adlected to the patriciate in 47: the first seems to have been McAlindon, 1957: 260.
25 Jones, 1984a: 7–11.
26 Mooney, 1930: 468.
27 Nicols argues convincingly that Vespasian and Sabinus II 'decided to split their support between the contending parties. . . . Vespasian chose to stand with Narcissus and suffered, consequently, by having to withdraw from court life for some years. . . . As it turned out, it was rather Flavius Sabinus who chose correctly' (1978: 22).
28 i.e. A. Plautius (*PIR¹* P 345), for allegedly aspiring to the empire with the help of Agrippina (*Nero* 35.4; Bradley, 1978b: 214–5) and Q. Plautius Lateranus (*PIR¹* P 354), the nephew of Claudius's legate, because of his involvement in the Pisonian conspiracy (*Ann.* 15.60).
29 On Petillius Cerialis, see Birley, 1981: 66–9 and Jones, 1984a: 29 n. 89. On L. Junius Caesennius Paetus, *PIR²* C 173; Houston, 1971: 38–41; and Nicols, 1978: 30–1. On Turpilianus, Birley, 1981: 57–8.
30 Birley, 1981: 57–8 with n. 5; Jones, 1984a: 30–1 with n. 109.
31 Raepsaet-Charlier, 1987: 107–10.
32 Jones, 1984a: 18.
33 The result was ill-feeling between the brothers: *Hist.* 3. 65. For some comments on Vespasian's trading activities, see Braithwaite, 1927: 30 and Mooney, 1930: 390–1.
34 Champlin, 1983: 262.
35 Jones, 1984a: 34–6; A.R. Birley, 1986: 66.
36 Champlin, 1983: 264.
37 Hardie, 1983: 7–11.

38 Millar refers to 'Domitian's total lack of literary culture' (1967: 19).

39 Walker, 1976: 20 (money) and Gsell, 1894: 80–7 (morals). As Carradice observes, 'Domitian's restoration of the Augustan coinage accords well with his many other actions' (1983: 161).

40 Platner and Ashby, 1929: 180.

41 Nicols, 1978: 83.

42 The 'alleged discrepancy' (Wellesley, 1956: 212); but, for Wiseman, the accounts of Tacitus and Suetonius are 'notoriously inconsistent' (1978: 173).

43 *arcem Capitolii insedit*: *Hist*. 3.69. Wiseman argues that (as Tacitus says) they occupied the *arx*, i.e. the northern and not the (universally accepted) south-western summit (1978: 163).

44 Wellesley, 1956: 211–14. Compare Barzano, 1982a: 11–20.

45 Wiseman, 1978: 163–78.

46 Wiseman also disposes of Wellesley's objection (1956: 212) to the procession of Isaic priests on the Capitol, stated by Tacitus and assumed in Suetonius (1978: 163–4): Wellesley had 'moved' it to another location.

47 Jones, 1984a: 209.

48 Evans, 1979: 198–202.

49 Jones, 1984a: 208.

50 Jones, 1984a: 93–8.

51 Evans's reconstruction of the incident (1978: 198–202) has been accepted in the text.

52 Gsell, 1894: 10, thinking of *Dom*. 2.1. Some believed that he even contemplated a war against Vespasian (*bellum adversus patrem*: *Hist*. 4.86).

53 i.e. Vespasian, Sabinus II, Titus, Vespasian's son-in-law Petillius Cerialis, Sabinus II's son-in-law Caesennius Paetus, the elder Trajan (married to the sister of Marcia Furnilla, Titus's wife) and L. Julius Lupus (prefect of Egypt).

54 Greenhalgh, 1975: 191–242.

55 Birley, 1973: 179–90.

56 Crook, 1951: 164–5.

57 Jones, 1984a: 209.

58 For his 'sheer incompetence', see Birley, 1973: 186.

59 Hannestad, 1986: 133–5. According to Last, the *adventus* scene showed that Vespasian was 'pleased with Domitian and that their relations were good' (1948: 12). As Rajak has noted, the Reliefs contain much the same message as the opening sections of *BJ* 7, i.e. the 'official version' of what had happened since December 69 (1983: 218).

60 Rejected by Jones, 1984a: 85–7.

61 Jones, 1984a: 79–85.

62 Hammond, 1959: 112–13 n. 133; Buttrey, 1980: 28–35; and Gallivan, 1981: 187–9. That he usually assumed his suffect posts *c*. 13 January appears from Buttrey's Table (1980: 28–9). His third consulship must be assigned to 75 (Buttrey, 1980: 33–4 and Gallivan, 1981: 188), not to 74 as in McCrum and Woodhead, 1966: 5.

63 Gsell, 1894: 18 – discussed by Buttrey, 1980: 32–3.

64 Gsell, 1894: 20.
65 Buttrey, 1980: 33.
66 B.W. Jones, 1971: 269 notes 38–44.
67 They appear in Crook's list of imperial *amici* (1955: 187, no. 328, i.e. Valerius Festus and 156, no. 75, i.e. Catullus Messallinus). The others were Pedius Cascus in 71 (Gallivan, 1981: 187) and Pasidienus Firmus in 75 (Gallivan, 1981: 188).
68 Suetonius repeats the fly-stabbing anecdote, but assigns it to the beginning of Domitian's reign (*Dom.* 3.1).
69 E.g. Pacorus who lost both his wife and his concubines (*BJ* 7.247) as well as Tiridates who nearly lost his wife (*BJ* 7.249).
70 Gsell, 1894: 28.
71 Gsell, 1894: 28–9.
72 It was Domitian who designated Sabinus (Eck, 1970: 48–54; Buttrey, 1980: 25–6, 34–5).
73 Jones, 1984a: 12–23.
74 For the date of his tribunician power, see the discussion of Hammond, 1956: 84–5 with notes 123, 124 and Buttrey, 1980: 35. It appears in the *Acta* of the Arval Brothers for 30 September (McCrum and Woodhead, 1966: 21, no. 12, lines 33–4), but that merely indicates a celebration of what had already been decided: so, in *ILS* 1995, he is holding tribunician power (for the second time) by 20 September 82. Gsell, 1894: 31 n. 1; Weynand, *RE* 6.2551 and Hammond, 1959: 97 n. 40, argue, on the basis of the numismatic evidence, that there was a delay before Domitian became chief priest: the notion should be discarded, as Buttrey shows (1980: 35–6). He also received the title 'father of his country' on 14 September: see Buttrey, 1980: 30.

2 COURT I

1 Talbert, 1984: 181.
2 For the *ab actis senatus* under Domitian, see Talbert, 1984: 311–12, and, for Junius Rusticus, Birley, 1981: 14.
3 I am heavily indebted to Professor Andrew Wallace-Hadrill for his insistence on the significance of the court and have tried to justify his dictum that 'Titus knew how to handle his court where Domitian did not' (1984: 1102). Detailed discussions of the imperial court are rare, the most accessible being Friedländer, 1907: (1) 30–97; Millar, 1977: 18–40 (*passim*); and Wallace-Hadrill, 1983: 73–96. In the brief survey that follows, I have, in the main, relied on Suetonius and Tacitus, rather than Epictetus and Dio of Prusa, both of whom should be mined for a more detailed coverage of the topic than can be justified here.
4 Millar discusses this, noting that the 'crucial shift from "Palatium", meaning the hill itself, to "Palatium" or "Palatia" meaning the imperial residence is already visible in the poetry of the reign of Augustus himself' (1977: 20).
5 See Talbert, 1984: 56.
6 Millar, 1977: 20.

7 Morton, 1964: 172. I am indebted to Mrs O. Peel for the reference.
8 The precise sense of Suetonius's *puerulus* is in dispute. As Janssen notes, the usual word for 'dwarf' is *nanus* or *pumilio* (1919: 19) and Vassileiou argues that Suetonius is really referring to Crispinus (1984: 40).
9 Friedländer, 1907: (4) 6–11.
10 According to Pliny, 'we have reached the point where almost all of us shall conform to the ways of a single man' (*Pan.* 45.5), referring (obviously) not to Domitian.
11 Cicero, *Ad Fam.* 15.4.6: 'I contrived that the king [*rex*] with the full authority of the court [*auctoritate aulae*] safeguarded, should remain in dignified possession of his kingdom'; and Tacitus, *Ann.* 6.43: '[Abdagaeses] who then ruled the court and the new king [*aula et novo rege*].
12 *AE* 1976: 653; Bérard, 1984: 300 n. 124.
13 Bérard, 1984: 300–4.
14 Walser, 1989: 449 n. 1; Lebek, 1989: 80 n. 93.
15 Eck, 1985b: 142 with n. 16.
16 McCrum and Woodhead, 1966: no. 466; Levick, 1982: 51–2.
17 Mooney, 1930: 527, 596; Blake, 1959: 134–8; Magi, 1973/4: 63–77; Crescenzi, 1978: 99–106; and Hersberg, 1978/80: 305–24.
18 McCrum and Woodhead, 1966: no. 462, translated (with comments) in Jones, 1984a: 171–2.
19 Sherwin-White, 1966; 283.
20 Crook, 1955: 50–2; Highet, 1954: 76–82, 256–62; Griffith, 1969: 134–40; Courtney, 1980: 195–229; Deroux, 1983: 283–98; and Vassileiou, 1984: 27–68.
21 Vassileiou, 1984: 66–7.
22 Millar, 1977: 79.
23 Vessey, 1973: 7–13. Both classicism and mannerism flourished under Domitian, Quintilian being the main exponent of the former (Bardon, 1962: 734), Statius of the latter.
24 E.g. Vessey, 1973: 11; Bardon, 1962: 740–1; Kähler, 1963: 126; and Hannestad, 1986: 132.
25 Vessey, 1970: 234 and 1973: 13.
26 Last, 1948: 9–14; McCann, 1972: 249–76 with the bibliography at 249, notes 1 and 2, 275 n. 115; Kazdova, 1979: 47–56; E. Simon, 1985: 543–55; and Hannestad, 1986: 132–7.
27 McCann, 1972: 271. Few scholars agree with her, as she admits on 249, n. 2, to which one might add Hannestad, who bluntly states that the Cancelleria Reliefs 'have an entirely different appearance' (1986: 132).
28 McCann, 1972: 254.
29 Garthwaite, 1978: 128.
30 *PIR*² E 282; Vessey, 1973: 28–35; White, 1975: 288–91; Garthwaite, 1978: 65–86, 91–129; and Ahl, 1984: 205–7. Martial wrote a number of epigrams in Earinus's honour in Book 9 (viz. 11, 12, 13, 16, 17 and 36), mainly on the eunuch's name, hair and beauty, describing him as the 'famous darling of the other Jupiter' (9.36.2).
31 On attaining manhood, Nero offered clippings from his first beard to Jupiter Capitolinus: *Nero* 12.

32 Garthwaite believes that Suetonius's statement is probably incorrect, basing his argument on Martial 5.49, an epigram intended for the emperor's eyes, where he laughs at a certain Labienus and his bald crown (1978: 93–4).

33 Martial 9.8.5. Domitian's legislation forbidding castration was frequently referred to, e.g. *Dom.* 7.1; Dio 67.2.3; *Vita Apoll.* 6.42; Martial 2.60, 6.2 and 9.6.

34 The passage is decidedly odd (but compare Vessey, 1983: 211). As Garthwaite observes, 'the reader is left with the bizarre and unlikely possibility that ... the happily married Domitia actually welcomed her husband's pederasty' (1978: 99). For ancient denunciations of pederasty, see Highet, 1954: 249.

35 Loeb trans.

36 Vessey, 1973: 35.

37 Trans. Ahl, 1984: 193.

38 'The very picture of the horde of young Ganymedes packed into the palace is a wry comment on the depiction of Domitian's concern for the protection of males in [Epigrams] 9.5 and 9.7' (Garthwaite, 1978: 84–5).

39 *PIR*[2] D 181; McDermott and Orentzel, 1979b: 69–86; Raepsaet-Charlier, 1987: 287–8, no. 327; and Vinson, 1989: 431–50.

40 Buttrey, 1980: 12.

41 The text of Suetonius is far from perfect at this point: see Mooney, 1930: 518. On Domitian's only son, see Desnier, 1979: 54–65.

42 *RP* 3: 1484 and 5: 729 (indices); *PIR*[2] A 678, 700 and 701; and Raepsaet-Charlier, 1987: 281–2, 444.

43 Jones, 1984a: 20.

44 Syme, 1958: 788–90; Nicols, 1978: 118–24.

45 *PIR*[1] P 95; Mooney, 1930: 519; and Highet, 1954: 24–6. According to Martial (11.13.3), he was 'the delight of the city and the wit of the Nile'.

46 Vinson, 1989: 440. Compare Iarbas's scornful description of Aeneas in *Aen.* 4, 215–16. For Paris's Egyptian origin, see Martial 11.13.3.

47 The *Lex Julia* is discussed in *RE* 1, 433–4; for the extracts in the text, see Lewis and Reinhold, 1966: 48–9.

48 Vinson, 1989: 445 n. 52.

49 Vinson, 1989: 438.

50 Vinson, 1989: 438–40.

51 The standard example comes from the late Republic (*Cat. min.* 25.2–5, 52.3.

52 Most scholars argue that he did, e.g. Humbert, 1972: 173 n. 83; *contra* McDermott and Orentzel, 1979b: 76–7 and Syme, 1986: 187.

53 Vinson, 1989: 444–5.

54 E.g. Castritius, 1969: 497–8; Baxter, 1974: *passim*; and McGuire, 1980: 174–8.

55 McGuire, 1980: 176.

56 Baxter, 1974: 11–12 (Ulpii, Vettuleni, Caesennii, Ti. Julius Alexander and Flavius Silva), 443 n. 148 (reason for Civica's execution) and 487 n. 146 (dismissal of Ursus and Pegasus).

57 McGuire, 1980: 152–4, 177.
58 Castritius, 1969: 497–8.
59 E.g. 'Enceinte une deuxième fois en 90 mais en vain': Raepsaet-Charlier, 1987: 28.
60 E.g. McDermott and Orentzel, 1979b: 78.
61 Garthwaite, 1978: 32. His suggestion has been followed in the text.
62 Garthwaite, 1990: 16–17.
63 I am indebted to Dr S. Dixon for drawing my attention to this passage.
64 Despite Scott, 1936: 83, she should not be identified with the *meretrix Augusta* of Juvenal 6.118. As Syme observed, she was not that 'noctivagous and indefatigable empress' (1937: 33).
65 *PIR²* F 426; McDermott and Orentzel, 1979b: 87–93; Jones, 1984a: 215 (index); Raepsaet-Charlier, 1987: 323–4, no. 371; and Vinson, 1989: 431–50.
66 Jones, 1984a: 209.
67 Martinet, 1981: 29–33, has rejected the argument of Castritius, 1969: 492–4, 498; the latter is retained in the text.
68 Josephus (*AJ* 19.191) attests to the close relationship between Arrecina's father (M. Arrecinus Clemens) and Julius Lupus.
69 For Marcia Furnilla's daughter, see Raepsaet-Charlier, 1987: 316–17, no. 362.
70 On 3 January 81, she appears as *Julia Augusta* (McCrum and Woodhead, 1966: 19).
71 Vinson, 1989: 431–50.
72 For 90 as the publication date of Martial's sixth book, see Garthwaite, 1990: 13–14. Julia died towards the end of 89 (Vinson, 1989: 436 n. 23).
73 See Ahl, 1984: 174–208.
74 Garthwaite, 1990: 15–16.
75 *PIR²* J 630; Houston, 1971: 563–7; and Raepsaet-Charlier, 1987: 36–7. Syme has discussed him on numerous occasions, e.g. 1958: 635–6, and his conclusions have been adopted in the text. Not all have agreed with Syme's reconstruction of Ursus's career and distinguish Ursus, prefect of Egypt, from the senatorial L. Julius Ursus (e.g. Pavis D'Escurac, 1976: 45, 52, 327).
76 Julius Lupus's career is outlined in *PIR²* J 388 and that of Arrecinus Clemens in *PIR²* A 1073 (together with his career inscription, *AE* 1976: 200); see also Raepsaet-Charlier, 1987: 108 (Clemens) and 109–10 (Lupus). For Lupus's sister, Julia, see Townend, 1961: 57–8 and Castritius, 1969: 494.
77 Cotton argues that he was promoted to Egypt while serving in the army besieging Masada (1989: 162).
78 Townend, 1961: 57.
79 Raepsaet-Charlier, 1987: 107–9, no. 92 (?Arrecina Clementina) and 109–10, no. 93 (Arrecina Tertulla).
80 Jones and Develin, 1976: 82.
81 Townend, 1961: 57.
82 Vidman, 1982: 44.

83 Syme, 1958: 635–6.
84 The phrase is taken from *Yes Minister* (Lynn and Jay, 1981: 112).
85 For Servianus and P. Julius Lupus, see Syme, 1958: 636. Arria Fadilla's first husband was T. Aurelius Fulvus, *cos. ord.* 89.
86 *AE* 1972: 574 (Classicus) and Carradice, 1979: 101–3 (Ti. Julius Aug. lib.).
87 *PIR²* A 1072; Jones, 1984a: 212 and Raepsaet-Charlier, 1987: 108.
88 i.e. Arrecina Tertulla to Titus and (?Arrecina Clementina) to Sabinus III.
89 Jones and Develin, 1976: 79–80; Mennella, 1981: 205–8 (= *AE* 1981: 335); Eck, 1982a: 288–9 n. 24 and 1983a: 197 n. 541.
90 Syme, 1979–88, *RP* 5: 613.
91 Bradley, 1978b: 224.
92 Townend, 1961: 57 n. 9; Jones and Develin, 1976: 83 with n. 40; and Raepsaet-Charlier, 1987: 257–8, no. 288.
93 Jones and Develin, 1976: 83; Syme, 1979–88, *RP* 5: 614–15. For the wording, compare *ob detecta scelera nefariorum* (22 September 87) and *ob detecta nefaria consilia* (27 October 39: of Lentulus and Gaetulicus).
94 Eck, 1970: 58 n. 21.
95 For a more detailed exposition, see Jones and Develin, 1976: 79–83. Syme, 1979–88, *RP* 5: 614–15 also discusses Clemens's fate.
96 Jones and Develin, 1976: 82–3; *contra*, Rodgers, 1982: 179–80.
97 *PIR²* F 355; Houston, 1971: 395–6; and Raepsaet-Charlier, 1987: 109.
98 'Imperial attendants (*aulici ministri*) wore a white tunic adorned with a border or lace of gold' (Mooney, 1930: 569). See also Mommsen, 1887–8: 2.1.780 n. 2.
99 According to Townend, Sabinus IV was born in 53 (1961: 62).
100 *PIR²* F 351 (Sabinus I), 352 (Sabinus II), 353/4 (Sabinus III), 355 (Sabinus IV) and 240 with addendum (Flavius Clemens). Townend has convincingly argued that Sabinus III was the son of Sabinus II and father of Sabinus IV (1961: 54–6); most have concurred. Wallace's comments (1987: 343–58) on the reluctance or cowardice of the Sabini also merit attention.
101 Birley, 1981: 27.
102 Townend, 1961: 54; Devreker, 1977: 231.
103 E.g. Gsell, 1894: 28 n. 9.
104 Eck, 1970: 48–54; Buttrey, 1980: 35.
105 During this period, consular *comitia* were probably held in March and October: see Talbert, 1984: 343 and n. 12.
106 Smallwood, 1967: 19–22, nos 20 and 21.
107 Gsell, 1894: 248 with n. 6; Stein, *RE* 6. 2614. 169; Groag in *PIR²* F 355; Townend, 1961: 55; Waters, 1964: 72; Houston, 1971: 395; and Syme, 1979–88, *RP* 4: 263. Not a few prefer the earlier date, e.g. Janssen, 1919: 55; Charlesworth, *CAH* 11: 24; Murray, 1967: 250; and Viscusi, 1973: 142.
108 Domitian assumed the title *Germanicus* at some time between 9 June 83 and 28 August 83 (Buttrey, 1980: 56). I am indebted to Mr Erik Estensen for drawing my attention to the fact that, by taking *Dom.* 22

and Dio 67.3.2 together, one can assign a fairly definite date to Sabinus IV's execution.

109 The latest possible date for Domitian's assumption of the title *Germanicus*.

110 *PIR²* F 240 and addenda; Houston, 1971: 394–5; and Raepsaet-Charlier, 1987: 109.

111 Townend, 1961: 54–7; it is now generally accepted – see Raepsaet-Charlier, 1987: 108.

112 *PIR¹* P 191; Birley, 1981: 66–9; and Raepsaet-Charlier, 1987: 321–2.

113 There is some doubt about the precise relationship between Cerialis (*cos. II suf.* 74) and Q. Petillius Rufus (*PIR¹* P 193). Some (e.g. Birley, 1981: 69 n. 31) identify them, making Rufus *cos. III ord.* rather than *II ord.* in 83. On the Petillii in general, see Bosworth, 1980: 267–77 (together with Dondin-Payre, 1983: 236–40) and Jones, 1984a: 3–4.

114 In the first year of Vespasian's reign, the ordinary consuls were Vespasian and Titus, whilst Titus and Domitian held the post in the first year of Titus's – in each case, the emperor and his heir.

115 *Inst. Or.* 4 *Praef.* 2. For the date, see Mooney, 1930: 580.

116 Hammond, 1959: 269 n. 22.

117 Similarly, 'If Fortune wishes it, you will become a consul after being a rhetor' (Juvenal, 7.97). These passages are discussed by McDermott and Orentzel, 1979b: 24 and Coleman, 1986: 3108–9.

118 Vidman, 1982: 45.

119 E.g. Keresztes, 1973: 7–15 (probably Jews) and Pergola, 1978: 407–23 (Christians).

120 Raepsaet-Charlier, 1987: 319–23, nos 367, 368 and 369.

121 Raepsaet-Charlier, 1987: 323 (cf. Fasola, 1960: 631).

122 For the relationship between Flavia Sabina and Paetus, see the discussion of *ILS* 995 (*Flaviae T.f. Sabinae Caesenni Paeti*) by Townend, 1961: 56. Paetus's full name was revealed in *AE* 1973, 141; for other aspects of his career, see *PIR²* C 173 and Houston, 1971: 38–41. Gregori has offered (1986a: 185–9) and then withdrawn (1986b: 239–44) the suggestion that Sabina's first husband was Cn. Pedanius Salinator with Pedanius Fuscus Salinator (= [Pedan]ius Flavius Sa[linator]) as their son.

123 For the younger Paetus, see *PIR²* C 174 and Houston, 1971: 41–2. Sospes's career has been restored by Syme, 1977: 38–49; note also *PIR¹* S 567 and Syme, 1979–88, *RP* 3: 1466 and 5: 720 (indices).

124 Eck, 1982a: 321 with n. 161.

3 COURT II

1 Crook, 1955; Millar, 1977: 110–22; and Devreker, 1977: 227–8.

2 Crook, 1955: 26.

3 i.e. Domitian's Cornelius Fuscus; for the presence of non-senators, see Crook, 1955: 23–4 and Millar, 1977: 116.

4 Devreker, 1977: 225.

5 The others are Arrecinus Clemens (*Hist.* 4.68; *Dom.* 11.1), Julius Bassus (*Ep.* 4.9.2) and Lucianus Proclus (Dio 67.11.5).

6 In the list that follows, the praetorian prefects have been added to the *amici* given by Devreker, 1977: 227–8.

7 Houston (1971: 328) and others (e.g. Vassileiou, 1984: 51) accept Groag's suggestion in *PIR²* A 62 that Aviola and the elder Glabrio are to be identified: but see Devreker, 1977: 227 n. 26 and Gallivan, 1978: 621–5.

8 On the elder Acilius, see *PIR²* A 62. In 1486, George Valla produced a commentary on Juvenal and included therein various comments of early scholars. On 4.94, he cites four lines from Statius's *De Bello Germanico*. '(Catullus Messallinus who had lost his) sight, the mild wisdom of Nestorian Crispus and Fabius Veiento (the purple marked them both out as powerful, they filled the mindful consular lists three times) and Acilius, almost as old as Caesar's palace'. See also Griffith, 1969: 138.

9 *PIR²* A 49; Crook, 1955: 148, no. 2; Houston, 1971: 1–2.

10 *PIR²* A 67; Crook, 1955: 148, no. 3; and Houston, 1971: 328.

11 Leclercq, 1921: 1392–401.

12 *PIR²* A 1510; Houston, 1971: 28–30; Modugno *et al.*, 1973: 87–108; and Syme, 1979–88, *RP* 5: 615–16.

13 Jones, 1984a: 208–9.

14 On the Spanish-Narbonensian connection, see Syme, 1958: 792–5 and 1979–88, *RP* 4: 397–417.

15 *PIR²* C 1227; Crook, 1955: 160, no. 108; and Houston, 1971: 56–8.

16 Houston, 1971: 56–8.

17 Syme, 1958: 636.

18 *PIR²* F 91; Crook, 1955: 164, no. 148; Syme, 1958: 5–6, 633 (Appendix 5); McDermott, 1970: 124–48; Houston, 1971: 87–90; McDermott and Orentzel, 1979b: 11–26; Vassileiou, 1984: 56–7 with n. 87.

19 See McDermott, 1970: 124–48. The only hint of this (despite, e.g., Garzetti, 1950: 50) occurs in the fourth-century Aurelius Victor, *De Caes.* 12.5, and he is absent from Tacitus's list of *delatores* in *Agr.* 45.1.

20 *PIR²* D 70; Crook, 1955: 162, no. 133; and Birley, 1981: 44–9.

21 *AE* 1945: 56 (AD 80) and Vidman, 1982: 77 (AD 83).

22 Houston, 1971: 89.

23 Syme, 1979–88, *RP* 3: 1127 and 4: 260.

24 *PIR²* C 1615; Highet, 1954: 260; and Griffith, 1969: 144 favour Curtius; *PIR²* J 781 and *PIR²* M 681 hesitatingly support Junius, but Syme has no doubts whatsoever (1979–88, *RP* 4: 260).

25 Syme, 1971: 200.

26 Gallivan, 1981: 215.

27 Another candidate for the honour could well be L. Sergius Paullus, from Antioch in Pisidia, whom some claim to have been consul in 70 (e.g. Syme, 1979–88, *RP* 4: 260.

28 *PIR¹* P 164; Crook, 1955: 177, no. 251; Houston, 1971: 178–80; Champlin, 1978: 269–78; and Vassileiou, 1984: 49 with n. 65. However, not everyone has accepted that Pegasus was indeed a [Plo]tius: Sturm thinks that he may have been a [Sex]tius or a [Ses]tius – or that more than three letters are missing from the name (1981: 108–9 with

n. 14). According to the *Digest* 1.2.2.53, he was made city prefect by Vespasian, whereas Juvenal attributes the appointment to Domitian.
29 Syme believes that what astonished the city was Pegasus's lowly origin (1979–88, *RP* 3: 1409). For yet another explanation, see Deroux, 1983: 289.
30 Syme, 1979–88, *RP* 5: 612–13. He suggests that Pegasus may have governed Upper Germany after Dalmatia.
31 Bosworth, 1980: 267–77.
32 For military tribunes serving under close relatives, see the sixteen examples given by Birley, 1981: 11. Bosworth convincingly argues that Firmus served in the *IV Flavia*, i.e. in Rubrius Gallus's Sarmatian campaign (1980: 273–4), whereas Maxfield prefers von Domaszewski's suggestion that the *IV Scythica* was his legion, thereby connecting him with Mucianus and Syria (1981: 153–4).
33 Evans, 1978: 121–3.
34 Champlin, 1978: 274, 276. For Nerva's father and grandfather, see *PIR²* C 1226 and 1227 respectively.
35 Similarly, Statius (*Silv.* 5.2.91) and Frontinus (*Strat.* 2.11.7): 'Obsequious flattery the comments of Statius and Frontinus may be, but the very fact that they chose that material suggests that Domitian prided himself on his justice' (Levick, 1982: 64).
36 *PIR¹* P 495; Houston, 1971: 207–9; Eck, 1972b: 259–75; and Vassileiou, 1984: 54–5 with notes 79–85. Eck's reconstruction of his career has been followed in the text.
37 So Eck, 1972b: 272–3. The candidate usually nominated is Cn. Pompeius Ferox Licinianus (Crook, 1955: 179, no. 266); but he was not consul until 98 and the other members of the *consilium* described by Juvenal are far older.
38 *PIR¹* R 167; Crook, 1955: 181, no. 287; Houston, 1971: 219–30; Hardie, 1983: 187–9, 195–8; Syme, 1979–88, *RP* 5: 514–20; and Eck, 1985a: 475–84. Both he and Pegasus were early Vespasianic consuls, and so probably about the same age. Statius's *Soteria* to Gallicus (*Silvae* 1.4.1–131) has survived.
39 Syme, 1979–88, *RP* 5: 516 and Eck, 1985a: 475. It used to be thought (e.g. Houston, 1971: 221–5 and Hardie, 1983: 183) that Gallicus was merely *legatus* to the proconsul of Asia.
40 Crook, 1955: 156, no. 75; Houston, 1971: 258–61; and Maxfield, 1981: 155–6.
41 Devreker, 1976: 182 and Howell, 1980: 282 – but not Eck, 1982a: 305.
42 *PIR¹* V 41; Crook, 1955: 187, no. 328; Sherwin-White, 1966: 300–1; Ogilvie and Richmond, 1967: 307; Houston, 1971: 257–8; and Vassileiou, 1984: 57 with notes 88 and 89. Syme discusses his antecedents (1979–88, *RP* 1: 265 and 5: 643).
43 *PIR¹* V 379 (*PIR²* J 847 is also this senator); Crook, 1955: 188, no. 340; Griffith, 1969: 139–40; Houston, 1971: 267–72; Syme, 1979–88, *RP* 5: 504; and Vassileiou, 1984: 50 with notes 67 to 70.
44 E.g. 'wealthier than Crispus' (Martial, 4.54.7).
45 Griffith, 1969: 139, translating Quint. 10.1.119· (*delectationi natus*).

46 For his personal charm, note Juvenal 4.81 and Quint. 5.13.48, 10.1.119 (*iucundus*); for his wit, *Dom.* 3.1.

47 A loose rendering of Juvenal 4.84–93.

48 Devreker, 1977: 227–8.

49 *PIR*[1] R 94; Crook, 1955: 181, no. 285; Houston, 1971: 218–19; and Vassileiou, 1984: 52.

50 Devreker, 1977: 228 n. 27; Syme, 1979–88, *RP* 1: 295.

51 *PIR*[2] J 126; Houston, 1971: 121–3 and Birley, 1981: 73–81. The bibliography on him is enormous – amongst the more recent work, note Hind, 1983: 1–18; Campbell, 1986: 197–200; and Hanson, 1987.

52 Birley, 1981: 80.

53 Syme, 1979–88 *RP* 1: 295.

54 Syme, 1979–88, *RP* 3: 1384.

55 Birley, 1981: 80–1.

56 *PIR*[2] J 322; Crook, 1955: 168, no. 176; Houston, 1971: 131–4; Birley, 1981: 69–72; and Eck, 1985b: 141–2.

57 Birley, 1981: 71 n. 18; but he may have held the Lower German post in 73/4 – see Eck, 1985b: 141–2.

58 'Domitian ... acted in the provinces' interests' (*Strat.* 1.1.8); '[the war] in which he earned the title *Conqueror of Germany* by beating the enemy' (*Strat.* 2.11.7) and 'the fame of his [Domitian's] justice' (*ibid.*).

59 On Domitian's accession, Rubrius would have been close to 60 (consul late Nero), Agricola 41 (born 40), Frontinus about 50 (consul *c*. 73), Lappius about 35 (consul 86) and Trajan not yet 30 (born 53 or 56: Houston, 1971: 275).

60 Assa, 1962: 31–9; Houston, 1971: 424–6; and *PIR*[2] L 84.

61 Champlin, 1983: 257–64. His reconstruction is disputed by Raepsaet-Charlier, 1987: 93–4.

62 Millar, 1977: 61–2; 122–31.

63 Millar, 1977: 129. But the court official more frequently in the emperor's presence would have been his *a cubiculo*.

64 On Fuscus, see *PIR*[2] C 1365; Crook, 1955: 160, no. 113; Pflaum, 1960: 77–80; Syme, 1971: 73–83 and Houston, 1971: 291–2. For L. Julius Ursus, see *PIR*[2] J 630; Houston, 1971: 563–7; and Syme, 1979–88, *RP* 5: 740; and, for L. Laberius Maximus, see *PIR*[2] L 8; Pflaum, 1960: 102–4; and Houston, 1971: 296–7.

65 *PIR*[2] C 462. He was prefect under both Domitian (*Vita Apoll.* 7.16; Dio 68.3.3) and Nerva (68.5.4) but not when Domitian was assassinated (67.15.2).

66 See C. P. Jones, 1970: 19.

67 For Norbanus, see Houston, 1971: 575 and *PIR*[2] N 162; for Petronius Secundus, *PIR*[1] P 226 and Houston, 1971: 577.

68 Townend, 1961: 62; Castritius, 1969: 492–4; Jones, 1984a: 19; and Raepsaet-Charlier, 1987: 107–10.

69 E.g. Garzetti, 1974: 294.

70 Titus must have appointed Ursus (Jones, 1984a: 169 n. 133).

71 Casperius Aelianus may have come from Amisus (Syme, 1958: 35 n. 4).

72 Boulvert, 1970 and 1974; Millar, 1977: 69; and Weaver, 1972.

73 Weaver, 1972: 5, 270.
74 Weaver, 1972: 274.
75 Dessau in *ILS* 1567 n. 2.
76 Sinnigen, 1962: 214–24.
77 See Weaver, 1972: 259. In addition, Capito remained in office for a considerable period, serving under Domitian, Nerva and Trajan (*ILS* 1448).
78 E.g. Friedländer, 1907: (4) 32–7 for the *a rationibus*, 37–9 (*a libellis*) and 40–50 (*ab epistulis*).
79 Weaver, 1972: 284–94; Evans, 1978: 102–28; and Carradice, 1979: 101–3.
80 *PIR²* A 1336; Houston, 1971: 594; and Weaver, 1972: 32.
81 *PIR²* F 194; Houston, 1971: 598; and Hardie, 1983: 183–7.
82 *PIR²* O 62; Pflaum, 1960: 143–5; and Sherwin-White, 1966: 124–6, 460, 645.
83 *PIR²* E 66; Houston, 1971: 597 and, for his part in the murder, Dio 67.15.1. Earlier, he had been *procurator aquarum* (*CIL* 15.7282).
84 Weaver, 1972: 261.
85 Nero's *a libellis*, Epaphroditus, was exiled by Domitian and, *c.* 95, executed (*Dom.* 14.4; Dio 67.14.4). Whether or not he held office after 68 cannot be determined.
86 He was concerned with legal inquiries and examinations. For Abascantus and Astectus, see Weaver, 1972: 261.
87 He had charge of the emperor's personal fortune: see Pflaum, 1960: 144.
88 Weaver (1980: 143–56) and Boulvert (1981: 267–77) discuss *AE* 1972: 574 where Classicus's career is outlined. Their conclusions have been attacked by Bruun, 1990: 271–85.
89 *PIR¹* P 101; Millar, 1977: 79 (Parthenius) and *PIR¹* S 500; Houston, 1971: 599 (Siger[i]us). The former was the *a cubiculo*, the latter one of his (subordinate) *cubicularii*: see Boulvert, 1970: 241–7 and Weaver, 1972: 223.
90 Millar, 1977: 85–6.
91 *quaedam ex maximis officiis inter libertinos equitesque R. communic-avit. Dom.* 7.2. This sentence has often been misinterpreted by students with little or no Latin and who have to rely on the standard translations, e.g. 'He opened some of the most important offices of the court [footnote: That is, those which had formerly been restricted to the senatorial orders] to freedmen and Roman knights' (Loeb) or 'He reserved half of the more important Court appointments, hitherto held by freedmen, for knights' (Penguin – Graves) or, better 'He divided some of the more important Court appointments between freedmen and knights' (Penguin – Grant/Graves).
92 Millar, 1977: 89.
93 Pflaum, 1960: 145.
94 Hardie, 1983: 185–7.
95 E.g. Weaver, 1972: 261 n. 5 as well as *PIR²* F 194 (the *ab epistulis*) and F 195 (the *a cognitionibus*).
96 So Hardie, 1983: 185.

97 See Crook, 1955: 49 n. 10 and Devreker, 1977: 232.
98 Birley, 1981: 80.
99 For his support for Vespasian, see *Vita Apoll.* 7.18.
100 *RE* 5. 848–77; *PIR*² D 93 and Crook, 1955: 162, no. 133a. There are more substantial accounts and/or discussions of various aspects of his work by von Arnim, 1898; Lemarchand, 1926; C.P. Jones, 1978; Moles, 1978: 78–100, 1983a: 130–4 and 1983b: 251–78.
101 But see Gowing, 1990: 49–54.
102 Loeb trans., Vol. 5, 375 (adapted). Moles refers to 'time-serving attacks on philosophy under Vespasian ... the melancholy but inevitable inference is that Dio, sycophantically outdoing Vespasian, who was content to exclude philosophers merely from Rome and Italy, lost his nerve and denounced his former friends with the most lurid of invective' (1978: 79, 85–6).
103 *RE* Suppl. 5. 730 (Stein); Jones, 1978: 16–17: Moles, 1978: 84; and *PIR*² M 448. On the other hand, Lemarchand argued that Melancomas was a purely fictitious figure (1926: 32).
104 Jones, 1978: 14, 164 n. 4.
105 He is often identified as T. Flavius Sabinus, grandson of Vespasian's brother, i.e. Sabinus IV – so von Arnim, 1898: 231; Janssen, 1919: 55; and Jones, 1978: 46. Most agree. Lemarchand, however, refused to be definite – the victim was 'un noble romain, parent de l'empereur' (1926: viii). But Dio's friend may have been M. Arrecinus Clemens: see Jones, 1990: 348–57.
106 Waters, 1969: 385–405; Devreker, 1977: 223–43.
107 Weaver, 1980: 150–5; Boulvert, 1981: 31–41; and Bruun, 1990: 271–85.
108 Weaver, 1980: 153.
109 Weaver, 1972: 6 and 1980: 153; Boulvert, 1970: 170–2 and 1974: 129–30.
110 Pflaum describes it as 'le poste le plus important du service personnel' (1960: 393). See also Weaver, 1972: 229; Boulvert, 1974: 130–1; Millar, 1977: 81–2; and Weaver, 1980: 153. For a discussion of the various holders of the post, see Boulvert, 1974: 252–5.
111 Tr. Smallwood, 1961.
112 Weaver, 1972: 282–94; Evans, 1978: 102–28; Carradice, 1979: 101–3; and Hardie, 1983: 181, 184.
113 *Ann.* 2.59; *Hist.* 3.5 and 3.48 (cited in Jones, 1984a: 133 and 166 notes 102–4).
114 Jones, 1984a: 131–4.
115 Carradice, 1979: 101–3 and 1983: 157–8.
116 *PIR*² C 1586; Highet, 1954: 260; Houston, 1971: 556; White, 1974a: 377–82; McDermott, 1978b: 117–22; Baldwin, 1979b: 109–14; Deroux, 1983: 283–98; and Vassileiou, 1984: 27–68.
117 White, 1974a: 377 n. 1; Vassileiou, 1984: 13–25.
118 White, 1974a: 382; Vassileiou, 1984: *passim*. For Courtney, he was an 'Egyptian dandy' (1980: 207).
119 Vassileiou, 1984: 30–1.
120 *PIR*² F 59; Giet, 1958: 321–34 and 1959: 1–17; McDermott and Orentzel, 1979a: 9–26; and Coleman, 1986: 3108–11.

121 *PIR²* L 129; Friedländer, 1907: (1) 60 and Mooney, 1930: 584–5.
122 *PIR¹* T 291; Baldwin, 1979a: 57–60; Coffey, 1979: 88–94; and Coleman, 1986: 3102 with n. 89.

4 ADMINISTRATION I

1 E.g. Garnsey and Saller, 1987: 20.
2 Hopkins, 1983: 186.
3 Rogers, 1984: 66 n. 26.
4 MacMullen, 1980: 453 with n. 7.
5 Gsell, 1894: 334; Syme, 1930: 55–70.
6 Sutherland, 1935: 150–62; Robathan, 1942: 130–44; Garzetti, 1974: 281–4; Carradice, 1983; and Rogers, 1984: 60–78.
7 The notion that Titus was financially incompetent should have been retired long ago: according to Dio, 'in money matters Titus was frugal and made no unnecessary expenditures' (66.19.3). See Carradice, 1983: 159 and Jones, 1984a: 140–3.
8 Syme, 1930: 62–3.
9 Rogers, 1984: 60–78. The figures cited in the text are his.
10 Carradice, 1983: 5.
11 Walker, 1976: 120; Carradice, 1983: 9–56.
12 Walker, 1976: 115.
13 Carradice, 1983: 159–60.
14 Carradice, 1983: 16, 21–2 and 142.
15 Walker, 1976: 117.
16 Carradice, 1983: 143.
17 Carradice, 1983: 157 with n. 34.
18 Carradice, 1983: 27, 29.
19 Syme, 1930: 67.
20 Carradice, 1983: 156.
21 'Ce fut donc à partir de 93 que les confiscations, les exils et les arrêts de mort se succédèrent presque sans interruption et qu'une période de terreur commença' (Gsell, 1894: 264).
22 Millar, 1977; 391–2; Sartori, 1981: 97–128; Levick, 1982: 66–73 (with a list of previous discussions at 67 n. 71); Garnsey and Saller, 1982: 31; Hardie, 1983: 175; Wallace-Hadrill, 1983: 134; Levick, 1985: 112–13; and Patterson, 1987: 115–18
23 Wallace-Hadrill, 1983: 134.
24 Levick, 1982: 66 n. 70 (vine edict); Eck, 1982a: 320 n. 153 (L. Antistius Rusticus).
25 Murray, 1969: 263–4.
26 Levick, 1982: 67.
27 Patterson, 1987: 116–17.
28 Levick, 1982: 69–72.
29 See Carradice, 1983: 165–6.
30 Robathan, 1942: 103–4 with notes 2 and 3.
31 In Platner and Ashby's chronological list of imperial buildings, Domitian has most entries (after Augustus), slightly more than Nero and about as many as Trajan and Hadrian combined (1929: 587–9).

32 E.g. McCrum and Woodhead, 1966: 422 (Thyatira) and 436 (Megalopolis).
33 Blake, 1959: 8; Blake and Bishop, 1973: 6.
34 Nash, 1962: 291–3, with the illustration no. 1054. Platner and Ashby suggest that the *Saepta* and *Diribitorium* may have been combined (1929: 151) and Nash discusses them as a unit.
35 *Forum Transitorium, Forum Traianum* and the *Mica Aurea.*
36 *Atria vii, Horrea Vespasiani, Templum Castorum et Minervae, Porta Capena, Gens Flavia, Minucia Vetus, Amphitheatrum, Palatium.*
37 For a survey of recent relevant archaeological work, see Anderson, 1983: 93–105, and, for the brickstamps, Blake, 1959: 87–141 (*passim*). For such details as concrete, mortar and types of tiles, see Blake, 1959: 158–63; for vaulting, Blake, 1959: 163–4 and MacDonald, 1982: 56–63.
38 Blake, 1959: 5–8.
39 Thanks to centuries of rebuilding (and plundering), a complete list of his work is, of course, impossible. The summary makes no such claim. Again, as well as the structures noted, some scholars have credited Domitian with, for instance, work on a number of temples, e.g. that of Jupiter Stator (see Blake, 1959: 115 with n. 213: the evidence is not convincing) and Apollo Sosianus (103 with n. 63), the one in the Via delle Botteghe Oscure now thought to have been dedicated to Diana and not Bellona (see Robathan, 1942: 137 and Blake, 1959: 104 with notes 67 to 69) and some in the *Argentina Area* (Robathan, 1942: 137–8 and Blake, 1959: 104 with n. 72).
40 Blake, 1959: 112 with notes 165–70.
41 Platner and Ashby, 1929: 45.
42 Statue: *superimposito moles geminata colosso* (*Silvae* 1.1.1), i.e. 'a gigantic statue redoubled by the huge form surmounting it' (according to Nash, 1961: 389, photo no. 476, the figure on one of Domitian's coins 'agrees with Statius's description'); victories: *Rhenus et attoniti ... Daci* (1.1.7), i.e. 'Rhine and the astounded Dacians'; dedicated: [*indulgentissimus imperator*] *dedicaverat ...* [*Praef.*], i.e. 'the most indulgent emperor had dedicated'. On the statue, see Gsell, 1894: 104 with notes 3 and 4; Hardie, 1983: 131–2 and Hannestad, 1986: 139–40.
43 Nash, 1961: 390 (photo no. 477).
44 The *Forum Nervae* is frequently mentioned in ancient sources, e.g. *Dom.* 5; *Silvae* 4.3.9–10; Eutropius 7.23 and Aurelius Victor, *De Caes.* 12.2. It is the fourth of the imperial *fora* (Martial 10.28.6, 10.51.12). At 1.2.8, though, Martial calls it the *forum Palladium*, not surprisingly given the temple of Minerva therein and Domitian's fondness for that deity (*Dom.* 15.3). Again, the 'new Forum' of Statius's *Silvae* 4.1.14–15 is presumably the *Forum Transitorium.*
45 Anderson, 1983: 94 with n. 3.
46 E.g. Gsell (1894: 105); Nash (1961: 433–4); and Kähler (1963: 112).
47 Blake, 1959: 105–6.
48 Platner and Ashby, 1929: 229.
49 Anderson, 1983: 97–8.

50 Blake, 1959: 114; *contra*, Ramage, 1983: 214.
51 Gsell, 1894: 108 n. 6. For the relevant section of the Severan marble plan, see Nash, 1961: 25 (photo no. 699) and, for the *ludus magnus*, 25–6 (photos nos 700, 701, 702). Domitian's plan for the latter was completed by Hadrian (Blake and Bishop, 1973: 34).
52 Blake, 1959: 120; Anderson, 1983: 99.
53 Its position is clear from *BMC* 2.262.190 and from photographs taken before its demolition in 1936 (e.g. Nash, 1962: 61, photo no. 747).
54 Nash, 1962: 63 (photo no. 749).
55 Gsell, 1894: 109–10 with n. 9.
56 Platner and Ashby, 1929: 371.
57 Scott, 1936: 62–3; Anderson, 1983: 96; and Nash, 1961: 304 (photo no. 361).
58 Platner and Ashby, 1929: 152.
59 Blake, 1959: 112 n. 159; Anderson, 1983: 96.
60 Blake, 1959: 113 notes 159 and 161.
61 Anderson, 1983: 97. Suetonius names the street *ad malum punicum* ('Pomegranate') and locates it on the Quirinal, in the sixth Region.
62 Gsell, 1894: 114 with n. 4.
63 E.g. Blake, 1959: 114.
64 *et fora tot numeras, Iane, quot ora geris*, i.e. 'You count as many fora, Janus, as you have faces' (10.28.6). See also Syme, 1979–88 *RP* 2: 1193.
65 Blake, 1959: 106; Nash, 1961: 505 (photos nos 621, 622).
66 Blake, 1959: 101 n. 34 (Conservatori) and n. 35 (Haterii).
67 Anderson, 1983: 97; Nash, 1962: 67 (photo no. 754).
68 A late coin of Domitian (94/6) shows a round temple of Minerva (*BMC* 2.346.241 = Nash, 1962: 66, photo no. 753) and the building on the Severan plan is circular.
69 Platner and Ashby, 1929: 41; Blake, 1959: 123–4; and Nash, 1961: 46 (photo no. 41).
70 Gsell, 1894: 101 with n. 6.
71 The reconstructed hut is illustrated in Nash, 1962: 164–5 (photos nos 885, 887).
72 On the *Curia*, see Anderson, 1981: 104 and 1983: 101; and Talbert, 1984: 114–5. Domitian's work was not completed until 94 (Platner and Ashby, 1929: 144).
73 Talbert, 1984: 115 n. 13.
74 See the illustrations in Platner and Ashby, 1929: 192 and Nash, 1961: 368, 369 and 371.
75 MacDonald, 1982: 47.
76 Robathan, 1942: 132.
77 Blake, 1959: 118.
78 For Domitian's work, see Blake, 1959: 102–3 and Anderson, 1983: 102 with notes 30 and 31.
79 Smallwood, 1966: 32 (*Fasti Ostienses*). For the temple of Venus Genetrix, see Nash, 1961: 424 (photo no. 519).
80 Nash, 1961: 477 (photo no. 584).
81 E.g. Platner and Ashby, 1929: 383.

82 Anderson, 1983: 99 with n. 20.
83 Platner and Ashby, 1929: 26 (*rivus Herculaneus*); Anderson, 1983: 101.
84 Blake, 1959: 97, 100.
85 Anderson, 1983: 97 with n. 15.
86 Blake, 1959: 103 notes 58 and 59.
87 For the relevant section of the Severan marble plan, see Nash, 1962: 293 (photo no. 1054).
88 E.g. Anderson, 1983: 100–1.
89 Nash, 1961: 201–11 (photos nos 239–41).
90 Anderson, 1983: 101.
91 Anderson, 1983: 100; Blake, 1959: 114–15.
92 E.g. *ILS* 1988 (27 October 90); Roxan, 1978: no. 4 (12 May 91) and no. 6 (12 July 96) together with others from subsequent reigns.
93 Blake, 1959: 124 n. 101.
94 Anderson, 1983: 96.
95 Nash, 1961: 119 (photo no. 124).
96 For a detailed discussion of the temple, Gsell, 1894: 92–3.
97 The *Acta* of the Arval Brethren for 7 December 80 refer to prayers offered for the *restitutionem et dedicationem Capitoli* (McCrum and Woodhead, 1966: 19, lines 13–4).
98 The sum in the text is based on Plutarch's figure of 12,000 talents (*Publ.* 15.3–5), i.e. 1 talent = 6,000 denari = HS 24,000 (Rogers, 1984: 68 with n. 36).
99 For the temple on the Haterii Relief, see Blake, 1959: 101 with notes 35 and 36 and Nash, 1961: 535 (with the illustration on 536 from the Relief).
100 E.g. Platner and Ashby, 1929: 386.
101 Anderson, 1983: 110.
102 Blake, 1959: 102. It is sometimes described as *inter duos lucos* (Vitruvius 4.8.4) or as *inter Arcum et Capitolium* (Gellius 5.12), e.g. Platner and Ashby give its title as *Templum Veiovis inter Duos Lucos* (1929: 548).
103 For the relevant section of the Severan marble plan, see Nash, 1962: 414 (photo no. 1205).
104 The conclusions of Anderson, 1983: 95 have been accepted in the text. Blake believes that Domitian's work can not be differentiated from Vespasian's and Titus's, that he may have added a fourth level and that he certainly completed the interior (1959: 91–6, 98–100, 109–10).
105 Nash, 1961: 134 (photo no. 144 = apotheosis) and 135 (nos 146–7 = triumph). For a detailed description, see Blake, 1959: 111–12.
106 Jones, 1984a: 156.
107 Gsell, 1894: 102–3; Anderson, 1983: 95.
108 McCrum and Woodhead, 1966: 25, line 52.
109 See the excellent illustration in Nash, 1962: 503.
110 Blake, 1959: 97–8; Anderson, 1983: 95.
111 For the *thermae Traianae*, see Anderson, 1983: 103–4; and, for the term *thermae Domitiani*, Platner and Ashby, 1929: 534. According to Paribeni, the *thermae* were more in the style of Rabirius: Blake and Bishop, 1973: 29 n. 156.

112 Anderson, 1983: 104.
113 Anderson, 1983: 103.
114 *[K. Ia]nuar. imp. Trianus forum suum et [bas]ilicam Ulpiam dedicavit* (Smallwood, 1966: 32, *Fasti Ostienses*).
115 On the palace, see Platner and Ashby, 1929: 158–66; Blake, 1959: 115–22; Nash, 1961: 316–38 (note particularly the bibliography on the various sections of the complex, 316–17); Kähler, 1963: 115–19; Pollitt, 1966: 161; and MacDonald, 1982: 47–74, 127–9 and 187, together with the works cited by him on 48–9 notes 5 and 6. Statius, *Silvae* 4.2, provides the most substantial ancient 'description' and Martial (7.56.2) expressly names Rabirius as the architect; parts of the complex appear on the Severan marble plan. In modern times, the brickstamps have proved invaluable and hence the importance of Bloch's work. That said, it must be recorded that a great deal of the archaeological investigation undertaken since the Second World War remains unpublished – consequently, MacDonald's account has been closely followed in the text.
116 Gsell, 1894: 95 n. 3.
117 For the evidence, see MacDonald, 1982: 47 with n. 3.
118 For a discussion of Rabirius's use of the magnificent site Domitian chose, see MacDonald, 1982: 70–1. Martial's assessment changed after 96; then, the palace was dismissed as the 'extravagance of a haughty king' (12.15.4–5).
119 MacDonald, 1982: 49.
120 Both spellings, *Augustana* (*CIL* 15.7246) and *Augustiana* (*CIL* 15.1860), are found in ancient as well as in modern sources.
121 MacDonald, 1982: 57. According to Statius, 'the view travels far upward, tired vision barely reaches the summit, one would think that it was the golden ceiling of the sky' (*Silvae* 4.2.30–1: Loeb, adapted). Martial similarly claims that the palace's 'pinnacle touches the stars' (8.36.11).
122 Blake and Bishop, 1973: 59–60; MacDonald, 1982: 56–63.
123 MacDonald, 1982: 63–4. For Statius's description, see *Silvae* 4.2.18–37 with the useful comments of Vessey, 1983: 215–17.
124 MacDonald, 1982: 66.
125 Diocletian made use of it when executing Christians: see the *Acta* of S. Sebastiani cited in Platner and Ashby, 1929: 162.
126 Platner and Ashby, 1929: 162–3.
127 MacDonald, 1982: 69.
128 MacDonald, 1982: 127, 128.
129 MacDonald, 1982: 71. Similarly, Vessey describes the palace as 'a complex symbol of the divine basis of the autocracy' (1983: 207) and as 'a visual statement of a complex imperial symbolism' (1983: 216).
130 Blake, 1959: 134; Magi, 1973/4: 63–77; and Hersberg, 1978/80: 305–24.
131 Blake, 1959: 134–8.
132 MacDonald, 1982: 70.
133 Blake, 1959: 138–40.
134 Blake, 1959: 140–1.

135 Strong, 1968b: 97–109.
136 Robathan, 1942: 144.

5 ADMINISTRATION II

1 Jones, 1984a: 121–2.
2 Fears, 1981: 76 with n. 371.
3 Fears, 1981: 78–80; Liebeschuetz, 1979: 173–4.
4 Momigliano, 1935: 165–71; Fears, 1981: 78 with n. 384a.
5 Mooney, 1930: 527–8, 583; Morawiecki, 1977: 185–93; and Girard, 1981: 233–45.
6 The standard reverse types show Minerva (a) advancing right with javelin and shield, (b) standing right on prow of ship with javelin, shield and owl at her feet, (c) standing left with thunderbolt, spear and shield and (4) standing left with spear (Carradice, 1978: 159–60). They appear with amazing regularity on both silver and gold coins (Carradice, 1983: 55n. 59).
7 Gsell, 1894: 125–6; Mooney, 1930: 527–8.
8 Liebeschuetz, 1979: 182.
9 Henrichs, 1968: 51–80.
10 *BMC* 2: 123, no. 572.
11 Ancient references to Domitian's relationship with the Vestals include *Dom.* 8.3–4; *Ep.* 4.11; Dio 67.3.3–4; *Silvae* 1.1.35–6; Plutarch, *Numa* 10.8 and *V Apoll.* 7.6. See also Gsell, 1894: 80–2; Mooney, 1930: 547–9; Scott, 1936: 187–8; Syme, 1958: 65; and Sherwin-White, 1966: 280–5.
12 That Domitian is meant is the contention of Hardie, 1983: 11, 203 n. 68 (and others).
13 The Oculatae may have belonged to the *gens Aelia* and Varronilla was probably related to either P. Tullius Varro or Cingonius Varro (Raepsaet-Charlier, 1987: 39, 611–12).
14 Mooney, 1930: 548.
15 Raepsaet-Charlier, 1987: 245. Crispinus's involvement with her (Juvenal 4.10) is hardly credible.
16 Gsell assigns the second trial to the period from 3.1.87 to 3.1.90, with the latter part of 89 being the most likely time (1894: 80–1 n. 9).
17 Technically, this was not incorrect, so not (as Pliny claims) an example of *immanitate tyranni* ('a tyrant's cruelty': *Ep.* 4.11.6).
18 Sherwin-White, 1966: 280–5; Vinson, 1989: 433–5.
19 So unattractive were the conditions that no candidates were interested in the position between 87 BC and the days of Augustus (*Aug.* 31.4).
20 Syme, 1958: 65 and 1980: 117, citing Plutarch, *Quaest. Rom.* 50.
21 *Dom.* 4.3; Gsell, 1894: 77–8; *BMC* 2: xcv–vi; Mooney, 1930: 524–5; and Syme, 1958: 65–6, 472 and 664. Statius (*Silvae* 1.4.17. 4.1.37) and Martial (4.1.7, 10.63.3) duly noted the event and it was also commemorated on an impressive series of coins (*BMC* 2: 392–6, nos 419–38). For the date, see Censorinus *De Die Natali* 17.11 (*Domitianus se XIIII et L. Minucio Rufo cons*) and, for an example of the ritual, *ILS* 5050 (partly translated by Lewis and Reinhold, 1955: 57–61).

22 Mooney, 1930: 524–5; Syme, 1958: 664.
23 In discussing Cladius's interpretation of the cycle, Syme notes that 'nobody was taken in' (1958: 472).
24 Syme, 1958: 65–6 n. 6.
25 *Dom.* 4.4; Gsell, 1894: 122–5; Friedländer, 1907: (2) 120–1, (4) 264–8; and Mooney, 1930: 526.
26 Friedländer, 1907: (2) 120 and (4) 548–9.
27 Juvenal 6.387 refers to Pollio who hoped for the *Capitolinam quercum* ('Capitoline oak-wreath') for his lyre playing; and, in *Silvae* 5.3, Statius mentions prizes at the *Quinquatria* (229) and at the *Ludi Capitolini* (233–4) presented by 'Caesar's hand'.
28 Friedländer, 1907: (4) 266.
29 Gsell, 1894: 125 n. 5.
30 Friedländer, 1907: (4) 264–5, for the Latin.
31 Friedländer, 1907: (4) 264–7.
32 Friedländer, 1907: (3) 46.
33 Mooney, 1930: 522.
34 Scorpus (*PIR*[1] S 203), the 'glory of the noisy circus' (Martial 10.54.1–4), was mentioned by Martial on four other occasions (5.25.9–10, 10.50, 10.53 and 11.1.16) and he is credited with 2,048 wins (*ILS* 5287). It used to be thought that it was his name on the tombstone of Domitian's freedman T. Flavius Abascantus (*ILS* 1679), but this was another Scorpus (see Syme, 1979–88, *RP* 3 1062–9).
35 Nerva reintroduced public performances (*Pan.* 46.1–2), but Trajan reverted to Domitian's practice, an apparent 'inconsistency' that Pliny was at considerable pains to justify (46.3–8).
36 The evidence is assembled in the relevant volumes of *PIR*[1] (except for Canus and Latinus in *PIR*[2] C 401 and L 129 respectively), i.e. P 95, T 140, P 64, G 177 and P 415.
37 Carradice, 1983: 27, 29.
38 Buttrey, 1980: 37.
39 Bauman, 1982: 121–4.
40 Hammond, 1959: 128–66.
41 Buttrey, 1980: 30–1.
42 Garthwaite, 1990: 13–15.
43 For those behaving like Phasis, see Garthwaite, 1990: 13–14, and for those neglecting the *lex Julia*, Thompson, 1984: 472 n. 36.
44 Janssen, 1919: 43–4; Bauman, 1982: 122 n. 197.
45 Janssen, 1919: 39; Mooney, 1930: 539. Bauman believes that it was done by edict (1982: 117 n. 171).
46 Bauman, 1982: 124.
47 But see Money, 1930: 546–7 and Bauman, 1982: 121–2.
48 Bauman, 1982: 117–24.
49 Janssen, 1919: 62–3; Gephardt, 1922: 85; Mooney, 1930: 571–2; Scott, 1936: 102–12; and Vessey, 1983: 217. Amongst the dissenters are Waters, 1964: 67 and Thompson, 1984: 469–75.
50 Scott, 1936: 108.
51 Hence Scott associated Domitian's alleged use of the title with his decision to 'turn to absolutism and to abandon the system of diarchy

(sic)' (1936: 103) – 'whatever that means' (Balsdon, 1938: 86, in a comment on this passage.

52 On all this, see Bowerstock, 1973: 180, 198.

53 Brunt, 1979: 173 and Vessey, 1983: 210. But, according to Syme, Pliny's view of Trajan as the vice-regent of Jupiter is 'not very different' from Statius's portrayal of Domitian (1979–88, *RP* 1: 78).

54 Compare *BMC* 2: 1xxxv (Domitian) and 3: 1xxv (Trajan).

55 For instances of Statius's and Martial's use of the title, see Scott, 1936: 102–12. Waters (1970: 70 n. 32) has pointed out that the flattery of Domitian assigned by Juvenal to his *amici* is paralleled almost exactly by Pliny in his references to Trajan in the *Panegyricus*: e.g. *dis aequa potestas* (Juv. 4.71) and *quem aequata dis immortalibus potestas* (*Pan.* 4.4).

56 Vessey, 1983: 217.

57 Fallows, 1990: 262.

58 E.g. Mooney, 1930: 544–5 and Pleket, 1961: 314; but not Brunt, 1961: 314 nor Levick, 1982: 63–4.

59 Gsell, 1894: 142.

60 Eck, 1982a: 328; and for Baebius Massa (*PIR²* B 26), see Houston, 1971: 34 and Eck, 1982a: 319 with n. 151.

61 Hopkins, 1983: 186.

62 On Book 12 of the Sibylline Oracles, see Pleket, 1961: 303; Waters, 1964: 50; and Levick, 1982: 61–2 (with n. 39).

63 Syme, 1979–88, *RP* 1: 10.

64 Williams, 1990: 201 n. 29.

65 Levick, 1982: 61 with n. 41.

66 Pleket, 1961: 296–315; Levick, 1982: 50–73.

67 Pleket, 1961: 304.

68 Pleket, 1961: 304–5; McCrum and Woodhead, 1966: no. 466; Lewis, 1968: 135–162; Bradley, 1978a: 336–42; Levick, 1982: 51–3; and Devreker, 1982: 514.

69 Jones, 1979: 61.

70 Pleket, 1961: 307–8; McCrum and Woodhead, 1966: no. 500; Levick, 1982: 53–6; Devreker, 1982: 514; and Levick, 1985: 196–7.

71 Pleket, 1961: 307–8; McCrum and Woodhead, 1966: no. 464; Levick, 1982: 57–8; Devreker, 1982: 514; and Levick, 1985: 111–12.

72 Levick, 1982: 57.

73 Levick, 1982: 58.

74 Pleket, 1961: 305.

75 Pleket, 1961: 305–6; Levick, 1982: 58–60; and Devreker, 1982: 514.

76 McCrum and Woodhead, 1966: no 463 (c) to (e).

77 McCrum and Woodhead, 1966: no. 121; Devreker, 1982: 515 n. 137.

78 Dvereker, 1982: 515 notes 138, 139.

79 Devreker, 1982: 515.

80 Devreker, 1982: 515–16; Levick, 1982: 61; and 1985: 86–7.

81 Dabrowa, 1980b: 73.

82 On these cities, see A.H.M. Jones, 1971: 81, 93, 159–60, 210 and Devreker, 1982: 513, 515.

83 Johnson *et al.* 1961: 153–9 (with fragments of two other Domitianic

[?] charters); Lewis and Reinhold, 1966: 321–6; and Levick, 1985: 25–30.

84 *AE* 1986: 333; Giminez-Candela, 1983: 125–40; Gonzalez, 1986: 147–243; Nony, 1986: 49–53; Mourgues, 1987: 78–87; Johnston, 1987: 62–77; Galsterer, 1987: 181–203, 1988: 78–90; and Horstkotte, 1989: 169–77.

85 Gonzalez suggests that the name was probably Irni, with Irnium as a possibility (1986: 147); Nony refers to it as Irnum (1986: 50).

86 Nony, 1986: 49.

87 The passage is discussed in detail by Bosworth, 1973: 53–5. Some have dissented from his interpretation.

88 Nony, 1986: 50.

89 For the relevant texts, see Gonzalez, 1986: 160 and 186–7 (ambassadors), 173 and 193 (revenue) together with 174 and 194–5 (games).

90 Garzetti, 1974: 278.

91 Garzetti, 1974: 652; Leglay, 1968: 221–2 (colonies) and 230–2 (commerce). In 87, Suellius Flaccus determined the boundaries between the Muduciuvii and the Zamucii to the east of the Serti (*IRT* 854).

92 Jones, 1976b: 256–7.

93 Syme, 1977: 38–49; Eck, 1982a: 321 n. 161; and Levick, 1985; 197.

94 Frankfort, 1962: 671; Schürer, 1973: 482.

95 *BMC* 2: xiii; *CAH*, 1936: 95–7; and Carradice, 1983: 2.

96 To cite but a very few, Pergola (1978: 407–23), Keresztes (1973: 1–28), Reicke (1980: 275–83) and Sordi (1960: 1–26, 1981: 137–52, 1985: 99–117) see Domitian as a persecutor. Doubters include Moreau (1953: 121–9), Saulnier (1984: 251–79) and Prigent (1974: 455–83). For earlier views, see Smallwood, 1956: 12 n. 2 and add Knudsen, 1943: *passim*.

97 Barzano has argued that Pliny's phrase *peregrinae superstitionis ministeria* (*Pan.* 49.8, i.e. 'ministrants of an oriental superstition') refers to the Christians who were in Domitian's court (1982b: 408–15)! Many years ago, Syme convincingly argued that they were 'clearly the ministrants of the cult of Isis' (1979–88 *RP* 1: 83).

98 Cross and Livingstone, 1984: 418–19.

99 Wallace, 1987: 343–58.

100 See Keresztes for some examples (1973: 8 n. 22).

101 Gsell, 1894: 294–5; Leclercq, 1921b and c: 1401–2; Fasola, 1960: 630–4: and Pergola, 1978: 413–15.

102 Smallwood, 1956: 8 (Domitilla) and 9 (Glabrio).

103 See Keresztes, 1973: 25 and Barnard, 1963–4: 251–60.

104 Keresztes, 1973: 20.

105 Bell, 1978: 96.

106 'It is perhaps unfortunate that improper emphasis ... was given ... to often very rhetorical passages by Melito, Tertullian ..., the consideration of whom is not essential at all' (Keresztes, 1973: 1).

107 Often identified as Hadrian's friend Bruttius Praesens: see Syme, 1979–88, *RP* 4: 29 n. 50 and 5: 563–78.

108 For Baronius, see Knudsen, 1943: 31–3.

109 Prigent (1974: 175–7), Collins (1977: 241–56) and Harris (1979: 15–25)

assign it to Domitian's reign, whereas Sanford (1937: 99) and Bell (1978: 93–102), for instance, prefer Nero's.

110 Newman, 1963: 138. Bell notes Irenaeus's confusion of the apostle James with James, the brother of Jesus (1979: 93).
111 Bell, 1978: 93–102.
112 With reference to the 'fifth head', Harris (who favours a Domitianic dating) argues as follows: 'It must be admitted that the straight-forward application of this points to Nero. . . . If, on the other hand, we choose a Domitianic date on other grounds and want the present "king" to be Domitian, we would have to start the list with Nero. . . . This version of course obliges us to explain why the list should start with Nero, which is difficult' (1979: 18).
113 Pringent, 1974: 471.
114 For the relevant extracts, see Williams, 1990: 205–6 with n. 68.
115 Smallwood, 1956: 8 with n. 35.
116 Smallwood, 1956: 8 with n. 36.
117 Gsell, 1894: 291–2; Smallwood, 1956: 10.
118 Gsell, 1894: 291; Smallwood, 1956: 9–10.
119 For a more detailed account, see Smallwood, 1956: 11 and Prigent, 1974: 483.
120 Smallwood, 1956: 1–13; Thompson, 1982: 329–42; Goodman, 1989: 41–4; and Williams, 1990: 196–211.
121 Williams's suggestion (1990: 200) has the merit of being clear and sensible.
122 Williams, 1990: 207–9.
123 'Treason' (R.S. Rogers, 1960: 23); 'defamatory compositions' (Bauman, 1974: 169).
124 Sherwin-White, 1966: 764.
125 On astrologers and astrology, see Cramer, 1951: 9–50 and Liebeschuetz, 1979: 119–26.
126 On all this, see Liebeschuetz, 1979: 121.
127 Syme, 1979–88, *RP* 1: 299.
128 *De Officio Proconsulis* 7, cited by Liebeschuetz, 1979: 124 n. 8.
129 Cramer, 1951: 12.
130 See *AE* 1936: 128 (=McCrum and Woodhead, 1966: no. 458), discussed by Forbes, 1955: 348–52 and Sherwin-White, 1966; 640–1. The Digest refers specifically to immunities that Vespasian granted to *philosophi* (50.4.18.30).
131 For Ti. Catius Asconius Silius Italicus, see Houston, 1971: 241–2; McDermott and Orentzel, 1977: 29–34; Liebeschuetz, 1979: 167–80 and Coleman, 1986: 3103–4. For the son, suffect consul in the last months of 94, see Houston, 1971: 496.
132 Liebeschuetz, 1979: 169–70.
133 Wistrand, 1979: 95.
134 Sherwin-White, 1966: 240
135 Birley, 1981: 81.
136 Bauman, 1974: 159–62; *contra* Rogers, 1960: 19–23.
137 Sherwin-White, 1966: 243, who discusses the background of all seven accused on 242–3.

138 For him, see Jones, 1979: 44–5; he had been proconsul of Asia in 80/1 (Eck, 1982a: 304 with n. 91).
139 Bauman, 1974: 159–62.
140 For a discussion of *Dom.* 8.3, see Bauman, 1974: 166 n. 202.
141 Bauman's suggestion that 'the good period probably lasted until the revolt of Antonius Saturninus' (1974: 167) is probably over-optimistic.
142 See Bauman, 1974: 165 n. 195. For the *humiliores*, the penalty was to be either burned alive or else thrown to the wild beasts.
143 Ballanti summarizes such evidence as exists and much more (1954: 74–95); for some sceptical comments, see Garzetti, 1974: 648–9.
144 Syme, 1958: 599–601; Birley, 1981: 85–7.
145 Starr, 1949: 20.
146 Waters, 1964: 70–1.
147 Ballanti (1954: 84–92) discusses Sulpicia and her role in the intellectual opposition to Domitian; Billault examines Chio's work (1977: 29–36), whilst Ballanti has discovered an 'affinità' between Chio and the 'mondo spirituale' of Sulpicia (1954: 92); and only Ballanti manages to link Seneca, St Paul and Domitian – on the grounds that Nero = Domitian (1954: 92–5).

6 WAR I

1 i.e *prosperae in Oriente, adversae in Occidente res: turbatum Illyricum, Galliae nutantes, perdomita Britannia et statim omissa: coortae in nos Sarmatarum ac Sueborum gentes, nobilitatus cladibus mutuis Dacus, mota prope etiam Parthorum arma falsi Neronis ludibrio (Hist.* 1.2: Loeb trans., adapted). Tacitus had already expressed similar sentiments in the *Agricola*, i.e. *tot exercitus in Moesia Daciaque et Germania et Pannonia temeritate aut per ignaviam ducum amissi* (41.2). Pliny, on the other hand, addressing one of Domitian's *duces* ('Trajan), naturally preferred not to mention their alleged cowardice (*ignavia*) and rashness (*temeritas*), but rather to criticize the attitude of the ordinary soldiers: at *Pan.* 18.2, he complained that *disciplinam castrorum* had to be restored by Trajan because of *inertia et contumacia et dedignatione parendi* (i.e. 'indifference, insolence and contempt for obedience').
2 For a detailed commentary on *Hist.* 1.2, see Syme, 1958: 214–15 and Chilver, 1979: 39–42.
3 Millar, 1982: 22; Murison, 1985: 33.
4 E.g. Walser, 1968: 499; Birley, 1974: 1–16; Luttwak, 1976: 68 and elsewhere; Millar, 1982: 1–23 with the bibliography at 3 n. 12; Garnsey and Saller, 1982: 9–10; and Hanson, 1989: 55–63.
5 Birley, 1974: 16, translating Walser, 1968: 499.
6 The names are confirmed not only by Juvenal but also by Statius in the surviving lines of his *De Bello Germanico*.
7 Millar, 1982: 14. On Frontinus (who presumably played a prominent role in the campaign), see Eck, 1985b: 141–2. For a full list of ancient laudatory references to Domitian's military ability, see Ramage, 1989: 704.

8 See Campbell, 1987: 28–9.
9 To the bibliography in Jones, 1973b: 79 n. 4, add Jones, 1982: 329–35 and Strobel, 1987a: 423–52 with 423 n. 1. For a full list of ancient references to the war, see Ramage, 1989: 703.
10 Hannestad, 1986: 136–7, with figure 85 at 135.
11 Walser, 1989: 449–56 (with the bibliography at 449 n. 1). He assigns the stone to 89, but Lebek prefers 83 (1989: 80 n. 93).
12 Evans, 1978: 121–4. For a list of those preferring 83, see Jones, 1973b: 80 n. 10.
13 Henderson, 1927: 100. The argument was first put forward by Gsell (1894: 184) and repeated by Weynand, *RE* 6.2556; Corradi, *DE* 2.1997 and Henderson (1927). In all of them, there is an interesting example of a received error, in that *A.d XII k. Octobr.* is incorrectly translated as 19 instead of 20 September.
14 See also Jones, 1982: 331.
15 CIL 16.35 and Roxan, 1978: 32, no. 3. See also Mann, 1972: 233–41.
16 Zonaras 11.19 p. 58, 16–25D (= Dio 67.3.5) and Xiphilinus 218, 22–9 (= Dio 67.3.4).
17 *Chronicorum Canonum, A. Abr.* 2098, i.e. 1 October 81/30 September 82.
18 Scott, 1936: 187.
19 Buttrey, 1980: 30–1
20 E.g. Evans, 1975: 124.
21 Syme, 1936: 164 n. 2.
22 Mommsen, 1887–8: 132–6; Hammond, 1959: 76–9, 108–11; and Maxfield, 1981: 101–3.
23 Kneissl, 1969: 43–57; Buttrey, 1980: 52–6; Martin, 1985: 168–73 and 1987: 73–82 (with bibliography).
24 On Macherus and Masada, see now Kennedy and Riley, 1990: 96–100 with figures 46–8; and, for Vespasian's salutations, Buttrey, 1980: 6–7.
25 Syme, 1936: 162–3. For a discussion of Frontinus's contributions, see Luttwak, 1976: 214 n. 103 and Perl, 1981: 563–83.
26 Schönberger, 1969: 159.
27 Isaac argues convincingly that the word *limes* at this time was not used in connection with frontier/border defence (1988: 127).
28 Compare the arguments of Kennedy, 1983: 189–91 and Strobel, 1986b: 257–64.
29 On the *ius gladii*, see Dio 53.13.6–7 and Pflaum, 1950: 119.
30 Syme, 1928: 41.
31 *Dom.* 7.3. Most scholars (e.g. Janssen, 1919: 41; Henderson, 1927: 104; Mooney, 1930: 542; Garzetti, 1974: 270; Nicols, 1978: 96; and Murison, 1985: 34 with n. 5) date the increase to *c.* 84. B. Campbell, however, despite Dio 67.3.5, assigns it to the period after the revolt of Saturninus, dismissing the coin of 84 with the legend *stip. Imp. Aug. Dom.* (1984: 185 n. 26).
32 Carradice, 1983: 161, 170 n. 46.
33 P.M. Rogers assesses the annual cost of a legion at 6.6 million HS (1984: 66). As for the total outlay on the army, Hopkins suggests a

figure of 450 million HS per year (1980: 116–17 and 124–5), whereas Rogers prefers 450–500 million (1984: 66 with n. 28).

34 Ostrand believes that the campaign was nothing more than a 'reconnaissance mission' (1984: 100); he refers to the 'concentration of coins for the years 81/82 and 82' (96), to the 'almost complete absence (of them) for the year 83' (94, with the tables on 131–48) and concludes that only 'minor fighting was involved in this war' (98). For Schönberger, the 'result was really rather poor', in view of the outlay of over 30,000 soldiers (1969: 158).

35 See Luttwak, 1976: 92.

36 Birley, 1981: 73–81. For his consulship, see now Campbell, 1986: 197–200.

37 For the different views, see Jones, 1984a: 177 n. 204. Since then, Pitts and St Joseph (1985: 264–7 – giving the arguments for both datings) and Strobel argue for 78–84 (1987b: 198–212), Hind for 77–83 (1985: 1), whereas Daniels is undecided (1989: 32).

38 Birley, 1981: 78–9.

39 Hind, 1985: 10.

40 'He must have been able to convince the new emperor that the *terminus Britanniae* was within his grasp' (Birley, 1981: 80–1).

41 Birley, 1981: 21.

42 See Pitts and St Joseph, 1985: 265, 272.

43 Martin, 1981: 45.

44 Hind feels that identifying Mons Graupius with Duncrub 'does make a good deal of sense' (1985: 13–14). Daniels, however, disagrees, arguing that its location 'has long been chased about the counties of Scotland and identified at Duncrub in Strathearn, Raedykes and Durno in Aberdeenshire and Knock Hill in Banff. Perhaps, it has even been suggested, it lay in Nairn, Inverness, or even beyond. While no site carries complete conviction, Duncrub has least of all' (1989: 33).

45 Hobley, 1989: 72–3. Daniels would put it even as early as 86 (1989: 32).

46 Hobley, 1989: 73.

47 Daniels, 1989: 34.

48 Hobley, 1989: 73.

49 Strong, 1968a: 73.

50 Eck, 1982a: 312–22.

51 Syme, 1980: 42–9.

52 See Jones and Conole, 1983: 632.

53 The inscription is discussed by Jarrett and Mann, 1970: 180; Davies, 1976; 115–21; and Jones and Conole 1983: 631. Maxfield finds the honours granted him unusually lavish and 'on an unprecedented scale . . . unparalleled by anything that came after' (1981: 164).

54 See Davies, 1976: 115–21; his hypothesis has been accepted in the text. Note also Speidel, 1978: 65, 126–7 and Jones and Conole, 1983: 629–33.

55 Maxfield, 1981: 155–6.

56 For units that were granted such titles, see Davies, 1976: 117 with n. 14.

57 For a discussion of the word *Britanniciani* see Speidel, who believes that Domitian had the *singulares* moved from Britain 'because of complicity in the "crime" of Governor Lucullus, whose new-fangled *Luculleae* lances may have been designed for his guard' (1978: 127).

58 Davies, 1976: 118.

59 Davies, 1976: 120–1.

60 Jarrett and Mann, 1970: 180.

61 Conole and Milns, 1983: 183–200.

62 For the details, see Mócsy, 1974: 80.

63 Syme, 1979–88, *RP* 5: 514–20; Eck, 1985a: 475–84.

64 Fulvus's career is discussed by Jones, 1984a: 111 n. 105 and by Syme, 1979–88, *RP* 5: 615–16.

65 For the Dacians after Burebista, see Mócsy, 1974: 19–24 and Luttwak, 1976: 97–101.

66 On the Sarmatians, see Bosworth, 1977: 220 n. 10; Conole and Milns, 1983: 183; and Wilkes, 1983: 256–8.

67 i.e. *ILS* 986 (Plautius Silvanus's inscription); see Wilkes, 1983: 259 and Conole and Milns, 1983: 183–200.

68 Such is the assessment of Wilkes, 1983: 263.

69 Compare the evidence from the archaeological reports listed by Mocsy (1974: 80–1) and those published subsequently (Wilkes, 1983: 266).

70 Mócsy, 1974: 81.

71 For the details, see Mocsy, 1974: 80–1 and Wilkes, 1983: 266.

72 On these, see Wilkes, 1983: 267, 280 n. 51.

73 Bérard, 1989: 138; Dorutiu-Boila, 1978: 289–96.

74 Wilkes, 1983: 267.

75 Syme, 1928: 55 and Wilkes, 1983: 265. The *V Alaudae* did not exist after 70; *contra* Syme, 1971: 82–3, 105 in *addenda* to earlier articles.

76 Modern attempts to reconstruct Domitian's Dacian wars include Syme, 1936: 168–78; Mócsy, 1974: 82–3; Visy, 1978: 37–60; Rossi, 1980/1; Wilkes, 1983: 268–70; and Strobel, 1989. The most substantial ancient account is to be found in Dio Cassius 67.5–7,10 and 68.9.3, with scattered comments in Suetonius, *Dom.* 6; Tacitus, *Agricola* 41; Orosius, 7.10.3–4; Jordanes, *Getica* 76; and Eutropius 7.23.4. Various passages in Statius and Martial, especially useful in dating the campaigns, are discussed by Gsell, 1894: 202–32. Buttrey, 1980: 30–1 and Carradice, 1983: 28–30, provide the most recent list of Domitian's salutations, valuable too for problems of chronology.

77 The date of Oppius Sabinus's disaster is hotly disputed. Syme (1936: 168) suggests that it occurred in the course of 85, as does Strobel, 1989: 116 and Alföldy and Halfmann, 1973: 356, whereas Mócsy's preference is for the traditional date (e.g. Gsell, 1894: 209–12), i.e. the end of 85 or early 86 (1974: 82) – less likely in view of the fact that salutations ten and eleven were announced in September/October 85.

78 Diurpaneus (*PIR²* D 110) could well be the Duras (*PIR²* D 208) who abdicated in favour of Decebalus (Dio 67.6.1): for the latter, see Speidel, 1970: 142–53.

79 Syme, 1936: 171 n. 1; Mócsy, 1974: 82; and Wilkes, 1983: 279 n. 42.

On Oppius Sabinus's family (from Auximum = modern Osimo), see Patterson, 1987: 131.

80 Rankov, 1990: 173; Alföldy and Halfmann, 1973: 331–73.

81 Dusanic argues for Scupi (1983: 18), but doubts are expressed by E. Birley, 1986: 209–16. Naissus was well situated for the division of Moesia into two provinces, and strategically significant as five roads met there (Syme, 1979–88, *RP* 3: 1003–4).

82 Syme, 1936: 169–70.

83 Wilkes, 1983: 280 n. 53.

84 For the substantial literature on this monument, see Wilkes, 1983: 287–8, notes 101–3.

85 Ogilvie and Richmond, 1967: 291.

86 Syme, 1971: 73, 82 and elsewhere: but Fuscus perished in Dacia itself, according to Juvenal 4.112.

87 Ogilvie and Richmond provide the standard view: 'One disaster, probably the first [i.e. Oppius Sabinus's] was commemorated on the altar of Adamklissi in the Dobrudja' (1967: 291). Wilkes firmly rejects such a notion (1983: 279 n. 42).

88 Carradice, 1983: 28.

89 Carradice has Domitian *censor perpetuus*, *IMP. XI* on the sixth (and last) issue of 85 (1983: 29).

90 Carradice, 1983: 29.

91 E.g. Hammond, 1959: 78; Baxter, 1974; 139; Rogers, 1984: 65 n. 24 and Campbell, who refers to triumphs for 'campaigns against the Chatti and again jointly over the Chatti and Dacians' (1984: 136).

92 E.g. Brandis, *RE* 4.2248; Janssen, 1919: 64–5; Mooney, 1930: 535; and Strobel, 1989: 116.

93 On Domitian's renaming of September and October, see Talbert, 1984: 360–2. Other emperors refused or accepted similar changes, e.g. *Julius* 76.1, *Aug.* 31.2, *Tib.* 26.2 and *Nero* 55, whilst Dio 72.15.3 has Commodus renaming all twelve. Eusebius assigns the changes to 1 October 86/30 September 87.

94 For what it is worth, the poets seem to support this argument. Throughout Book 6, Martial lauds Domitian the Censor and, at 6.4.2, finds that Rome 'already owes you so many triumphs'; similarly, Statius, *Thebaid* 1.18–20.

95 For Maternus and Flaccus, see *CAH* 11: 145 and Wood, 1941: 21–2. Desanges identifies Septimius and Suellius Flaccus (1964: 713–25), but not very convincingly, as Eck argues (1982a: 313 n. 130).

96 For Flaccus, see *PIR*[1] S 398; *RE* 4 A.581; and Strobel, 1986c: 273 n. 46 (bibliography). Eck argues for 86/7 as Flaccus's first year in the Numidian command on the basis of *IRT* 854, assigned to the period 1 January/13 September 87 (1982a: 313 n. 130). Dio (67.4.6) incorrectly refers to him as the governor of Numidia: but the province did not then officially exist, and it is better to regard Flaccus as commanding the *III Augusta*.

97 Walker, 1976: 120; Carradice, 1983: 159–61.

98 *CAH* 11: 147–8.

99 *AE* 1954, 137 reveals the existence of a new permanent camp in stone

for a detachment of the *III Augusta*; perhaps the entire legion was stationed there by Domitian's time.

100 *PIR*¹ 291; *RE* Suppl. 9.1368.8; Pflaum, 1960: 116 n. 7 and 1962: 1235; and Houston, 1971: 237–40. He had previously commanded the *III Augusta* in Numidia in 73/4 and 74/5, according to Eck, 1982a: 293, 295.

101 Compare Kennedy, 1983: 185, 195–6 and Strobel, 1986c: 279–80.

102 Kennedy, 1983: 194

103 *Isdem cos . . . [id]us Ianuar. in aedem Concordiae astantibus fratribus Arva[libus] magisterio [imp.] Caesaris Domitiani Aug. Germanici, promag. L. Veratio Quadra[to]*: McCrum and Woodhead, 1966: 23, no. 13, lines 26–30.

104 For the Games, see Censorinus, *De Die Natali: quorum agonum primus a Domitiano institutus fuit, duodecimo eius et Ser. Corneli Dolabellae consulatu*, i.e. 86, and, for the time of the year, Friedländer, 1907: (4) 549.

105 See Pflaum, 1960: 79.

106 Buttrey, 1980: 31; Carradice, 1983: 30 and 32 (i.e. *IMP. XV* by the second issue of 88).

107 Carradice, 1979: 101–3.

108 Evans, 1978: 102–28 and Eck, 1982a: 302–14.

109 For Nigrinus's decorations, see Maxfield, 1981: 151; for Vettoninaus's, Wilkes, 1983: 283 n. 67, and, for the date of the salutations, Carradice, 1983: 30.

110 For the three legions and their possible destinations, see Wilkes, 1983: n. 67 and 283–4 n. 74. Syme prefers Singidunum for *II Adiutrix* and Viminacium for *IV Flavia* (1928: 55). It was certainly there later (Wilkes, 1983: 285 n. 85), but there is no clear evidence to identify the Upper Moesian base which housed it. On the whole question, see also Mócsy, 1974: 86.

111 Eck, 1982a: 302–14.

112 Domitian was *IMP. XIV* in January 88, *XV* by September, *XVII* a month later and *XXI* by September of the following year. Gsell assigned Julianus's campaign to 89 (1894: 218), but most scholars prefer the previous year, e.g. Syme, 1936: 172 (Autumn 88).

113 Gsell, 1894: 77.

114 Carradice, 1983; 30.

115 Campbell tends to prefer the second alternative, i.e. the edict 'states in formal terms and links specifically with his own name a privilege that was already established but . . . bestowed on an *ad hoc* basis' (1984: 443).

116 For the text, see McCrum and Woodhead, 1966: 111, no. 404.

117 Strobel, 1989: 119.

118 i.e. June–September 88 (Strobel, 1989: 118).

7 WAR II

1 For the details of the uprising (not generally disputed), see Assa, 1962: 31–9; Walser, 1968: 497–507; Winkler, 1972: 495–8; Syme, 1979–88,

RP 3: 1070–84: 12–21; Jones, 1979: 30–6; Murison, 1985: 31–49; and Strobel, 1986a: 203–20.

2 The exact date depends on the interpretation of a number of items in the *Acta Fratrum Arvalium* of 88–9 (*CIL* 6.2066).

3 Murison argues that, whilst the destruction later caused by the Chatti is attested archaeologically, Saturninus's alleged invitation might simply be 'post-mortem vilification of him' (1985: 37).

4 Assa, 1962; *PIR²* L 84; and Eck, 1985b: 149–51.

5 Winkler, 1972: 495–8; *PIR²* N 162. The so-called epitomator of Aurelius Victor incorrectly conflated the consular Lappius and the equestrian Norbanus, an error corrected by *AE* 1961: 319 but retained by Sherwin-White, 1966: 643 and *OCD²*, 1970: 738. Norbanus, procurator of Rhaetia in 88/9, may have become prefect of Egypt later in Domitian's reign and was then promoted to the most senior equestrian post, the prefecture of the praetorian guard, a post he held when the emperor was assassinated (Dio 67.15.2).

6 See Janssen, 1919: 41; Mooney, 1930: 542; and Garzetti, 1974: 270 for the pay rise and, for the privileges granted in September/October 88, McCrum and Woodhead, 1966: 111, no. 404. Campbell (1984: 185, 234), however, links the pay rise to the aftermath of the revolt and argues that it coincided with the privileges edict.

7 *PIR²* J 14 and Eck, 1985b: 42–3. He had been suffect consul with Lappius in 86.

8 Pitts and St Joseph, 1985.

9 Walser, 1968: 500; Birley, 1974: 16.

10 Vidman, 1982: 77.

11 Syme, 1928: 42.

12 Syme, 1936: 173. Looking at marching rates and chronological indications alone, Murison argues for somewhere very close to the same area (1985: 39–40).

13 For the various routes available to messengers from Germany to Rome, from Rome to Germany and from Spain to Germany, see Walser, 1968: 503 and Murison, 1985: 38–44.

14 Walser, 1989: 455.

15 E.g. 'Hinter Saturninus stand eine grossere Verschwörung aus Kreisen des Senats und der Generalität' (Walser, 1968: 498); 'doubtless L. Antonius Saturninus' conspiracy brought on an intensification of the persecution [of the senatorial order]' (Applebaum, 1974: 116); similarly, Gsell, 1894: 261 and others listed by Jones, 1979: 30 n. 1 and 31 n. 16.

16 Syme, 1979–88, *RP* 3: 1070–84.

17 Murray, 1967: 250.

18 Devreker, 1980: 257–68.

19 According to Dio 67.11.2–3, Lappius burned many incriminating documents before the emperor could reach Mainz, and thereby saved from execution anyone who had given Saturninus written evidence of their support: but the story should be rejected, according to Jones, 1979: 30–6. Murison, on the other hand, suggests that Lappius and Norbanus (who both helped to suppress the revolt) were, in fact, the 'villains who prospered', i.e. they pretended to Saturninus that

they would support him, but turned on him so as to gain influence with Domitian and then burned the evidence (1985: 46–7), a highly speculative reconstruction, as Murison recognizes (48 n. 41).

20 Jones, 1979: 30.

21 For the interval between praetorship and consulship, see Birley, 1981: 24–5 with n. 6.

22 Gallivan, 1981: 191.

23 For an alternative explanation, see Jones, 1979: 35.

24 Walser, 1968: 505 with n. 46; Maxfield, 1981: 234.

25 Wilkes, 1983: 283 n. 74, 285 n. 83. The *XIV Gemina* retained its revolutionary spirit, playing a significant role in the proclamation of Septimius Severus a century later, in 193 (Walser, 1968: 505–6).

26 Walser, 1968: 506 with notes 53–6.

27 See Pflaum for the *procuratores provinciarum Galliae Belgicae et duarum Germanicarum* (1960: 1056–7). Walser, 1968: 507 and Raepsaet-Charlier, 1973: 158–61 discuss the administrative arrangements for the area.

28 Schönberger comments on the destruction of a number of forts and watch-towers on the *limes* (1969: 159), discussed also by Syme, 1936: 175; Murison, 1985: 37; and Strobel, 1986: 215–16.

29 Walser prefers 89 (1989: 449–56), whereas Lebek favours 83 (1989: 80 n. 93).

30 'An old and well-tried policy' (Gordon, 1949: 61). According to Garzetti, 'the terms . . . were no different from those normally granted to client kingdoms, even down to the clause, which seemed scandalous, granting financial and technical aid to build fortifications and works of public utility' (1974: 290). Naturally, Pliny scorned it. At *Pan.* 12.2, he proclaimed that, under Trajan, Romans no longer had to pay for hostages nor spend large sums of money in order to buy peace or to be named as conquerors.

31 The month and year (November 89) were established by Gsell, 1894: 198–200.

32 So Syme, 1936: 178.

33 Mócsy, 1974: 83 and Wilkes, 1983: 264. Baxter, on the other hand, argues that Dacia was the main enemy all the time (1974: 547–9).

34 See Gsell, 1894: 224–5.

35 Syme, 1936: 177.

36 Gsell, 1894: 225–7.

37 Kennedy, 1983: 183–96; Strobel, 1986c: 265–86.

38 Syme, 1936: 177; Mócsy, 1974; 83–4; and Wilkes, 1983; 283–4 n. 74.

39 So Syme, 1977: 38, in his reconstruction of Sospes' career, accepted by Eck, 1982a: 320 but not by Sherk, 1980: 1029–33.

40 Gsell, 1894: 227. His arguments were apparently not considered by Mócsy, who assigns the war to either 92 or 93 (1974: 83–4).

41 See *RE* 7.499–500; Hammond, 1959: 35–6, 52–4, 78; and Maxfield, 1981: 101–3.

42 For the text, see Dusanic and Vasic, 1977: 291–2; *AE* 1977: 722; and Roxan, 1978: 36–7, no. 6.

43 Dusanic and Vasic, 1977: 296 n. 32.

44 Dusanic and Vasic reject (1977: 296–7 with notes 36–8) the old explanation, i.e. as expressed by Syme, that it was 'not transfer of regiments back and forth, but a change of status for the region' (1971: 206).

45 Dusanic, 1983: 13–21.

46 Dusanic, 1983: 17.

47 So Birley, 1986: 209–16.

48 E.g. Eck, 1970: 145 and Syme, 1971: 185, 208 (but compare Eck, 1982a: 326). Trajan may have governed the province some years earlier, c. 92–3, according to Dusanic, 1983: 18 n. 24 and AE 1985: 722; but compare Eck, 1982a: 320 n. 154, for L. Neratius Priscus in Pannonia during the same period.

49 E.g. Syme, 1971: 204–5, 221. On Trajan and Servianus, see Eck, 1985b: 45–8.

50 Dusanic and Vasic, 1977: 303 with notes 75 and 76.

51 Dusanic and Vasic, 1977: 303–4 and, for their bases, 301–2. It used to be argued that a complement of four was the maximum likely, e.g. Syme believes that five legions in Pannonia at that time was 'excessive . . . not tolerable. . . . One imagines what Domitian would have thought of the notion' (1971: 206).

52 See Schieber, 1976; Dabrowa, 1980b: 379–88; the articles in ANRW 2.7.1; and also Grosso, 1954: 117–79 (with caution) for both Flavian policy in general and individual nations such as the Alani, Iberi, Albani and Hyrcani.

53 Luttwak, 1976: 113.

54 For the annexation of Armenia Minor and Commagene, see Schieber, 1976: 278–85; Bosworth, 1976: 66 with n. 24; and Mitford, 1980: 1180–2. The Cappadocia–Galatia complex is discussed by Schieber, 1976: 68–73; Bosworth, 1976: 63; and Sherk, 1980b: 991–8. For Melitene and Satala, see Dabrowa, 1980b: 381–2; Mitford, 1980: 1186–7, 1220–4; and Sherk, 1980: 996–7 n. 114: their location in relationship to the Parthian empire is clearly shown in Luttwak, 1976: 109 (map no. 2.8). For road-building both in the province and behind it, in Asia, see McCrum and Woodhead, 1966: nos 86 (Melik Scherif), 93 (Samosata to Rum-Kaleh in Syria), 105 (Ancyra to Dorylaeum), 117 (Derbe to Lystra), 421 (Prusa in Bithynia), 422 (Thyatira in Asia) and 438 (Seleucea on the Cilician coast).

55 Grosso, 1954: 144–62; Bosworth, 1976: 73–4 and 1977: 224–5; Schieber, 1976: 79–95, 232 n. 1; and RE Suppl. 9.1899–911.

56 For the text, see McCrum and Woodhead, 1966: 72, no. 237 (trans. Jones and Milns, 1984: 37). Its significance is discussed by Schieber, 1976: 90–1 (with others from the same area) and Dabrowa, 1980b: 387 with n. 60. On ancient Harmozica (= modern Metskheta), see Magie, 1950: 1438 n. 2; RE 2.1177 and Grosso, 1954: 129.

57 E.g. by McCrum and Woodhead, 1966: 72 and Sherk, 1980: 997 n. 118, who consign it to Armenia Maior.

58 Schieber, 1976: 99–106.

59 Magie, 1950: 1225–6 n. 13; Bosworth; 1976: 73–4; and Schieber, 1976: 96–9.

60 Bejuk Dagh is a small hill some 70 kilometres north (almost certainly)

of Baku. Bosworth observes that 'the Soviet publication carefully concealed the exact location, leaving it open whether it was north or south of Baku' (1976: 75).

61 *AE* 1951: 263 = McCrum and Woodhead, 1966: 100, no. 369: Grosso provides a clear photograph (1954: 119). For a discussion of its significance, see (with patience) Grosso, 1954: 117–79 but especially 118–20; Schieber, 1976: 120–5; and Bosworth, 1977: 226.

62 Bosworth, 1977: 227 with n. 39. Schieber, however, is somewhat sceptical of its strategic significance (1976: 124). Grosso thinks that Bejuk Dagh is in the area of Kilyazi (1954: 124 n. 1).

63 Grosso, 1954: 124. It was found by an enthusiast named V.A. Petrov and soon lost; possibly, though, it is to be assigned to the reign of Marcus Aurelius (129).

64 For the inscription, see *AE* 1968: 145, together with *AE* 1972: 151; Kreiler, 1975: 85 with n. 5; Dabrowa, 1980b: 387 with notes 61–4; Sherk, 1980: 1000–1; and *PIR²* N 56. Schieber suggests the connection between *AE* 1968: 145 and the Bejuk Dagh inscription (1976: 118–19).

65 As Bosworth points out, 'it is questionable whether the Alani ever posed a serious frontier problem for the Romans. Their previous history ... suggests that their depredations in general served the interests of Rome' (1977: 220). On the Alani in general, see *CAH* 11: 94–7; Schieber, 1976; Bosworth, 1977; and Yarshater, 1983.

66 For a discussion of the entire passage, see Warmington, 1977: 117–18 and Bradley, 1978b: 294–5.

67 McCrum and Woodhead, 1966: 27, no. 14, lines 61–2.

68 Eck, 1982a: 314 with n. 133 (Cerialis) and 315 with n. 135 (Florus). Most scholars now favour 87/8 for the pretender (e.g. Eck, 1970: 86; Kreiler, 1975: 48–9; and Schieber, 1976: 145–6). For the older view (i.e. 88/9), see Ogilvie and Richmond, 1967: 294. The first to suggest the earlier year seems to have been Gephardt, 1922: 67.

69 The argument advanced here is developed more fully in Jones, 1983: 516–21.

70 Roxan, 1978: 32–3, no. 3; Holder, 1980: 204.

71 Roxan, 1978: 34, no. 4; Holder, 1980: 205.

72 It is unlikely that they were involved in executing Cerialis. *ILS* 1374 indicates that C. Minicius Italus, Domitian's procurator, was to govern Asia in place of Cerialis and, presumably, he was responsible for the execution (so Syme, 1979–88, *RP* 3: 330).

73 For Patruinus in Syria, see Eck, 1982a: 312–15 (AD 86–8). Kreiler argued for the Cappadocian–Galatian position (1975: 88–9), an 'attractive conjecture' according to Syme, 1980: 28 and accepted by Eck, 1982a: 307–11 (AD 83–5).

74 Grosso, 1955: 65; Carradice, 1983: 34; and Strobel, 1989: 34.

75 Debevoise believed that an expedition was planned (1938: 210): others are rightly more sceptical, e.g. Schieber, 1976: 145–6 and Bosworth, 1977: 227. Grosso provides an exhaustive list of passages apparently similar to *Silvae* 4.4.63–4 (1955: 36–55). At 4.4.30–1, for instance, one gains the opposite impression from the lines *et sontes operit pharetras*

arcumque retendit Parthus: on the whole poem, see Hardie, 1983: 164–71.

8 ARISTOCRACY I

1 For Nerva and the *fiscus Iudaicus*, see Mooney, 1930: 567; Thompson, 1982: 329–42; and Goodman, 1989: 40–4.
2 Waters, 1969: 385–405; Devreker, 1977: 223–43.
3 Ehrhardt, 1987: 18–19.
4 *Dom.* 3.1; *BMC* 2: 311, nos 60–7; and McDermott and Orentzel, 1979b: 75. The title *Augusta* appears in the *Acta* of the Arval Brethren of 1 October 81.
5 Scott, 1936: 84; McDermott and Orentzel, 1979b: 75.
6 *BMC* 2: 311, nos 62–3. On the emperor's son, see Mooney, 1930: 518; Desnier, 1979: 54–65; and Garthwaite, 1978: 30–1.
7 On his designation as consul for ten years, see Hammond, 1959: 83, 118 n. 163 and Buttrey, 1980: 37; on the perpetual censorship, Hammond, 1959: 86–7, 121–3 notes 180–3 and Buttrey, 1980: 38 with table 3.
8 Scott, 1936: 158–65.
9 Millar, 1977: 67–8.
10 Scott, 1936: 75–7; Garthwaite, 1978: 36–43; and Jones, 1984a: 19, 155–6.
11 Champlin, 1983: 257–64.
12 The non-Flavian ordinary consuls were Nerva (in 71), Catullus Messallinus (73), D. Junius Novius Priscus with L. Ceionius Commodus (78) and L. Flavius Silva with L(?). Asinius Pollio (81). For the evidence, see Gallivan, 1981: 187–9.
13 Gallivan, 1981: 189–90 (for Cerialis and Sabinus IV); Vidman, 1982: 77 (Vibius Crispus and Veiento); and Eck, 1972b: 259–76 (Pompeius Silvanus).
14 Jones and Develin, 1976: 79–83; Syme, 1979–88, *RP* 5: 614–15.
15 For patricians, see Hammond, 1959: 250–1 and 274–6 with notes 40–9; also Pistor, 1965: *passim*.
16 Hopkins, 1983: 137–8.
17 Eck, 1970: 63, notes 40–4. Thirteen of the thirty consulships were held by Domitian (ten) and his relatives (three).
18 Eck, 1970: 63 n. 44, 108.
19 Eck, 1970: 64 n. 10.
20 Houston, 1971: 364–5 and Syme, 1979–88, *RP* 4: 153, 310 (Calpurnius); Raepsaet-Charlier, 1987: 421 (Volusius and Licinia).
21 For Libo Frugi's full name, see Syme, 1979–88, *RP* 4: 153 and, for the relationship, Raepsaet-Charlier, 1987: 591.
22 Raepsaet-Charlier, 1987: 203, 552.
23 Jones, 1979: 73. To these eleven should be added P. Herennius Pollio and C. Cilnius Proculus: see Modugno *et al.*, 1973: 96; Gallivan, 1981: 190 and Jones, 1984a: 29 n. 80.
24 'Contempt' (1979–88, *RP* 4.266); 'sympathy' (Eck, 1970: 67).
25 Hahn and Leunissen, 1990: 74 with n. 35.
26 Eck, 1970: 67.

27 Jones, 1979: 72, table 12.
28 Jones, 1984a: 19–20.
29 Jones, 1973a: 86–8.
30 Raepsaet-Charlier, 1987: 354–5.
31 Jones, 1973a: 89–90.
32 Quietus was a friend of Thrasea Paetus (*Ep.* 6.29.1) and of Arria and Fannia (9.13.16). When Groag wrote the article on Quietus in *PIR*² A 1410, the date of his consulship was not known, and it was regarded as 'scarcely credible' that Quietus could have been given the *fasces* by Domitian. So according to Groag, he must have held them in 97.
33 For a fuller statement of the case, see Jones, 1973a: 79–91.
34 Hopkins, 1983: 123–7; but rejected (or regarded as 'non-proven') by Hahn and Leunissen, 1990: 60–81.
35 Hopkins, 1983: 194–6.
36 Quoted from Hopkins, 1983: 171 n. 66.
37 They were 'held in low esteem' (Syme, 1958: 67) and 'seldom came to anything' (1971: 200). To illustrate this, Syme notes that only about six proconsuls from praetorian provinces between 70 and 120 (i.e out of a possible 400 or so) are known to have subsequently governed a military province (1971: 200).
38 Cornutus Tertullus's appointment to Pontus–Bithynia could, by no stretch of the imagination, be described as 'military', for only recently had the province been up-graded to consular status, a temporary measure made necessary by the financial problems of the area.
39 Jones, 1979: 74–6.
40 Jones, 1975b: 631–2.
41 Eck, 1974: 227–8.
42 Eck, 1982a: 316 with notes 143 and 144.
43 Syme, 1958: 67–8.
44 For his origin, see Syme, 1980: 51.
45 Eck, 1970: 138.
46 Syme, 1980: 27–8.
47 See Devreker, 1982: 492–516.
48 Devreker, 1980: 496–8.
49 Bloch, 1948: 340; similarly, Hammond, 1957: 79.
50 Syme, 1979–88, *RP* 3: 1301; Chastagnol, 1980: 276–7.
51 Syme, 1979–88, *RP* 5: 558–9; Houston, 1971: 606.
52 Syme, 1979–88, *RP* 5: 552–3.
53 Devreker, 1980: 257–68; cf. Jones, 1979: 91–143.
54 See Devreker, 1980: 263.
55 Eck, 1982a: 306; for Vettonianus's origin, Syme, 1979–88, *RP* 5: 82.
56 Eck, 1982a: 326.
57 In this regard, Raepsaet-Charlier, 1987, is particularly valuable. To avoid a proliferation of footnotes, references to her work will be given in each instance in the text. The dates for senators' provincial posts are those of Eck, 1982a and 1983a.
58 According to Syme (1979–88, *RP* 5: 526 n. 33), he was the son of Ti. Julius Lupus, prefect of Egypt early in Vespasian's reign and so related to the Flavians through the Arrecini (*AJ* 19.191).

59 See Eck, 1970: 76.
60 His term will have been shorter if Trajan was also governor of Pannonia during this period.
61 Houston, 1971: 391–2.
62 Syme, 1958: 68.
63 Jones, 1979: 99.
64 Eck, 1985b: 39.
65 Pflaum, 1950: 50–4 and 1974: 14–16. Compare Brunt, 1983: 42–75, especially his view of 'the inadequacy of prosopographic evidence . . . and the fragility of some conclusions based on it' (68).
66 Pflaum, 1974: 13–14.
67 *Ep.* 7.31.2–4; Pflaum, 1960: 124–6, no. 54.
68 Pflaum, 1960: 126–8, no. 55.
69 Gsell, 1894: 108–9.
70 *AE* 1939, 60; Pflaum, 1960: 128–36, no. 56.
71 Ferrill, 1985: 353–71, especially 367 n. 34.
72 The document is translated in full (together with comments) in Jones, 1984a: 171–2.
73 Syme, 1958: 635–6.
74 Chastagnol argues for 84 (1980: 272–3) but the numismatic evidence is clear – he became censor in April 85 (Carradice, 1983: 27).
75 Jones, 1984a: 35–6.
76 Jones, 1979: 25.
77 For a more detailed discussion, see Jones, 1983: 516–21.

9 ARISTOCRACY II

1 *PIR²* B 26; *PIR²* M 562 and *PIR¹* V 41.
2 Gsell, 1894: 269 notes 8–10.
3 Hopkins, 1983: 27–30.
4 Jones and Develin, 1976: 83, a reconstruction described as 'coherent yet to be avowed hazardous' (Syme, 1979–88, *RP* 5: 614–15).
5 Ogilvie and Richmond, 1967: 294.
6 Jones, 1983: 516–21.
7 *PIR²* C 1444 (father) and C 1445 (son). See also *IRT* 341 (Africa) and Bradley, 1978b: 222.
8 Syme, 1979–88, *RP* 2: 812; *PIR¹* P564 (Pomponius Secundus) and *Ann.* 13.43 (involvement in the conspiracy).
9 For a novel interpretation, see Jackson, 1984: 25–32.
10 E.g. Leclercq, 1921a: 1391.
11 *PIR²* A 205; Houston, 1971: 5–7; Courtney, 1980: 229; Jones, 1984a: 125–6; and Raepsaet-Charlier, 1987: 33.
12 Possibly, he was his son (Houston, 1971: 5–6).
13 Syme, 1979–88, *RP* 1: 327; Jones, 1984a: 164 n. 76.
14 Gallivan, 1981: 198.
15 *PIR¹* S 110; Houston, 1971: 487.
16 Syme, 1979–88, *RP* 1: 254; 2: 667–8 (consul *c.* 80); Houston, 1971: 487; and Raepsaet-Charlier, 1987: 235.
17 *PIR²* M 570; Houston, 1971: 159–60; and Baxter, 1974: 114, 333. He

is not to be identified with the *praefectus aerarii Saturni* L. Pompusius Mettius (Braithwaite, 1927: 57).

18 Arnaud, 1983: 677–99.
19 *PIR*[1] S 63 and Houston, 1971: 484–5. For speculation on his identity, see Syme, 1980: 42–9 ('P. Sallustius Aburius Lucullus' or 'P. Sallustius Blaesus Aburius Lucullus' are amongst the possibilities discussed). Birley examines such evidence as we have about him (1981: 82–3).
20 Walser, 1968: 500; Birley, 1974: 16.
21 Rusticus was suffect consul in 92, the younger Helvidius in 93 or before 87 (Gallivan, 1981: 218 and 220).
22 The fate of Sabinus and the other two imperial relatives (Arrecinus and Flavius Clemens) is discussed in chapter 2, pp. 42–8.
23 Barnes, 1981: 382–4 and 1986: 225–44. On the other hand, R. Martin rejects even the identification of Tacitus's and Dio's Maternus (1981: 250 n. 37).
24 Eck, 1982a: 224 n. 172.
25 Syme, 1979–88, *RP* 5: 641.
26 Vinson, 1989: 431–50.
27 For the varying degrees of exile (*relegatio* and *deportatio*), see Sherwin-White, 1966: 165, 281–2.
28 Sherwin-White, 1966: 764.
29 Jones, 1978: 48 (Dio Chrysostom); Sherwin-White, 1966: 764–5 (late sources on expulsions).
30 *PIR*[2] J 205; Houston, 1971: 404–5.
31 *PIR*[2] B 26; Sherwin-White, 1966: 445; and Houston, 1971: 34.
32 *PIR*[1] S 105; Houston, 1971: 233–5; McDermott, 1973: 335–51; Syme, 1980: 25–6, 31–4; and Birley, 1981: 211–12, 404–7.
33 Pleket, 1961: 309–10.
34 Birley, 1981: 404. The chronology of Liberalis's career is disputed: see Houston, 1971: 233–4 and Birley, 1981: 211–12.
35 Eck, 1982a: 307 with n. 112 on 308.
36 See Birley, 1981: 11, no. 14 and 15 n. 11. The relevant inscription (*CIL* 6365, from Urbs Salvia) is acephalous, but almost certainly refers to Salvius Vitellianus.
37 *PIR*[2] F 368; Houston, 1971: 94; McDermott, 1973: 335–51; and Jones, 1984a: 215.
38 Sherwin-White doubts whether he was ever exiled (1966: 237), but he clearly was (Syme, 1930: 31).
39 Syme, 1980: 31.
40 For the younger Plotius and the possible exile of the father, see Bérard, 1984: 259–324.
41 Jones, 1979: 27.
42 So Hardie, 1983: 69.
43 See Bérard, 1984: 264–72.
44 Bérard, 1984: 263.
45 Eck, 1980: 58–60; *PIR*[2] M 566–71.
46 Eck, 1985b: 44.
47 Houston, 1971: 572–3.

48 Eck, 1982a: 332 with n. 207 and 1983a: 186–7 n. 475.
49 *RE* 15.1502; Pflaum, 1960: 119; and Sherwin-White, 1966: 97.

10 CONCLUSION

1 *xiii k. Oct. Domitianus o[ccisus]/eodem die M. Cocceius N[erva]/im-perator appellatu[s est]*: see Jones, 1979: 48.
2 See Jones, 1979: 46–7: an alliance of praetorian prefects and senators is often assumed. Waters believes that the assassination was 'the work of the senate' (1963: 217). Similarly, Ambrosio, whilst arguing that Suetonius's account is correct, maintains (as the sub-title of his article indicates) that it was 'a case of senatorial treason' (1980: 232–41).
3 Jones, 1979: 47–8. Syme is more cautious: 'conspirators, it should seem, ought not to have gone ahead without enlisting the Prefects of the Guard or deciding on the choice of the next emperor. Conspirators are not always given the requisite leisure' (1983b: 137).
4 Syme, 1958: 3; see also Jones, 1979: 48–9.
5 Eck, 1982a: 326.
6 A civil servant's summary of the ideal prime minister: Lynn and Jay, 1986: 29.
7 They are conveniently collected by Gephardt, 1922: 89.
8 Hassall, 1984: 265.
9 Vessey, 1983: 212.
10 Coleman, 1986: 3096–100.

BIBLIOGRAPHY

Ahl, F., 1984, 'The art of safe criticism in Greece and Rome', *AJPh* 105: 174–208.

Alföldy, G., 1969, 'Die Generalität des römischen Heeres', *BJ* 169: 233–46.

Alföldy, G. and Halfmann, H., 1973, 'M. Cornelius Nigrinus Curiatius Maternus, General Domitians und Rivale Trajans', *Chiron* 3: 331–73.

Ambrosio, F.G. D', 1980, 'End of the Flavians. The case for senatorial treason', *RIL* 114: 232–41.

Anderson, J.C., 1981, 'Domitian's building programme. Forum Julium and markets of Trajan', *ArchN* 10: 41–8.

——1982, 'Domitian, the Argiletum, and the temple of Peace', *AJA* 86: 101–10.

——1983, 'A topographical tradition in the fourth century chronicles. Domitian's building programme', *Historia* 32: 93–105.

——1985, 'The date of the Thermae Trajani and the topography of the Oppius Mons', *AJA* 89: 499–509.

Applebaum, S., 1974, 'Domitian's assassination. The Jewish aspect', *SCI* 1: 116–23.

Arias, P.E., 1945, *Domiziano*, Catania: G. Crisafulli.

Arnaud, P., 1983, 'L'affaire Mettius Pompusianus ou le crime de cartographie', *MEFR* 95: 677–99.

Arnim, H. von, 1898, *Leben und Werke des Dio von Prusa*, Berlin: Wiedmann.

Assa, J., 1962, 'Aulus Bucius Lappius Maximus', *Akten des IV. internationalen Kongresses für griechische und lateinische Epigraphik*, Vienna: Böhlau, 31–9.

Baldwin, B., 1979a, 'Turnus the satirist', *Eranos* 77: 57–60.

——1979b, 'Juvenal's Crispinus', *AClass* 22: 109–14.

Balland, A., 1980, 'Un concours lycien en l'honneur de Domitien?' *Mélanges de littérature et d'épigraphie latines, d'histoire ancienne et d'archéologie. Hommage à la mémoire de P. Wuilleumier*, Paris: Les Belles Lettres, 11–15.

Ballanti, A., 1954, 'Documenti sull'opposizione degli intellettuali a Domiziano', *AFLN* 4: 75–95.

Balsdon, J.P.V.D., 1938, Review of K. Scott, 1936, *The Imperial Cult under the Flavians*, *JRS* 28: 86–7.

238

Bardon, H., 1962, 'Le goût à l'époque des Flaviens', *Latomus* 21: 732–48.
Barnard, L.W., 1963–4, 'Clement of Rome and the persecution of Domitian', *NTS* 10: 251–60.
Barnes, T.D., 1974, 'Who were the nobility of the Roman empire?' *Phoenix* 28: 444–9.
——1976, 'The horoscope of Licinius Sura', *Phoenix* 30: 76–9.
——1981, 'Curiatius Maternus', *Hermes* 109: 382–4.
——1986, 'The significance of Tacitus's *Dialogus de Oratoribus*', *HSCPh* 90: 225–44.
Barzano, A., 1982a, 'Domiziano e il bellum Capitolinum', *RIL* 116; 11–20.
——1982b, 'Plinio il Giovane e i cristiani alla corte di Domiziano', *RSCI* 36: 408–15.
Bauman, R.A., 1968, 'Some remarks on the structure and survival of the *Quaestio de Adulteriis*", *Antichthon* 2: 68–93.
——1974, Impietas in Principem. *A Study of Treason against the Roman Emperor with Special Reference to the First Century* AD, Munich: C.H. Beck.
——1982, 'The résumé of legislation in Suetonius', *ZSS* 99: 81–127.
Baxter, T.F., 1974, 'Domitian and the senate', dissertation, University of Toronto.
Bell, A.A., 1978, 'The date of John's Apocalypse. The evidence of some Roman historians reconsidered', *NTS* 25: 93–102.
Bengston, H., 1979, *Die Flavier. Vespasian, Titus, Domitian. Geschichte eines römischen Kaiserhauses*, Munich: C.H. Beck.
Bérard, F., 1984, 'La carrière de Plotius Grypus et le ravitaillement de l'armée impériale en campagne', *MEFR* 96: 259–324.
——1989, 'La cohorte *I Cilicum*, la *classis flavia moesica* et les vexillations de l'armée de Mésie inférieure: à propos d'une inscription de Montana', *ZPE* 79: 129–38.
Berchem, D. van, 1978, 'Un banquier chez les Helvètes', *Ktèma* 3: 267–74.
——1983, 'Une inscription flavienne du musée d'Antioche', *MH* 40: 185–96.
Billault, A., 1977, 'Les lettres de Chion d'Héraclée', *REG* 90: 29–37.
Birley, A.R., 1962, 'The oath not to put senators to death', *CR* 12: 197–9.
——1973, 'Petillius Cerialis and the conquest of Brigantia', *Britannia* 4: 179–90.
——1974, 'Roman frontiers and Roman frontier policy: some reflections on Roman imperialism', *Transactions of the Architectural and Archaeological Society of Durham and Northumberland* 3: 13–25.
——1976, 'The Date of Mons Graupius', *LCM* 1: 11–14.
——1981, *The Fasti of Roman Britain*, Oxford: Clarendon Press.
——1984, Review of A. Hardie, 1983, *Statius and the* Silvae. *Poets, Patrons and* Epideixis *in the Graeco-Roman World*, *LCM* 9: 26–7.
——1986, Review of B.W. Jones, 1984a, *The Emperor Titus, Ancient Society* 16: 63–7.
Birley, E., 1953, 'Senators in the emperors' service', *PBA* 39: 197–214.
——1983, 'The enigma of Calvisius Ruso', *ZPE* 51: 263–9.
——1986, 'The Flavian *colonia* at Scupi', *ZPE* 64: 209–16.

239

Blake, M.E., 1959, *Roman Construction in Italy from Tiberius through the Flavians*, Washington: Carnegie Institute of Washington.

Blake, M.E. and Bishop, D.T., 1973, *Roman Construction in Italy from Nerva through the Antonines*, Philadelphia: American Philosophical Society.

Bloch, H., 1948, Review of S.J. de Laet, 1941, 'De Samenstelling Van Den Romeinschen Senaat Gedurende de Eerste Eeuw het Principaat', *AJPh* 69: 337–40

Boren, H.C., 1983, 'Studies relating to the *stipendium militum*', *Historia* 32: 427–60.

Bosworth, A.B., 1973, 'Vespasian and the provinces: some problems of the early 70's AD', *Athenaeum* 51: 49–78.

——1976, 'Vespasian's reorganisation of the north-east frontier', *Antichthon* 10: 49–78.

——1977, 'Arrian and the Alani', *HSCPh* 81: 217–55.

——1980, 'Firmus of Arretium', *ZPE* 39: 267–77.

Boulvert, G., 1970, *Esclaves et affranchis impériaux sous le haut-empire romain: rôle politique et administratif*, Naples: Jovene.

——1974, *Domestique et fonctionnaire sous le haut-empire romain: la condition de l'affranchi et de l'esclavage du prince*, Paris: Les Belles Lettres.

——1981, 'La carrière de Tiberius Claudius Augusti libertus Classicus', *AE* 1972: 574, *ZPE* 43: 31–41.

Bowersock, G.W., 1973, 'Greek intellectuals and the imperial cult in the second century AD', *Le culte des souverains dans l'empire romain*, Entretiens sur l'antiquité classique: 20, Geneva: Fondation Hardt.

Bradley, K.R., 1978a, 'Claudius Athenodorus', *Historia* 27: 336–42.

——1978b, *Suetonius' Life of Nero: An Historical Commentary*, Collection Latomus 157, Brussels: Société-d'Etudes Latines.

Braithwaite, A.W., 1927, *C. Suetonii Tranquilli Divus Vespasianus with an Introduction and Commentary*, Oxford: Clarendon Press.

Braund, D., 1984, 'Berenice in Rome', *Historia* 33: 120–3.

Breeze, D.J., 1982, *The Northern Frontiers of Roman Britain*, London: B.T. Batsford.

Breissmann, A., 1955, *Tacitus und das flavische Geschichtsbild*, Hermes Einzelschriften 10, Wiesbaden: F. Steiner.

Brind'Amour, P., 1981, 'Problèmes astrologiques et astronomiques soulevés par le récit de la mort de Domitien chez Suétone', *Phoenix* 35: 338–44.

Brunt, P.A., 1961, 'Charges of provincial maladministration under the early Principate', *Historia* 10: 189–227.

——1975, 'The administrators of Roman Egypt', *JRS* 65: 124–47.

——1979, Review of J.R. Fears, 1977, '*Princeps a diis electus*: The divine election of the emperor as a political concept at Rome', *JRS* 69: 168–75.

——1983, '*Princeps* and *Equites*', *JRS* 73: 42–75.

Bruun, C., 1990, 'Some comments on the status of imperial freedmen. (The case of Ti. Claudius Aug. lib. Classicus)', *ZPE* 82: 271–85.

Burton, G., 1977, Review of G. Boulvert, 1970 and 1974, *JRS* 67: 163–4.

Buttrey, T.V., 1975, 'Domitian's perpetual censorship and the numismatic evidence', *CJ* 71: 26–34.

——1980 *Documentary Evidence for the Chronology of the Flavian Titulature*, Beiträge für Klassischen Philologie 112, Meisenheim: A. Hain.

BIBLIOGRAPHY

Camodeca, G. 1976, 'La Carriera del giurista L. Neratius Priscus', *AAN* 87: 19–38.
Campbell, B., 1975, 'Who were the *Viri Militares*?' *JRS* 65: 11–31.
——1984, *The Emperor and the Roman Army: 31 BC–AD 235*, Oxford: Clarendon Press.
——1987, 'Teach yourself how to be a general,' *JRS* 77: 13–29.
Campbell, D., 1986, 'The consulship of Agricola', *ZPE* 63: 197–200.
Carradice, I.A., 1978, 'A Denarius of AD 92', *ZPE* 28: 159–60.
——1979, 'The banishment of the father of Claudius Etruscus: numismatic evidence', *LCM* 4: 101–3.
——1983, *Coinage and Finances in the Reign of Domitian, AD 81–96*, BAR International Series 178, Oxford: British Archaeological Reports.
Castritius, H., 1969, 'Zu den Frauen der Flavier', *Historia* 18: 492–502.
Champlin, E., 1978, 'Pegasus', *ZPE* 32: 269–78.
——1983, *'Figlinae Marcianae'*, *Athenaeum* 61: 257–64.
Chastagnol, A., 1980 'Les *homines novi* entrés au sénat sous le règne de Domitien', *Studien zur antiken Sozialgeschichte, Festschrift Friedrich Vittinghoff*, hrsg. von Eck, W., Galsterer, H. und Wolff, H., Kölner hist. Abh. 28, Böhlau Köln, 269–81.
Chilver, G.E.F., 1979, *A Historical Commentary on Tacitus' Histories I and II*, Oxford: Clarendon Press.
Coffey, M., 1979, 'Turnus and Juvenal', *BICS* 26: 88–94.
Coleman, K.M., 1986, 'The emperor Domitian and literature', *ANRW* 2.32.5: 3087–115.
Collins, A.Y., 1977, 'The political perspective of the Revelation to John', *JBL* 96: 241–56.
Condurachi, E., 1980, 'Alcune considerazioni sull'altare funerario di Tropaeum Traiani', *QC* 2: 101–24.
Conole, P. and Milns, R.D., 1983, 'Neronian frontier policy in the Balkans: the career of Ti. Plautius Silvanus', *Historia* 32: 183–200.
Cotton, H.M., 1989, 'The date of the fall of Masada', *ZPE* 78: 157–62.
Courtney, E., 1980, *A Commentary on the Satires of Juvenal*, London: Athlone Press.
Cramer, F.C., 1951, 'Expulsion of astrologers from ancient Rome', *Classica et Mediaevalia* 12: 9–50.
Crescenzi, L., 1978, 'La villa di Domiziano a Castel Gandolfo', *Secondo incontro di studio del Comitato per l'archeologia etrusco-italica*. Roma: Cons. naz. delle ric., 99–106.
Crook, J., 1951, 'Titus and Berenice', *AJPh* 72: 162–75.
——1955, *Consilium Principis. Imperial Councils and Counsellors from Augustus to Dicoletian*, Cambridge: Cambridge University Press.
Cross, F.L. and Livingstone, E.A., (eds), 1984, *The Oxford Dictionary of the Christian Church* 2nd edn, Oxford: Oxford University Press.
Dabrowa, E., 1980a, *L'Asie mineure sous les Flaviens*, Cracow: Polska Akademia Nauk.
——1980b, 'Le limes anatolien et la frontière caucasienne au temps des Flaviens', *Klio* 62: 379–88.
——1982, 'Sur la création de la légion XVI Flavia', *Latomus* 41: 614–19.
Daniels, C., 1989, 'The Flavian and Trajanic northern frontier', in M.

241

Todd (ed.), *Research on Roman Britain: 1960–1989*, Britannia Monograph Series No. 11, London: Society for the Promotion of Roman Studies: 31–4.

Daube, D., 1976, 'Martial, father of three', *AJAH* 1: 145–7.

Davies, R.W., 1976, 'Military decorations and the British war', *AClass* 19: 115–21.

Debevoise, N.C., 1938, *A Political History of Parthia*, Chicago: University of Chicago Press.

Deroux, C., 1983, *Domitian, the Kingfish and the Prodigies: A Reading of Juvenal's Fourth Satire*, Collection Latomus 180, Brussels.

Desanges, J., 1964, 'Note sur la datation de l'expédition de Julius Maternus au pays d'Agisymba', *Latomus* 23: 713–25.

Desnier, J.L., 1979, '*Divus Caesar Imp Domitiani F.*', *REA* 81: 54–65.

Devreker, J., 1976, Review of B. Kreiler, 1975, 'Die Statthalter Kleinasiens unter den Flaviern', *Epigraphica* 38: 179–88.

——1977, 'La continuité dans le *consilium principis* sous les Flaviens', *Ancient Society* 8: 223–43.

——1980, 'La composition du sénat romain sous les Flaviens', *Studien zur antiken Sozialgeschichte, Festschrift Friedrich Vittinghoff, hsrg. von Eck, W., Galsterer, H. und Wolff H.*, Kölner hist. Abh. 28, Böhlau Köln, 257–68.

——1982, 'Les Orientaux aux sénat romain d'Auguste à Trajan', *Latomus* 41: 492–516.

Dondin-Payre, M., 1983, 'Firmus d'Arretium: Légat préquestorien?' *ZPE* 52: 236–40.

Dorutiu-Boila, E., 1978, 'Der Niedermoesische Limes unter Domitian zu einer Inschrift aus Ephesos', *Studien zu den Militärgrenzen Roms* 2: 289–96.

Dudley, D.R. (ed.), 1972, *Neronians and Flavians: Silver Latin I*, London and Boston: Routledge and Kegan Paul.

Dunkle, J.R., 1971, 'The rhetorical tyrant in Roman historiography: Sallust, Livy and Tacitus', *CW* 64: 12–20.

Dusanic, S., 1983, 'Moesia and Pannonia in Domitian's last war on the Danube', *ZA* 33: 13–21.

Dusanic, S. and Vasic, M.R., 1977, 'An Upper Moesian diploma of AD 96', *Chiron* 7: 291–304.

Eck, W., 1970, *Senatoren von Vespasian bis Hadrian*, Munich: C.H. Beck.

——1972a, Review of P. Kneissl, 1969, *Die Siegestitulatur der römischen Kaiser; Untersuchungen zu den Siegerbeinamen des ersten und zweiten Jahrhunderts Gnomon* 44: 171–6

——1972b, 'M. Pompeius Silvanus, *consul designatus tertium* – ein Vertrauter Vespasians und Domitians', *ZPE* 9: 259–76.

——1974, 'Beförderungskriterien innerhalb der senatorischen Laufbahn, dargestellt in der Zeit von 69 bis 138 n. Chr.', *ANRW* 2.1: 158–228.

——1975, 'Ergänzungen zu den *fasti consulares* des 1.u.2. Jh. n. Chr.', *Historia* 24: 324–44.

——1980, 'Epigraphische Untersuchungen zu Konsuln und Senatoren des 1.-3. Jh. n. Chr.', *ZPE* 37: 31–68.

——1982a, 'Jahres- und Provinzalfasten der senatorischen Statthalter von 69/70 bis 138/139 (I)', *Chiron* 12: 281–362.

——1982b, 'Proconsuln von Asia in der flavisch-trajanischen Zeit', *ZPE* 45: 139–53.

——1983a, 'Jahres- und Provinzialfasten der senatorischen Statthalter von 69/70 bis 138/139 (II)', *Chiron* 13: 147–237.

——1983b, '*CIL* VI 1444 and *CIL* XII 3169: Die Laufbahn des D. Terentius Scaurianus?' *ZPE* 52: 151–6.

——1985a, 'Statius *Silvae* 1.4 und C. Rutilius Gallicus als Proconsul Asiae II', *AJPh* 106: 475–84.

——1985b, *Die Statthalter der germanischen Provinzen vom 1.–3. Jahrhundert*, Cologne: Rheinland-Verlag.

Ehrhardt, C.T.H.R., 1987, 'Nerva's background', *LCM* 12: 18–20.

Elias, N., 1983, *The Court Society* (trans. of *Die höfische Gesellschaft* by E. Jephcott), Oxford: B. Blackwell.

Evans, J.K., 1975, 'The dating of Domitian's war against the Chatti again', *Historia* 24: 121–4.

——1978, 'The role of *suffragium* in imperial political decision-making: a Flavian example', *Historia* 27: 102–28.

——1979, 'The trial of P. Egnatius Celer', *CQ* 29: 198–202.

Fallows, D., 1990, Review of Purcell, 'Ode for the Birthday of the Duke of Gloucester', *Gramophone* 68: 262.

Fasola, U., 1960, 'Domitilla', in R. Aubert and E. van Cauwenbergh (eds), Paris: Letouzey et Ané, *Dictionnaire d'Histoire et de Géographie Ecclésiastiques*, Vol. 14: 630–4.

Fears, J.R., 1981, 'Jupiter and Roman imperial ideology: the role of Domitian', *ANRW* 2.17.1: 233–45.

Ferril, A., 1985, 'The senatorial aristocracy in the early Roman empire', in J.W. Eadie and J. Ober (eds), *The Craft of the Ancient Historian: Essays in Honour of Chester G. Starr*, Lanham, New York and London: University Press of America.

Fitton, J., 1974, 'Domitian and Saint John in Malalas', *Byzantion* 44: 193–4.

Forbes, C.A., 1955, 'The education and training of slaves,' *TAPhA* 86: 3–60.

Franke, P.R., 1979, 'Zur Chronologie der Statthalter von Cappadocia–Galatia 91–107 n. Chr.', *Chiron* 9: 377–82.

Frankfort, T., 1962, 'Le royaume d'Agrippa II et son annexion par Domitien', *Collection Latomus* 58: 659–72.

Frere, S.S., 1980, 'Hyginus and the first cohort', *Britannia* 11: 51–60.

Friedländer, F., 1907, *Roman Life and Manners under the Early Empire* (trans. of *Darstellungen aus Sittengeschichte Roms in der Zeit von August bis zum Ausgang der Antonine*, 7th edn, by L.A. Magnus), George Routledge and Sons (repr. Routledge and Kegan Paul, London, 1968).

Gallivan, P.A., 1978, 'Who was Acilius?' *Historia* 27: 621–5.

——1981, 'The Fasti for AD 70–96', *CQ* 31: 186–220.

Galsterer, H., 1987, 'La loi municipale des Romains: chimère ou réalité?' *RHD* 65: 181–203.

——1988, '*Municipium Flauium Irnitanum*. A Latin town in Spain', *JRS* 78: 78–90.

Garnsey, P. and Saller, R., 1982, *The Early Principate: Augustus to Trajan*, Greece and Rome, New Surveys in the Classics No. 15, Oxford: Clarendon Press.

——1987, *The Roman Empire. Economy, Society and Culture*, London: Duckworth.

Garthwaite, J., 1978, 'Domitian and the Court Poets Martial and Statius', dissertation, Cornell University, Ithaca, New York.

——1990, 'Martial, Book 6, on Domitian's Moral Censorship', *Prudentia* 22: 13–22.

Garzetti, A., 1950, *Nerva*, Rome: Angelo Signorelli.

——1974, *From Tiberius to the Antonines: A History of the Roman Empire, 14–192*, trans. J.R. Foster, London: Methuen.

Gascou, J., 1976, 'Suétone et l'ordre equestre', *REL* 54: 257–77.

Gephardt, R.F.C., 1922, 'C. Suetonii Tranquilli Vita Domitiani: Suetonius' *Life of Domitian* with Notes and Parallel Passages', dissertation, University of Pennsylvania, Philadelphia.

Giet, S., 1958, 'Quintilien et les jeunes Flaviens, I', *RSR* 32: 321–34.

——1959, 'Quintilien et les jeunes Flaviens, II', *RSR* 33: 1–17.

Gimenez-Candela, T., 1983, 'La *lex Irnitana*. Une nouvelle loi municiale de la Bétique', *RIDA* 30: 125–40.

Girard, J.-L., 1981, 'Domitien et Minerve: une prédilection impériale', *ANRW* 2.17.1: 233–45.

Gonzalez, J., 1986, 'The *lex Irnitana*. A new copy of the Flavian municipal law', *JRS* 76: 147–243.

Goodman, M., 1989, 'Nerva, the *Fiscus Judaicus* and the Jewish identity', *JRS* 79: 41–4.

Gordon, C.D., 1949, 'Subsidies in Roman imperial defence,' *Phoenix* 3: 660–9.

Gowing, A., 1990, 'Dio's name', *CPh* 85: 49–54.

Greenhalgh, P.A.L., 1975, *The Year of the Four Emperors*, London: Weidenfeld and Nicolson.

Gregori, G.L., 1986a, 'Pedanii Flavii Salinatores!', *ZPE* 62: 185–9.

——1986b, 'Pedanii Flavii Salinatores?', *ZPE* 65: 239–44.

Grelle, F., 1980, 'La *Correctio morum* nella legislazione flavia', *ANRW* 2.13: 340–65.

Griffin, M., 1975, *Seneca. A Philosopher in Politics*, Oxford: Clarendon Press.

Griffith, J.G., 1969, 'Juvenal, Statius and the Flavian establishment', *Greece and Rome* 16: 134–50.

Grosso, F., 1954, 'Aspetti della politica orientale di Domiziano, I', *Epigraphica* 16: 117–79.

——1955, 'Aspetti della politica orientale di Domiziano, II', *Epigraphica* 17: 33–78.

Gsell, S., 1894, *Essai sur le règne de l'empereur Domitien.*, Paris: Thorin.

Hahn, J., and Leunissen, P.M.M., 1990, 'Statistical method and inheritance of the consulate under the early Roman empire', *Phoenix* 44: 60–81.

Halfmann, H., 1979, *Die Senatoren aus dem östlichen Teil des* Imperium Romanum *bis zum Ende des 2. Jh. n. Chr.*, Göttingen: Hubert.

Hammond, M., 1956, 'The transmission of the imperial powers of the

Roman emperor from the death of Nero in AD 68 to that of Alexander Severus in AD 235', *MAAR* 24: 63–133.

——1957, 'Composition of the senate, AD 68–235', *JRS* 47: 74–81.

——1959, *The Antonine Monarchy*, Rome: American Academy in Rome.

Hannestad, N., 1986, *Roman Art and Imperial Policy*, Jutland Archaeological Society Publications 19, Aarhus: Aarhus University Press.

Hanson, W.S., 1987, *Agricola and the Conquest of the North*, London: B.T. Batsford.

——1989, 'The nature and function of Roman frontiers', BAR International Series 471, Oxford: British Archaeological Reports, 55–63.

Hardie, A., 1983, *Statius and the Silvae. Poets, Patrons and* Epideixis *in the Graeco-Roman World*, ARCA Classical and Medieval Texts, Papers and Monographs 9, Liverpool: Francis Cairns.

Harris, B.F., 1977, 'Stoic and cynic under Vespasian', *Prudentia* 9: 105–14.

——1979, 'Domitian, the emperor cult and *Revelation*', *Prudentia* 11: 15–25.

Hassall, M., 1984, 'Epigraphy and the Roman army in Britain', *BAR* British Series 136, Oxford: British Archaeological Reports, 265–77.

Henderson, B.W., 1927, *Five Roman Emperors (Vespasian–Trajan, AD 69–117)*, Cambridge: Cambridge University Press.

Henrichs, A., 1968, 'Vespasian's visit to Alexandria', *ZPE* 3: 51–80.

Herrmann, L., 1979, 'Babrius et Titus', *REG* 92: 113–19.

Hersberg, H. von, 1978/80, 'Zur Datierung des Theaters in der Domitiansvilla von Castel Gandolfo', *RPAA* 51–2: 305–24.

Highet, G., 1954, *Juvenal the Satirist* (repr. 1955), Oxford: Oxford University Press.

Hind, J.G.F., 1983, 'Caledonia and its occupation under the Flavians', *Proceedings of the Society of Antiquaries of Scotland* 113: 373–8.

——1985, 'Summers and winters in Tacitus' account of Agricola's campaigns in Britain', *Northern History* 21: 1–18.

Hobley, A.S., 1989, 'The numismatic evidence for the post-Agricolan abandonment of the Roman frontier in northern Scotland', *Britannia* 20: 69–74.

Holder, P.A., 1977, 'Domitian and the title Germanicus', *LCM* 2: 151.

——1980, *Studies in the* Auxilia *of the Roman Army from Augustus to Trajan*, BAR International Series 70, Oxford: British Archaeological Reports.

Homo, L., 1949, *Vespasien, l'empereur du bon sens.*, Paris: A. Michel.

Hopkins, K., 1980, 'Taxes and trade in the Roman empire (200 BC–AD 400)', *JRS* 70: 101–25.

——1983, *Death and Renewal: Sociological Studies in Roman History, II*, Cambridge: Cambridge University Press.

Horstkotte, H., 1989, 'Dekurionat und römisches Bürgerrecht nach der Lex Irnitana', *ZPE* 78: 169–77.

Houston, G.W., 1971 'Roman imperial administrative personnel during the principates of Vespasian and Titus', dissertation, University of North Carolina, Chapel Hill.

——1977, 'Vespasian's adlection of men *in senatum*', *AJPh* 98: 35–63.

Howell, P., 1980, *A Commentary on Book One of the Epigrams of Martial*, London: Athlone Press.

Humbert, M., 1972, *Le remariage à Rome. Etude d'histoire juridique et sociale*, Milan: A. Guiffrè.

Isaac, B., 1988, 'The meaning of the terms *limes* and *limitanei*', *JRS* 78: 125–47.

Isaac, B. and Roll, I., 1976, 'A milestone of AD 69 from Judaea: the elder Trajan and Vespasian', *JRS* 66: 15–9.

Jackson, S., 1984, 'Apollonius and the emperors', *Hermathena* 137: 25–32.

Janssen, J.C., 1919, 'C. Suetonii Tranquilli Vita Domitiani', dissertation, University of Amsterdam.

Jarrett, M.G. and Mann, J.C., 1970, 'Britain from Agricola to Gallienus', *BJ* 170: 178–210.

Johnson, A.C., Coleman-Norton, P.R. and Bourne, F.C., 1961, *Ancient Roman Statutes*, Austin: University of Texas Press.

Johnston, D., 1987, 'Three thoughts on Roman private law and the *Lex Irnitana*', *JRS* 77: 62–77.

Jones, A.H.M., 1971, *The Cities of the Eastern Roman Provinces*, 2nd edn, Oxford: Clarendon Press.

Jones, B.W., 1971, 'Preparation for the Principate', *La parola del passato* 139: 264–70.

——1972, 'La Chute de M. Arrecinus Clemens', *La parola del passato* 146: 320–1.

——1973a, 'Domitian's attitude to the senate', *AJPh* 94: 70–90.

——1973b, 'The dating of Domitian's war against the Chatti', *Historia* 22: 79–90.

——1974, 'Senatorial influence in the revolt of Saturninus', *Latomus* 33: 529–35.

——1975a, 'Titus and some Flavian *Amici*', *Historia* 24: 453–62.

——1975b, 'Praetorian proconsuls under Domitian', *Historia* 24: 631–2.

——1976a, 'The consuls of AD 90', *Historia* 25: 499–501.

——1976b, 'Dalmatia again', *CPh* 71: 256–7.

——1979, *Domitian and the Senatorial Order. A Prosopographical Study of Domitian's Relationship with the Senate, AD 81–96*, Philadelphia: American Philosophical Society.

——1982, 'Domitian's advance into Germany and Moesia', *Latomus* 41: 329–35.

——1983, 'C. Vettulenus Civica Cerialis and the "False Nero" of AD 88', *Athenaeum* 61: 516–21.

——1984a, *The Emperor Titus*, London: Croom Helm.

——1984b, 'The diminishing role of patricians, AD 70–96', *Athenaeum* 62: 635–40.

——1984c, 'Agrippina and Vespasian,' *Latomus* 43: 581–3.

——1990, 'Domitian and the exile of Dio of Prusa', *La parola del passato* 254: 348–57.

Jones, B.W. and Conole, P., 1983, 'Sallustius Lucullus', *Latomus* 42: 629–33.

Jones, B.W. and Develin, R., 1976, 'M. Arrecinus Clemens', *Antichthon* 10: 79–83.

Jones, B.W. and Milns, R.D., 1984, *The Use of Documentary Evidence in the Study of Roman Imperial History*, Sydney: Sydney University Press.

Jones, C.P., 1970, *Philostratus, Life of Apollonius*, trans. and ed. G.W. Bowersock, Harmondsworth: Penguin Books.

——1971, *Plutarch and Rome*, Oxford: Clarendon Press.

——1978, The Roman World of Dio Chrysostom, Cambridge, Mass. and London: Harvard University Press.

Kähler, H., 1963, *Rome and Her Empire*, trans. J.R. Foster, London: Methuen.

Kazdova, E., 1979, 'The Domitianic reliefs of the Cancelleria', *SPFB* 24: 47–56.

Keller, E., 1967, 'Studien zu den Cancellaria Reliefs', *Klio* 49: 193–217.

Kennedy, D., 1983, 'C. Velius Rufus', *Britannia* 14: 183–96.

Kennedy, D. and Riley, D., 1990, *Rome's Desert Frontier from the Air*, London: B.T. Batsford.

Keresztes, P., 1973, 'The Jews, the Christians and the emperor Domitian', *VChr* 27: 1–28.

Kindstrand, J.F., 1978 'The date of Dio of Prusa's Alexandrian oration – a Reply', *Historia* 27: 378–83.

Klose, D.O.A., 1984, 'Ouespasianos neoteros', *Chiron* 14: 193–5.

Kneissl, P., 1969, *Die Siegestitulatur der römischen Kaiser, Untersuchungen zu den Siegerbeinamen des ersten und zweiten Jahrhunderts*, Göttingen: Hubert.

Knudsen, J.H.V., 1943. 'The treatment of the Domitian persecution in the history of modern research', dissertation, Hartford Theological Seminary, Hartford, Connecticut.

Koeppel, G., 1969, 'Profectio und Adventus', *BJ* 169: 130–94.

Kreiler, B., 1975, *Die Statthalter Kleinasiens unter den Flaviern*, dissertation, Ludwig-Maximilians-Universität, Munich.

Last, H., 1948, 'On the Flavian reliefs from the Palazzo della Cancellaria', *JRS* 38: 9–14.

Lebek, W.D., 1989, 'Die mainzer Ehrungen für Germanicus, den älteren Drusus und Domitian (Tab. Siar. Frg. 1 26–34; Suet. *Claud.* 1, 3)', *ZPE* 78: 45–82.

Leclercq, H., 1921a, 'Domitien', *Dictionnaire d'Archéologie chrétienne et de Liturgie*, Paris: Letouzey et Ané, 1388–401.

——1921b, 'Domitille (Flavie)', *Dictionnaire d'Archéologie chrétienne et de Liturgie*, Paris: Letouzey et Ané, 1401–4.

——1921c, 'Domitille (Cimitière de)', *Dictionnaire d'Archéologie chrétienne et de Liturgie*, Paris: Letouzey et Ané, 1404–42.

Leglay, M., 1968, 'Les Flaviens et l'Afrique', *MEFR* 80: 201–46.

Lemarchand, L., 1926, *Dion de Pruse – Les oeuvres d'avant l'exil*, Paris: de Gigord.

Levick, B.M., 1982, 'Domitian and the provinces', *Latomus* 41: 50–73.

——1985, *The Government of the Roman Empire: A Sourcebook*, London and Sydney: Croom Helm.

Levin, S. 1985, 'Plutarch's part in the *damnatio memoriae* of the emperor Domitian', *La Béotie antique*, Lyon-Saint-Etienne, 16–20 mai 1983, Colloque internationale du CNRS, Paris, 283–7.

Lewis, N., 1968, 'Domitian's order on requisitioned transport and lodgings', *RIDA* 15: 135–42.

Lewis, N. and Reinhold, M., 1966, *Roman Civilization: Sourcebook II, the Empire*, New York: Harper and Row.
Liebeschuetz, J.H.W.G., 1979, *Continuity and Change in Roman Religion*, Oxford: Clarendon Press.
Luttwak, E.N., 1976, *The Grand Strategy of the Roman Empire from the First Century to the Third*, Baltimore and London: Johns Hopkins University Press.
Lynn, J. and Jay, A., 1981, *Yes Minister: The Diaries of a Cabinet Minister by the Rt Hon. James Hacker MP*, vol. 1, London: British Broadcasting Corporation.
——1986, *Yes Prime Minister: The Diaries of the Right Hon. James Hacker*, vol. 1, London: BBC Publications.
McAlindon, D., 1957, 'Senatorial advancement in the age of Claudius', *Latomus* 16: 252–62.
McCann, A., 1972, 'A re-dating of the reliefs from the Palazzo della Cancellaria', *MDAI(R)* 79: 249–76.
McCrum, M. and Woodhead, A.G., 1966, *Select Documents of the Principates of the Flavian Emperors including the Year of Revolution AD 68–96*, Cambridge: Cambridge University Press.
McDermott, W.C., 1970, 'Fabricius Veiento', *AJPh* 91: 124–48.
——1973, 'Flavius Silva and Salvius Liberalis', *CW* 66: 335–51.
——1978a, 'Pliny, *Epistulae* IV. 22', *Antichthon* 12: 78–82.
——1978b, '*Ecce Iterum Crispinus*', *RSA* 8: 117–22.
McDermott, W.C. and Orentzel, A., 1977, 'Silius Italicus and Domitian', *AJPh* 98: 23–34.
——1979a, 'Quintilian and Domitian', *Athenaeum* 57: 9–26.
——1979b, *Roman Portraits: The Flavian-Trajanic Period*, Columbia and London: University of Missouri Press.
MacDonald, W.L., 1982, *The Architecture of the Roman Empire I. An Introductory Study*, Rev. edn, New Haven and London: Yale University Press.
McGuire, M.E., 1980, 'A historical commentary on Suetonius' *Life of Titus*', dissertation, Johns Hopkins University, Baltimore.
MacMullen, R., 1966, *Enemies of the Roman Order: Treason, Unrest and Alienation in the Empire*, Cambridge, Mass.: Harvard University Press.
——1980, 'How big was the Roman imperial army?' *Klio* 62: 451–60.
Magi, F., 1973/4, 'I marmi del teatro di Domiziano a Castel Gandolfo', *RPAA* 46: 63–77.
Magie, D., 1950, *Roman Rule in Asia Minor to the end of the Third Century after Christ*, Princeton: Princeton University Press.
Mann, J.C., 1972, 'The development of auxiliary and fleet diplomas', *ES* 9: 233–41.
Martin, A., 1985, 'Quelques réflexions autour de la titulature papyrologique de Domitien', *CE* 60: 168–73.
——1987, 'Domitien *Germanicus* et les documents grecs d'Egypte', *Historia* 36: 73–82.
Martin, R., 1981, *Tacitus*, London: B.T. Batsford.
Martinet, H., 1981, *C. Suetonius Tranquillus, Divus Titus; Kommentar*, Beiträge für Klassischen Philologie 123, Meisenheim: A. Hain.

Maxfield, V.A., 1972, 'C. Minicius Italus', *ES* 9: 243–5.

——1981, *The Military Decorations of the Roman Army*, London: B.T. Batsford.

Mennella, G., 1981, 'Ancora sulla carriera di M. Arrecino Clemente', *Athenaeum* 59: 205–8.

Merkelbach, R., 1979, 'Warum Domitians Siegername "Germanicus" eradiert worden ist', *ZPE* 34: 62–4.

Millar, F., 1967, 'Emperors at work', *JRS* 57: 9–19.

——1977, *The Emperor in the Roman World*, London: Duckworth.

——1982, 'Emperors, frontiers and foreign relations, 31 BC to AD 378', *Britannia* 13: 1–23.

Mitford, T.B., 1974, 'Some inscriptions from the Cappadocian *limes*', *JRS* 64: 160–75.

——1980, 'Cappadocia and Armenia Minor', *ANRW* 2.7.2: 1169–228.

Mócsy, A., 1974, *Pannonia and Upper Moesia. A History of the Middle Danube Provinces of the Roman Empire*, trans. S. Frere, London and Boston: Routledge and Kegan Paul.

Modugno, S., Panciera, S., and Zevi, F., 1973, 'Osservazioni sui consoli dell' 85 d. C.', *RSA* 3: 87–108.

Moles, J.L., 1978, 'The career and conversion of Dio Chrysostom', *JHS* 98: 79–100.

——1983a, 'Dio Chrysostom. Exile, Tarsus, Nero and Domitian', *LCM* 8: 130–4

——1983b, 'The date and purpose of the fourth kingship oration of Dio Chrysostom', *CIAnt* 2: 251–78.

Momigliano, A., 1935, '*Sodales Flaviales Titiales* e culto di Giove', *BCAC* 63: 165–71.

Mommsen, Th., 1873, *Etude sur Pline le Jeune*, trans. C. Morel, Paris: A. Franck.

——1887–8, *Römisches Stattsrecht*, 3 vols, Leipzig: Hirzel.

——1974, *The Provinces of the Roman Empire from Caesar to Diocletian*, trans. W.P. Dickson, Chicago: Ares Reprint.

Mooney, G.W., 1930, *C. Suetoni Tranquilli De Vita Caesarum. Libri VII–VIII*, London: Longmans, Green; Dublin: Hodges, Figgis.

Morawiecki, L., 1977, 'The symbolism of Minerva on the coins of Domitianus', *Klio* 59: 185–93.

Moreau, J., 1953, 'A propos de la persécution de Domitien', *La Nouvelle Clio* 5: 121–9.

Morford, M.P.O., 1968, 'The training of three Roman emperors', *Phoenix* 22: 57–72.

Morton, H.V., 1964, *A Traveller in Italy*, London: Methuen.

Mourgues, J.-L., 1987, 'The so-called letter of Domitian at the end of the *Lex Irnitana*' *JRS* 77: 78–87.

Murison, C.L., 1985, 'The revolt of Saturninus in Upper Germany', *ECM* 29: 31–49.

Murray, O., 1967, Review of B.Grenzheuser, 1964, 'Kaiser und Senat in der Zeit von Nero bis Nerva', dissertation, Münster, *JRS* 57: 250–1.

——1969, Review of R. MacMullen, 1966, *Enemies of the Roman Order: Treason, Unrest and Alienation in the Empire*, *JRS* 59: 261–5.

Nash, E., 1961–62, *Pictorial Dictionary of Ancient Rome*, 2 vols, London: A. Zwemmer.

Newman, B., 1963, 'The fallacy of the Domitian hypothesis. Critique of the Irenaeus source as a witness for the contemporary-historical approach to the interpretation of the Apocalypse', *NTS* 10: 133–9.

Nicols, J., 1975, 'Antonia and Sejanus', *Historia* 24: 48–58.

——1978, *Vespasian and the Partes Flavianae*, Historia Einzelschriften 28, Wiesbaden: F. Steiner.

Nodet, E., 1985, 'Jésus et Jean-Baptiste selon Josèphe', *RBi* 92: 321–48 and 497–524.

Nony, D., 1986, 'Domitien et les cités de Bétique', in B. Rémy (ed.), *Recherches épigraphiques. Documents relatifs à l'histoire des institutions et de l'administration de l'empire romain*, Centre Jean-Palerne Mémoires 7: 49–53.

Ogilvie, R.M., and Richmond, I., 1967, *Cornelii Taciti de Vita Agricolae*, Oxford: Clarendon Press.

Ostrand, K.D., 1984, 'Aspects of the Reign of the Emperor Domitian', dissertation, University of Missouri, Columbia.

Patterson, J.R., 1987, 'Crisis: What crisis? Rural change and urban development in imperial Appennine Italy', *PBSR* 55: 115–46.

Pavis D'Escurac, H., 1976, *La préfecture de l'annone. Service administratif impérial d'Auguste à Constantin*, Rome: Ecole Française de Rome, Palais Farnèse.

Pergola, P., 1978, 'La condamnation des Flaviens "Chrétiens" sous Domitien: Persécution religieuse ou répression à caractère politique?' *MEFR* 90: 407–23.

Perl, G., 1981 'Frontin und "der limes": zu *Strat* 1,3,10 und 2,11,7', *Kilo* 63: 563–83.

Pflaum, H.-G., 1950, *Les procurateurs équestres sous le haut-empire romain*, Paris: A. Maisonneuve.

——1951, 'A propos des préfets d'Egypte d'Arthur Stein', *Latomus* 10: 471–7.

——1960, *Les carrières procuratoriennes équestres sous le haut-empire romain*, Paris: P. Geuthner.

——1962, 'Légats impériaux à l'intérieur de provinces sénatoriales', *Collection Latomus* 58: 1232–42.

——1974, *Abrégé des procurateurs équestres: d'après l'article paru en allemand dans l'Encyclopédie classique (Pauly-Wissowa)* by S. Ducroix, Paris: De Boccard.

Pistor, H.H., 1965, 'Prinzeps und Patriziat in der Zeit von Augustus bis Commodus', dissertation, Albert-Ludwigs-Universität, Freiburg.

Pitts, L.F., and St Joseph, J.K., 1985, *Inchtuthil: The Roman Legionary Fortress*, Britannia Monograph Series No. 6, London: Society for the Promotion of Roman Studies.

Platner, M., and Ashby, T., 1929, *A Topographical Dictionary of Ancient Rome*, Oxford: Oxford University Press.

Pleket, H.W., 1961 'Domitian, the senate and the provinces', *Mnemosyne* 14: 296–315.

Pollitt, J.J., 1966, *The Art of Rome c. 753 BC–337 AD*, Englewood Cliffs, New Jersey: Prentice-Hall.
Prigent, P., 1974, 'Au temps de l'Apocalypse I: Domitien', *RHPhR* 54: 455–83.
Raepsaet-Charlier, M.T., 1973, 'Germania inferior et Germania superior', *Latomus* 32: 158–61.
——1987, *Prosopographie des femmes de l'ordre sénatorial* (Ier–IIe siècles), Louvain: Peeters.
Rajak, T., 1983, *Josephus*, London: Duckworth.
Ramage, E.S., 1983, 'Denigration of predecessor under Claudius, Galba and Vespasian', *Historia* 32: 200–14.
——1989, 'Juvenal and the establishment: denigration of predecessor in the "Satires"', *ANRW* 2.33.1: 640–707.
Rankov, N.B., 1990, '*Singulares legati legionis*: a problem in the interpretation of the Ti. Claudius Maximus inscription from Philippi', *ZPE* 80: 165–75.
Reicke, B., 1980, 'The inauguration of catholic martyrdom according to St John the Divine', *Augustinianum* 20: 275–83.
Rémy, B., 1983, 'La carrière de P. Calvisius Ruso Iulius Frontinus, gouverneur de Cappadoce–Galatie. A propos de l'inscription *MAMA* VII, 193', *MEFR* 95: 163–82.
Ritter, H.W., 1972, 'Zur Lebensgeschichte der Flavia Domitilla, der Frau Vespasians', *Historia* 21: 759–61.
Robathan, D.M., 1942, 'Domitian's Midas touch', *TAPhA* 73: 130–44.
Rodgers, R.H., 1982, '*Curatores Aquarum*', *HSCPh* 86: 171–80.
Rogers, P.M., 1980, 'Titus, Berenice and Mucianus', *Historia* 29: 86–95.
——1984, 'Domitian and the finances of state', *Historia* 33: 60–78.
Rogers, R.S., 1960, 'A group of Domitianic treason trials', *CPh* 55: 19–23.
Rossi, L., 1980–81, 'Guerra e vittoria dacica di Domiziano nell' 88–89(?) AD. Breve riesame delle fonti', *CRDAC* 11: 441–5.
Roxan, M.M., 1978, *Roman Military Diplomas 1954–1977*, London: Institute of Archaelogy, Occasional Papers 2.
Saller, R.P., 1980, 'Promotion and patronage in equestrian careers', *JRS* 70: 44–63.
——1982 *Personal Patronage under the Early Caesars*, Cambridge: Cambridge University Press.
Sanford, E.M., 1937, 'Nero and the East' *HSCPh* 48: 75–103.
Sartori, A., 1981, 'L'editto di Domiziano sulla viticoltura: indistintamente repressivo o accortamente selettivo?' *RIL* 115: 97–128.
Saulnier, C., 1984, 'La persécution des chrétiens et la théologie du pouvoir à Rome (Ier–IVe s.)', *RSR* 58: 251–79.
Schieber, A.S., 1976, 'The Flavian eastern policy', dissertation, State University of New York, Buffalo.
Schönberger, H., 1969, 'The Roman frontier in Germany: an archaeological survey', *JRS* 59: 144–64.
Schürer, E., 1973, *The History of the Jewish People in the Age of Jesus Christ (175 BC–AD 135)*, Rev. and ed. G. Vermes and F. Millar, Edinburgh: T. and T. Clark.

Scott, K., 1936, *The Imperial Cult under the Flavians*, Stuttgart and Berlin: Kohlhammer.

Shackleton-Bailey, D.R., 1987, 'The *Silvae* of Statius', *HSCPh* 91: 273–82.

Sherk, R.K., 1980, 'Roman Galatia', *ANRW* 2.7.2: 954–1052.

Sherwin-White, A.N., 1966, *The Letters of Pliny. A Historical and Social Commentary*, Oxford: Clarendon Press.

Simon, E., 1985, 'Virtus und Pietas. Zu den Friesen A und B von der Cancellaria', *JDAI* 100: 543–55.

Simon, S.J., 1975, 'Domitian, patron of letters', *CB* 51: 58–9.

Sinnigen, W.G., 1962, 'The origins of the *Frumentarii*', *MAAR* 27: 214–24.

Smallwood, E.M., 1956, 'Domitian's attitude to the Jews and Judaism', *CPh* 51: 1–13.

——1961, *Philonis Alexandrini Legatio ad Gaium. Edited with an Introduction, Translation and Commentary*, Leiden: E.J. Brill.

——1966, *Documents illustrating the Principates of Nerva, Trajan and Hadrian*, Cambridge: Cambridge University Press.

——1967, *Documents illustrating the Principates of Gaius, Claudius and Nero*, Cambridge: Cambridge University Press.

——1976, *The Jews under Roman Rule from Pompey to Diocletian*, Leiden: E.J. Brill.

Sordi, M., 1960, 'La persecuzione di Domiziano', *RSCI* 14: 1–26.

——1981, 'I Flavi et il Christianesimo', *Atti del Congresso internazionale di Studi Vespasiani*, Rieti: Centro di Studi Varroniani, 137–52.

——1985, 'Il cristianesimo nella cultura romana dell'età postflavia', *CCC* 6: 99–117.

Speidel, M., 1970, 'The captor of Decebalus', *JRS* 60: 142–53.

——1978, *Guards of the Roman Armies: An Essay on the singulares of the Provinces*, Bonn: Habelt.

Starr, C.J., 1949, 'Epictetus and the tyrant', *CPh* 44: 20–9.

Strobel, K., 1986a, 'Der Aufstand des L. Antonius Saturninus und der sogenannte zweite Chattenkrieg Domitians', *Tyche* 1: 203–20.

——1986b, 'Zu den Vexillationsziegelstempeln von Mirebeau bei Dijon', *ZPE* 64: 257–64.

——1986c, 'Zur Rekonstruktion der Laufbahn des C. Velius Rufus', *ZPE* 64: 265–86.

——1987a, 'Der Chattenkrieg Domitians: historische und politische Aspekte', *Germania* 65: 423–52.

——1987b, 'Nochmals zur Datierung der Schlacht am *Mons Graupius*', *Historia* 36: 198–212.

——1989, *Die Donaukriege Domitians*, Bonn: Dr Rudolf Habelt.

Strong, D.E., 1968a, *Fifth Report on the Excavations of the Roman Fort at Richborough, Kent*, Reports of the Research Committee of the Society of Antiquaries of London 23.

——1968b, 'The administration of public building in Rome during the late republic and early empire' *BICS* 15:97–109.

Sturm, F., 1981, 'Pegaso: un guireconsulto dell'epoca di Vespasiano', *Atti del Congresso internazionale di Studi Vespasiani*, Rieti: Centro di Studi Varroniani, 105–36.

Sutherland, C.H.V., 1935, 'The state of the imperial treasury at the death of Domitian', *JRS* 25: 150–62.

Syme, R. 1928, 'Rhine and Danubian legions under Domitian', *JRS* 18: 41–55.

——1930, 'The imperial finances under Domitian, Nerva and Trajan', *JRS* 20: 55–70.

——1936, 'Flavian wars and frontiers', *CAH* 11: 131–67.

——1937, Review of K. Scott, 1936, *The Imperial Cult under the Flavians*, *CR* 51: 32–3.

——1958, *Tacitus*, Oxford: Clarendon Press.

——1971, *Danubian Papers*, Bucharest: AIESEE.

——1977, 'The enigmatic Sospes', *JRS* 67: 38–49.

——1979–88, *Roman Papers*, vols 1–5, ed. E. Badian (1–2) and A.R. Birley (3–5), Oxford: Oxford University Press.

——1980, *Some Arval Brethren*, Oxford: Clarendon Press.

——1981, 'Governors dying in Syria', *ZPE* 41: 125–44.

——1983a, 'Antistius Rusticus. A consular from Corduba', *Historia* 32: 359–34.

——1983b, 'Domitian, the last years', *Chiron* 13: 121–46.

——1984a, 'P. Calvisius Ruso. One person or two?' *ZPE* 56: 173–92.

——1984b, 'Statius on Rutilius Gallicus', *Arctos* 18: 149–56.

——1986, *The Augustan Aristocracy*, Oxford: Clarendon Press.

Szelest, H. 1974, 'Domitian und Martial', *Eos* 62: 105–14.

Talbert, R.J.A., 1984, *The Senate of Imperial Rome*, Princeton: Princeton University Press.

Thompson, L., 1982, 'Domitian and the Jewish tax', *Historia* 31: 329–42.

——1984, '*Domitianus Dominus*. A gloss on Statius *Silvae* 1.6.84', *AJPh* 105: 469–75.

Townend, G.B., 1961, 'Some Flavian connections', *JRS* 51: 54–62.

——1987, 'The restoration of the Capitol in AD 70', *Historia* 36: 243–8.

Urban, R., 1971, 'Historische Untersuchungen zum Domitianbild des Tacitus', dissertation, Ludwig-Maximilians-Universität, Munich.

Vassileiou, A., 1984, 'Crispinus et les conseillers du prince (Juvénal, *Satires* IV)', *Latomus* 43: 27–68.

Vessey, D.W.T.C., 1970, 'Lucan, Statius and the baroque epic', *CW* 63: 232–4.

——1973, *Statius and the* Thebaid, Cambridge: Cambridge University Press.

——1974, 'Pliny, Martial and Silius Italicus', *Hermes* 102: 109–16.

——1983, '*Mediis discumbere in astris*. Statius *Silvae* IV. 2', *AC* 52: 206–20.

Veyne, P., 1962, 'Les honneurs posthumes de Flavia Domitilla et les dédicaces grecques et latines', *Latomus* 21: 49–98.

Vidman, L., 1982, *Fasti Ostienses*, Prague: Academiae Scientiarum Bohemoslovacae.

Vinson, M.P., 1989, 'Domitia Longina, Julia Titi, and the literary tradition', *Historia* 38: 431–50.

Viscusi, P.L., 1973, 'Studies on Domitian', dissertation, University of Delaware.

Visy, Z., 1978, 'Der Beginn der Donau–Kriege des Domitian', *AArchHung* 30: 37–60.

Walker, D.R., 1976, *The Metrology of the Roman Silver Coinage. Part I; From Augustus to Domitian*, BAR Supplementary Series 5, Oxford: British Archaeological Reports.

Wallace, K.G., 1987, 'The Flavii Sabini in Tacitus', *Historia* 36: 343–58.

Wallace-Hadrill, A., 1983, *Suetonius: The Scholar and his Caesars*, London: Duckworth.

——1984, Review of B.W. Jones, 1984a, *The Emperor Titus*, *TLS* 28.9: 1102

——(ed.), 1989, *Patronage in Ancient Society*, London: Routledge.

Walser, G., 1968, 'Der Putsch des Saturninus gegen Domitian', *Festschrift für R. Laur-Belart, Provincialia* 40: 497–507.

——1989, 'Kaiser Domitian in Mainz', *Chiron* 19: 449–56.

Warmington, B.H., 1977, *Suetonius Nero*, Bristol: Bristol Classical Press.

Waters, K.H., 1963, 'The second dynasty of Rome', *Phoenix* 17: 198–218.

——1964, 'The character of Domitian', *Phoenix* 18: 49–77.

——1969, '*Traianus Domitiani Continuator*', *AJPh* 90: 385–405.

——1970, 'Juvenal and the reign of Trajan,' *Antichthon* 4: 62–77.

——1974, 'Trajan's character in the literary tradition', in J.A.S. Evans (ed.), *Polis and Imperium. Studies in Honour of E.T. Salmon*, Hakkert: Toronto; 233–49.

Weaver, P.C., 1964, '*Augustorum libertus*', *Historia* 13: 188–98.

——1965, 'The father of Claudius Etruscus: Statius *Silvae* 3.3', *CQ* 15: 145–54.

——1967, 'Social mobility in the early Roman empire. The evidence of the imperial freedmen and slaves', *P. and P.* 37: 3–20.

——1972, Familia Caesaris: *A Social Study of the Emperor's Freedmen and Slaves*, Cambridge: Cambridge University Press.

——1979, 'Misplaced officials', *Antichthon* 13: 70–102.

——1980, 'Two freedman careers', *Antichthon* 14: 143–56.

Wellesley, K., 1956, 'Three historical puzzles in Tacitus *Histories III*: (3) The escape of Domitian from the Capitol', *CQ* 6: 211–14.

Wells, C., 1984, *The Roman Empire*, Glasgow: Fontana.

White, P., 1974a, '*Ecce Iterum Crispinus*', *AJPh* 95: 377–82.

——1974b, 'The presentation and dedication of the *Silvae* and the *Epigrams*', *JRS* 64: 40–61.

——1975, 'The friends of Martial, Statius and Pliny, and the dispersal of patronage', *HSCPh* 79: 265–300.

Wilkes, J.J., 1983, 'Romans, Dacians and Sarmatians in the first and early second centuries', in B. Hartley and J. Wacher (eds), *Rome and her Northern Provinces*, Gloucester: Alan Sutton.

Williams, M.H., 1990, 'Domitian, the Jews and the "Judaizers" – a simple matter of cupiditas and maiestas?' *Historia* 39: 196–211.

Wiseman, T.P., 1978, 'Flavians on the Capitol', *AJAH* 3: 163–78.

Winkler, G., 1972, 'Norbanus, ein bisher unbekannter Prokurator von Raetien', *Akten des VI. internationalen Kongresses für griechesche und lateinische Epigraphik*: 495–8.

Wistrand, E., 1979, 'The stoic opposition to the principate', *Studii Classice* 18: 92–101.

Wood, Jr, F.M., 1941, 'Some imperial virtues of Domitian', dissertation, Duke University, Durham, N.C.

Yarshater, E. (ed.), 1983, *The Cambridge History of Iran: The Seleucid, Parthian and Sasanian Periods*, Cambridge: Cambridge University Press.

Zucchelli, B., 1986, 'A proposito dell'epistolario di Chèone d'Eraclea', *Paideia* 41: 13–24.

PERSONS INDEX

Unless otherwise indicated, all dates are AD *and all consulships are* suffect.

Abdagaeses (Parthian king) 25, 203 n.11

Achilleus (Christian martyr; servant of Flavius Clemens's wife, Flavia Domitilla) 115

Acilii Glabriones, the 51

M'. Acilius Aviola (*cos. c. ord.* 54) 44, 51, 59, 208 n.7

M'. Acilius Glabrio (?father of *cos. ord.* 91) 51, 208 n.7, 208 n.8

M'. Acilius Glabrio (*cos. ord.* 91) 36, 51, 71, 115, 127, 184, 188, 193, 221 n.102

L. Aconius Statura (fought in a 'German and Sarmatian War') 153

(Aelia) Domitia Paulina (Hadrian's sister; wife of L. Julius Ursus Servianus) 42, 52, 174

Aelia Paetina (Claudius's wife) 8

Aeliae Oculatae (Vestals) 101, 189, 218 n.13

Aelius Aristides (orator) 108

L. (Aelius) Lamia Aelianus (*cos.* 116) 184–5

L. Aelius Lamia Plautius Aelianus (*cos.* 80; Domitia Longina's first husband) 20, 33, 36, 294

L. Aelius Sejanus (praetorian prefect) 4

M. Aemillius Lepidus (Gaius's

nominated successor) 7, 8

Sex. Afranius Burrus (praetorian prefect) 60

Agrippa I *See* (M). Julius Agrippa I

Agrippina *See* Julia Agrippina

Akiba (rabbi) 118

Alexander the Alabarch (father of Ti. and M. Julius Alexander) 6

Andromachus (court physician to Domitian) 70

L. Annaeus Seneca (*cos.* 56; philosopher) 122, 223 n.147

Annia Quartilla (wife of Galeo Tettienus Severus . . . Ti. Caepio Hispo) 174

P. Annius Florus (poet) 104

Ap. Annius Marsus (Flavian senator) 174

Annius Pollio (brother of Annius Vinicianus; husband of Barea Soranus's daughter, Servilia) 34

Annius Vinicianus (brother-in-law of Domitia Longina) 34

L. Antistius Rusticus (from Baetica; *cos.* 90) 78, 111, 176

Antonia Caenis (freedwoman of Antonia Minor; Vespasian's mistress) 4, 5, 19

Antonia Minor (Mark Antony's

257

AUTHOR INDEX

161; *986* 34, 226 n.73; *995* 207
n.122; *1006* 150; *1010* 53; *1025*
131; *1374* 114, 158, 232 n.72;
1397 178; *1447* 64, 178; *1448* 64,
178; *1567* 62, 64; *1679* 65, 219
n.34; *1763* 62; *1839* 47; *1988* 216
n.92; *1992* 88; *1995* 128, 129,
202 n.74; *1996* 129; *1998* 100,
145; *2720* 155; *3512* 88; *4914*
80, 84, 102; *5050* 219 n.21; *5177*
103, 104; *5178* 103; *5287* 219
n.34; *5759a* 161; *8905* 112; *9150*
134; *9200* 130, 140, 152

Irenaeus
Adversus Haereses (Adv. haer.):
5.30.3 116
*The Inscriptions of Roman
Tripolitania (IRT)*: *341* 235
n.7; *854* 221 n.91

John
Revelation: *13.3* 117; *17.9–11*
116
Jordanes
Getica: *76* 226 n.76; *77* 141
Josephus
Antiquitates Iudaicae (AJ):
18.3.4 92; *18.143* 5; *18.156*
5; *18.165* 5, 6; *18.180–4* 4;
18.182 8; *19.191* 40, 205 n.68,
235 n.58; *19.276* 6; *19.277* 5;
19.360 5; *20.100* 6; *20.145* 6;
20.146 6; *159–60* 6
Bellum Iudaicum (BJ): *2.217* 5;
2.221 5; *3.66–9* 11; *4.645–9*
14; *5.498* 16; *6.132–3* 16; *7*
201 n.59; *7.85* 17; *7.91–5* 135;
7.92–5 58; *7.94–5* 137; *7.123*
101; *7.244–51* 157; *7.244–54*
156; *7.247* 157, 202 n.69;
7.249 157, 202 n.69; *8.158* 92
Vita: *429* 37
Justinian
Digest: *1.2.2.53* 208 n.28;
12.2.52 43; *50.4.18.30*
222 n.130
Juvenal (Juv.)
Satires (Sat.): *1.26–9* 70; *1.35*
189; *2.29–33* 36, 39; *4* 135;

4.1–33 70; *4.65* 29; *4.71* 220
n.55; *4.73* 29; *4.75* 29; *4.77*
54, 135, 190; *4.78–81* 55; *4.81*
210 n.46; *4.81–93* 57; *4.84*
57; *4.84–93* 210 n.47; *4.93*
58; *4.94* 208 n.8; *4.99* 28;
4.99–101 97; *4.105* 135; *4.106*
58; *4.107* 135; *4.108–9* 70;
4.110 55, 135; *4.112* 135, 227
n.86; *4.113* 57; *4.124–5* 53;
4.130–5 29; *4.137* 54; *4.138*
54; *4.144–6* 127; *4.145* 27;
4.146 29; *4.145–7* 28; *4.152*
185; *6.118* 205 n.64; *6.387*
219 n.27; *7.86–8* 70; *7.88* 35;
9.22 92

Livy
2.42.5 91

Macrobius
Saturnalia (Sat.): *2.4.11*
199 n.13;
Martial
De Spectaculis (De Spect.):
2.5–8 94
Epigrammata (Epig.): *1.2.5* 92;
1.4.7 107; *1.5.1–2* 86; *1.8.1*
121; *1.43.10* 25; *1.78.10* 56,
135; *1.104* 105; *2.14.5* 91;
2.14.7 92; *2.57.2* 91; *2.59.2*
86; *2.60* 204 n.33; *3.36.6* 94;
4.1.7 218 n.21; *4.3* 37; *4.5.7*
25; *4.8.7* 62; *4.8.10* 32; *4.11*
147; *4.30* 97; *4.35.1–5* 105;
4.45 24, 62; *4.54.1* 103; *4.54.7*
209 n.44; *5.1* 97; *5.1.1* 28;
5.3 150; *5.5.1–2* 24; *5.5.7* 12;
5.6.2 61; *5.8.1–3* 107; *5.19.3*
151; *5.25.1–10* 219 n.34; *5.49*
204 n.32; *5.53.1–2* 91, 100; *6.2*
39, 204 n.33; *6.3* 37, 39; *6.3.1*
39; *6.3.5* 39; *6.4* 39; *6.4.2*
151, 227 n.94; *6.10.8* 151;
6.46.1–2 104; *6.76* 151; *6.76.1*
50; *7.56.2* 217 n.115; *7.60* 62;
7.99 70; *8.15.5–6* 152; *8.36.1*
196; *8.36.5* 95; *8.36.11* 217
n.121; *8.48* 70; *8.65* 84; *8.65.8*

60; *3.44* 17; *3.48* 212 n.113;
3.50 135; *3.52* 55; *3.66* 4; *3.69*
13, 14, 47, 201 n.43; *3.70–2*
14; *3.74* 14, 88, 101; *3.75* 13;
3.83 14; *4.2* 15, 17, 33; *4.3* 15;
4.7 10, 11, 34, 50, 168, 183;
4.11 15; *4.39* 15, 191; *4.40*
12, 15; *4.46* 15; *4.49* 56; *4.50*
56; *4.51* 33; *4.52* 17; *4.53* 102;
4.59 14; *4.68* 15, 40, 43, 60,
164, 207 n.108; *4.69* 14; *4.70*
14; *4.74* 14; *4.80* 15; *4.81* 101;
4.86 12, 14, 16, 201 n.52; *5.1*
126; *5.5* 117

Ulpian
  De Officio Proconsulis: *7*
  222 n.128

Valerius Flaccus
  Argonautica (Argon.): *1.10–12*
  12
Vergil
  Aeneid (Aen.): *4.215–16*
  204 n.46
Vitruvius
  4.8.4 216 n.102; *6.5.2* 24; *9.6* 120

Zosimus
  5.38.4 9

GENERAL INDEX

Abortion 36, 39
Achaia 191
Acmonia (Phrygia) 111,
ab actis 176
Adamklissi 138, 139
Adana 104
Administration
  Domitian 72–125, 178, 197, 198;
  financial 149; officials 60, 72,
  107, 109, 110, 111, 160, 170;
  provincial 109–10, 111, 112, 113,
  114, 170; system 72
Adony 137
Adultery 35
  Imperial 34, 35, 42, 46, 205 n.64
Aedes
  Caesarum 91; Castoris 91;
  Divorum 91; Titus 87, 136
  Vespasian 87, 136
Aediles 7
Aerarium Saturni 104
Africa 9, 10, 13, 56, 57, 78, 104,
  113, 134, 139, 140, 158, 170,
  174, 175, 176, 177, 183
Ala Claudia nova 137
Ala Praetoria 144
Alani, the 19, 114, 126,
  136, 156, 157, 231 n.52,
  232 n.65
Albania 156, 157, 159
Albani, the/Albanians 155, 156,
  231 n.52
Albanum (*See also* Domitian –
  Alban 'villa') 96

Alexandria 5, 6, 13, 52, 54, 100,
  104, 178
Alimenta 73
Altars 82, 84, 102, 138, 139
Amici (See also Domitian – *amici*;
  Titus – *amici*; Vespasian – *amici*)
  11, 16, 65, 66, 122, 168, 169,
  195, 196; Imperial 6, 28, 50,
  51, 53, 55, 58, 61, 66, 70, 120,
  202 n.67, 212 n.102, 220 n.55,
  221 n.107
Amisus 210 n.71
Ammaedara 140
Amphitheatrum Flavianum 80, 82,
  84, 85, 87, 93, 105, 214 n.36
Anabazus 112
Ancyra 172, 231 n.54
Andernach 146
Antioch 104
Antioch in Pisidia 78, 208 n.27
Antium 97
Anxur 97
Aqua Claudia 136
Aquae Cutiliae 2
Aquincum 137, 142
Arabia 85
Arcar (Ratiaria) 137
Arch of Titus 30, 82, 93
Arcus Neroniana 82, 136
Ardoch 133
Argiletum 89, 92
Arles 191
Armenia 155, 156, 157; Maior 156,
  232 n.57; Minor 155, 231 n.54

281

n.31, 225 n.34, 235 n.74; oratory
12; persecutor 115–24, 221 n.96;
regard for 110, 112; religion,
interest in (*See also* priesthoods
– Domitian) 53, 56, 57, 72, 99,
102, 109, 117; reputation 17, 26,
32–3, 160, 164, 169, 180, 181;
seduction 194; skills 27, 187;
succession 40, 68; Titus 8–9, 13,
18, 19, 20–1, 93; triumphs 128,
129, 131, 132, 138, 139, 151,
152; upbringing 9–10; Vespasian
13, 16, 17, 18, 19, 33, 80, 201
n.52, 201 n.59; Vestals 28, 46,
47, 101, 102, 107, 128, 189, 218
n.11; wife *See* Domitia Longina
and Persons Index
Donji Milanovac 137
Dorylaeum 231 n.54
Dwarfs 25, 105, 203 n.8

Economic policy (*See also*
Economy)
Domitian 72–9, 193; 'vine
edict' 77–9
Economy (*See also* Economic
policy) 113–49
Education
Domitian *See* Domitian
– education; Imperial 48;
Senatorial 13, 15; Titus *See* Titus
– education
Egypt 5, 6, 62, 69, 70, 85, 103,
113, 178, 184, 205 n.77
Ephesus 137
ab epistulis 62, 63, 64, 65, 107,
178, 211 n.78, 211 n.95
Equestrians (*See also* Procurators
– equestrian) 7, 10, 29, 40, 42,
50, 59, 60, 61, 63, 64, 65, 67, 68,
70, 102, 107, 109, 110, 118, 119,
127, 130, 137, 144, 147, 160,
169, 177, 178, 179, 182, 190,
191, 192, 211 n.91, 229 n.5
Equus Domitiani 82, 85, 151,
214 n.42
Esquiline 84
Ethiopia 139
Eunuchs (*See also* Domitian –

concern for protection of males)
31, 32, 62, 65, 70, 115, 203 n.30
Euphrates, the 158
Executions 123, 185, 189; Claudius
122, 165, 192, 196; Commodus
68; Diocletian 217 n.125;
Domitian 35, 36, 39, 44, 46, 47,
48, 51, 65, 67, 70, 77, 102, 114,
115, 116, 117, 120, 121, 122,
123, 125, 147, 148, 158, 161,
167, 179, 180–8, 192, 193, 195,
196, 205 n.56, 213 n.21, 230
n.19, 232 n.72; Gaius 7; Hadrian
124, 166; Nero 122, 165, 168,
183; Pliny/Trajan 181; Vespasian
122, 166, 168
Exile 8, 10, 11, 34, 35, 42, 43,
47, 48, 53, 65, 67, 69, 77, 102,
115, 116, 117, 119, 120, 121,
122, 124, 125, 166, 180, 181,
183, 184, 186, 187, 188–91, 195,
211 n.85, 213 n.21, 236 n.29,
237 n.40

Falacrina 2
Falerienses, the 28
familia Caesaris (*See also*
Freedmen – Imperial) 61, 62
Festivals (*See also* Games;
Shows) 100
Fires 79, 80, 91; 83 BC 92; AD 64
79, 84, 136, 89, 92, 102; AD 80
80, 81, 84, 89, 90, 91, 92, 93; AD
203 90; AD 217 87
Firmani, the 28
fiscus Iudaicus 74, 76, 110, 114,
118, 119, 160, 233 n.1
Flavian emperors (*See also*
Domitian; Titus; Vespasian *and*
Persons Index) 7, 46, 53, 136,
100; accession 14, 46, 58, 103
Flavians
clients 14, 39, 52, 55, 100;
contact with Julio–Claudians 4,
5, 8, 99; family (*See also* Persons
Index) 1–3, 18, 28, 32, 40, 41,
43, 44, 45, 55, 67ff., 127, 164,
199 n.5, 200 n.33, 201 n.53, 206
n.99, 206 n.100, 212 n.105, 235